P9-DTZ-855

WITHDRAWN

MASTERY

ALSO BY ROBERT GREENE

The 50th Law (with 50 Cent)

The 33 Strategies of War
(A Joost Elfers Production)

The Art of Seduction
(A Joost Elfers Production)

The 48 Laws of Power
(A Joost Elfers Production)

ROBERT GREENE

MASTERY

VIKING

VIKING
Published by the Penguin Group
Penguin Group (USA) Inc., 375 Hudson Street, New York, New York 10014,
U.S.A. • Penguin Group (Canada), 90 Eglinton Avenue East, Suite 700,
Toronto, Ontario, Canada M4P 2Y3 (a division of Pearson Penguin
Canada Inc.) • Penguin Books Ltd, 80 Strand, London WC2R 0RL,
England • Penguin Ireland, 25 St. Stephen's Green, Dublin 2, Ireland
(a division of Penguin Books Ltd) • Penguin Books Australia Ltd, 250
Camberwell Road, Camberwell, Victoria 3124, Australia (a division
of Pearson Australia Group Pty Ltd) • Penguin Books India Pvt Ltd,
11 Community Centre, Panchsheel Park, New Delhi–110 017, India
• Penguin Group (NZ), 67 Apollo Drive, Rosedale, Auckland
0632, New Zealand (a division of Pearson New Zealand Ltd) •
Penguin Books (South Africa) (Pty) Ltd, 24 Sturdee Avenue,
Rosebank, Johannesburg 2196, South Africa

Penguin Books Ltd, Registered Offices:
80 Strand, London WC2R 0RL, England

First published in 2012 by Viking Penguin,
a member of Penguin Group (USA) Inc.
1 3 5 7 9 10 8 6 4 2

Copyright © Robert Greene, 2012
All rights reserved

Library of Congress Cataloging-
in-Publication Data
Greene, Robert.
Mastery / Robert Greene.
p.   cm.
Includes bibliographical references (p.)
and index.
ISBN 978-0-670-02496-4
Export ISBN 978-0-670-02630-2
1. Successful people. 2. Success.
3. Self-actualization (Psychology) I. Title.
BF637.S8G695 2012
158—dc23   2012027195

Printed in the
United States of America
Set in Baskerville
Designed by Daniel Lagin

No part of this book may be reproduced, scanned, or distributed in
any printed or electronic form
without permission. Please do
not participate in or encourage piracy of copyrighted
materials in violation of the
author's rights. Purchase
only authorized editions.

ALWAYS LEARNING   PEARSON

To Anna

CONTENTS

mastery is always inward–learning who you really are and reconnecting with that innate force. Knowing it with clarity, you will find your way to the proper career path and everything else will fall into place. It is never too late to start this process.

II.
SUBMIT TO REALITY:
THE IDEAL APPRENTICESHIP   47

After your formal education, you enter the most critical phase in your life–a second, practical education known as The Apprenticeship. Before it is too late you must learn the lessons and follow the path established by the greatest Masters, past and present–a kind of Ideal Apprenticeship that transcends all fields. In the process you will master the necessary skills, discipline your mind, and transform yourself into an independent thinker, prepared for the creative challenges on the way to mastery.

III.
ABSORB THE MASTER'S POWER:
THE MENTOR DYNAMIC   93

Life is short, and your time for learning and creativity is limited. Without any guidance, you can waste valuable years trying to gain knowledge and practice from various sources. Instead, you must follow the example set by Masters throughout the ages and find the proper mentor. Choose the mentor who best fits your needs and connects to your Life's Task. Once you have internalized their knowledge, you must move on and never remain in their shadow. Your goal is always to surpass your mentors in mastery and brilliance.

IV.
SEE PEOPLE AS THEY ARE:
SOCIAL INTELLIGENCE   125

Often the greatest obstacle to our pursuit of mastery comes from the emotional drain we experience in dealing with the resistance and manipulations of the people around us. We misread their intentions and react in ways that cause confusion or conflict. Social intelligence is the ability to see people in the most realistic light possible. Navigating smoothly through the social environment, we have more time and energy to focus on learning and acquiring skills. Success attained without this intelligence is not true mastery, and will not last.

V.
AWAKEN THE DIMENSIONAL MIND:
THE CREATIVE-ACTIVE 167

As you accumulate more skills and internalize the rules that govern your field, your mind will want to become more active, seeking to use this knowledge in ways that are more suited to your inclinations. Instead of feeling complacent about what you know, you must expand your knowledge to related fields, giving your mind fuel to make new associations between different ideas. In the end, you will turn against the very rules you have internalized, shaping and reforming them to suit your spirit. Such originality will bring you to the heights of power.

VI.
FUSE THE INTUITIVE WITH
THE RATIONAL: MASTERY

All of us have access to a higher form of intelligence, one that can allow us to see more of the world, to anticipate trends, to respond with speed and accuracy to any circumstance. This intelligence is cultivated by deeply immersing ourselves in a field of study and staying true to our inclinations, no matter how unconventional our approach might seem to others. This power is what our brains were designed to attain, and we will be naturally led to this type of intelligence if we follow our inclinations to their ultimate ends.

THE THIRD TRANSFORMATION
Marcel Proust

KEYS TO MASTERY
Examples of Masters seeing more–the fingertip feel–a power that is mystified–high-level intuition–the Dynamic–gaining an intuitive feel for the whole–Jane Goodall's feel for chimpanzees–Erwin Rommel's feel for battle–the fusing of the rational and the intuitive–mastery at 20,000 hours–time as a crucial factor–make study time qualitatively rich–interpretation of Proust story

The Roots of Masterly Intuition
The Ammophila wasp–intuition and our primitive ancestors–mnemonic networks in the brain–Bobby Fischer and memory traces–engaging with complexity–gaining a tolerance for chaos–increasing memory capacity–examples of high-level intuition and youthfulness

The Return to Reality
Overview of evolution from the beginning–the interconnectedness of all life–the ultimate reality–our modern Renaissance–returning to the whole–the altered brain of the Master

STRATEGIES FOR ATTAINING MASTERY

1. **Connect to your environment—Primal Powers**
   The Caroline Islanders

2. **Play to your strengths—Supreme Focus**
   A. Albert Einstein
   B. Temple Grandin

INTRODUCTION

THE ULTIMATE POWER

Everyone holds his fortune in his own hands, like a sculptor the raw material he will fashion into a figure. But it's the same with that type of artistic activity as with all others: We are merely born with the capability to do it. The skill to mold the material into what we want must be learned and attentively cultivated.

—JOHANN WOLFGANG VON GOETHE

There exists a form of power and intelligence that represents the high point of human potential. It is the source of the greatest achievements and discoveries in history. It is an intelligence that is not taught in our schools nor analyzed by professors, but almost all of us, at some point, have had glimpses of it in our own experience. It often comes to us in a period of tension—facing a deadline, the urgent need to solve a problem, a crisis of sorts. Or it can come as the result of constant work on a project. In any event, pressed by circumstances, we feel unusually energized and focused. Our minds become completely absorbed in the task before us. This intense concentration sparks all kinds of ideas—they come to us as we fall asleep, out of nowhere, as if springing from our unconscious. At these times, other people seem less resistant to our influence; perhaps we are more attentive to them, or we appear to have a special power that inspires their respect. We might normally experience life in a passive mode, constantly reacting to this or that incident, but for these days or weeks we feel like we can determine events and make things happen.

We could express this power in the following way: Most of the time we live in an interior world of dreams, desires, and obsessive thoughts. But in this period of exceptional creativity, we are impelled by the need to get something done that has a practical effect. We force ourselves to step outside our inner chamber of habitual thoughts and connect to the world, to other people, to reality. Instead of flitting here and there in a state of perpetual distraction, our minds focus and penetrate to the core of something real. At these moments, it is as if our minds—turned outward—are now flooded with light from the world around us, and suddenly exposed to new details and ideas, we become more inspired and creative.

Once the deadline has passed or the crisis is over, this feeling of power and heightened creativity generally fades away. We return to our distracted state and the sense of control is gone. If only we could manufacture this feeling, or somehow keep it alive longer . . . but it seems so mysterious and elusive.

The problem we face is that this form of power and intelligence is either ignored as a subject of study or is surrounded by all kinds of myths and misconceptions, all of which only add to the mystery. We imagine that creativity and brilliance just appear out of nowhere, the fruit of natural talent, or perhaps of a good mood, or an alignment of the stars. It would be an immense help to clear up the mystery—to name this feeling of power, to examine its roots, to define the kind of intelligence that leads to it, and to understand how it can be manufactured and maintained.

Let us call this sensation *mastery*—the feeling that we have a greater command of reality, other people, and ourselves. Although it might be something we experience for only a short while, for others—Masters of their field—it becomes their way of life, their way of seeing the world. (Such Masters include Leonardo da Vinci, Napoleon Bonaparte, Charles Darwin, Thomas Edison, and Martha Graham, among many others.) And at the root of this power is a simple *process* that leads to mastery—one that is accessible to all of us.

The process can be illustrated in the following manner: Let us say we are learning the piano, or entering a new job where we must acquire certain skills. In the beginning, we are outsiders. Our initial impressions of the piano or the work environment are based on prejudgments, and often contain an element of fear. When we first study the piano, the keyboard looks rather intimidating—we don't understand the relationships between the keys, the chords, the pedals, and everything else that goes into creating music. In a new job situation, we are ignorant of the power relationships between people, the psychology of our boss, the rules and procedures that are considered critical for success. We are confused—the knowledge we need in both cases is over our heads.

Although we might enter these situations with excitement about what we can learn or do with our new skills, we quickly realize how much hard work there is ahead of us. The great danger is that we give in to feelings of boredom, impatience, fear, and confusion. We stop observing and learning. The process comes to a halt.

If, on the other hand, we manage these emotions and allow time to take its course, something remarkable begins to take shape. As we continue to observe and follow the lead of others, we gain clarity, learning the rules and seeing how things work and fit together. If we keep practicing, we gain fluency; basic skills are mastered, allowing us to take on newer and more exciting challenges. We begin to see connections that were invisible to us before. We slowly gain confidence in our ability to solve problems or overcome weaknesses through sheer persistence.

At a certain point, we move from student to practitioner. We try out our own ideas, gaining valuable feedback in the process. We use our expanding knowledge in ways that are increasingly creative. Instead of just learning how others do things, we bring our own style and individuality into play.

As years go by and we remain faithful to this process, yet another leap takes place—to mastery. The keyboard is no longer something outside of us; it is internalized and becomes part of our nervous system, our fingertips. In our career, we now have a feel for the group dynamic, the current state of business. We can apply this feel to social situations, seeing deeper into other people and anticipating their reactions. We can make decisions that are rapid and highly creative. Ideas come to us. We have learned the rules so well that we can now be the ones to break or rewrite them.

In the process leading to this ultimate form of power, we can identify three distinct phases or levels. The first is the *Apprenticeship;* the second is the *Creative-Active;* the third, *Mastery.* In the first phase, we stand on the outside of our field, learning as much as we can of the basic elements and rules. We have only a partial picture of the field and so our powers are limited. In the second phase, through much practice and immersion, we see into the inside of the machinery, how things connect with one another, and thus gain a more comprehensive understanding of the subject. With this comes a new power—the ability to experiment and creatively play with the elements involved. In the third phase, our degree of knowledge, experience, and focus is so deep that we can now see the whole picture with complete clarity. We have access to the heart of life—to human nature and natural phenomena. That is why the artwork of Masters touches us to the core; the artist has captured something of the essence of reality. That is why the brilliant scientist can uncover a new law of physics, and the inventor or entrepreneur can hit upon something no one else has imagined.

We can call this power intuition, but intuition is nothing more than a sudden and immediate seizing of what is real, without the need for words or formulas. The words and formulas may come later, but this flash of intuition is what ultimately brings us closer to reality, as our minds suddenly become illuminated by some particle of truth previously hidden to us and to others.

An animal has the capacity to learn, but it largely relies on its instincts to connect to its surroundings and save itself from danger. Through instinct, it can act quickly and effectively. The human relies instead on thinking and rationality to understand its environment. But such thinking can be slow, and in its slowness can become ineffective. So much of our obsessive, internal thought process tends to disconnect us from the world. Intuitive powers at the mastery level are a mix of the instinctive and the rational, the conscious and the unconscious, the human and the animal. It is our way of making sudden and powerful connections to the environment, to feeling or thinking inside things. As children we had some of this intuitive power and spontaneity, but it is generally drummed out of us by all of the information that overloads our minds over time. Masters return to this childlike state, their works displaying degrees of spontaneity and access to the unconscious, but at a much higher level than the child.

If we move through the process to this endpoint, we activate the intuitive power latent in every human brain, one that we may have briefly experienced when we worked so deeply on a single problem or project. In fact, often in life we have glimpses of this power—for instance, when we have an inkling of what will come next in a particular situation, or when the perfect answer to a problem comes to us out of nowhere. But these moments are ephemeral and not based on enough experience to make them repeatable. When we reach mastery, this intuition is a power at our command, the fruit of working through the lengthier process. And because the world prizes creativity and this ability to uncover new aspects of reality, it brings us tremendous practical power as well.

Think of mastery in this way: Throughout history, men and women have felt trapped by the limitations of their consciousness, by their lack of contact with reality and the power to affect the world around them. They have sought all kinds of shortcuts to this expanded consciousness and sense of control, in the form of magic rituals, trances, incantations, and drugs. They have devoted their lives to alchemy, in search of the philosopher's stone—the elusive substance that transformed all matter into gold.

This hunger for the magical shortcut has survived to our day in the form of simple formulas for success, ancient secrets finally revealed in which a mere change of attitude will attract the right energy. There is a grain of truth and practicality in all of these efforts—for instance, the emphasis in magic on deep focus. But in the end all of this searching is centered on something that doesn't exist—the effortless path to practical power, the quick and easy solution, the El Dorado of the mind.

At the same time that so many people lose themselves in these endless fantasies, they ignore the one real power that they actually possess. And unlike magic or simplistic formulas, we can see the material effects of this power in history—the great discoveries and inventions, the magnificent buildings and works of art, the technological prowess we possess, all works of the masterful mind. This power brings to those who possess it the kind of connection to reality and the ability to alter the world that the mystics and magicians of the past could only dream of.

Over the centuries, people have placed a wall around such mastery. They have called it genius and have thought of it as inaccessible. They have seen it as the product of privilege, inborn talent, or just the right alignment of the stars. They have made it seem as if it were as elusive as magic. But that wall is imaginary. This is the real secret: the brain that we possess is the work of six million years of development, and more than anything else, this evolution of the brain was designed to lead us to mastery, the latent power within us all.

THE EVOLUTION OF MASTERY

For three million years we were hunter-gatherers, and it was through the evolutionary pressures of that way of life that a brain so adaptable and creative eventually emerged. Today we stand with the brains of hunter-gatherers in our heads.

—RICHARD LEAKEY

It is hard for us to imagine now, but our earliest human ancestors who ventured out onto the grasslands of East Africa some six million years ago were remarkably weak and vulnerable creatures. They stood less than five feet tall. They walked upright and could run on their two legs, but nowhere near as fast as the swift predators on four legs that pursued them. They were skinny—their arms could not provide much defense. They had no claws or fangs or poison to resort to if under attack. To gather fruits, nuts, and insects, or to scavenge dead meat, they had to move out into the open savanna where they became easy prey to leopards or packs of hyenas. So weak and small in number, they might have easily become extinct.

And yet within the space of a few million years (remarkably short on the time scale of evolution), these rather physically unimpressive ancestors of ours transformed themselves into the most formidable hunters on the planet. What could possibly account for such a miraculous turnaround?

Some have speculated that it was their standing on two legs, which freed up the hands to make tools with their opposable thumbs and precision grip. But such physical explanations miss the point. Our dominance, our mastery does not stem from our hands but from our brains, from our fashioning the mind into the most powerful instrument known in nature—far more powerful than any claw. And at the root of this *mental* transformation are two simple biological traits—the *visual* and the *social*—that primitive humans leveraged into power.

Our earliest ancestors were descended from primates who thrived for millions of years in a treetop environment, and who in the process had evolved one of the most remarkable visual systems in nature. To move quickly and efficiently in such a world, they developed extremely sophisticated eye and muscle coordination. Their eyes slowly evolved into a full-frontal position on the face, giving them binocular, stereoscopic vision. This system provides the brain a highly accurate three-dimensional and detailed perspective, but is rather narrow. Animals that possess such vision—as opposed to eyes on the side or half side—are generally efficient predators like owls or cats. They use this powerful sight to home in on prey in the distance. Tree-living primates evolved this vision for a different purpose—to navigate branches, and to spot fruits, berries, and insects with greater effectiveness. They also evolved elaborate color vision.

When our earliest human ancestors left the trees and moved to the open grasslands of the savanna, they adopted an upright stance. Possessing already this powerful visual system, they could see far into the distance (giraffes and elephants might stand taller, but their eyes are on the sides, giving them instead panoramic vision). This allowed them to spot dangerous predators far away on the horizon and detect their movements even in twilight. Given a few seconds or minutes, they could plot a safe retreat. At the same time, if they focused on what was nearest at hand, they could identify all kinds of important details in their environment—footprints and signs of passing predators, or the colors and shapes of rocks that they could pick up and perhaps use as tools.

In the treetops, this powerful vision was built for speed—seeing and reacting quickly. On the open grassland, it was the opposite. Safety and finding food relied upon slow, patient observation of the environment, on the ability to pick out details and focus on what they might mean. Our ancestors' survival depended on the intensity of their attention. The longer and harder they looked, the more they could distinguish between an opportunity and a danger. If they simply scanned the horizon quickly they could see a lot more, but this would overload the mind with information—too many details for such sharp vision. The human visual system is not built for scanning, as a cow's is, but for depth of focus.

Animals are locked in a perpetual present. They can learn from recent events, but they are easily distracted by what is in front of their eyes. Slowly, over a great period of time, our ancestors overcame this basic animal weakness. By looking long enough at any object and refusing to be distracted—even for a few seconds—they could momentarily detach themselves from their immediate surroundings. In this way they could notice patterns, make generalizations, and think ahead. They had the mental distance to think and reflect, even on the smallest scale.

These early humans evolved the ability to detach and think as their primary advantage in the struggle to avoid predators and find food. It connected them to a reality other animals could not access. Thinking on this level was the single greatest turning point in all of evolution—the emergence of the conscious, reasoning mind.

The second biological advantage is subtler, but equally powerful in its implications. All primates are essentially social creatures, but because of their intense vulnerability in open areas, our earliest ancestors had a much greater need for group cohesion. They depended on the group for vigilant observation of predators and the gathering of food. In general, these early hominids had many more social interactions than other primates. Over the course of hundreds of thousands of years, this social intelligence became increasingly sophisticated, allowing these ancestors to cooperate with one another on a high level. And as with our understanding of the natural environment, this intelligence depended on deep attention and focus. Misreading the social signs in a tight-knit group could prove highly dangerous.

Through the elaboration of these two traits—the *visual* and the *social*—our primitive ancestors were able to invent and develop the complex skill of hunting some two to three million years ago. Slowly, they became more creative, refining this complex skill into an art. They became seasonal hunters and spread throughout the Euro-Asian landmass, managing to adapt themselves to all kinds of climates. And in the process of this rapid evolution, their brains grew to virtually modern human size, some 200,000 years ago.

In the 1990s a group of Italian neuroscientists discovered something that could help explain this increasing hunting prowess of our primitive ancestors, and in turn something about mastery as it exists today. In studying the brains of monkeys, they found that particular motor-command neurons will not only fire when they execute a very specific action—such as pulling a lever to get a peanut or taking hold of a banana—but that these neurons will also fire when monkeys observe another performing the same actions. These were soon dubbed *mirror neurons*. This neuronal firing meant that these primates would experience a similar sensation in both doing and observing the same deed, allowing them to put themselves in the place of another and perceive its movements as if they were doing them. It would account for the ability of many primates to imitate others, and for the pronounced abilities of chimpanzees to anticipate the plans and actions of a rival. Such neurons, it is speculated, evolved because of the social nature of primate life.

Recent experiments have demonstrated the existence of such neurons in humans, but on a much higher level of sophistication. A monkey or primate can see an action from the point of view of the performer and imagine its intentions, but we can take this further. Without any visual cues or any action on the part of others, we can place ourselves *inside their minds* and imagine what they might be thinking.

For our ancestors, the elaboration of mirror neurons would allow them to read each other's desires from the subtlest of signs and thus elevate their social skills. It would also serve as a critical component in toolmaking—one could learn to fashion a tool by imitating the actions of an expert. But perhaps most important of all, it would give them the ability to *think inside* everything around them. After years of studying particular animals, they could identify with and think like them, anticipating behavioral patterns and heightening their ability to track and kill prey. This *thinking inside* could be applied to the inorganic as well. In fashioning a stone tool, expert toolmakers would feel as one with their instruments. The stone or wood they cut with became an extension of their hand. They could feel it as if it were their own flesh, permitting much greater control of the tools themselves, both in making and in using them.

This power of the mind could be unleashed only after years of experience. Having mastered a particular skill—tracking prey, fashioning a tool—it was now automatic, and so while practicing the skill the mind no longer had to focus on the specific actions involved but instead could concentrate on something higher—what the prey might be thinking, how the tool could be felt as part of the hand. This *thinking inside* would be a preverbal version of third-level intelligence—the primitive equivalent of Leonardo da Vinci's intuitive feel for anatomy and landscape or Michael Faraday's for electromagnetism. Mastery at this level meant our ancestors could make decisions rapidly and effectively, having gained a complete understanding of their environment and their prey. If this power had not evolved, the minds of our ancestors would have become easily overwhelmed by the mass of information they had to process for a successful hunt. They had developed this intuitive power hundreds of thousands of years before the invention of language, and that is why when we experience this intelligence it seems like something preverbal, a power that transcends our ability to put it into words.

Understand: This long stretch of time played a critical, elemental role in our mental development. It fundamentally altered our relationship to time. For animals, time is their great enemy. If they are potential prey, wandering too long in a space can spell instant death. If they are predators, waiting too long will only mean the escape of their prey. Time for them also represents physical decay. To a remarkable extent, our hunting ancestors reversed this process. The longer they spent observing something, the deeper their understanding and connection to reality. With experience, their hunting skills would progress. With continued practice, their ability to make effective tools would improve. The body could decay but the mind would continue to learn and adapt. Using time for such effect is the essential ingredient of mastery.

In fact, we can say that this revolutionary relationship to time fundamentally altered the human mind itself and gave it a particular quality or *grain*. When we take our time and focus in depth, when we trust that going through a process of months or years will bring us mastery, we work with the grain of this marvelous instrument that developed over so many millions of years. We infallibly move to higher and higher levels of intelligence. We see more deeply and realistically. We practice and make things with skill. We learn to think for ourselves. We become capable of handling complex situations without being overwhelmed. In following this path we become *Homo magister*, man or woman the Master.

To the extent that we believe we can skip steps, avoid the process, magically gain power through political connections or easy formulas, or depend on our natural talents, we move against this grain and reverse our natural powers. We become *slaves* to time—as it passes, we grow weaker, less capable, trapped in some dead-end career. We become captive to the opinions and fears of others. Rather than the mind connecting us to reality, we become disconnected and locked in a narrow chamber of thought. The human that depended on focused attention for its survival now becomes the distracted scanning animal, unable to think in depth, yet unable to depend on instincts.

It is the height of stupidity to believe that in the course of your short life, your few decades of consciousness, you can somehow rewire the configurations of your brain through technology and wishful thinking, overcoming the effect of six million years of development. To go against the grain might bring temporary distraction, but time will mercilessly expose your weakness and impatience.

The great salvation for all of us is that we have inherited an instrument that is remarkably plastic. Our hunter-gatherer ancestors, over the course of time, managed to craft the brain into its present shape by creating a culture that could learn, change, and adapt to circumstances, that wasn't a prisoner to the incredibly slow march of natural evolution. As modern individuals, our brains have the same power, the same plasticity. At any moment we can choose to shift our relationship to time and work with the grain, knowing of its existence and power. With the element of time working for us, we can reverse the bad habits and passivity, and move up the ladder of intelligence.

Think of this shift as a return to your radical, deep past as a human, connecting to and maintaining a magnificent continuity with your hunter-gatherer ancestors in a modern form. The environment we operate in may be different, but the brain is essentially the same, and its power to learn, adapt, and master time is universal.

KEYS TO MASTERY

A man should learn to detect and watch that gleam of light which flashes across his mind from within, more than the luster of the firmament of bards and sages. Yet he dismisses without notice his thought, because it is his. In every work of genius we recognize our own rejected thoughts; they come back to us with a certain alienated majesty.

—RALPH WALDO EMERSON

If all of us are born with an essentially similar brain, with more or less the same configuration and potential for mastery, why is it then that in history only a limited number of people seem to truly excel and realize this potential power? Certainly, in a practical sense, this is the most important question for us to answer.

The common explanations for a Mozart or a Leonardo da Vinci revolve around natural talent and brilliance. How else to account for their uncanny achievements except in terms of something they were born with? But thousands upon thousands of children display exceptional skill and talent in some field, yet relatively few of them ever amount to anything, whereas those who are less brilliant in their youth can often attain much more. Natural talent or a high IQ cannot explain future achievement.

As a classic example, compare the lives of Sir Francis Galton and his older cousin, Charles Darwin. By all accounts, Galton was a super-genius with an exceptionally high IQ, quite a bit higher than Darwin's (these are estimates done by experts years after the invention of the measurement). Galton was a boy wonder who went on to have an illustrious scientific career, but he never quite mastered any of the fields he went into. He was notoriously restless, as is often the case with child prodigies.

Darwin, by contrast, is rightly celebrated as the superior scientist, one of the few who has forever changed our view of life. As Darwin himself admitted, he was "a very ordinary boy, rather below the common standard in intellect. . . . I have no great quickness of apprehension. . . . My power to follow a long and purely abstract train of thought is very limited." Darwin, however, must have possessed something that Galton lacked.

In many ways, a look at the early life of Darwin himself can supply an answer to this mystery. As a child Darwin had one overriding passion—collecting biological specimens. His father, a doctor, wanted him to follow in his footsteps and study medicine, enrolling him at the University of Edinburgh. Darwin did not take to this subject and was a mediocre student. His father, despairing that his son would ever amount to anything, chose for him a career in the church. As Darwin was preparing for this, a former professor of his told him that the HMS *Beagle* was to leave port soon to sail around the world, and that it needed a ship's biologist to accompany the crew in order to collect specimens that could be sent back to England. Despite his father's protests, Darwin took the job. Something in him was drawn to the voyage.

Suddenly, his passion for collecting found its perfect outlet. In South America he could collect the most astounding array of specimens, as well as fossils and bones. He could connect his interest in the variety of life on the planet with something larger—major questions about the origins of species. He poured all of his energy into this enterprise, accumulating so many specimens that a theory began to take shape in his mind. After five years at sea, he returned to England and devoted the rest of his life to the single task of elaborating his theory of evolution. In the process he had to deal with a tremendous amount of drudgery—for instance, eight years exclusively studying barnacles to establish his credentials as a biologist. He had to develop highly refined political and social skills to handle all the prejudice against such a theory in Victorian England. And what sustained him throughout this lengthy process was his intense love of and connection to the subject.

The basic elements of this story are repeated in the lives of all of the great Masters in history: a youthful passion or predilection, a chance encounter that allows them to discover how to apply it, an apprenticeship in which they come alive with energy and focus. They excel by their ability to practice harder and move faster through the process, all of this stemming from the intensity of their desire to learn and from the deep connection they feel to their field of study. And at the core of this intensity of effort is in fact a quality that is genetic and inborn—not talent or brilliance, which is something that must be developed, but rather a deep and powerful *inclination* toward a particular subject.

This inclination is a reflection of a person's uniqueness. This uniqueness is not something merely poetic or philosophical—it is a scientific fact that genetically, every one of us is unique; our exact genetic makeup has never happened before and will never be repeated. This uniqueness is revealed to us through the preferences we innately feel for particular activities or subjects of study. Such inclinations can be toward music or mathematics, certain sports or games, solving puzzle-like problems, tinkering and building, or playing with words.

With those who stand out by their later mastery, they experience this inclination more deeply and clearly than others. They experience it as an inner calling. It tends to dominate their thoughts and dreams. They find their way, by accident or sheer effort, to a career path in which this inclination can flourish. This intense connection and desire allows them to withstand the pain of the process—the self-doubts, the tedious hours of practice and study, the inevitable setbacks, the endless barbs from the envious. They develop a resiliency and confidence that others lack.

In our culture we tend to equate thinking and intellectual powers with success and achievement. In many ways, however, it is an emotional quality that separates those who master a field from the many who simply work at a job. Our levels of desire, patience, persistence, and confidence end up playing a much larger role in success than sheer reasoning powers. Feeling motivated and energized, we can overcome almost anything. Feeling bored and restless, our minds shut off and we become increasingly passive.

In the past, only elites or those with an almost superhuman amount of energy and drive could pursue a career of their choice and master it. A man was born into the military, or groomed for the government, chosen among those of the right class. If he happened to display a talent and desire for such work it was mostly a coincidence. Millions of people who were not part of the right social class, gender, and ethnic group were rigidly excluded from the possibility of pursuing their calling. Even if people wanted to follow their inclinations, access to the information and knowledge pertaining to that particular field was controlled by elites. That is why there are relatively few Masters in the past and why they stand out so much.

These social and political barriers, however, have mostly disappeared. Today we have the kind of access to information and knowledge that past Masters could only dream about. Now more than ever, we have the capacity and freedom to move toward the inclination that all of us possess as part of our genetic uniqueness. It is time that the word "genius" becomes demystified and de-rarefied. We are all closer than we think to such intelligence. (The word "genius" comes from the Latin, and originally referred to a guardian spirit that watched over the birth of each person; it later came to refer to the innate qualities that make each person uniquely gifted.)

Although we may find ourselves at a historical moment rich in possibilities for mastery, in which more and more people can move toward their inclinations, we in fact face one last obstacle in attaining such power, one that is cultural and insidiously dangerous: The very concept of mastery has become denigrated, associated with something old-fashioned and even unpleasant. It is generally not seen as something to aspire to. This shift in value is rather recent, and can be traced to circumstances peculiar to our times.

We live in a world that seems increasingly beyond our control. Our livelihoods are at the whim of globalized forces. The problems that we face—economic, environmental, and so on—cannot be solved by our individual actions. Our politicians are distant and unresponsive to our desires. A natural response when people feel overwhelmed is to retreat into various forms of passivity. If we don't try too much in life, if we limit our circle of action, we can give ourselves the illusion of control. The less we attempt, the less chances of failure. If we can make it look like we are not really responsible for our fate, for what happens to us in life, then our apparent powerlessness is more palatable. For this reason we become attracted to certain narratives: it is genetics that determines much of what we do; we are just products of our times; the individual is just a myth; human behavior can be reduced to statistical trends.

Many take this change in value a step further, giving their passivity a positive veneer. They romanticize the self-destructive artist who loses control of him- or herself. Anything that smacks of discipline or effort seems fussy and passé: what matters is the feeling behind the artwork, and any hint of craftsmanship or work violates this principle. They come to accept things that are made cheaply and quickly. The idea that they might have to expend much effort to get what they want has been eroded by the proliferation of devices that do so much of the work for them, fostering the idea that they deserve all of this—that it is their inherent right to have and to consume what they want. "Why bother working for years to attain mastery when we can have so much power with very little effort? Technology will solve everything." This passivity has even assumed a moral stance: "mastery and power are evil; they are the domain of patriarchal elites who oppress us; power is inherently bad; better to opt out of the system altogether," or at least make it look that way.

If you are not careful, you will find this attitude infecting you in subtle ways. You will unconsciously lower your sights as to what you can accomplish in life. This can diminish your levels of effort and discipline below the point of effectiveness. Conforming to social norms, you will listen more to others than to your own voice. You may choose a career path based on what peers and parents tell you, or on what seems lucrative. If you lose contact with this inner calling, you can have some success in life, but eventually your lack of true desire catches up with you. Your work becomes mechanical. You come to live for leisure and immediate pleasures. In this way you become increasingly passive, and never move past the first phase. You may grow frustrated and depressed, never realizing that the source of it is your alienation from your own creative potential.

Before it is too late you must find your way to your inclination, exploiting the incredible opportunities of the age that you have been born into. Knowing the critical importance of desire and of your emotional connection to your work, which are the keys to mastery, you can in fact make the passivity of these times work in your favor and serve as a motivating device in two important ways.

First, you must see your attempt at attaining mastery as something extremely necessary and positive. The world is teeming with problems, many of them of our own creation. To solve them will require a tremendous amount of effort and creativity. Relying on genetics, technology, magic, or being nice and natural will not save us. We require the energy not only to address practical matters, but also to forge new institutions and orders that fit our changed circumstances. We must create our own world or we will die from inaction. We need to find our way back to the concept of mastery that defined us as a species so many millions of years ago. This is not mastery for the purpose of dominating nature or other people, but for determining our fate. The passive ironic attitude is not cool or romantic, but pathetic and destructive. You are setting an example of what can be achieved as a Master in the modern world. You are contributing to the most important cause of all—the survival and prosperity of the human race, in a time of stagnation.

Second, you must convince yourself of the following: people get the mind and quality of brain that they deserve through their actions in life. Despite the popularity of genetic explanations for our behavior, recent discoveries in neuroscience are overturning long-held beliefs that the brain is genetically hardwired. Scientists are demonstrating the degree to which the brain is actually quite plastic—how our thoughts determine our mental landscape. They are exploring the relationship of willpower to physiology, how profoundly the mind can affect our health and functionality. It is possible that more and more will be discovered about how deeply we create the various patterns of our lives through certain mental operations—how we are truly responsible for so much of what happens to us.

People who are passive create a mental landscape that is rather barren. Because of their limited experiences and action, all kinds of connections in the brain die off from lack of use. Pushing against the passive trend of these times, you must work to see how far you can extend control of your circumstances and create the kind of mind you desire—not through drugs but through action. Unleashing the masterful mind within, you will be at the vanguard of those who are exploring the extended limits of human will-power.

In many ways, the movement from one level of intelligence to another can be considered as a kind of ritual of transformation. As you progress, old ideas and perspectives die off; as new powers are unleashed, you are initiated into higher levels of seeing the world. Consider *Mastery* as an invaluable tool in guiding you through this transformative process. The book is designed to lead you from the lowest levels to the highest. It will help to initiate you into the first step—discovering your *Life's Task*, or vocation, and how to carve out a path that will lead you to its fulfillment on various levels. It will advise you how to exploit to the fullest your apprenticeship—the various strategies of observation and learning that will serve you best in this phase; how to find the perfect mentors; how to decipher the unwritten codes on political behavior; how to cultivate social intelligence; and finally, how to recognize when it is time to leave the apprenticeship nest and strike out for yourself, entering the active, creative phase.

It will show you how to continue the learning process on a higher level. It will reveal timeless strategies for creative problem solving, for keeping your mind fluid and adaptable. It will show you how to access more unconscious and primitive layers of intelligence, and how to endure the inevitable barbs of envy that will come your way. It will spell out the powers that will come to you through mastery, pointing you in the direction of that intuitive, inside feel for your field. Finally, it will initiate you into a philosophy, a way of thinking that will make it easier to follow this path.

The ideas in the book are based on extensive research in the fields of neuro- and cognitive science, studies on creativity, as well as the biographies of the greatest Masters in history. These include Leonardo da Vinci, the Zen Master Hakuin, Benjamin Franklin, Wolfgang Amadeus Mozart, Johann Wolfgang von Goethe, the poet John Keats, the scientist Michael Faraday, Charles Darwin, Thomas Edison, Albert Einstein, Henry Ford, the writer Marcel Proust, the dancer Martha Graham, the inventor Buckminster Fuller, the jazz artist John Coltrane, and the pianist Glenn Gould.

To make it clear how this form of intelligence can be applied to the modern world, nine contemporary Masters have been interviewed at length as well. They are neuroscientist V. S. Ramachandran; anthropologist-linguist Daniel Everett; computer engineer, writer, and tech-startup mastermind Paul Graham; architect-engineer Santiago Calatrava; former boxer and now trainer Freddie Roach; robotics engineer and green technology designer

Yoky Matsuoka; visual artist Teresita Fernández; professor of animal husbandry and industrial designer Temple Grandin; and U.S. Air Force fighter pilot ace Cesar Rodriguez.

The life stories of these various contemporary figures dispel the notion that mastery is somehow passé or elitist. They come from all different backgrounds, social classes, and ethnicities. The power they have achieved is clearly the result of effort and process, not genetics or privilege. Their stories also reveal how such mastery can be adapted to our times, and the tremendous power it can bring us.

The structure of *Mastery* is simple. There are six chapters, moving sequentially through the process. Chapter 1 is the starting point—discovering your calling, your Life's Task. Chapters 2, 3, and 4 discuss different elements of the Apprenticeship Phase (learning skills, working with mentors, acquiring social intelligence). Chapter 5 is devoted to the Creative-Active Phase, and chapter 6 to the ultimate goal—Mastery. Each chapter begins with the story of an iconic historical figure who exemplifies the chapter's overall concept. The section that follows, Keys to Mastery, gives you a detailed analysis of the phase involved, concrete ideas on how to apply this knowledge to your circumstances, and the mind-set that is necessary to fully exploit these ideas. Following the Keys is a section detailing the strategies of Masters—contemporary and historical—who have used various methods to advance them through the process. These strategies are designed to give you an even greater sense of the practical application of the ideas in the book, and to inspire you to follow in the footsteps of these Masters, showing how their power is eminently attainable.

For all of the contemporary Masters and some of the historical ones, their stories will continue over several chapters. In such cases there may be a slight repetition of biographical information in order to recap what happened in the previous phase of their lives. Page numbers in parentheses will refer back to these earlier narrations.

Finally, you must not see this process of moving through levels of intelligence as merely linear, heading toward some kind of ultimate destination known as mastery. Your whole life is a kind of apprenticeship to which you apply your learning skills. Everything that happens to you is a form of instruction if you pay attention. The creativity that you gain in learning a skill so deeply must be constantly refreshed, as you keep forcing your mind back to a state of openness. Even knowledge of your vocation must be revisited throughout the course of your life as changes in circumstance force you to adapt its direction.

In moving toward mastery, you are bringing your mind closer to reality and to life itself. Anything that is alive is in a continual state of change and movement. The moment that you rest, thinking that you have attained the level you desire, a part of your mind enters a phase of decay. You lose your hard-earned creativity and others begin to sense it. This is a power and intelligence that must be continually renewed or it will die.

Do not talk about giftedness, inborn talents! One can name great men of all kinds who were very little gifted. They acquired greatness, became "geniuses" (as we put it), through qualities the lack of which no one who knew what they were would boast of: they all possessed that seriousness of the efficient workman which first learns to construct the parts properly before it ventures to fashion a great whole; they allowed themselves time for it, because they took more pleasure in making the little, secondary things well than in the effect of a dazzling whole.

—FRIEDRICH NIETZSCHE

I

DISCOVER YOUR CALLING: THE LIFE'S TASK

You possess a kind of inner force that seeks to guide you toward your Life's Task—what you are meant to accomplish in the time that you have to live. In childhood this force was clear to you. It directed you toward activities and subjects that fit your natural inclinations, that sparked a curiosity that was deep and primal. In the intervening years, the force tends to fade in and out as you listen more to parents and peers, to the daily anxieties that wear away at you. This can be the source of your unhappiness—your lack of connection to who you are and what makes you unique. The first move toward mastery is always inward—learning who you really are and reconnecting with that innate force. Knowing it with clarity, you will find your way to the proper career path and everything else will fall into place. It is never too late to start this process.

THE HIDDEN FORCE

Toward the end of April 1519, after months of illness, the artist Leonardo da Vinci felt certain that his death was only a few days away. For the past two years Leonardo had been living in the château of Cloux in France, the personal guest of the French king, François I. The king had showered him with money and honors, considering him the living embodiment of the Italian Renaissance, which he had wanted to import to France. Leonardo had been most useful to the king, advising him on all kinds of important matters. But now, at the age of sixty-seven, his life was about to end and his thoughts turned toward other things. He made out his will, received the holy sacrament in church, and then returned to his bed, waiting for the end to come.

As he lay there, several of his friends—including the king—visited him. They noticed that Leonardo was in a particularly reflective mood. He was not someone who usually liked to talk about himself, but now he shared memories from his childhood and youth, dwelling on the strange and improbable course of his life.

Leonardo had always had a strong sense of fate, and for years he had been haunted by one particular question: is there some kind of force from within that makes all living things grow and transform themselves? If such a force in nature existed, he wanted to discover it, and he looked for signs of it in every thing he examined. It was an obsession. Now, in his final hours, after his friends had left him alone, Leonardo would have almost certainly applied this question in some form or another to the riddle of his own life, searching for signs of a force or a fate that had brought about his own development and guided him to the present.

Leonardo would have begun such a search by first thinking back to his childhood in the village of Vinci, some twenty miles outside Florence. His father, Ser Piero da Vinci, was a notary and staunch member of the powerful bourgeoisie, but since Leonardo had been born out of wedlock, he was barred from attending the university or practicing any of the noble professions. His schooling therefore was minimal, and so as a child Leonardo was left mostly to himself. He liked most of all to wander through the olive groves around Vinci or to follow a particular path that led to a much different part of the landscape—dense forests full of wild boar, waterfalls cascading over fast-moving streams, swans gliding through pools, strange wildflowers growing out of the sides of cliffs. The intense variety of life in these forests enthralled him.

One day, sneaking into his father's office, he grabbed some sheets of paper—a rather rare commodity in those days, but as a notary his father had a large supply. He took the sheets on his walk into the forest, and sitting upon a rock he began to sketch the various sights around him. He kept returning day after day to do more of the same; even when the weather was bad, he would sit under some kind of shelter and sketch. He had no teachers, no paintings to look at; he did everything by eye, with nature as the model. He noticed that in drawing things he had to observe them much more closely and catch the details that made them come to life.

Once he sketched a white iris, and in observing it so closely he was struck by its peculiar shape. The iris begins as a seed, and then it proceeds through various stages, all of which he had drawn over the past few years. What makes this plant develop through its stages and culminate in this magnificent flower, so unlike any other? Perhaps it possesses a force that pushes it through these various transformations. He would wonder about the metamorphosis of flowers for years to come.

Alone on his deathbed, Leonardo would have thought back to his earliest years as an apprentice in the studio of the Florentine artist Andrea del Verrocchio. He had been admitted there at the age of fourteen because of the remarkable quality of his drawings. Verrocchio instructed his apprentices in all of the sciences that were necessary to produce the work of his studio—engineering, mechanics, chemistry, and metallurgy. Leonardo was eager to learn all of these skills, but soon he discovered in himself something else: he could not simply do an assignment; he needed to make it something of his own, to invent rather than imitate the Master.

One time, as part of his studio work, he was asked to paint an angel in a larger biblical scene designed by Verrocchio. He had decided that he would make his portion of the scene come to life in his own way. In the foreground in front of the angel he painted a flowerbed, but instead of the usual generalized renderings of plants, Leonardo depicted the flower specimens that he had studied in such detail as a child, with a kind of scientific rigor no one had seen before. For the angel's face, he experimented with his paints and mixed a new blend that gave it a kind of soft radiance that expressed the angel's sublime mood. (To help capture this mood, Leonardo had spent time in the local church observing those in fervent prayer, the expression of one young man serving as the model for the angel.) And finally, he determined that he would be the first artist to create realistic angelic wings.

For this purpose, he went to the marketplace and purchased several birds. He spent hours sketching their wings, how exactly they merged into their bodies. He wanted to create the sensation that these wings had organically grown from the angel's shoulders and would bring it natural flight. As usual, Leonardo could not stop there. After his work was completed he became obsessed with birds, and the idea brewed in his mind that perhaps a human could really fly, if Leonardo could figure out the science behind avian flight. Now, several hours every week, he read and studied everything he could about birds. This was how his mind naturally worked—one idea flowed into another.

Leonardo would certainly have recalled the lowest point in his life—the year 1481. The Pope asked Lorenzo de' Medici to recommend to him the finest artists in Florence to decorate a chapel he just had built, the Sistine Chapel. Lorenzo complied and sent to Rome all of the best Florentine artists, excluding Leonardo. They had never really gotten along. Lorenzo was a literary type, steeped in the classics. Leonardo could not read Latin and had little knowledge of the ancients. He had a more scientific bent to his nature. But at the root of Leonardo's bitterness at this snub was something else—he had come to hate the dependence forced upon artists to gain royal favor, to live from commission to commission. He had grown tired of Florence and the court politics that reigned there.

He made a decision that would change everything in his life: He would establish himself in Milan, and he would devise a new strategy for his livelihood. He would be more than an artist. He would pursue all of the crafts and sciences that interested him—architecture, military engineering, hydraulics, anatomy, sculpture. For any prince or patron that wanted him, he could serve as an overall adviser and artist, for a nice stipend. His mind, he decided, worked best when he had several different projects at hand, allowing him to build all kinds of connections between them.

Continuing his self-examination, Leonardo would have thought back to the one great commission that he accepted during this new phase of his life—an enormous bronze equestrian statue in memory of Francesco Sforza, the father of the current duke of Milan. The challenge for him was too irresistible. It would be of a scale no one had seen since the days of ancient Rome, and to cast something so large in bronze would require an engineering feat that had baffled all of the artists of his time. Leonardo worked on the design for months, and to test it out he built a clay replica of the statue and displayed it in the most expansive square in Milan. It was gigantic, the size of a large building. The crowds that gathered to look at it were awestruck—its size, the impetuous stance of the horse that the artist had captured, its terrifying aspect. Word spread throughout Italy of this marvel and people anxiously awaited its realization in bronze. For this purpose, Leonardo invented a totally new way of casting. Instead of breaking up the mold for the horse into sections, Leonardo would construct the mold as one seamless piece (using an unusual mix of materials he had concocted) and cast it as a whole, which would give the horse a much more organic, natural appearance.

A few months later, however, war broke out and the duke needed every bit of bronze he could lay his hands on for artillery. Eventually, the clay statue was taken down and the horse was never built. Other artists had scoffed at Leonardo's folly—he had taken so long to find the perfect solution that naturally, events had conspired against him. One time even Michelangelo himself taunted Leonardo: "You who made a model of a horse you could never cast in bronze and which you gave up, to your shame. And the stupid people of Milan had faith in you?" He had become used to such insults about his slowness at work, but in fact he regretted nothing from this experience. He had been able to test out his ideas on how to engineer large-scale projects; he would apply this knowledge elsewhere. Anyway, he didn't care so much about the finished product; it was the search and process in creating something that had always excited him.

Reflecting on his life in this way, he would have clearly detected the workings of some kind of hidden force within him. As a child this force had drawn him to the wildest part of the landscape, where he could observe the most intense and dramatic variety of life. This same force compelled him to steal paper from his father and devote his time to sketching. It pushed him to experiment while working for Verrocchio. It guided him away from the courts of Florence and the insecure egos that flourished among artists. It compelled him to an extreme of boldness—the gigantic sculptures, the attempt to fly, the dissection of hundreds of corpses for his anatomical studies—all to discover the essence of life itself.

Seen from this vantage point, everything in his life made sense. It was in fact a blessing to have been born illegitimate—it allowed him to develop in his own way. Even the paper in his house seemed to indicate some kind of destiny. What if he had rebelled against this force? What if, after the Sistine Chapel rejection, he had insisted on going to Rome with the others and forced his way into the Pope's good graces instead of seeking his own path? He was capable of that. What if he had devoted himself to mostly painting in order to make a good living? What if he had been more like the others, finishing his works as fast as possible? He would have done well, but he would not have been Leonardo da Vinci. His life would have lacked the purpose that it had, and inevitably things would have gone wrong.

This hidden force within him, like that within the iris he had sketched so many years before, had led to the full flowering of his capacities. He had faithfully followed its guidance to the very end and, having completed his course, now it was time to die. Perhaps his own words, written years before in his notebook, would have come back to him in such a moment: "Just as a well-filled day brings blessed sleep, so a well-employed life brings a blessed death."

KEYS TO MASTERY

Among his various possible beings each man always finds one which is his genuine and authentic being. The voice which calls him to that authentic being is what we call "vocation." But the majority of men devote themselves to silencing that voice of the vocation and refusing to hear it. They manage to make a noise within themselves . . . to distract their own attention in order not to hear it; and they defraud themselves by substituting for their genuine selves a false course of life.

—JOSÉ ORTEGA Y GASSET

Many of the greatest Masters in history have confessed to experiencing some kind of force or voice or sense of destiny that has guided them forward. For Napoleon Bonaparte it was his "star" that he always felt in ascendance when he made the right move. For Socrates, it was his daemon, a voice that he heard, perhaps from the gods, which inevitably spoke to him in the negative—telling him what to avoid. For Goethe, he also called it a daemon— a kind of spirit that dwelled within him and compelled him to fulfill his destiny. In more modern times, Albert Einstein talked of a kind of inner voice that shaped the direction of his speculations. All of these are variations on what Leonardo da Vinci experienced with his own sense of fate.

Such feelings can be seen as purely mystical, beyond explanation, or as hallucinations and delusions. But there is another way to see them—as eminently real, practical, and explicable. It can be explained in the following way:

All of us are born unique. This uniqueness is marked genetically in our DNA. We are a one-time phenomenon in the universe—our exact genetic makeup has never occurred before nor will it ever be repeated. For all of us, this uniqueness first expresses itself in childhood through certain primal inclinations. For Leonardo it was exploring the natural world around his village and bringing it to life on paper in his own way. For others, it can be an early attraction to visual patterns—often an indication of a future interest in mathematics. Or it can be an attraction to particular physical movements or spatial arrangements. How can we explain such inclinations? They are *forces* within us that come from a deeper place than conscious words can express. They draw us to certain experiences and away from others. As these forces move us here or there, they influence the development of our minds in very particular ways.

This primal uniqueness naturally wants to assert and express itself, but some experience it more strongly than others. With Masters it is so strong that it feels like something that has its own external reality—a force, a voice, destiny. In moments when we engage in an activity that corresponds to our deepest inclinations, we might experience a touch of this: We feel as if the words we write or the physical movements we perform come so quickly and easily that they are coming from outside us. We are literally "inspired," the Latin word meaning something from the outside breathing within us.

Let us state it in the following way: At your birth a seed is planted. That seed is your uniqueness. It wants to grow, transform itself, and flower to its full potential. It has a natural, assertive energy to it. Your Life's Task is to bring that seed to flower, to express your uniqueness through your work. You have a destiny to fulfill. The stronger you feel and maintain it—as a force, a voice, or in whatever form—the greater your chance for fulfilling this Life's Task and achieving mastery.

What weakens this force, what makes you not feel it or even doubt its existence, is the degree to which you have succumbed to another force in life—social pressures to conform. This *counterforce* can be very powerful. You want to fit into a group. Unconsciously, you might feel that what makes you different is embarrassing or painful. Your parents often act as a counterforce as well. They may seek to direct you to a career path that is lucrative and comfortable. If these counterforces become strong enough, you can lose complete contact with your uniqueness, with who you really are. Your inclinations and desires become modeled on those of others.

This can set you off on a very dangerous path. You end up choosing a career that does not really suit you. Your desire and interest slowly wane and your work suffers for it. You come to see pleasure and fulfillment as something that comes from outside your work. Because you are increasingly less engaged in your career, you fail to pay attention to changes going on in the field—you fall behind the times and pay a price for this. At moments when you must make important decisions, you flounder or follow what others are doing because you have no sense of inner direction or radar to guide you. You have broken contact with your destiny as formed at birth.

At all cost you must avoid such a fate. The process of following your Life's Task all the way to mastery can essentially begin at any point in life. The hidden force within you is always there and ready to be engaged.

The process of realizing your Life's Task comes in three stages: First, you must connect or reconnect with your inclinations, that sense of uniqueness. The first step then is always inward. You search the past for signs of that inner voice or force. You clear away the other voices that might confuse you—parents and peers. You look for an underlying pattern, a core to your character that you must understand as deeply as possible.

Second, with this connection established, you must look at the career path you are already on or are about to begin. The choice of this path—or redirection of it—is critical. To help in this stage you will need to enlarge your concept of work itself. Too often we make a separation in our lives—there is work and there is life outside work, where we find real pleasure and fulfillment. Work is often seen as a means for making money so we can enjoy that second life that we lead. Even if we derive some satisfaction from our careers we still tend to compartmentalize our lives in this way. This is a depressing attitude, because in the end we spend a substantial part of our waking life at work. If we experience this time as something to get through on the way to real pleasure, then our hours at work represent a tragic waste of the short time we have to live.

Instead you want to see your work as something more inspiring, as part of your *vocation*. The word "vocation" comes from the Latin meaning to call or to be called. Its use in relation to work began in early Christianity—certain people were called to a life in the church; that was their vocation. They could recognize this literally by hearing a voice from God, who had chosen them for this profession. Over time, the word became secularized, referring to any work or study that a person felt was suited to his or her interests, particularly a manual craft. It is time, however, that we return to the original meaning of the word, for it comes much closer to the idea of a Life's Task and mastery.

The voice in this case that is calling you is not necessarily coming from God, but from deep within. It emanates from your individuality. It tells you which activities suit your character. And at a certain point, it calls you to a particular form of work or career. Your work then is something connected deeply to who you are, not a separate compartment in your life. You develop then a sense of your vocation.

Finally, you must see your career or vocational path more as a journey with twists and turns rather than a straight line. You begin by choosing a field or position that roughly corresponds to your inclinations. This initial position offers you room to maneuver and important skills to learn. You don't want to start with something too lofty, too ambitious—you need to make a living and establish some confidence. Once on this path you discover certain side routes that attract you, while other aspects of this field leave you cold. You adjust and perhaps move to a related field, continuing to learn more about yourself, but always expanding off your skill base. Like Leonardo, you take what you do for others and make it your own.

Eventually, you will hit upon a particular field, niche, or opportunity that suits you perfectly. You will recognize it when you find it because it will spark that childlike sense of wonder and excitement; it will feel right. Once found, everything will fall into place. You will learn more quickly and more deeply. Your skill level will reach a point where you will be able to claim your independence from within the group you work for and move out on your own. In a world in which there is so much we cannot control, this will bring you the ultimate form of power. You will determine your circumstances. As your own Master, you will no longer be subject to the whims of tyrannical bosses or scheming peers.

This emphasis on your uniqueness and a Life's Task might seem a poetic conceit without any bearing on practical realities, but in fact it is extremely relevant to the times that we live in. We are entering a world in which we can rely less and less upon the state, the corporation, or family or friends to help and protect us. It is a globalized, harshly competitive environment. We must learn to develop ourselves. At the same time, it is a world teeming with critical problems and opportunities, best solved and seized by entrepreneurs—individuals or small groups who think independently, adapt quickly, and possess unique perspectives. Your individualized, creative skills will be at a premium.

Think of it this way: What we lack most in the modern world is a sense of a larger purpose to our lives. In the past, it was organized religion that often supplied this. But most of us now live in a secularized world. We human animals are unique—we must build our own world. We do not simply react to events out of biological scripting. But without a sense of direction provided to us, we tend to flounder. We don't how to fill up and structure our time. There seems to be no defining purpose to our lives. We are perhaps not conscious of this emptiness, but it infects us in all kinds of ways.

Feeling that we are called to accomplish something is the most positive way for us to supply this sense of purpose and direction. It is a religious-like quest for each of us. This quest should not be seen as selfish or antisocial. It is in fact connected to something much larger than our individual lives. Our evolution as a species has depended on the creation of a tremendous diversity of skills and ways of thinking. We thrive by the collective activity of people supplying their individual talents. Without such diversity, a culture dies.

Your uniqueness at birth is a marker of this necessary diversity. To the degree you cultivate and express it you are fulfilling a vital role. Our times might emphasize equality, which we then mistake for the need for everyone to be the same, but what we really mean by this is the equal chance for people to express their differences, to let a thousand flowers bloom. Your vocation is more than the work that you do. It is intimately connected to the deepest part of your being and is a manifestation of the intense diversity in nature and within human culture. In this sense, you must see your vocation as eminently poetic and inspiring.

Some 2,600 years ago the ancient Greek poet Pindar wrote, "Become who you are by learning who you are." What he meant is the following: You are born with a particular makeup and tendencies that mark you as a piece of fate. It is who you are to the core. Some people never become who they are; they stop trusting in themselves; they conform to the tastes of others, and they end up wearing a mask that hides their true nature. If you allow yourself to learn who you really are by paying attention to that voice and force within you, then you can become what you were fated to become—an individual, a Master.

STRATEGIES FOR FINDING YOUR LIFE'S TASK

The misery that oppresses you lies not in your profession but in yourself! What man in the world would not find his situation intolerable if he chooses a craft, an art, indeed any form of life, without experiencing an inner calling? Whoever is born with a talent, or to a talent, must surely find in that the most pleasing of occupations! Everything on this earth has its difficult sides! Only some inner drive—pleasure, love—can help us overcome obstacles, prepare a path, and lift us out of the narrow circle in which others tread out their anguished, miserable existences!

—Johann Wolfgang von Goethe

It might seem that connecting to something as personal as your inclinations and Life's Task would be relatively simple and natural, once you recognize their importance. But in fact it is the opposite. It requires a good deal of planning and strategizing to do it properly, since so many obstacles will present themselves. The following five strategies, illustrated by stories of Masters, are designed to deal with the main obstacles in your path over time—the voices of others infecting you, fighting over limited resources, choosing false paths, getting stuck in the past, and losing your way. Pay attention to all of them because you will almost inevitably encounter each one in some form.

1. Return to your origins—The primal inclination strategy

For Masters, their inclination often presents itself to them with remarkable clarity in childhood. Sometimes it comes in the form of a simple object that triggers a deep response. When Albert Einstein (1879–1955) was five, his father gave him a compass as a present. Instantly, the boy was transfixed by the needle, which changed direction as he moved the compass about. The idea that there was some kind of magnetic force that operated on this needle, invisible to the eyes, touched him to the core. What if there were other forces in the world equally invisible yet equally powerful—ones that were undiscovered or not understood? For the rest of his life all of his interests and ideas would revolve around this simple question of hidden forces and fields, and he would often think back to the compass that had sparked the initial fascination.

When Marie Curie (1867–1934), the future discoverer of radium, was four years old she wandered into her father's study and stood transfixed before a glass case that contained all kinds of laboratory instruments for chemistry and physics experiments. She would return to that room again and again to stare at the instruments, imagining all sorts of experiments she could conduct with these tubes and measuring devices. Years later, when she entered a real laboratory for the first time and did some experiments herself, she reconnected immediately with her childhood obsession; she knew she had found her vocation.

When the future film director Ingmar Bergman (1918–2007) was nine years old his parents gave his brother for Christmas a cinematograph—a moving picture machine with strips of film that projected simple scenes. He had to have it for himself. He traded his own toys to get it and once it was in his possession, he hurried into a large closet and watched the flickering images it projected on the wall. It seemed like something had magically come to life each time he turned it on. To produce such magic would become his lifelong obsession.

Sometimes this inclination becomes clear through a particular activity that brings with it a feeling of heightened power. As a child, Martha Graham (1894–1991) felt intensely frustrated by her inability to make others understand her in a deep way; words seemed inadequate. Then one day, she saw her first dance performance. The lead dancer had a way of expressing certain emotions through movement; it was visceral, not verbal. She started dance lessons soon thereafter and immediately understood her vocation.

Only when dancing could she feel alive and expressive. Years later she would go on to invent a whole new form of dance and revolutionize the genre.

Sometimes it is not an object or activity but rather something in culture that sparks a deep connection. The contemporary anthropologist-linguist Daniel Everett (b. 1951) grew up on the California-Mexico border, in a cowboy town. From a very early age, he found himself drawn to the Mexican culture around him. Everything about it fascinated him—the sound of the words spoken by the migrant workers, the food, the manners that were so different from the Anglo world. He immersed himself as much as he could in their language and culture. This would transform into a lifelong interest in the Other—the diversity of cultures on the planet and what that means about our evolution.

And sometimes one's true inclinations can be revealed through an encounter with an actual Master. As a young boy growing up in North Carolina, John Coltrane (1926–67) felt different and strange. He was much more serious than his schoolmates; he experienced emotional and spiritual longings he did not know how to verbalize. He drifted into music more as a hobby, taking up the saxophone and playing in his high school band. Then a few years later he saw the great jazz saxophonist Charlie "Bird" Parker perform live, and the sounds Parker produced touched Coltrane to the core. Something primal and personal came through Parker's saxophone, a voice from deep within. Coltrane suddenly saw the means for expressing his uniqueness and giving a voice to his own spiritual longings. He began to practice the instrument with such intensity that within a decade he transformed himself into perhaps the greatest jazz artist of his era.

You must understand the following: In order to master a field, you must love the subject and feel a profound connection to it. Your interest must transcend the field itself and border on the religious. For Einstein, it was not physics but a fascination with invisible forces that governed the universe; for Bergman, it was not film but the sensation of creating and animating life; for Coltrane, it was not music but giving voice to powerful emotions. These childhood attractions are hard to put into words and are more like sensations—that of deep wonder, sensual pleasure, power, and heightened awareness. The importance of recognizing these preverbal inclinations is that they are clear indications of an attraction that is not infected by the desires of other people. They are not something embedded in you by your parents, which come with a more superficial connection, something more verbal and conscious. Coming instead from somewhere deeper, they can only be your own, reflections of your unique chemistry.

As you become more sophisticated, you often lose touch with these signals from your primal core. They can be buried beneath all of the other subjects you have studied. Your power and future can depend on reconnecting with this core and returning to your origins. You must dig for signs of such inclinations in your earliest years. Look for its traces in visceral reactions to something simple; a desire to repeat an activity that you never tired of; a subject that stimulated an unusual degree of curiosity; feelings of power attached to particular actions. It is already there within you. You have nothing to create; you merely need to dig and refind what has been buried inside of you all along. If you reconnect with this core at any age, some element of that primitive attraction will spark back to life, indicating a path that can ultimately become your Life's Task.

2. Occupy the perfect niche—The Darwinian strategy

A. As a child growing up in Madras, India, in the late 1950s, V. S. Ramachandran knew he was different. He was not interested in sports or the other usual pursuits of boys his age; he loved to read about science. In his loneliness he would often wander along the beach, and soon he became fascinated by the incredible variety of seashells that washed up on shore. He began to collect them and study the subject in detail. It gave him a feeling of power—here was a field he had all to himself; nobody in school could ever know as much as he did about shells. Soon he was drawn to the strangest varieties of seashells, such as the Xenophora, an organism that collects discarded shells and uses them for camouflage. In a way, he was like the Xenophora—an anomaly. In nature, these anomalies often serve a larger evolutionary purpose—they can lead to the occupation of new ecological niches, offering a greater chance of survival. Could Ramachandran say the same about his own strangeness?

Over the years, he transferred this boyhood interest into other subjects—human anatomical abnormalities, peculiar phenomena in chemistry, and so on. His father, fearing that the young man would end up in some esoteric field of research, convinced him to enroll in medical school. There he would be exposed to all sides of science and he would come out of it with a practical skill. Ramachandran complied.

Although the studies in medical school interested him, after a while he grew restless. He disliked all of the rote learning. He wanted to experiment and discover, not memorize. He began to read all kinds of science journals and books that were not on the reading list. One such book was *Eye and*

Brain, by the visual neuroscientist Richard Gregory. What particularly intrigued him were experiments on optical illusions and blind spots—anomalies in the visual system that could explain something about how the brain itself functioned.

Stimulated by this book, he conducted his own experiments, the results of which he managed to get published in a prestigious journal, which in turn led to an invitation to study visual neuroscience in the graduate department at Cambridge University. Excited by this chance to pursue something more suited to his interests, Ramachandran accepted the invitation. After a few months at Cambridge, however, he realized that he did not fit in this environment. In his boyhood dreams, science was a great romantic adventure, an almost religious-like quest for the truth. But at Cambridge, for the students and faculty, it seemed to be more like a job; you put in your hours, you contributed some small piece to a statistical analysis, and that was that.

He soldiered on, finding his own interests within the department, and completed his degree. A few years later he was hired as an assistant professor in visual psychology at the University of California at San Diego. As had happened so many times before, after a few years his mind began to drift to yet another subject—this time to the study of the brain itself. He became intrigued by the phenomenon of phantom limbs—people who have had an arm or leg amputated and yet still feel a paralyzing pain in the missing limb. He proceeded to conduct experiments on phantom limb subjects. These experiments led to some exciting discoveries about the brain itself, as well as a novel way to relieve such patients of their pain.

Suddenly the feeling of not fitting in, of restlessness, was gone. Studying anomalous neurological disorders would be the subject to which he could devote the rest of his life. It opened up questions that fascinated him about the evolution of consciousness, the origin of language, and so on. It was as if he had come full circle to the days of collecting the rarest forms of seashells. This was a niche he had all to himself, one he could command for years to come, that corresponded to his deepest inclinations and would serve best the cause of scientific advancement.

B. For Yoky Matsuoka, childhood was a period of confusion and blur. Growing up in Japan in the 1970s, everything seemed laid out for her in advance. The school system would funnel her into a field that was appropriate for girls, and the possibilities were rather narrow. Her parents, believing in the importance of sports in her development, pushed her into competitive swimming at a very early age. They also had her take up the piano. For other children in Japan it may have been comforting to have their lives directed in such a fashion, but for Yoky it was painful. She was interested in all kinds of subjects—particularly math and science. She liked sports but not swimming. She had no idea what she wanted to become or how she could possibly fit into such a regimented world.

At the age of eleven she finally asserted herself. She had had enough of swimming and wanted to take up tennis. Her parents agreed to her wishes. Being intensely competitive, she had great dreams for herself as a tennis player, but she was starting out in the sport rather late in life. To make up for lost time she would have to undergo an almost impossibly rigorous practice schedule. She traveled outside Tokyo for training and so would do her homework on the ride back at night. Often having to stand up in the crowded car, she would crack open her math and physics books and work out the equations. She loved solving puzzles, and in doing this homework her mind would become so completely absorbed in the problems that she was barely aware of the time passing. In a strange way, it was similar to the sensation she felt on the tennis court—a deep focus where nothing could distract her.

In the few free moments on the train Yoky would think about her future. Science and sports were the two great interests in her life. In them she could express all of the different sides of her character—her love of competing, working with her hands, moving gracefully, analyzing and solving problems. In Japan you had to choose a career that was generally quite specialized. Whatever she chose would require sacrificing her other interests, which depressed her to no end. One day she daydreamed about inventing a robot that could play tennis with her. Inventing and playing against such a robot would satisfy all of the different sides of her character, but it was only a dream.

Although she had risen through the ranks to become one of the top tennis prospects in Japan, she quickly realized that this was not to be her future. In practice, no one could beat her, but in competition she would often freeze up, overthink the situation, and lose to inferior players. She also suffered some debilitating injuries. She would have to focus on academics and not on sports. After attending a tennis academy in Florida, she convinced her parents to let her stay in the States and apply to the University of California at Berkeley.

At Berkeley she could not decide on a major—nothing seemed to quite fit her wide-ranging interests. For lack of anything better, she settled on electrical engineering. One day she confided to a professor in her department about her youthful dream to build a robot to play tennis with her. Much to her surprise the professor did not laugh, but instead invited her to join his graduate lab for robotics. Her work there showed so much promise that she was later admitted to graduate school at MIT, where she joined the artificial-intelligence lab of robotics pioneer Rodney Brooks. They were developing a robot with artificial intelligence, and Matsuoka volunteered to design the hand and arms.

Ever since she was a child she had pondered her own hands while she was playing tennis or the piano or while scribbling out math equations. The human hand was a miracle of design. Although this was not exactly sports, she would be working with her hands to construct the hand. Finding at last something that suited a larger range of her interests, she worked night and day on building a new kind of robotic limb, one that possessed as much as possible the delicate grasping power of the human hand. Her design dazzled Brooks—it was years ahead of anything anyone had ever developed.

Feeling that there was a critical lack in her knowledge, she decided to gain an additional degree in neuroscience. If she could better understand the connection between the hand and the brain, she could design a prosthetic limb that would feel and respond like a human hand. She continued this process, adding new fields of science to her résumé, culminating in the creation of a completely new field, one that she would dub *neurobotics*—the design of robots that possessed simulated versions of human neurology, bringing them closer to life itself. Forging this field would bring her great success in science and put her in the ultimate position of power—the ability to freely combine all of her interests.

———◆———

The career world is like an ecological system: People occupy particular fields within which they must compete for resources and survival. The more people there are crowded into a space, the harder it becomes to thrive there. Working in such a field will tend to wear you out as you struggle to get attention, to play the political games, to win scarce resources for yourself. You spend so much time at these games that you have little time left over for true mastery. You are seduced into such fields because you see others there making a living, treading the familiar path. You are not aware of how difficult such a life can be.

The game you want to play is different: to instead find a niche in the ecology that you can dominate. It is never a simple process to find such a niche. It requires patience and a particular strategy. In the beginning you choose a field that roughly corresponds to your interests (medicine, electrical engineering). From there you can go in one of two directions. The first is the Ramachandran path. From within your chosen field, you look for side paths that particularly attract you (in his case the science of perception and optics). When it is possible, you make a move to this narrower field. You continue this process until you eventually hit upon a totally unoccupied niche, the narrower the better. In some ways, this niche corresponds to your uniqueness, much as Ramachandran's particular form of neurology corresponds to his own primal sense of feeling like an exception.

The second is the Matsuoka path. Once you have mastered your first field (robotics), you look for other subjects or skills that you can conquer (neuroscience), on your own time if necessary. You can now combine this added field of knowledge to the original one, perhaps creating a new field, or at least making novel connections between them. You continue this process as long as you wish—in Matsuoka's case, she never stops expanding. Ultimately you create a field that is uniquely your own. This second version fits in well with a culture where information is so widely available, and in which connecting ideas is a form of power.

In either direction, you have found a niche that is not crowded with competitors. You have freedom to roam, to pursue particular questions that interest you. You set your own agenda and command the resources available to this niche. Unburdened by overwhelming competition and politicking, you have time and space to bring to flower your Life's Task.

3. Avoid the false path—The rebellion strategy

In 1760, at the age of four, Wolfgang Amadeus Mozart took up the piano under his father's instruction. It was Wolfgang who asked to start lessons at this precocious age; his sister, age seven, had already started on the instrument. Perhaps it was partly out of sibling rivalry that he had taken such initiative, seeing the attention and love that his sister received for her playing and wanting it for himself.

After the first few months of practice, his father, Leopold—a talented player, composer, and teacher himself—could see that Wolfgang was exceptional. Most strange for his age, the boy loved to practice; at night his parents had to drag him away from the piano. He began to compose his own pieces at the age of five. Soon, Leopold took this prodigy and his sister on the road to perform in all the capitals of Europe. Wolfgang dazzled the royal audiences for whom he performed. He played with assurance and could improvise all kinds of clever melodies. He was like a precious toy. The father was now earning a nice income for the family, as more and more courts wanted to see the child genius in action.

As the patriarch of the family, Leopold demanded total obedience from his children, even though it was now young Wolfgang who was essentially supporting them all. Wolfgang willingly submitted—he owed everything to his father. But as he entered adolescence something else stirred within him. Was it playing the piano that he enjoyed, or simply attracting all of this attention? He felt confused. After so many years composing music he was finally developing his own style, and yet his father insisted that he focus on writing the more conventional pieces that pleased the royal audiences and brought the family money. The city of Salzburg, where they lived, was provincial and bourgeois. In general, he yearned for something else, to be on his own. With each passing year, Wolfgang felt increasingly stifled.

Finally, in 1777, the father allowed Wolfgang—now twenty-one—to leave for Paris, accompanied by his mother. There he must try to gain a prominent position as conductor, so that he could continue supporting his family. But Wolfgang did not find Paris to his liking. The jobs he was offered seemed beneath his talents. And then his mother fell ill while there and died on the way back home. The trip was a disaster in all possible ways. Wolfgang returned to Salzburg, chastened and prepared to submit to his father's will. He accepted a rather uninteresting position as the court organist, but he could not completely suppress his unease. He despaired of spending his life in this mediocre position, writing music to please these petty provincials. At one point, he wrote his father: "I am a composer. . . . I neither can nor ought to bury the talent for composition with which God in his goodness has so richly endowed me."

Leopold reacted to these increasingly frequent complaints of his son with anger, reminding him of the debt he owed him for all of the training he had received and the expenses the father had incurred in their endless travels. Finally, in a flash, it came to Wolfgang: it was never really the piano that was his love, nor even music per se. He did not enjoy performing before others like a puppet. It was composing that he was destined for; but more than that, he had an intense love for the theater. He wanted to compose operas—that was his true voice. He would never realize this if he remained in Salzburg. It was his father who represented more than an obstacle; he was in fact ruining his life, his health, his confidence. It was not just about money; his father was actually jealous of his son's talents, and whether consciously or not, he was trying to stifle his progress. Wolfgang had to take a step, however painful, before it was too late.

On a trip to Vienna in 1781, Wolfgang made the fateful decision to stay. He would never return to Salzburg. As if Wolfgang had broken some great taboo, his father could never forgive him for this; his son had abandoned the family. The rift between them would never be repaired. Feeling that he had lost so much time under his father's thumb, Wolfgang composed at a furious pace, his most famous operas and compositions pouring out of him as if he were possessed.

———

A false path in life is generally something we are attracted to for the wrong reasons—money, fame, attention, and so on. If it is attention we need, we often experience a kind of emptiness inside that we are hoping to fill with the false love of public approval. Because the field we choose does not correspond with our deepest inclinations, we rarely find the fulfillment that we crave. Our work suffers for this, and the attention we may have gotten in the beginning starts to fade—a painful process. If it is money and comfort that dominate our decision, we are most often acting out of anxiety and the need to please our parents. They may steer us toward something lucrative out of care and concern, but lurking underneath this can be something else— perhaps a bit of envy that we have more freedom than they had when they were young.

Your strategy must be twofold: first, to realize as early as possible that you have chosen your career for the wrong reasons, before your confidence takes a hit. And second, to actively rebel against those forces that have pushed you away from your true path. Scoff at the need for attention and approval—they will lead you astray. Feel some anger and resentment at the parental forces that want to foist upon you an alien vocation. It is a healthy part of your development to follow a path independent of your parents and to establish your own identity. Let your sense of rebellion fill you with energy and purpose. If it is the father figure, the Leopold Mozart, that is blocking your path, you must slay him and clear the way.

4. Let go of the past—The adaptation strategy

From the time he was born in 1960, Freddie Roach was groomed to be a boxing champion. His father had been a professional fighter himself, and his mother a boxing judge. Freddie's older brother began learning the sport at an early age, and when Freddie was six he was promptly taken to the local gym in south Boston to begin a rigorous apprenticeship in the sport. He trained with a coach several hours a day, six days a week.

By the age of fifteen he felt like he was burned out. He made more and more excuses to avoid going to the gym. One day his mother sensed this and said to him, "Why do you fight anyway? You just get hit all the time. You can't fight." He was used to the constant criticism from his father and brothers, but to hear such a frank assessment from his mother had a bracing effect. Clearly, she saw his older brother as the one destined for greatness. Now Freddie determined that he would somehow prove her wrong. He returned to his training regimen with a vengeance. He discovered within himself a passion for practice and discipline. He enjoyed the sensation of getting better, the trophies that began to pile up, and, more than anything, the fact that he could now actually beat his brother. His love for the sport was rekindled.

As Freddie now showed the most promise of the brothers, his father took him to Las Vegas to help further his career. There, at the age of eighteen, he met the legendary coach Eddie Futch and began to train under him. It all looked very promising—he was chosen for the United States boxing team and began to climb up the ranks. Before long, however, he hit another wall. He would learn the most effective maneuvers from Futch and practice them to perfection, but in an actual bout it was another story. As soon as he got hit in the ring, he would revert to fighting instinctually; his emotions would get the better of him. His fights would turn into brawls over many rounds, and he would often lose.

After a few years, Futch told Roach it was time to retire. But boxing had been his whole life; retire and do what? He continued to fight and to lose, until finally he could see the writing on the wall and retired. He took a job in telemarketing and began to drink heavily. Now he hated the sport—he had given it so much and had nothing to show for his efforts. Almost in spite of himself, one day he returned to Futch's gym to watch his friend Virgil Hill spar with a boxer about to fight for a title. Both fighters trained under Futch, but there was nobody in Hill's corner helping him, so Freddie brought him water and gave him advice. He showed up the following day to help Hill again, and soon became a regular at Futch's gym. He was not being paid, so he kept his telemarketing job, but something in him smelled opportunity—and he was desperate. He showed up on time and stayed later than anyone else. Knowing Futch's techniques so well, he could teach them to all of the fighters. His responsibilities began to grow.

In the back of his mind he could not shake his resentment of boxing, and he questioned how long he could keep this up. It was a dog-eat-dog career and trainers rarely lasted very long in the business. Would this turn into yet another routine in which he would endlessly repeat the same exercises he had learned from Futch? A part of him yearned to return to fighting—at least fighting was not so predictable.

One day Virgil Hill showed him a technique he had picked up from some Cuban fighters: Instead of working with a punching bag, they mostly trained with the coach, who wore large padded mitts. Standing in the ring, the fighters half-sparred with the coach and practiced their punches. Roach tried it with Hill and his eyes lit up. It brought him back into the ring, but there was something else. Boxing, he felt, had become stale, as had its training methods. In his mind, he saw a way to adapt the mitt work for more than just punching practice. It could be a way for a trainer to devise an entire strategy in the ring and demonstrate it to his fighter in real time. It could revolutionize and revitalize the sport itself. Roach began to develop this with the stable of fighters that he now trained. He instructed them in maneuvers that were much more fluid and strategic.

Soon he left Futch to work on his own. He quickly established a reputation for preparing his boxers better than anyone else, and within a few years he rose to become the most successful trainer of his generation.

In dealing with your career and its inevitable changes, you must think in the following way: You are not tied to a particular position; your loyalty is not to a career or a company. You are committed to your Life's Task, to giving it full expression. It is up to you to find it and guide it correctly. It is not up to others to protect or help you. *You are on your own.* Change is inevitable, particularly in such a revolutionary moment as ours. Since you are on your own, it is up to you to foresee the changes going on right now in your profession. You must adapt your Life's Task to these circumstances. You do not hold on to past ways of doing things, because that will ensure you will fall behind and suffer for it. You are flexible and always looking to adapt.

If change is forced upon you, as it was for Freddie Roach, you must resist the temptation to overreact or feel sorry for yourself. Roach instinctively found his way back to the ring because he understood that what he loved was not boxing per se, but competitive sports and strategizing. Thinking in this way, he could adapt his inclinations to a new direction *within* boxing. Like Roach, you don't want to abandon the skills and experience you have gained, but to find a new way to apply them. Your eye is on the future, not the past. Often such creative readjustments lead to a superior path for us—we are shaken out of our complacency and forced to reassess where we are headed. Remember: your Life's Task is a living, breathing organism. The moment you rigidly follow a plan set in your youth, you lock yourself into a position, and the times will ruthlessly pass you by.

5. Find your way back—The life-or-death strategy

As a very young child Buckminster Fuller (1895–1983) knew that he experienced the world differently than others. He was born with extreme nearsightedness. Everything around him was a blur, and so his other senses developed to compensate for this—particularly touch and smell. Even after he was prescribed glasses at the age of five, he continued to perceive the world around him with more than just his eyes. He had a tactile form of intelligence.

Fuller was an extremely resourceful child. He once invented a new kind of oar to help propel him across the lakes in Maine where he spent his summers delivering mail. Its design was modeled after the motion of jellyfish, which he had observed and studied. He could envision the dynamics of their movement with more than his eyes—he *felt* the movement. He reproduced this motion in his newfangled oar and it functioned beautifully. During such summers he would dream of other interesting inventions—these would be his life's work, his destiny.

Being different, however, had its painful side. He had no patience for the usual forms of education. Although he was very bright and had been admitted to Harvard University, he could not adapt to its strict style of learning. He skipped classes, began to drink, and led a rather bohemian lifestyle. The officials at Harvard expelled him twice—the second time for good.

After that he bounced from job to job. He worked at a meatpacking plant and then, during World War I, he secured a good position in the navy. He had an incredible feel for machines and how their parts worked in concert. But he was restless, and could not stay too long in one place. After the war he had a wife and child to support, and despairing of ever being able to care for them properly, he decided to take a high-paying position as a sales manager. He worked hard, did a decent job, but after three months the company folded. He had found the work extremely unsatisfying, but it seemed that such jobs were all he could expect from life.

Finally, a few months later, a chance appeared out of nowhere. His father-in-law had invented a way of producing materials for houses that would end up making them more durable and better insulated, and at a much lower cost. But the father could not find investors or anyone willing to help him set up a business. Fuller thought his idea brilliant. He had always been interested in housing and architecture, and so he offered to take charge of implementing this new technology. He put everything he could into the effort and was even able to improve on the materials to be used. Fuller's father-in-law supported his work, and together they formed the Stockade Building System. Money from investors, mostly family members, allowed them to open factories. The company struggled—the technology was too new and radical, and Fuller was too much of a purist to compromise his desire to revolutionize the construction industry. After five years the company was sold and Fuller was fired as president.

Now the situation looked bleaker than ever. The family had been living well in Chicago on his salary, beyond its means. In those five years he had not managed to save anything. Winter was approaching and his prospects for work seemed very slim—his reputation was in tatters. One evening he walked along Lake Michigan and thought of his life up until then. He had disappointed his wife, and he had lost money for his father-in-law and his friends who had invested in the enterprise. He was useless at business and a burden to everyone. Finally he decided upon suicide as the best option. He would drown himself in the lake. He had a good insurance policy, and his wife's family would take better care of her than he had been able to. As he walked toward the water, he mentally prepared himself for death.

Suddenly something stopped him in his tracks—what he would describe later as a voice, coming from nearby or perhaps from within him. It said, "From now on you need never await temporal attestation to your thought. You think the truth. You do not have the right to eliminate yourself. You do not belong to you. You belong to Universe. Your significance will remain forever obscure to you, but you may assume that you are fulfilling your role if you apply yourself to converting your experiences to the highest advantage of others." Never having heard voices before, Fuller could only imagine it as something real. Stunned by these words, he turned away from the water and headed home.

On the way there he began to ponder the words and to reassess his life, now in a different light. Perhaps what he had perceived moments earlier as his mistakes were not mistakes at all. He had tried to fit into a world (business) in which he did not belong. The world was telling him this if he only listened. The Stockade experience was not all a waste—he had learned some invaluable lessons about human nature. He should have no regrets. The truth was that he *was* different. In his mind he imagined all kinds of inventions—new kinds of cars, houses, building structures—that reflected his unusual perceptual skills. It struck him, as he looked around at row after row of apartment housing on his way back, that people suffered more from sameness, from the inability to think of doing things differently, than from nonconformity.

He swore that from that moment on he would listen to nothing except his own experience, his own voice. He would create an alternative way of making things that would open people's eyes to new possibilities. The money would eventually come. Whenever he thought of money first, disaster followed. He would take care of his family, but they would have to live frugally for the moment.

Over the years, Fuller kept to this promise. The pursuit of his peculiar ideas led to the design of inexpensive and energy-efficient forms of transportation and shelter (the Dymaxion car and Dymaxion house), and to the invention of the geodesic dome—a whole new form of architectural structure. Fame and money soon followed.

No good can ever come from deviating from the path that you were destined to follow. You will be assailed by varieties of hidden pain. Most often you deviate because of the lure of money, of more immediate prospects of prosperity. Because this does not comply with something deep within you, your interest will lag and eventually the money will not come so easily. You will search for other easy sources of money, moving further and further away from your path. Not seeing clearly ahead of you, you will end up in a dead-end career. Even if your material needs are met, you will feel an emptiness inside that you will need to fill with any kind of belief system, drugs, or diversions. There is no compromise here, no way of escaping the dynamic. You will recognize how far you have deviated by the depth of your pain and frustration. You must listen to the message of this frustration, this pain, and let it guide you as clearly as Fuller's voice guided him. It is a matter of life and death.

The way back requires a sacrifice. You cannot have everything in the present. The road to mastery requires patience. You will have to keep your focus on five or ten years down the road, when you will reap the rewards of your efforts. The process of getting there, however, is full of challenges and pleasures. Make your return to the path a resolution you set for yourself, and then tell others about it. It becomes a matter of shame and embarrassment to deviate from this path. In the end, the money and success that truly last come not to those who focus on such things as goals, but rather to those who focus on mastery and fulfilling their Life's Task.

REVERSAL

Some people do not become aware of inclinations or future career paths in their childhood, but instead are made painfully aware of their limitations. They are not good at what others seem to find easy or manageable. The idea of a calling in life is alien to them. In some cases they internalize the judgments and criticisms of others, and come to see themselves as essentially deficient. If they are not careful, this can become a self-fulfilling prophecy.

Nobody faced this fate more powerfully than Temple Grandin. In 1950, at the age of three, she was diagnosed with autism. She had yet to make any progress in learning language, and it was thought that this would remain her condition—and that she would need to be institutionalized her entire life. But her mother wanted to try one last option before giving up: she sent Temple to a speech therapist, who miraculously, slowly managed to teach her language, which allowed her to attend school and begin to learn what other children were learning.

Despite this improvement, Temple's future appeared limited at best. Her mind functioned in a different way—she thought in terms of images, not words. In order to learn a word she had to be able to picture it in her mind. This made it hard to understand abstract words or learn mathematics. She was also not good at socializing with other children, who often made fun of her for her differences. With such learning disabilities, what could she hope to do in life beyond some kind of menial job? To make matters worse, she had an extremely active mind, and without something to concentrate on, she would give in to feelings of intense anxiety.

Whenever she felt troubled, Temple instinctively retreated to two activities that were comfortable to her: interacting with animals and building things with her hands. With animals, particularly horses, she had an uncanny ability to sense their feelings and thoughts. She became an expert horseback rider. Because she tended to think first in images, when it came to making things with her hands (like sewing or woodwork), she could envision the finished product in her mind and then easily put it together.

At the age of eleven, Temple went to visit an aunt who had a ranch in Arizona. There she realized that she had an even greater sense of empathy for cattle than she did for horses. One day she watched with particular interest as some of the cattle were placed in a squeeze chute that pressed them on their sides to relax them before their vaccination shots. Throughout her childhood Temple had had the desire to be held tightly, but could not stand being held by an adult—she felt like she had no control in such a situation, and would panic. She pleaded with her aunt to allow her to be put into the squeeze device herself. The aunt agreed, and for thirty minutes Temple gave in to the feeling of pressure she had always dreamed of. Once it was over, she felt an enormous sense of calmness. After that experience she became obsessed with the machine, and several years later managed to build her own primitive version of it that she could use at home.

Now she was obsessed with the subject of cattle, squeeze chutes, and the effect of touch and pressure on autistic children. In order to satisfy her curiosity, she had to develop reading and researching skills. Once she did, she found she had unusually high powers of concentration—she could read for hours on one subject without getting the slightest bit bored. Her research slowly expanded into books on psychology, biology, and science in general. Because of the intellectual skills she had developed, she was admitted into a university. Her horizons were slowly expanding.

Several years later, she found herself pursuing a master's degree in Animal Sciences at Arizona State University. There, her obsession with cattle resurfaced—she wanted to do a detailed analysis of feedlots and cattle chutes in particular, to help understand the behavioral responses of the animals. Her professors there could not understand such an interest, and told her it was not possible. Never being one to take no for an answer, she found professors in another department who would sponsor her. She did her study, and in the process finally caught a glimpse of her Life's Task.

She was not destined for a life in the university. She was a practical person who liked to build things and yet needed constant mental stimulation. She decided she would carve out her own peculiar career path. Starting off freelance, she offered her services to various ranches and feedlots, designing cattle chutes that were much more suited to the animals and more efficient. Slowly, with her visual sense of design and engineering, she taught herself the rudiments of the business. She expanded her services to designing more humane slaughterhouses and systems for managing farm animals.

With this career solidly in place, she proceeded to go further: she became a writer; she returned to the university as a professor; she transformed herself into a gifted lecturer on animals and autism. Somehow she had managed to overcome all of the seemingly insurmountable obstructions in her path and find her way to the Life's Task that suited her to perfection.

When you are faced with deficiencies instead of strengths and inclinations, this is the strategy you must assume: ignore your weaknesses and resist the temptation to be more like others. Instead, like Temple Grandin, direct yourself toward the small things you are good at. Do not dream or make grand plans for the future, but instead concentrate on becoming proficient at these simple and immediate skills. This will bring you confidence and become a base from which you can expand to other pursuits. Proceeding in this way, step by step, you will hit upon your Life's Task.

Understand: Your Life's Task does not always appear to you through some grand or promising inclination. It can appear in the guise of your deficiencies, making you focus on the one or two things that you are inevitably good at. Working at these skills, you learn the value of discipline and see the rewards you get from your efforts. Like a lotus flower, your skills will expand outward from a center of strength and confidence. Do not envy those who seem to be naturally gifted; it is often a curse, as such types rarely learn the value of diligence and focus, and they pay for this later in life. This strategy applies as well to any setbacks and difficulties we may experience. In such moments, it is generally wise to stick to the few things we know and do well, and to reestablish our confidence.

If someone like Temple Grandin, with so much against her at birth, can find her way to her Life's Task and to mastery, it means it must be a power accessible to us all.

Sooner or later something seems to call us onto a particular path. You may remember this "something" as a signal calling in childhood when an urge out of nowhere, a fascination, a peculiar turn of events struck like an annunciation: This is what I must do, this is what I've got to have. This is who I am . . . If not this vivid and sure, the call may have been more like gentle pushings in the stream in which you drifted unknowingly to a particular spot on the bank. Looking back, you sense that fate had a hand in it. . . . A calling may be postponed, avoided, intermittently missed. It may also possess

you completely. Whatever; eventually it will out. It makes its claim. . . .
Extraordinary people display calling most evidently. Perhaps that's why
they fascinate. Perhaps, too, they are extraordinary because their calling
comes through so clearly and they are so loyal to it. . . . Extraordinary people
bear the better witness because they show what ordinary mortals simply
can't. We seem to have less motivation and more distraction. Yet our destiny
is driven by the same universal engine. Extraordinary people are not a
different category; the workings of this engine in them are simply more
transparent. . . .

—JAMES HILLMAN

II

SUBMIT TO REALITY: THE IDEAL APPRENTICESHIP

After your formal education, you enter the most critical phase in your life—a second, practical education known as The Apprenticeship. Every time you change careers or acquire new skills, you reenter this phase of life. The dangers are many. If you are not careful, you will succumb to insecurities, become embroiled in emotional issues and conflicts that will dominate your thoughts; you will develop fears and learning disabilities that you will carry with you throughout your life. Before it is too late you must learn the lessons and follow the path established by the greatest Masters, past and present—a kind of Ideal Apprenticeship that transcends all fields. In the process you will master the necessary skills, discipline your mind, and transform yourself into an independent thinker, prepared for the creative challenges on the way to mastery.

THE FIRST TRANSFORMATION

From early in his life, Charles Darwin (1809–82) felt the presence of his father bearing down on him. The father was a successful and wealthy country doctor who had high hopes for his two sons. But Charles, the youngest, seemed to be the one who was less likely to meet his expectations. He was not good at Greek and Latin, or algebra, or really anything in school. It wasn't that he lacked ambition. It was just that learning about the world through books did not interest him. He loved the outdoors—hunting, scouring the countryside for rare breeds of beetles, collecting flower and mineral specimens. He could spend hours observing the behavior of birds and taking elaborate notes on their various differences. He had an eye for such things. But these hobbies did not add up to a career, and as he got older he could sense his father's growing impatience. One day, his father rebuked him with words Charles would never forget: "You care for nothing but shooting, dogs, and rat-catching, and you will be a disgrace to yourself and all your family."

When Charles turned fifteen, his father decided to become more actively involved in his life. He sent him off to medical school in Edinburgh, but Charles could not stand the sight of blood and so had to drop out. Determined to find some career for him, the father then secured for his son a future position in the church as a country parson. For this Charles would be well paid, and he would have plenty of spare time to pursue his mania for collecting specimens. The only requirement for such a position was a degree from an eminent university, and so Charles was enrolled at Cambridge. Once again, he had to confront his disinterest in formal schooling. He tried his best. He developed an interest in botany and became good friends with his instructor, Professor Henslow. He worked as hard as he could, and to his father's relief he managed, barely, to earn his Bachelor of Arts in May 1831.

Hoping that his schooling was forever over, Charles left on a tour of the English countryside where he could indulge in all of his passions for the outdoors and forget about the future, for the time being.

When he returned home in late August, he was surprised to see a letter waiting for him from Professor Henslow. The professor was recommending Charles for a position as an unpaid naturalist on the HMS *Beagle*, which was to leave in a few months on a several-year journey around the globe, surveying various coastlines. As part of his job, Charles would be in charge of collecting life and mineral specimens along the way and sending them back to England for examination. Evidently, Henslow had been impressed by the young man's remarkable skill in collecting and identifying plant specimens.

This offer confused Charles. He had never thought of traveling that far, let alone pursuing a career as a naturalist. Before he really had time to consider it, his father weighed in—he was dead set against his accepting the offer. Charles had never been to sea and would not take to it well. He was not a trained scientist, and lacked the discipline. Moreover, taking several years on this voyage would jeopardize the position his father had secured for him in the church.

His father was so forceful and persuasive that Charles could not help but agree, and he decided to turn the offer down. But over the next few days he thought about this voyage and what it could be like. And the more he imagined it, the more it appealed to him. Perhaps it was the lure of adventure after leading such a sheltered childhood, or the chance to explore a possible career as a naturalist, seeing along the way almost every possible life form the planet could offer. Or maybe he needed to get away from his overbearing father and find his own way. Whatever the reason, he soon decided that he had changed his mind and wanted to accept the offer. Recruiting an uncle to his cause, he managed to get his father to give his very reluctant consent. On the eve of the ship's departure, Charles wrote to the captain of the *Beagle*, Robert FitzRoy: "My second life will then commence, and it shall be as a birthday for the rest of my life."

The ship set sail in December of that year and almost instantly young Darwin regretted his decision. The boat was rather small and strongly buffeted by the waves. He was continually seasick and could not hold his food. His heart ached at the thought that he would not see his family for so long, and that he would have to spend so many years cooped up with all of these strangers. He developed heart palpitations and felt like he was dangerously ill. The sailors sensed his lack of seaworthiness and eyed him strangely. Captain FitzRoy proved to be a man of wildly swinging moods, suddenly turning furious over the most seemingly trivial events. He was also a religious fanatic who believed in the literal truth of the Bible; it was Darwin's duty, FitzRoy told him, to find in South America evidence of the Flood and the creation of life as described in Genesis. Darwin felt like a fool for going against his father, and his sense of loneliness was crushing. How could he endure this cramped existence for months on end, living in close quarters with a captain who seemed half-insane?

A few weeks into the journey, feeling somewhat desperate, he decided upon a strategy. Whenever he experienced such inner turmoil at home, what always calmed him down was to head outdoors and observe the life around him. In that way he could forget himself. This now was his world. He would observe life on board this ship, the characters of the various sailors and the captain himself, as if he were taking note of the markings of butterflies. For instance, he noticed that no one grumbled about the food or the weather or the tasks at hand. They valued stoicism. He would try to adopt such an attitude. It seemed that FitzRoy was slightly insecure and needed constant validation about his authority and high position within the navy. Darwin would supply that to no end. Slowly, he began to fit into the daily scheme of life. He even picked up some of the mannerisms of the sailors. All of this distracted him from his loneliness.

Several months later the *Beagle* arrived in Brazil, and now Darwin understood why he had wanted so badly to go on this voyage. He was completely mesmerized by the intense variety of the vegetation and wildlife—this was a naturalist's paradise. It was not like anything he had observed or collected in England. One day on a walk through a forest, he stood to the side and witnessed the most bizarre and cruel spectacle he had ever seen: a march of tiny black ants, their columns over a hundred yards long, devouring every living thing in their path. Everywhere he turned he saw some example of the fierce struggle for survival in forests with overabundant life. In attending to his work, he quickly realized that he also faced a problem: All of the birds, the butterflies, the crabs, and the spiders he caught were so unusual. Part of his job was to choose judiciously what to send back, but how could he possibly distinguish what was worth collecting?

He would have to expand his knowledge. Not only would he have to spend endless hours studying everything in his sight on his walks, and take copious notes, but he would have to find a way to organize all of this information, catalog all of these specimens, bring some order to his observations. It would be a herculean task, but unlike schoolwork, it excited him. These were living creatures, not vague notions in books.

As the ship headed south along the coast, Darwin realized that there were interior parts of South America that no naturalist had yet explored. Determined to see every form of life that he could possibly find, he began a series of treks into the Pampas of Argentina, accompanied only by gauchos, collecting all kinds of unusual animal and insect specimens. Adopting the same strategy as on the ship, he observed the gauchos and their ways, fitting into their culture as if one of them. On these and other jaunts, he would brave marauding Indians, poisonous insects, and jaguars lurking in the forests. Without thinking of it, he had developed a taste for adventure that would have shocked his family and friends.

A year into the voyage, on a beach some 400 miles south of Buenos Aires, Darwin discovered something that would set his mind to thinking for many years to come. He came upon a cliff with streaks of white amid the rock. Seeing that they were enormous bones of some sort, he began to chip away at the rock, extracting as many of these remains as possible. They were of a size and kind he had never seen before—the horns and armor of what seemed to be a giant armadillo, the huge teeth of a mastodon, and then, most surprisingly, the tooth of a horse. When the Spaniards and Portuguese had first arrived in South America there were no horses to be found, and yet this tooth was quite old and predated their arrival. He began to wonder—if such species had died off long ago, the idea of all of life being created at once and for good seemed illogical. More important, how could so many species become extinct? Could life on the planet be in a state of constant flux and development?

Months later he was trekking through the high Andes, looking for rare geological specimens to send back. At an elevation of about 12,000 feet he discovered some fossilized seashells and deposits of marine rocks—a rather surprising find at such an altitude. As he examined them and the surrounding flora, he speculated that these mountains had once stood in the Atlantic Ocean. A series of volcanoes, thousands of years ago, must have raised them higher and higher. Instead of relics to support the stories in the Bible, he was finding evidence for something shockingly different.

As the journey progressed, Darwin noted some obvious changes in himself. He used to find almost any kind of work boring, but now he could labor all hours of the day; in fact, with so much to explore and learn, he hated wasting a single minute of the voyage. He had cultivated an incredible eye for the flora and fauna of South America. He could identify local birds by their songs, the markings on their eggs, their manner of taking flight. All of this information he could catalog and organize in an efficient manner. More important, his whole way of thinking had changed. He would observe something, read and write about it, then develop a theory after even more observation, the theories and observations feeding off one another. Full of details about so many facets of the world he was exploring, ideas were sprouting up out of nowhere.

In September 1835, the *Beagle* left the Pacific Coast of South America and headed west for the journey home. Their first stop along the way was a series of virtually unoccupied islands known as the Galápagos. The islands were famous for their wildlife, but nothing could prepare Darwin for what he would find there. Captain FitzRoy gave him one week to explore one of the islands, and then they would be on their way. From the moment he stepped on the island, Darwin realized something was different: this small speck of land was crammed with life that was not like anywhere else— thousands of black marine iguanas swarming around him, on the beach and in the shallow water; 500-pound tortoises lumbering about the shore; seals, penguins, and flightless cormorants, all cold-water creatures, inhabiting a tropical island.

By the end of the week, he had counted twenty-six unique species of land birds on this one island alone. His jars began to fill up with the most bizarre plants, snakes, lizards, fish, and insects. Back on board the *Beagle*, he began to catalog and categorize the remarkable number of specimens he had collected. He was struck by the fact that almost all of them represented completely new species. He then made an even more remarkable discovery: the species differed from island to island, even though they were only some fifty miles apart. The tortoise shells had different markings, and the finches had developed different types of beaks, each designed for a specific kind of food on their particular island.

Suddenly, as if the four years of this voyage and all of his observations had distilled in him a deeper way of thinking, a radical theory took shape in his mind: These islands, he speculated, had first been pushed up out of the water by volcanic eruptions, much like the Andes. In the beginning, there was no life to be found on them. Slowly, birds visited and deposited seeds. Various animals arrived by sea—lizards or insects floating on logs; tortoises, originally of a marine variety, swam over. Over thousands of years, each creature adapted to the food and predators that were found there, changing their shape and appearance in the process. Animals that failed to adapt died out, like the fossils of those giant creatures Darwin had unearthed in Argentina. It was a ruthless struggle for survival. Life was not created on these islands at one time and for good by some divine being. The creatures here had ever so slowly evolved to their present form. And these islands represented a microcosm of the planet itself.

On the journey home Darwin began to develop this theory further, so revolutionary in its implications. To prove his theory would now be his life's work.

Finally, in October 1836, the *Beagle* returned to England after nearly five years at sea. Darwin hurried home, and when his father first saw him he was astonished. Physically, he had changed. His head seemed larger. His whole manner was different—a seriousness of purpose and sharpness could be read in his eyes, almost the opposite look of the lost young man who had gone to sea years before. Clearly, the voyage had transformed his son in body and spirit.

KEYS TO MASTERY

One can have no smaller or greater mastery than mastery of oneself.

—LEONARDO DA VINCI

In the stories of the greatest Masters, past and present, we can inevitably detect a phase in their lives in which all of their future powers were in development, like the chrysalis of a butterfly. This part of their lives—a largely self-directed apprenticeship that lasts some five to ten years—receives little attention because it does not contain stories of great achievement or discovery. Often in their Apprenticeship Phase, these types are not yet much different from anyone else. Under the surface, however, their minds are transforming in ways we cannot see but contain all of the seeds of their future success.

Much of how such Masters navigate this phase comes from an intuitive grasp of what is most important and essential for their development, but in studying what they did right we can learn some invaluable lessons for ourselves. In fact, a close examination of their lives reveals a pattern that transcends their various fields, indicating a kind of *Ideal Apprenticeship* for mastery. And to grasp this pattern, to follow it in our own ways, we must understand something about the very idea and necessity for passing through an apprenticeship.

In childhood we are inculcated in culture through a long period of dependency—far longer than any other animal. During this period we learn language, writing, math, and reasoning skills, along with a few others. Much of this happens under the watchful and loving guidance of parents and teachers. As we get older, greater emphasis is placed on book learning—absorbing as much information as possible about various subjects. Such knowledge of history, science, or literature is abstract, and the process of learning largely involves passive absorption. At the end of this process (usually somewhere between the ages of eighteen and twenty-five) we are then thrust into the cold, harsh work world to fend for ourselves.

When we emerge from the youthful state of dependency, we are not really ready to handle the transition to an entirely independent phase. We carry with us the habit of learning from books or teachers, which is largely unsuited for the practical, self-directed phase of life that comes next. We tend to be somewhat socially naïve and unprepared for the political games people play. Still uncertain as to our identity, we think that what matters in the work world is gaining attention and making friends. And these misconceptions and naïveté are brutally exposed in the light of the real world.

If we adjust over time, we might eventually find our way; but if we make too many mistakes, we create endless problems for ourselves. We spend too much time entangled in emotional issues, and we never quite have enough detachment to reflect and learn from our experiences. The apprenticeship, by its very nature, must be conducted by each individual in his or her own way. To follow *precisely* the lead of others or advice from a book is self-defeating. This is the phase in life in which we finally declare our independence and establish who we are. But for this second education in our lives, so critical to our future success, there are some powerful and essential lessons that we all can benefit from, that can guide us away from common mistakes and save us valuable time.

These lessons transcend all fields and historical periods because they are connected to something essential about human psychology and how the brain itself functions. They can be distilled into one overarching *principle* for the Apprenticeship Phase, and a process that loosely follows three steps.

The principle is simple and must be engraved deeply in your mind: the goal of an apprenticeship is not money, a good position, a title, or a diploma, but rather the *transformation* of your mind and character—the first transformation on the way to mastery. You enter a career as an outsider. You are naïve and full of misconceptions about this new world. Your head is full of dreams and fantasies about the future. Your knowledge of the world is subjective, based on emotions, insecurities, and limited experience. Slowly, you will ground yourself in reality, in the objective world represented by the knowledge and skills that make people successful in it. You will learn how to work with others and handle criticism. In the process you will transform yourself from someone who is impatient and scattered into someone who is disciplined and focused, with a mind that can handle complexity. In the end, you will master yourself and all of your weaknesses.

This has a simple consequence: you must choose places of work and positions that offer the greatest possibilities for learning. Practical knowledge is the ultimate commodity, and is what will pay you dividends for decades to come—far more than the paltry increase in pay you might receive at some seemingly lucrative position that offers fewer learning opportunities. This means that you move toward challenges that will toughen and improve you, where you will get the most objective feedback on your performance and progress. You do not choose apprenticeships that seem easy and comfortable.

In this sense you must see yourself as following in the footsteps of Charles Darwin. You are finally on your own, on a voyage in which you will craft your own future. It is the time of youth and adventure—of exploring the world with an open mind and spirit. In fact, whenever you must learn a new skill or alter your career path later in life, you reconnect with that youthful, adventurous part of yourself. Darwin could have played it safe, collecting what was necessary, and spending more time on board studying instead of actively exploring. In that case, he would not have become an illustrious scientist, but just another collector. He constantly looked for challenges, pushing himself past his comfort zone. He used danger and difficulties as a way to measure his progress. You must adopt such a spirit and see your apprenticeship as a kind of journey in which you will transform yourself, rather than as a drab indoctrination into the work world.

The Apprenticeship Phase—The Three Steps or Modes

With the *principle* outlined above guiding you in your choices, you must think of three essential steps in your apprenticeship, each one overlapping the other. These steps are: *Deep Observation (The Passive Mode), Skills Acquisition (The Practice Mode)*, and *Experimentation (The Active Mode)*. Keep in mind that an apprenticeship can come in many different forms. It can happen at one place over several years, or it can consist of several different positions in different places, a kind of compound apprenticeship involving many different skills. It can include a mix of graduate school and practical experience. In all of these cases, it will help you to think in terms of these steps, although you may need to give added weight to a particular one depending on the nature of your field.

Step One: Deep Observation—The Passive Mode

When you enter a career or new environment, you move into a world with its own rules, procedures, and social dynamic. For decades or even centuries, people have compiled knowledge of how to get things done in a particular field, each generation improving on the past. In addition, every workplace has its own conventions, rules of behavior, and work standards. There are also all kinds of power relationships that exist between individuals. All of this represents a reality that transcends your individual needs and desires. And so your task upon entering this world is to *observe* and absorb its reality as *deeply* as possible.

The greatest mistake you can make in the initial months of your apprenticeship is to imagine that you have to get attention, impress people, and prove yourself. These thoughts will dominate your mind and close it off from the reality around you. Any positive attention you receive is deceptive; it is not based on your skills or anything real, and it will turn against you. Instead, you will want to acknowledge the reality and *submit* to it, muting your colors and keeping in the background as much as possible, remaining passive and giving yourself the space to observe. You will also want to drop any preconceptions you might have about this world you are entering. If you impress people in these first months, it should be because of the seriousness of your desire to learn, not because you are trying to rise to the top before you are ready.

You will be observing two essential realities in this new world. First, you will observe the rules and procedures that govern success in this environment—in other words, "this is how we do things here." Some of these rules will be communicated to you directly—generally the ones that are superficial and largely a matter of common sense. You must pay attention to these and observe them, but what is of more interest are the rules that are unstated and are part of the underlying work culture. These concern style and values that are considered important. They are often a reflection of the character of the man or woman on top.

You can observe such rules by looking at those who are on their way up in the hierarchy, who have a golden touch. More tellingly, you can observe those who are more awkward, who have been chastised for particular mistakes or even been fired. Such examples serve as negative trip wires: do things this way and you will suffer.

The second reality you will observe is the power relationships that exist within the group: who has real control; through whom do all communications flow; who is on the rise and who is on the decline. (For more on this element of social intelligence, please see chapter 4.) These procedural and political rules may be dysfunctional or counterproductive, but your job is not to moralize about this or complain, but merely to understand them, to get a complete lay of the land. You are like an anthropologist studying an alien culture, attuned to all of its nuances and conventions. You are not there to change that culture; you will only end up being killed, or in the case of work, fired. Later, when you have attained power and mastery, you will be the one to rewrite or destroy these same rules.

Every task you are given, no matter how menial, offers opportunities to observe this world at work. No detail about the people within it is too trivial. Everything you see or hear is a sign for you to decode. Over time, you will begin to see and understand more of the reality that eluded you at first. For instance, a person whom you initially thought had great power ended up being someone with more bark than bite. Slowly, you begin to see behind the appearances. As you amass more information about the rules and power dynamics of your new environment, you can begin to analyze why they exist, and how they relate to larger trends in the field. You move from observation to analysis, honing your reasoning skills, but only after months of careful attention.

We can see how Charles Darwin followed this step quite clearly. By spending the first few months studying life on board the ship and perceiving the unwritten rules, he made his time for science much more productive. By enabling himself to fit in, he was able to avoid needless battles that would have later disrupted his scientific work, not to mention the emotional turmoil these would have presented to him. He later practiced the same technique with gauchos and other local communities he came in contact with. This allowed him to extend the regions he could explore and the specimens he could collect. On another level, he slowly transformed himself into perhaps the most astute observer of nature the world has ever known. Emptying himself of any preconceptions about life and its origins, Darwin trained himself to see things as they are. He did not theorize or generalize about what he was seeing until he had amassed enough information. *Submitting to and absorbing the reality of all aspects of this voyage*, he ended up piercing one of the most fundamental realities of all—the evolution of all living forms.

Understand: there are several critical reasons why you must follow this step. First, knowing your environment inside and out will help you in navigating it and avoiding costly mistakes. You are like a hunter: your knowledge of every detail of the forest and of the ecosystem as a whole will give you many more options for survival and success. Second, the ability to observe any unfamiliar environment will become a critical lifelong skill. You will develop the habit of stilling your ego and looking outward instead of inward. You will see in any encounter what most people miss because they are thinking of themselves. You will cultivate a keen eye for human psychology, and strengthen your ability to focus. Finally, you will become accustomed to observing first, basing your ideas and theories on what you have seen with your eyes, and then analyzing what you find. This will be a very important skill for the next, creative phase in life.

Step Two: Skills Acquisition—The Practice Mode

At some point, as you progress through these initial months of observation, you will enter the most critical part of the apprenticeship: *practice toward the acquisition of skills.* Every human activity, endeavor, or career path involves the mastering of skills. In some fields, it is direct and obvious, like operating a tool or machine or creating something physical. In others, it is more of a mix of the physical and mental, such as the observing and collecting of specimens for Charles Darwin. In still others, the skills are more nebulous, such as handling people or researching and organizing information. As much as possible, you want to reduce these skills to something simple and essential—the core of what you need to get good at, skills that can be practiced.

In acquiring any kind of skill, there exists a natural learning process that coincides with the functioning of our brains. This learning process leads to what we shall call *tacit knowledge*—a feeling for what you are doing that is hard to put into words but easy to demonstrate in action. And to understand how this learning process operates, it is useful to look at the greatest system ever invented for the training of skills and the achievement of tacit knowledge—the apprenticeship system of the Middle Ages.

This system arose as a solution to a problem: As business expanded in the Middle Ages, Masters of various crafts could no longer depend on family members to work in the shop. They needed more hands. But it was not worth it for them to bring in people who would come and go—they needed stability and time to build up skills in their workers. And so they developed the apprenticeship system, in which young people from approximately the ages of twelve to seventeen would enter work in a shop, signing a contract that would commit them for the term of seven years. At the end of this term, apprentices would have to pass a *master test*, or produce a *master work*, to prove their level of skill. Once passed, they were now elevated to the rank of journeymen and could travel wherever there was work, practicing the craft.

Because few books or drawings existed at the time, apprentices would learn the trade by watching Masters and imitating them as closely as possible. They learned through endless repetition and hands-on work, with very little verbal instruction (the word "apprentice" itself comes from the Latin *prehendere*, meaning to grasp with the hand). Because resources such as textiles, wood, and metals were expensive and could not be wasted on practice runs, apprentices would spend most of their time working directly on materials that would be used for the final product. They had to learn how to focus deeply on their work and not make mistakes.

If one added up the time that apprentices ended up working directly on materials in those years, it would amount to more than 10,000 hours, enough to establish exceptional skill level at a craft. The power of this form of tacit knowledge is embodied in the great Gothic cathedrals of Europe—masterpieces of beauty, craftsmanship, and stability, all erected without blueprints or books. These cathedrals represented the accumulated skills of numerous craftsmen and engineers.

What this means is simple: language, oral and written, is a relatively recent invention. Well before that time, our ancestors had to learn various skills—toolmaking, hunting, and so forth. The natural model for learning, largely based on the power of mirror neurons, came from watching and imitating others, then repeating the action over and over. Our brains are highly suited for this form of learning.

In an activity such as riding a bicycle, we all know that it is easier to watch someone and follow their lead than to listen to or read instructions. The more we do it, the easier it becomes. Even with skills that are primarily mental, such as computer programming or speaking a foreign language, it remains the case that we learn best through practice and repetition—the natural learning process. We learn a foreign language by actually speaking it as much as possible, not by reading books and absorbing theories. The more we speak and practice, the more fluent we become.

Once you take this far enough, you enter a *cycle of accelerated returns* in which the practice becomes easier and more interesting, leading to the ability to practice for longer hours, which increases your skill level, which in turn makes practice even more interesting. Reaching this cycle is the goal you must set for yourself, and to get there you must understand some basic principles about skills themselves.

First, it is essential that you begin with one skill that you can master, and that serves as a foundation for acquiring others. You must avoid at all cost the idea that you can manage learning several skills at a time. You need to develop your powers of concentration, and understand that trying to multitask will be the death of the process.

Second, the initial stages of learning a skill invariably involve tedium. Yet rather than avoiding this inevitable tedium, you must accept and embrace it. The pain and boredom we experience in the initial stage of learning a skill toughens our minds, much like physical exercise. Too many people believe that everything must be pleasurable in life, which makes them constantly search for distractions and short-circuits the learning process. The pain is a kind of challenge your mind presents—will you learn how to focus and move past the boredom, or like a child will you succumb to the need for immediate pleasure and distraction? Much as with physical exercise, you can even get a kind of perverse pleasure out of this pain, knowing the benefits it will bring you. In any event, you must meet any boredom head-on and not try to avoid or repress it. Throughout your life you will encounter tedious situations, and you must cultivate the ability to handle them with discipline.

In practicing a skill in the initial stages, something happens neurologically to the brain that is important for you to understand. When you start something new, a large number of neurons in the frontal cortex (the higher, more conscious command area of the brain) are recruited and become active, helping you in the learning process. The brain has to deal with a large amount of new information, and this would be stressful and overwhelming if only a limited part of the brain were used to handle it. The frontal cortex even expands in size in this initial phase, as we focus hard on the task. But once something is repeated often enough, it becomes hardwired and automatic, and the neural pathways for this skill are delegated to other parts of the brain, farther down the cortex. Those neurons in the frontal cortex that we needed in the initial stages are now freed up to help in learning something else, and the area goes back to its normal size.

In the end, an entire network of neurons is developed to remember this single task, which accounts for the fact that we can still ride a bicycle years after we first learned how to do so. If we were to take a look at the frontal cortex of those who have mastered something through repetition, it would be remarkably still and inactive as they performed the skill. All of their brain activity is occurring in areas that are lower down and require much less conscious control.

This process of hardwiring cannot occur if you are constantly distracted, moving from one task to another. In such a case, the neural pathways dedicated to this skill never get established; what you learn is too tenuous to remain rooted in the brain. It is better to dedicate two or three hours of intense focus to a skill than to spend eight hours of diffused concentration on it. You want to be as immediately present to what you are doing as possible.

Once an action becomes automatic, you now have the mental space to observe yourself as you practice. You must use this distance to take note of your weaknesses or flaws that need correction—to analyze yourself. It helps also to gain as much feedback as possible from others, to have standards against which you can measure your progress so that you are aware of how far you have to go. People who do not practice and learn new skills never gain a proper sense of proportion or self-criticism. They think they can achieve anything without effort and have little contact with reality. Trying something over and over again grounds you in reality, making you deeply aware of your inadequacies and of what you can accomplish with more work and effort.

If you take this far enough, you will naturally enter the cycle of accelerated returns: As you learn and gain skills you can begin to vary what you do, finding nuances that you can develop in the work, so that it becomes more interesting. As elements become more automatic your mind is not exhausted by the effort and you can practice harder, which in turn brings greater skill and more pleasure. You can look for challenges, new areas to conquer, keeping your interest at a high level. As the cycle accelerates, you can reach a point where your mind is totally absorbed in the practice, entering a kind of flow in which everything else is blocked out. You become one with the tool or instrument or thing you are studying. Your skill is not something that can be put into words; it is embedded in your body and nervous system—it becomes tacit knowledge. Learning any kind of skill deeply prepares you for mastery. The sensation of flow and of being a part of the instrument is a precursor to the great pleasures that mastery can bring.

In essence, when you practice and develop any skill you transform yourself in the process. You reveal to yourself new capabilities that were previously latent, that are exposed as you progress. You develop emotionally. Your sense of pleasure becomes redefined. What offers immediate pleasure comes to seem like a distraction, an empty entertainment to help pass the time. Real pleasure comes from overcoming challenges, feeling confidence in your abilities, gaining fluency in skills, and experiencing the power this brings. You develop patience. Boredom no longer signals the need for distraction, but rather the need for new challenges to conquer.

Although it might seem that the time necessary to master the requisite skills and attain a level of expertise would depend on the field and your own talent level, those who have researched the subject repeatedly come up with the number of 10,000 hours. This seems to be the amount of quality practice time that is needed for someone to reach a high level of skill and it applies to composers, chess players, writers, and athletes, among others. This number has an almost magical or mystical resonance to it. It means that so much practice time—no matter the person or the field—leads to a qualitative change in the human brain. The mind has learned to organize and structure large amounts of information. With all of this tacit knowledge, it can now become creative and playful with it. Although the number of hours might seem high, it generally adds up to seven to ten years of sustained, solid practice—roughly the period of a traditional apprenticeship. In other words, concentrated practice over time cannot fail but produce results.

Step Three: Experimentation—The Active Mode

This is the shortest part of the process, but a critical component nonetheless. As you gain in skill and confidence, you must make the move to a more *active* mode of *experimentation*. This could mean taking on more responsibility, initiating a project of some sort, doing work that exposes you to the criticisms of peers or even the public. The point of this is to gauge your progress and whether there are still gaps in your knowledge. You are observing yourself in action and seeing how you respond to the judgments of others. Can you take criticism and use it constructively?

With Charles Darwin, as the voyage progressed and he began to entertain the notions that would lead to his theory of evolution, he decided to expose his ideas to others. First, on the *Beagle*, he discussed them with the captain and patiently absorbed his vehement criticisms of the idea. This, Darwin told himself, would be more or less the reaction of the public, and he would have to prepare himself for that. He also began to write letters to various scientists and scientific societies back in England. The responses he received indicated he was on to something, but that he would need some more research. For Leonardo da Vinci, as he progressed in his studio work for Verrocchio, he began to experiment and to assert his own style. He found to his surprise that the Master was impressed with his inventiveness. For Leonardo, this indicated that he was near the end of his apprenticeship.

Most people wait too long to take this step, generally out of fear. It is always easier to learn the rules and stay within your comfort zone. Often you must force yourself to initiate such actions or experiments *before you think you are ready*. You are testing your character, moving past your fears, and developing a sense of detachment to your work—looking at it through the eyes of others. You are getting a taste for the next phase in which what you produce will be under constant scrutiny.

You will know when your apprenticeship is over by the feeling that you have nothing left to learn in this environment. It is time to declare your independence or move to another place to continue your apprenticeship and expand your skill base. Later in life, when you are confronted with a career change or the need to learn new skills, having gone through this process before, it will become second nature. You have learned how to learn.

———

Many people might find the notion of an apprenticeship and skill acquisition as quaint relics of bygone eras when work meant making things. After all, we have entered the information and computer age, in which technology makes it so we can do without the kinds of menial tasks that require practice and repetition; so many things have become virtual in our lives, making the craftsman model obsolete. Or so the argument goes.

In truth, however, this idea of the nature of the times we are living in is completely incorrect, even dangerous. The era we have entered is not one in which technology will make everything easier, but rather a time of increased complexity that affects every field. In business, competition has become globalized and more intense. A businessperson must have a command of a much larger picture than in the past, which means more knowledge and skills. The future in science does not lie in increased specialization, but rather in the combining and cross-fertilization of knowledge in various fields. In the arts, tastes and styles are changing at an accelerated rate. An artist must be on top of this and be capable of creating new forms, always remaining ahead of the curve. This often requires having more than just a specialized knowledge of that particular art form—it requires knowing other arts, even the sciences, and what is happening in the world.

In all of these areas, the human brain is asked to do and handle more than ever before. We are dealing with several fields of knowledge constantly intersecting with our own, and all of this chaos is exponentially increased by the information available through technology. What this means is that all of us must possess different forms of knowledge and an array of skills in different fields, and have minds that are capable of organizing large amounts of information. The future belongs to those who learn more skills and combine them in creative ways. And the process of learning skills, no matter how virtual, remains the same.

In the future, the great division will be between those who have trained themselves to handle these complexities and those who are overwhelmed by them—those who can acquire skills and discipline their minds and those who are irrevocably distracted by all the media around them and can never focus enough to learn. The Apprenticeship Phase is more relevant and important than ever, and those who discount this notion will almost certainly be left behind.

Finally, we live in a culture that generally values intellect and reasoning with words. We tend to think of working with the hands, of building something physical, as degraded skills for those who are less intelligent. This is an extremely counterproductive cultural value. The human brain evolved in intimate conjunction with the hand. Many of our earliest survival skills depended on elaborate hand-eye coordination. To this day, a large portion of our brain is devoted to this relationship. When we work with our hands and build something, we learn how to sequence our actions and how to organize our thoughts. In taking anything apart in order to fix it, we learn problem-solving skills that have wider applications. Even if it is only as a side activity, you should find a way to work with your hands, or to learn more about the inner workings of the machines and pieces of technology around you.

Many Masters in history intuited this connection. Thomas Jefferson, who himself was an avid tinkerer and inventor, believed that craftspeople made better citizens because they understood how things functioned and had practical common sense—all of which would serve them well in handling civic needs. Albert Einstein was an avid violinist. He believed that working with his hands in this way and playing music helped his thinking process as well.

In general, no matter your field, you must think of yourself as a builder, using actual materials and ideas. You are producing something tangible in your work, something that affects people in some direct, concrete way. To build anything well—a house, a political organization, a business, or a film— you must understand the building process and possess the necessary skills. You are a craftsman learning to adhere to the highest standards. For all of this, you must go through a careful apprenticeship. You cannot make anything worthwhile in this world unless you have first developed and transformed yourself.

STRATEGIES FOR COMPLETING
THE IDEAL APPRENTICESHIP

Do not think that what is hard for you to master is humanly impossible; and if it is humanly possible, consider it to be within your reach.

—Marcus Aurelius

Throughout history, Masters in all fields have devised for themselves various strategies to help them pursue and complete an Ideal Apprenticeship. The following are eight classic strategies, distilled from the stories of their lives and illustrated with examples. Although some might seem more relevant than others to your circumstances, each of them relates fundamental truths about the learning process itself that you would be wise to internalize.

1. Value learning over money

In 1718, Josiah Franklin decided to bring his twelve-year-old son Benjamin into his lucrative, family-run candle-making business in Boston as an apprentice. His idea was that after a seven-year apprenticeship and a little experience, Benjamin would take over the business. But Benjamin had other ideas. He threatened to run away to sea if his father did not give him the choice of where he could apprentice. The father had already lost another son who had run away, and so he relented. To the father's surprise, his son chose to work in an older brother's recently opened printing business. Such a business would mean harder work and the apprenticeship would last nine instead of seven years. Also, the printing business was notoriously fickle, and it was quite a risk to bank one's future on it. But that was his choice, his father decided. Let him learn the hard way.

What young Benjamin had not told his father was that he was determined to become a writer. Most of the work in the shop would involve manual labor and operating machines, but every now and then he would be asked to proofread and copyedit a pamphlet or text. And there would always be new books around. Several years into the process, he discovered that some of his favorite writing came from the English newspapers the shop would reprint. He asked to be the one to oversee the printing of such articles, giving him the chance to study these texts in detail and teach himself how to imitate their style in his own work. Over the years he managed to turn this into a most efficient apprenticeship for writing, with the added benefit of having learned the printing business well.

After graduating from the Zurich Polytechnic in 1900, the twenty-one-year-old Albert Einstein found his job prospects extremely meager. He had graduated near the bottom of the class, almost certainly nullifying any chance to obtain a teaching position. Happy to be away from the university, he now planned to investigate, on his own, certain problems in physics that had haunted him for several years. It would be a self-apprenticeship in theorizing and thought experiments. But in the meantime, he would have to make a living. He had been offered a job in his father's dynamo business in Milan as an engineer, but such work would not leave him any free time. A friend could land him a well-paid position in an insurance company, but that would stultify his brain and sap his energy for thinking.

Then, a year later, another friend mentioned a job opening up in the Swiss Patent Office in Bern. The pay was not great, the position was at the bottom, the hours were long, and the work consisted of the rather mundane task of looking over patent applications, but Einstein leaped at the chance. It was everything he wanted. His task would be to analyze the validity of patent applications, many of which involved aspects of science that interested him. The applications would be like little puzzles or thought experiments; he could try to visualize how the ideas would actually translate into inventions. Working on them would sharpen his reasoning powers. After several months on the job, he became so good at this mental game that he could finish his work in two or three hours, leaving him the rest of the day to engage in his own thought experiments. In 1905 he published his first theory of relativity, much of the work having been done while he was at his desk in the Patent Office.

Martha Graham (see pages 30–31 for more on her early years) first trained as a dancer at the Denishawn School in Los Angeles, but after several years she determined she had learned enough and needed to go elsewhere to sharpen her skills. She ended up in New York, and in 1924 was offered a two-year stint as a dancer in a follies' show; it was well paid, and so she accepted. Dancing is dancing, she thought, and she could always work on her own ideas in her free time. But near the end of the term, she decided she would never again accept commercial work. It drained her of all of her creative energy and destroyed her desire to work on her own time. It also made her feel dependent on a paycheck.

What is important when you are young, she decided, is to train yourself to get by with little money and make the most of your youthful energy. For the next few years she would work as a dance teacher, keeping her hours to the minimum for survival. The rest of the time she would train herself in the new style of dancing she wanted to create. Knowing the alternative was slavery to some commercial job, she made the most of every free minute, creating in these few years the groundwork for the most radical revolution in modern dance.

As previously narrated in chapter 1 (see page 39), when Freddie Roach's career as a boxer came to an end in 1986, he took a job as a telemarketer in Las Vegas. One day, he entered the gym where he himself had trained under the legendary coach Eddie Futch. He found many boxers there who were not receiving any personalized attention from Futch. Even though he was not asked, he began to hang around the gym every afternoon and help out. It turned into a job for which he was not paid, so he held on to his telemarketing position. Working the two jobs left just enough time to sleep. It was almost unbearable, but he could withstand it because he was learning the trade for which he knew was destined. Within a few years he had impressed enough young boxers with his knowledge to set up his own business, and was soon to become the most successful boxing trainer of his generation.

———◆———

It is a simple law of human psychology that your thoughts will tend to revolve around what you value most. If it is money, you will choose a place for your apprenticeship that offers the biggest paycheck. Inevitably, in such a place you will feel greater pressures to prove yourself worthy of such pay, often before you are really ready. You will be focused on yourself, your insecurities, the need to please and impress the right people, and not on acquiring skills. It will be too costly for you to make mistakes and learn from them, so you will develop a cautious, conservative approach. As you progress in life, you will become addicted to the fat paycheck and it will determine where you go, how you think, and what you do. Eventually, the time that was not spent on learning skills will catch up with you, and the fall will be painful.

Instead, you must value learning above everything else. This will lead you to all of the right choices. You will opt for the situation that will give you the most opportunities to learn, particularly with hands-on work. You will choose a place that has people and mentors who can inspire and teach you. A job with mediocre pay has the added benefit of training you to get by with less—a valuable life skill. If your apprenticeship is to be mostly on your own time, you will choose a place that pays the bills—perhaps one that keeps your mind sharp, but that also leaves you the time and mental space to do valuable work on your own. You must never disdain an apprenticeship with no pay. In fact, it is often the height of wisdom to find the perfect mentor and offer your services as an assistant for free. Happy to exploit your cheap and eager spirit, such mentors will often divulge more than the usual trade secrets. In the end, by valuing learning above all else, you will set the stage for your creative expansion, and the money will soon come to you.

2. Keep expanding your horizons

For the writer Zora Neale Hurston (1891–1960), her childhood represented a kind of Golden Age. She grew up in Eatonville, Florida, a town that was something of an anomaly in the South. It had been founded as an all-black township in the 1880s, governed and managed by its citizens. Its only struggles and sufferings came at the hands of its own inhabitants. For Zora, racism had no meaning. A spirited and strong-willed girl, she spent a lot of her time alone, wandering through the town.

She had two great passions in those years. First, she loved books and reading. She read everything she could get her hands on, but she was particularly drawn to books on mythology—Greek, Roman, and Norse. She identified with the strongest characters—Hercules, Odysseus, Odin. Second, she would spend much of her time listening to the stories of locals as they gathered on porches and gossiped or related folk tales, many of them dating back to the years of slavery. She loved their manner of telling stories—the rich metaphors, the simple lessons. In her mind, the Greek myths and the stories of Eatonville citizens all blended into one reality—human nature revealed in its most naked form. Walking alone, her imagination would take flight, and she would begin telling her own strange tales to herself. Someday she would write all of this down and become the Homer of Eatonville.

Then in 1904 her mother died, and the Golden Age came to an abrupt end. It was her mother who had always protected and sheltered Zora from her father, who thought her strange and unlikeable. Eager to have her out of the house, he shipped her off to a school in Jacksonville. A few years later, he stopped paying her tuition and essentially abandoned her to the world. For five years she wandered from one relative's house to another. She took up all kinds of jobs to support herself, mostly housekeeping.

Thinking back to her childhood, she could remember a sense of expansion—learning about other cultures and their history, learning about her own culture. There seemed to be no limits to what she could explore. Now, it was the opposite. Worn down by work and depression, everything was tightening around her until all she could think about was her own tiny world and how sorry it had become. Soon it would be hard to imagine anything besides cleaning houses. But the paradox is that the mind is essentially free. It can travel anywhere, across time and space. If she kept it confined to her narrow circumstances, it would be her own fault. No matter how impossible it seemed, she could not let go of her dream to become a writer. To realize this dream, she would have to educate herself and keep her mental horizons expanding by whatever means necessary. A writer needs knowledge of the world. And so, thinking in this way, Zora Neale Hurston proceeded to create for herself one of the most remarkable self-directed apprenticeships in history.

Since the only jobs she could get at that moment were housecleaning, she managed to land work in the homes of the wealthiest white people in town—there she would find plenty of books. Snatching a few moments here and there, she would read portions of these books on the sly, quickly memorizing passages so she could have something to go over in her head in her free time. One day, she discovered a discarded copy of Milton's *Paradise Lost* in a garbage can. It was as good as gold for her. She took it wherever she went, and read it over and over. In this way, her mind did not stagnate; she had created for herself a strange sort of literary education.

In 1915, she landed a job as a lady's maid to the lead singer of an all-white traveling troupe of performers. For most, this would mean yet another subservient position, but for Hurston it was a godsend. Many of the members of the troupe were well educated. There were books everywhere to read and interesting conversations to overhear. By observing closely, she could see what passed for sophistication in the white world, and how she could make herself charming to them with her stories of Eatonville and her knowledge of literature. As part of the job, they had her trained as a manicurist. She would later use this skill to find jobs in the barbershops in Washington D.C., near the Capitol. The clientele included the most powerful politicians of the time, and they would often gossip as if she weren't even there. For her, this was almost as good as reading any book—it taught her more about human nature, power, and the inner workings of the white world.

Her world was slowly expanding, but still there were severe limitations on where she could work, on the books she could find, on the people she could meet and associate with. She was learning, but her mind was unstructured and her thoughts unorganized. What she needed, she decided, was formal education and the discipline this would bring her. She could try to patch a degree together in various night schools, but what she really wanted was to regain what had been taken away from her by her father. At twenty-five she looked young for her age, and so chopping off ten years in her application, she gained admittance to a free public high school in Maryland as a freshman.

She would have to make the most of this schooling—her future depended on it. She would read many more books than were required, and work particularly hard on any writing assignments. She would befriend teachers and professors with the charm she had established over the years, making the kinds of connections that had eluded her in the past. In this way, a few years later, she gained admittance to Howard University, the leading institution of black higher learning, and made the acquaintance of key figures in the black literary world. With the discipline she had gained in school, she began to write short stories. Now, with the help of one of her connections, she got a short story published in a prestigious Harlem literary journal. Seizing opportunities whenever they appeared, she decided to leave Howard and move to Harlem, where all of the leading black writers and artists were living. This would add another dimension to the world she was finally able to explore.

Over the years, Hurston had made a study of powerful, important people—black and white—and how to impress them. Now in New York, she used this skill to great effect, charming several wealthy white patrons of the arts. Through one of these patrons she was offered the opportunity to enroll in Barnard College, where she could finish her college education. She would be the first and only black student there. It had been her strategy to keep moving, keep expanding—the world could quickly close in on you if you stayed put or stagnated. And so she accepted the offer. The white students at Barnard were intimidated in her presence—her knowledge of so many fields far exceeded their own. Several professors in the anthropology department fell under her spell, and sent her on a tour through the South to gather folk tales and stories. She used the trip to immerse herself in hoodoo, the southern black version of voodoo, and in other ritual practices. She wanted to deepen her knowledge of black culture in all of its richness and variety.

In 1932, with the Depression raging in New York and her employment opportunities drying up, she decided to return to Eatonville. There she could live cheaply, and the atmosphere would be inspiring. Borrowing money from friends, she proceeded to work on her first novel. From somewhere deep inside, all of her past experiences, her lengthy and multifaceted apprenticeship, rose to the surface—the stories from her childhood, the books she had read here and there over the years, the various insights into the dark side of human nature, the anthropological studies, every encounter that she had paid attention to with so much intensity. This novel, *Jonah's Gourd Vine*, would recount the relationship of her parents, but it was really the distillation of all of her life's work. It spilled out of her in a few intense months.

The novel was published the following year and became a great success. Over the next few years she wrote more novels at a furious pace. She soon became the most famous black writer of her time, and the first black female writer ever to make a living from her work.

◆

Zora Neale Hurston's story reveals in its barest form the reality of the Apprenticeship Phase—no one is really going to help you or give you direction.

In fact, the odds are against you. If you desire an apprenticeship, if you want to learn and set yourself up for mastery, you have to do it yourself, and with great energy. When you enter this phase, you generally begin at the lowest position. Your access to knowledge and people is limited by your status. If you are not careful, you will accept this status and become defined by it, particularly if you come from a disadvantaged background. Instead, like Hurston, you must struggle against any limitations and continually work to expand your horizons. (In each learning situation you will submit to reality, but that reality does not mean you must stay in one place.) Reading books and materials that go beyond what is required is always a good starting point. Being exposed to ideas in the wide world, you will tend to develop a hunger for more and more knowledge; you will find it harder to remain satisfied in any narrow corner, which is precisely the point.

The people in your field, in your immediate circle, are like worlds unto themselves—their stories and viewpoints will naturally expand your horizons and build up your social skills. Mingle with as many different types of people as possible. Those circles will slowly widen. Any kind of outside schooling will add to the dynamic. Be relentless in your pursuit for expansion. Whenever you feel like you are settling into some circle, force yourself to shake things up and look for new challenges, as Hurston did when she left Howard for Harlem. With your mind expanding, you will redefine the limits of your apparent world. Soon, ideas and opportunities will come to you and your apprenticeship will naturally complete itself.

3. Revert to a feeling of inferiority

Attending high school in the late 1960s, Daniel Everett was a bit of a lost soul. He felt trapped in the California border town of Holtville, where he grew up, and totally disconnected to the local cowboy way of life. As narrated in chapter 1 (see page 31), Everett had always been drawn to the Mexican culture that existed among the migrant workers on the margins of the town. He loved their rituals and way of life, the sound of their language, and their songs. He seemed to have a knack for learning a foreign language and picked up Spanish rather quickly, gaining a bit of entrée into their world. To him, their culture represented a glimpse of a more interesting world beyond Holtville, but sometimes he despaired of ever really getting away from his hometown. He began to take drugs—for the time being, at least, they offered an escape.

Then, when he was seventeen, he met Keren Graham, a fellow student at his high school, and everything seemed to change. Keren had spent much of her childhood in northeastern Brazil, where her parents had served as Christian missionaries. He loved to hang out with her and listen to her stories of life in Brazil. He met her family and became a regular guest at their dinners. He admired their sense of purpose and dedication to their missionary work. A few months after meeting Keren he became a born-again Christian, and a year later they were married. Their goal was to start a family and become missionaries themselves.

Everett graduated from the Moody Bible Institute of Chicago with a degree in Foreign Missions, and in 1976 he and his wife enrolled in the Summer Institute of Linguistics (SIL)—a Christian organization that instructs future missionaries in the necessary linguistic skills to translate the Bible into indigenous languages and spread the Gospel. After going through the course work, he and his family (which now included two children) were sent to SIL's jungle camp in the region of Chiapas, in southern Mexico, to prepare them for the rigors of missionary life. For a month the family had to live in a village and learn as best they could the indigenous language, a Mayan dialect. Everett passed all of the tests with flying colors. Based on his success in the program, the faculty at SIL decided to offer him and his family the greatest challenge of them all—to live in a Pirahã village, deep in the heart of the Amazon.

The Pirahã are among the oldest inhabitants of the Amazon. When the Portuguese arrived in the area in the early eighteenth century, most of the tribes learned their language and adopted many of their ways, but the Pirahã resisted and retreated further into the jungle. They lived in deep isolation, with little contact with outsiders. By the time missionaries arrived in their villages in the 1950s, there were only some 350 Pirahã still alive, scattered in the area. The missionaries who tried to learn their language found it impossible. The Pirahã spoke no Portuguese, had no written language, and their words, to Westerners, all sounded alike. SIL had sent a couple in 1967 to learn the language and finally translate part of the Bible into Pirahã, but they could make little progress. After more than ten years of struggling with the language, they were driven half-mad by the task and wanted to leave. Hearing all of this, Everett was more than happy to accept the challenge. He and his wife were determined to be the first ones to crack the code of Pirahã.

He and his family arrived at a Pirahã village in December 1977. In his first few days there, Everett used all of the strategies he had been taught— for instance, holding up a stick and asking for their word for it, then dropping the stick and asking for the phrase to describe the action. In the months to come, he made good progress learning basic vocabulary. The method he had learned at SIL worked well, and he worked assiduously. Every time he heard a new word, he wrote it down on three-by-five note cards. He punched holes in the corners of the cards, carried dozens of them on the loop of his pants, and repeatedly practiced them with villagers. He tried to apply these words and phrases in different contexts, sometimes making the Pirahã laugh. Whenever he felt frustrated, he would look at the Pirahã children who picked up the language with ease. If they could learn it, so could he, he kept telling himself. But every time he felt like he was learning more phrases, he had the equal sensation that he was really getting nowhere. He began to understand the frustration of the couple that had preceded him.

For instance, he kept hearing a word over and over again that seemed to translate as "just now," as in "the man had just now left." But later, hearing it in a different context, he realized that it in fact referred to the precise moment when something appears or disappears—a person, a sound, anything. The phrase was really about the experience of such transitory moments, he decided, which seemed to resonate a lot with the Pirahã. "Just now" did not begin to cover the rich meanings of it. This started to happen with all kinds of words he thought he had understood. He also began to discover things that were missing in their language that went against all of the linguistic theories he had been taught. They had no words for numbers, no concept of right and left, no simple words that designated colors. What could this mean?

One day, after more than a year living there, he decided to accompany some Pirahã men deep into the jungle, and to his surprise he discovered a whole other side to their existence and language. They acted and spoke differently; they employed a different form of communication, talking to one another in elaborate whistles that clearly replaced spoken language, making them stealthier in their hunting forays. Their ability to navigate this dangerous environment was impressive.

Suddenly something became clear to Everett: his decision to confine himself to village life and simply to learn their language was the source of his problem. Their language could not be separated from their method of hunting, their culture, their daily habits. He had unconsciously internalized a sense of superiority to these people and their way of life—living among them like a scientist studying ants. His inability to pierce the secret of their language, however, revealed the inadequacies of his method. If he wanted to learn Pirahã as the children did, he would have to become like a child— dependent on these people for survival, participating in their daily activities, entering their social circles, feeling in fact inferior and in need of their support. (Losing any sense of superiority would later lead to a personal crisis, in which he would lose faith in his role as a missionary and leave the church for good.)

He began to enact this strategy on all levels, entering a realm of their lives that had been hidden to him. Soon all kinds of ideas about their strange language came to him. The linguistic oddities of Pirahã reflected the unique culture that they had evolved from living in isolation for so long.

Participating in their lives as if he was one of their children, the language came alive from within, and he began to make the kind of progress in Pirahã that had eluded everyone else before him.

In his apprenticeship in the jungles of the Amazon that would later lead to his career as a groundbreaking linguist, Daniel Everett came upon a truth that has application far beyond his field of study. What prevents people from learning, even something as difficult as Pirahã, is not the subject itself—the human mind has limitless capabilities—but rather certain learning *disabilities* that tend to fester and grow in our minds as we get older. These include a sense of smugness and superiority whenever we encounter something alien to our ways, as well as rigid ideas about what is real or true, often indoctrinated in us by schooling or family. If we feel like we know something, our minds close off to other possibilities. We see reflections of the truth we have already assumed. Such feelings of superiority are often unconscious and stem from a fear of what is different or unknown. We are rarely aware of this, and often imagine ourselves to be paragons of impartiality.

Children are generally free of these handicaps. They are dependent upon adults for their survival and naturally feel *inferior.* This sense of inferiority gives them a hunger to learn. Through learning, they can bridge the gap and not feel so helpless. Their minds are completely open; they pay greater attention. This is why children can learn so quickly and so deeply. Unlike other animals, we humans retain what is known as neoteny—mental and physical traits of immaturity—well into our adult years. We have the remarkable capability of returning to a childlike spirit, especially in moments in which we must learn something. Well into our fifties and beyond, we can return to that sense of wonder and curiosity, reviving our youth and apprenticeships.

Understand: when you enter a new environment, your task is to learn and absorb as much as possible. For that purpose you must try to revert to a childlike feeling of inferiority—the feeling that others know much more than you and that you are dependent upon them to learn and safely navigate your apprenticeship. You drop all of your preconceptions about an environment or field, any lingering feelings of smugness. You have no fears. You interact with people and participate in the culture as deeply as possible. You are full of curiosity. Assuming this sensation of inferiority, your mind will open up and you will have a hunger to learn. This position is of course only temporary. You are reverting to a feeling of dependence, so that within five to ten years you can learn enough to finally declare your independence and enter full adulthood.

4. Trust the process

Cesar Rodriguez's father was a lifelong officer in the U.S. Army, but when Cesar (b. 1959) chose to attend the Citadel, the Military College of South Carolina, it was not because he was determined to follow in his father's footsteps. He was probably heading toward a career in business. He decided, however, that he needed some discipline in life, and there was no more rigorous environment than the Citadel.

One morning in 1978, during his sophomore year, Rodriguez's roommate told him that he was going to take the exams that the army, navy, and air force were offering for entrance into the aviation branches of their forces. Rodriguez decided to come along and take the exams just for the hell of it. To his surprise, a few days later he was notified that he had been accepted by the air force for their pilot training program. The initial training, to take place while he was still at the Citadel, meant taking flying lessons in a Cessna. Figuring that would be fun, he entered the program, not entirely sure how far he would take it. He passed the training exams rather easily. He enjoyed the mental challenge, the complete focus that flying required. Perhaps it would be interesting to take the next step. And so, after graduating from the Citadel in 1981, he was sent to the ten-month pilot instruction school at Vance Air Force Base in Oklahoma.

At Vance, however, he discovered that he was suddenly in over his head. Now they were training on a subsonic jet, the T-37. He had to wear a ten-pound helmet and a forty-pound parachute on his back. The cockpit was unbearably small and hot. The instructor sat uncomfortably close in the seat beside him, observing his every move. The stress of performing, the heat, the physical pressures of flying at such speeds would make him sweat profusely and shake. He felt as though the jet itself was pounding and beating him as he flew. And then there were so many more variables to be aware of in flying a jet.

Working on the simulator, he could fly with relative confidence and feel as if he were in control. But once he was strapped into the jet itself he could not suppress a feeling of panic and uncertainty—his mind could not keep up with all of the information he had to process, and it was difficult to prioritize his tasks. Much to his dismay, several months into training he received failing marks on two consecutive flights, and was benched from flying for an entire week.

He had never failed at anything before; it was a matter of pride that he had conquered everything that had been presented to him so far in life. Now he faced a possibility that would devastate him. Seventy students had started out in the course, but almost every week one of them was cut from the program. It was a ruthless, whittling-down process. It looked as if he would be the next one to be cut, and such cuts were final. Once he was allowed back into the plane, he would only have a few chances to prove himself. He had already been trying his hardest. Where had he gone wrong? Perhaps unconsciously, he had become intimidated and afraid of the flying process itself. Now he was more afraid of failing.

He thought back to his days in high school. Despite his relatively short height, he had managed to become the quarterback of his high school football team. Back then he had also experienced moments of doubt and even panic. He had discovered, however, that through rigorous training—mental and physical—he could overcome his fear and almost any deficiency in his skill level. In football practice, placing himself in circumstances that had made him feel uncertain had helped him to become familiar with the situation and not so afraid. What was necessary was to trust the process and the results that would come from more practice. This would have to be the way forward in his current situation.

He tripled his time with the simulator, habituating his mind to the sensation of so many stimuli. He spent his off-hours visualizing himself in the cockpit, repeating the maneuvers he was weakest at. Once he was allowed back in the plane, he focused much harder, knowing he would have to make the most of each precious session. Whenever there was a chance to have more air time, for instance when another student was sick, he grabbed it. Slowly, day by day, he found a way to calm himself in the pilot seat and get a better handle on all of the complex operations. In the two weeks after being allowed back into the plane, he had managed to rescue his position for the time being; he was now ranked somewhere in the middle of the group.

With ten weeks remaining in the program, Rodriguez took stock of the situation. He had come too far not to succeed. He enjoyed the challenge, he loved flying, and now what he wanted more than anything in life was to become a fighter pilot. That would mean graduating from the program near the very top. Among his group were several "golden boys"—young men who had a natural flair for flying. They not only handled the intense pressures, they fed off of them. He was the opposite of a golden boy, but that had been the story of his life. He had succeeded through his determination before, and now it would have to be the same. In these final weeks he was to train on the supersonic T-38, and he asked his new instructor, Wheels Wheeler, to work him to death—he had to move up in the rankings and he was prepared to do whatever it took.

Wheeler obliged him. He made Rodriguez repeat the same maneuver ten times more than the golden boys, until he was physically sick. He homed in on all of Rodriguez's flying weaknesses and made him practice on the things he hated the most. His criticisms were brutal. One day, however, as he was flying the T-38, Rodriguez had a strange and wonderful sensation—it seemed like he could feel the plane itself at the edge of his fingertips. This is how it must be for the golden boys, he thought, only for him it had taken nearly ten months of intense training. His mind no longer felt mired in all of the details. It was vague, but he could sense the possibility of a higher way of thinking—seeing the larger picture of flying in formation, while also commanding the complex operations in the cockpit. This sensation would come and go, but the feeling made all of the work worthwhile.

In the end Rodriguez graduated third in his class, and was promoted to fighter-pilot lead-in training. The same process would now repeat itself in an even more competitive environment. He would have to outdo the golden boys through practice and sheer determination. In this manner, he slowly rose through the ranks to become a colonel in the U.S. Air Force. During the 1990s, his three air-to-air kills in active duty brought him closer to the designation of ace than any American pilot since the Vietnam War, and earned him the nickname the Last American Ace.

———

What separates Masters from others is often something surprisingly simple. Whenever we learn a skill, we frequently reach a point of frustration—what we are learning seems beyond our capabilities. Giving in to these feelings, we unconsciously quit on ourselves before we actually give up. Among the dozens of pilots in Rodriguez's class who never made the cut, almost all of them had the same talent level as he did. The difference is not simply a matter of determination, but more of trust and faith. Many of those who succeed in life have had the experience in their youth of having mastered some skill—a sport or game, a musical instrument, a foreign language, and so on. Buried in their minds is the sensation of overcoming their frustrations and entering the cycle of accelerated returns. In moments of doubt in the present, the memory of the past experience rises to the surface. Filled with trust in the process, they trudge on well past the point at which others slow down or mentally quit.

When it comes to mastering a skill, time is the magic ingredient. Assuming your practice proceeds at a steady level, over days and weeks certain elements of the skill become hardwired. Slowly, the entire skill becomes internalized, part of your nervous system. The mind is no longer mired in the details, but can see the larger picture. It is a miraculous sensation and practice will lead you to that point, no matter the talent level you are born with. The only real impediment to this is yourself and your emotions—boredom, panic, frustration, insecurity. You cannot suppress such emotions—they are normal to the process and are experienced by everyone, including Masters. What you can do is have faith in the process. The boredom will go away once you enter the cycle. The panic disappears after repeated exposure. The frustration is a sign of progress—a signal that your mind is processing complexity and requires more practice. The insecurities will transform into their opposites when you gain mastery. Trusting this will all happen, you will allow the natural learning process to move forward, and everything else will fall into place.

5. Move toward resistance and pain

A. Bill Bradley (b. 1943) fell in love with the sport of basketball somewhere around the age of ten. He had one advantage over his peers—he was tall for his age. But beyond that, he had no real natural gift for the game. He was slow and gawky, and could not jump very high. None of the aspects of the game came easily to him. He would have to compensate for all of his inadequacies through sheer practice. And so he proceeded to devise one of the most rigorous and efficient training routines in the history of sports.

Managing to get his hands on the keys to the high school gym, he created for himself a schedule—three and a half hours of practice after school and on Sundays, eight hours every Saturday, and three hours a day during the summer. Over the years, he would keep rigidly to this schedule. In the gym, he would put ten-pound weights in his shoes to strengthen his legs and give him more spring to his jump. His greatest weaknesses, he decided, were his dribbling and his overall slowness. He would have to work on these and also transform himself into a superior passer to make up for his lack of speed.

For this purpose, he devised various exercises. He wore eyeglass frames with pieces of cardboard taped to the bottom, so he could not see the basketball while he practiced dribbling. This would train him to always look around him rather than at the ball—a key skill in passing. He set up chairs on the court to act as opponents. He would dribble around them, back and forth, for hours, until he could glide past them, quickly changing direction. He spent hours at both of these exercises, well past any feelings of boredom or pain.

Walking down the main street of his hometown in Missouri, he would keep his eyes focused straight ahead and try to notice the goods in the store windows, on either side, without turning his head. He worked on this endlessly, developing his peripheral vision so he could see more of the court. In his room at home, he practiced pivot moves and fakes well into the night— such skills that would also help him compensate for his lack of speed.

Bradley put all of his creative energy into coming up with novel and effective ways of practicing. One time his family traveled to Europe via transatlantic ship. Finally, they thought, he would give his training regimen a break—there was really no place to practice on board. But below deck and running the length of the ship were two corridors, 900 feet long and quite narrow—just enough room for two passengers. This was the perfect location to practice dribbling at top speed while maintaining perfect ball control. To make it even harder, he decided to wear special eyeglasses that narrowed his vision. For hours every day he dribbled up one side and down the other, until the voyage was done.

Working this way over the years, Bradley slowly transformed himself into one of the biggest stars in basketball—first as an All-American at Princeton University and then as a professional with the New York Knicks. Fans were in awe of his ability to make the most astounding passes, as if he had eyes on the back and sides of his head—not to mention his dribbling prowess, his incredible arsenal of fakes and pivots, and his complete gracefulness on the court. Little did they know that such apparent ease was the result of so many hours of intense practice over so many years.

B. When John Keats (1795–1821) was eight years old, his father died in a riding accident. His mother never quite got over the loss and died seven years later—essentially leaving John, his two brothers, and one sister orphaned and homeless in London. John, the eldest of the children, was taken out of school by the appointed trustee and guardian of the estate, and enrolled as an apprentice to a surgeon and apothecary—he would have to earn a living as quickly as possible, and this seemed the best career for that.

In his last few terms at school, Keats had developed a love for literature and reading. To continue his education, he would return to his school in his off-hours and read as many books as he could in the library. Sometime later, he had the desire to try his hand at writing poetry, but lacking any kind of instructor or literary circle he could frequent, the only way he knew to teach himself to write was to read the works of all of the greatest poets of the seventeenth and eighteenth centuries. He then wrote his own poems, using the poetic form and style of the particular writer he was trying to model himself after. He had a knack for imitation, and soon he was creating verses in dozens of different styles, always tweaking them a little with his own voice.

Several years into this process, Keats came to a fateful decision—he would devote his life to writing poetry. That was his calling in life and he would find a way to make a living at it. To complete the rigorous apprenticeship he had already put himself through, he decided that what he needed was to write a very long poem, precisely 4,000 lines. The poem would revolve around the ancient Greek myth of Endymion. "*Endymion*," he wrote a friend, "will be a test, a trial of my Powers of Imagination and chiefly of my invention . . .—by which I must make 4000 lines of some circumstances and fill them with Poetry." He gave himself a rather impossible deadline—seven months—and a task of writing fifty lines a day, until he had a rough draft.

Three-quarters of the way through, he came to thoroughly hate the poem he was writing. He would not quit, however, willing his way to the end, meeting the deadline he had set. What he did not like about *Endymion* was the flowery language, the overwriting. But it was only by means of this exercise that he could discover what worked for him. "In *Endymion*," he later wrote, "I leaped headlong into the Sea and thereby became better acquainted with the Soundings, the quicksands and the rocks, than if I had stayed upon the green shore and . . . took tea and comfortable advice."

In the aftermath of writing what he considered to be a mediocre poem, Keats took stock of all of the invaluable lessons he had learned. Never again would he suffer from writer's block—he had trained himself to write past any obstacle. He had acquired now the habit of writing quickly, with intensity and focus—concentrating his work in a few hours. He could revise with equal speed. He had learned how to criticize himself and his overly romantic tendencies. He could look at his own work with a cold eye. He had learned that it was in the actual writing of the poem that the best ideas would often come to him, and that he had to boldly keep writing or he would miss such discoveries. Most important of all, as a counterexample to *Endymion,* he had hit upon a style that suited him—language as compact and dense with imagery as possible, with not a single wasted line.

With these lessons in hand, in the years 1818 to 1819, before he became gravely ill, Keats would produce some of the most memorable poems in the English language, including all of his greatest odes. This added up to perhaps the most productive two years of writing in the history of Western literature—all of it set up by the rigorous self-apprenticeship he had put himself through.

By nature, we humans shrink from anything that seems possibly painful or overtly difficult. We bring this natural tendency to our practice of any skill. Once we grow adept at some aspect of this skill, generally one that comes more easily to us, we prefer to practice this element over and over. Our skill becomes lopsided as we avoid our weaknesses. Knowing that in our practice we can let down our guard, since we are not being watched or under pressure to perform, we bring to this a kind of dispersed attention. We tend to also be quite conventional in our practice routines. We generally follow what others have done, performing the accepted exercises for these skills.

This is the path of amateurs. To attain mastery, you must adopt what we shall call Resistance Practice. The principle is simple—you go in the opposite direction of all of your natural tendencies when it comes to practice.

First, you *resist* the temptation to be nice to yourself. You become your own worst critic; you see your work as if through the eyes of others. You recognize your weaknesses, precisely the elements you are not good at. Those are the aspects you give precedence to in your practice. You find a kind of perverse pleasure in moving past the pain this might bring. Second, you *resist* the lure of easing up on your focus. You train yourself to concentrate in practice with double the intensity, as if it were the real thing times two. In devising your own routines, you become as creative as possible. You invent exercises that work upon your weaknesses. You give yourself arbitrary deadlines to meet certain standards, constantly pushing yourself past perceived limits. In this way you develop your own standards for excellence, generally higher than those of others.

In the end, your five hours of intense, focused work are the equivalent of ten for most people. Soon enough you will see the results of such practice, and others will marvel at the apparent ease in which you accomplish your deeds.

6. Apprentice yourself in failure

One day in 1885, the twenty-three-year old Henry Ford got his first look at the gas-powered engine, and it was instant love. Ford had apprenticed as a machinist and had worked on every conceivable device, but nothing could compare to his fascination with this new type of engine, one that created its own power. He envisioned a whole new kind of horseless carriage that would revolutionize transportation. He made it his Life's Task to be the pioneer in developing such an automobile.

Working the night shift at the Edison Illuminating Company as an engineer, during the day he would tinker with the new internal-combustion engine he was developing. He built a workshop in a shed behind his home and started constructing the engine from pieces of scrap metal he salvaged from anywhere he could find them. By 1896, working with friends who helped him build a carriage, he completed his first prototype, which he called the Quadricycle, and debuted it on the streets of Detroit.

At the time there were many others working on automobiles with gas-powered engines. It was a ruthlessly competitive environment in which new companies died by the day. Ford's Quadricycle looked nice and ran well, but it was too small and incomplete for large-scale production. And so he began work on a second automobile, thinking ahead to the production end of the process. A year later he completed it, and it was a marvel of design. Everything was geared toward simplicity and compactness. It was easy to drive and maintain. All that he needed was financial backing and sufficient capital to mass-produce it.

To manufacture automobiles in the late 1890s was a daunting venture. It required a tremendous amount of capital and a complex business structure, considering all of the parts that went into production. Ford quickly found the perfect backer: William H. Murphy, one of the most prominent businessmen in Detroit. The new company was dubbed the Detroit Automobile Company, and all who were involved had high hopes. But problems soon arose. The car Ford had designed as a prototype needed to be reworked—the parts came from different places; some of them were deficient and far too heavy for his liking. He kept trying to refine the design to come closer to his ideal. But it was taking far too long, and Murphy and the stockholders were getting restless. In 1901, a year and a half after it had started operation, the board of directors dissolved the company. They had lost faith in Henry Ford.

In analyzing this failure, Ford came to the conclusion that he had been trying to make his automobile serve too many consumer needs. He would try a second time, starting out with a lightweight and smaller vehicle. He convinced Murphy to give him another chance, something rare in the fledgling automobile business. Still believing in Ford's genius, he agreed, and together they formed the Henry Ford Company. Right from the start, however, Ford felt the pressure from Murphy to get the automobile ready for production so as to avoid the problems he'd had with the first company. Ford resented the interference from people who knew nothing about design or the high standards he was trying to establish for the industry.

Murphy and his men brought in an outsider to supervise the process. This was the breaking point—less than a year after its establishment, Ford left the company. The break with Murphy this time was final. In the car business, everyone wrote Henry Ford off. He had blown his two chances and nobody was ever given a third, not with the amount of money at stake. But to friends and family, Ford himself seemed blithely unconcerned. He told everyone that these were all invaluable lessons to him—he had paid attention to every glitch along the way, and like a watch or an engine, he had taken apart these failures in his mind and had identified the root cause: no one was giving him enough time to work out the bugs. The people with money were meddling in mechanical and design affairs. They were injecting their mediocre ideas into the process and polluting it. He resented the idea that having money gave them certain rights, when all that mattered was a perfect design.

The answer was to find a way to maintain complete independence from the financiers. This was not the usual way of doing business in America, which was becoming increasingly bureaucratic. He would have to invent his own form of organization, his own business model, one that suited his temperament and needs—including an efficient team he could trust, and the right to the final word on every decision.

Considering his reputation, it would be almost impossible to find backing, but several months into the search he found an ideal partner—Alexander Malcomson, an émigré from Scotland who had made his fortune in the coal business. Like Ford, he had an unconventional streak and was a risk taker. He agreed to finance this latest venture and to not meddle in the manufacturing process. Ford worked at creating a new kind of assembly plant that would give him more control over the car he wanted to design, now known as the Model A. The Model A would be the lightest car ever made, simple and durable. It was the culmination of all of his tinkering and designing. It would be assembled along a line that would ensure speed of production.

With the assembly plant ready, Ford worked hard at getting the team of workers to churn out fifteen cars a day—a rather high number back then. He oversaw every aspect of the production—it was his car from the inside out. He even worked on the assembly line, endearing himself to the workers. Orders started pouring in for the well made yet inexpensive Model A, and by 1904 the Ford Motor Company had to expand its operations. Soon it would be one of the few survivors from the early era of the automobile business, and a giant in the making.

Henry Ford had one of those minds that was naturally attuned to the mechanical. He had the power of most great inventors—the ability to visualize the parts and how they functioned together. If he had to describe how something worked, Ford would inevitably take a napkin and sketch out a diagram rather than use words. With this type of intelligence, his apprenticeships on machines were easy and fast. But when it came to mass-producing his inventions, he had to confront the fact that he did not have the requisite knowledge. He needed an additional apprenticeship in becoming a businessman and entrepreneur. Fortunately, working on machines had developed in him a kind of practical intelligence, patience, and way of solving problems that could be applied to anything.

When a machine malfunctions you do not take it personally or grow despondent. It is in fact a blessing in disguise. Such malfunctions generally show you inherent flaws and means of improvement. You simply keep tinkering until you get it right. The same should apply to an entrepreneurial venture. Mistakes and failures are precisely your means of education. They tell you about your own inadequacies. It is hard to find out such things from people, as they are often political with their praise and criticisms.

Your failures also permit you to see the flaws of your ideas, which are only revealed in the execution of them. You learn what your audience really wants, the discrepancy between your ideas and how they affect the public. Pay close attention to the structure of your group—how your team is organized, the degree of independence you have from the source of capital. These are design elements as well, and such management issues are often hidden sources of problems.

Think of it this way: There are two kinds of failure. The first comes from never trying out your ideas because you are afraid, or because you are waiting for the perfect time. This kind of failure you can never learn from, and such timidity will destroy you. The second kind comes from a bold and venturesome spirit. If you fail in this way, the hit that you take to your reputation is greatly outweighed by what you learn. Repeated failure will toughen your spirit and show you with absolute clarity how things must be done. In fact, it is a curse to have everything go right on your first attempt. You will fail to question the element of luck, making you think that you have the golden touch. When you do inevitably fail, it will confuse and demoralize you past the point of learning. In any case, to apprentice as an entrepreneur you must act on your ideas as early as possible, exposing them to the public, a part of you even hoping that you'll fail. You have everything to gain.

7. Combine the "how" and the "what"

At a very early age, Santiago Calatrava (b. 1951) developed a love for drawing. He carried his pencils wherever he went. A certain paradox in drawing began to obsess him. In Valencia, Spain, where he grew up, the harsh Mediterranean sunlight would place in sharp relief the things he liked to draw— rocks, trees, buildings, people. Their outlines would slowly soften as the day progressed. Nothing he drew was ever really static; everything is in a state of change and motion—that is the essence of life. How could he capture this movement on paper, in an image that was perfectly still?

He took classes and learned techniques for creating the various illusions of something caught in the moment of movement, but it was never quite enough. As part of this impossible quest he taught himself aspects of mathematics, such as descriptive geometry, that could help him understand how to represent his objects in two dimensions. His skill improved and his interest in the subject deepened. It seemed he was destined for a career as an artist, and so in 1969 he enrolled in art school in Valencia.

A few months into his studies, he had a seemingly minor experience that would change the course of his life: browsing for supplies in a stationery store, his eye was drawn to a beautifully designed booklet describing the work of the great architect Le Corbusier. Somehow this architect had managed to create completely distinctive shapes. He turned even something as simple as a stairway into a dynamic piece of sculpture. The buildings he designed seemed to defy gravity, creating a feeling of movement in their still forms. Studying this booklet, Calatrava now developed a new obsession—to learn the secret of how such buildings came about. As soon as he could, he transferred to the one architecture school in Valencia.

Graduating from the school in 1973, Calatrava had gained a solid education in the subject. He had learned all of the most important design rules and principles. He was more than capable of taking his place in some architecture firm and working his way up. But he felt something elemental was missing in his knowledge. In looking at all of the great works of architecture that he most admired—the Pantheon in Rome, the buildings of Gaudí in Barcelona, the bridges designed by Robert Maillart in Switzerland—he had no solid idea about their actual construction. He knew more than enough about their form, their aesthetics, and how they functioned as public buildings, but he knew nothing about how they stood up, how the pieces fit together, how the buildings of Le Corbusier managed to create that impression of movement and dynamism.

It was like knowing how to draw a beautiful bird but not understanding how it could fly. As with drawing, he wanted to go beyond the surface, the design element, and touch upon the reality. He felt that the world was changing; something was in the air. With advances in technology and new materials, revolutionary possibilities had emerged for a new kind of architecture, but to truly exploit that he would have to learn something about engineering. Thinking in this direction, Calatrava made a fateful decision—he would virtually start over and enroll at the Federal Institute of Technology in Zurich, Switzerland, to gain a degree in civil engineering. It would be an arduous process, but he would train himself to think and draw like an engineer. Knowing how buildings were constructed would liberate him and give him ideas about how to slowly expand the boundaries of what could be made.

In the first few years he grounded himself in the rigors of engineering—all of the mathematics and physics required for the field. But as he progressed, he found himself returning to that paradox that he had been obsessed with in childhood—how to express movement and change. In architecture, the golden rule was that buildings had to be stable and stationary. Calatrava felt the desire to break up this rigid convention. For his PhD dissertation, he decided to explore the possibilities of bringing actual movement into architecture. Inspired by NASA and its designs for space travel, as well as the folding bird wings designed by Leonardo da Vinci, Calatrava chose as his topic the foldability of structures—how through advanced engineering structures could move and transform themselves.

Completing his dissertation in 1981, he finally entered the work world—after fourteen years of a university apprenticeship in art, architecture, and engineering. In the coming years he would experiment in designing new kinds of collapsible doors, windows, and roofs that would move and open up in new ways, altering the shape of the building. He designed a drawbridge in Buenos Aires that moved outward instead of up. In 1996 he took all of this a step further with his design and construction of an extension to the Milwaukee Art Museum. It consisted of a long glass-and-steel reception hall with an eighty-foot ceiling, all shaded by an enormous moveable sunscreen on the roof. The screen had two ribbed panels that opened and closed like the wings of a giant seagull, putting the entire edifice into motion, and giving the sense of a building that could take flight.

———

We humans live in two worlds. First, there is the outer world of appearances—all of the forms of things that captivate our eye. But hidden from our view is another world—how these things actually function, their anatomy or composition, the parts working together and forming the whole. This second world is not so immediately captivating. It is harder to understand. It is not something visible to the eye, but only to the mind that glimpses the reality. But this "how" of things is just as poetic once we understand it—it contains the secret of life, of how things move and change.

This division between the "how" and the "what" can be applied to almost everything around us—we see the machine, not how it works; we see a group of people producing something as a business, not how the group is structured or how the products are manufactured and distributed. (In a similar fashion, we tend to be mesmerized by people's appearances, not the psychology behind what they do or say.) As Calatrava discovered, in overcoming this division, in combining the "how" and the "what" of architecture, he gained a much deeper, or rather more rounded knowledge of the field. He grasped a larger portion of the reality that goes into making buildings. This allowed him to create something infinitely more poetic, to stretch the boundaries, to break the conventions of architecture itself.

Understand: we live in the world of a sad separation that began some five hundred years ago when art and science split apart. Scientists and technicians live in their own world, focusing mostly on the "how" of things. Others live in the world of appearances, using these things but not really understanding how they function. Just before this split occurred, it was the ideal of the Renaissance to combine these two forms of knowledge. This is why the work of Leonardo da Vinci continues to fascinate us, and why the Renaissance remains an ideal. This more rounded knowledge is in fact the way of the future, especially now that so much more information is available to all of us.

As Calatrava intuited, this should be a part of our apprenticeship. We must make ourselves study as deeply as possible the technology we use, the functioning of the group we work in, the economics of our field, its lifeblood. We must constantly ask the questions—how do things work, how do decisions get made, how does the group interact? Rounding our knowledge in this way will give us a deeper feel for reality and the heightened power to alter it.

8. Advance through trial and error

Growing up in a suburb of Pittsburgh, Pennsylvania, in the early 1970s, Paul Graham (b. 1964) became fascinated with the depiction of computers in television and film. They were like electronic brains with limitless powers. In the near future, or so it seemed, you would be able to talk to your computer, and it would do everything you wanted.

In junior high school he had been admitted into a program for gifted students that provided them with the chance to work on a creative project of their choosing. Graham decided to focus his project on the school's computer, an IBM mainframe that was used for printing out grade reports and class schedules. This was the first time he had gotten his hands on a computer, and although it was primitive and had to be programmed with punch cards, it seemed like something magical—a portal to the future.

Over the next few years, he taught himself how to program by consulting the few books then written on the subject, but mostly he learned by trial and error. Like painting on a canvas, he could see the results immediately of what he had done—and if the programming worked, it had a certain aesthetic rightness to it. The process of learning through trial and error was immensely satisfying. He could discover things on his own, without having to follow a rigid path set up by others. (This is the essence of being a "hacker.") And the better he got at programming, the more he could make it do.

Deciding to pursue his studies further, he chose to attend Cornell University, which at the time had one of the best computer science departments in the country. Here he finally received instruction in the basic principles of programming, cleaning up many of the bad hacking habits he had developed on his own. He became intrigued by the recently developed field of artificial intelligence—the key to designing the kinds of computers he had dreamed about as a child. To be on the frontier of this new field, he applied and was accepted to the graduate school in computer science at Harvard University.

At Harvard Graham finally had to confront something about himself— he was not cut out for academia. He hated writing research papers. The university way of programming took all the fun and excitement out of it— the process of discovering through trial and error. He was a hacker at heart, one who liked to figure things out for himself. He found a fellow hacker at Harvard, Robert Morris, and together they began to explore the intricacies of the programming language Lisp. It seemed like the most potentially powerful and fluid language of them all. Understanding Lisp made you understand something essential about programming itself. It was a language suited for high-level hackers, a language specifically made for investigation and discovery.

Disillusioned with the computer science department at Harvard, Graham decided to design his own graduate school program: he would take a wide range of classes and discover what interested him the most. To his surprise, he found himself attracted to art—to painting, and to the subject of art history itself. What this meant to him was that he should follow this interest and see where it would lead. After completing his PhD at Harvard in computer science, he enrolled in the Rhode Island School of Design, then attended a painting program at the Accademia in Florence, Italy. He returned to the States broke but determined to try his hand at painting. He would pay for his lifestyle with intermittent consulting work in programming.

As the years went by, he would occasionally reflect on the course of his life. Artists in the Renaissance would go through clear-cut apprenticeships, but what could he say about his own apprenticeship? There seemed to be no real design or direction to his life. It was like the "cheesy hacks" he did in high school, patching things together, figuring things out through constant trial and error, finding out what worked by doing it. Shaping his life in this haphazard way, he learned what to avoid—academia; working for large companies; any political environment. He liked the process of *making* things. What really mattered to him in the end was having possibilities—being able to go in this or that direction, depending on what life presented to him. If over the years he had undergone an apprenticeship, it was almost by default.

One afternoon in 1995, he heard on the radio a story about Netscape—the company itself was touting its future and discussing how someday most businesses would be selling their products on the Internet itself, with Netscape leading the way. With his bank account getting desperately low again, yet dreading the idea of returning to another consulting job, he recruited his old hacker friend Robert Morris to help him create software for running an online business. Graham's idea was to design a program that would run directly on the web server instead of having to be downloaded. No one had thought of this before. They would write the program in Lisp, taking advantage of the speed with which they could make changes to it. They called their business Viaweb, and it would be the first of its kind, the pioneer of online commerce. Just three years later they sold it to Yahoo! for $45 million.

In the years to come Graham would continue on the path set in his twenties, moving to where his interests and skills converged, to wherever he could see possibilities. In 2005 he gave a talk at Harvard about his experiences with Viaweb. The students, excited by his advice, pleaded with him to start up some kind of consulting firm. Intrigued by the idea, he created Y Combinator, an apprenticeship system for young entrepreneurs in technology, with his company taking a stake in each successful startup. Over the years he would refine the system, learning as he went along. In the end, Y Combinator represented his ultimate hack—something he came upon by accident and improved through his own process of trial and error. The company is now valued at close to $500 million.

Each age tends to create a model of apprenticeship that is suited to the system of production that prevails at the time. In the Middle Ages, during the birth of modern capitalism and the need for quality control, the first apprenticeship system appeared, with its rigidly defined terms. With the advent of the Industrial Revolution, this model of apprenticeship became largely outmoded, but the idea behind it lived on in the form of self-apprenticeship—developing yourself from within a particular field, as Darwin did in biology. This suited the growing individualistic spirit of the time. We are now in the computer age, with computers dominating nearly all aspects of commercial life. Although there are many ways in which this could influence the concept of apprenticeship, it is the hacker approach to programming that may offer the most promising model for this new age.

The model goes like this: You want to learn as many skills as possible, following the direction that circumstances lead you to, but only if they are related to your deepest interests. Like a hacker, you value the process of self-discovery and making things that are of the highest quality. You avoid the trap of following one set career path. You are not sure where this will all lead, but you are taking full advantage of the openness of information, all of the knowledge about skills now at our disposal. You see what kind of work suits you and what you want to avoid at all cost. You move by trial and error. This is how you pass your twenties. You are the programmer of this wide-ranging apprenticeship, within the loose constraints of your personal interests.

You are not wandering about because you are afraid of commitment, but because you are expanding your skill base and your possibilities. At a certain point, when you are ready to settle on something, ideas and opportunities will inevitably present themselves to you. When that happens, all of the skills you have accumulated will prove invaluable. You will be the Master at combining them in ways that are unique and suited to your individuality.

You may settle on this one place or idea for several years, accumulating in the process even more skills, then move in a slightly different direction when the time is appropriate. In this new age, those who follow a rigid, singular path in their youth often find themselves in a career dead end in their forties, or overwhelmed with boredom. The wide-ranging apprenticeship of your twenties will yield the opposite—expanding possibilities as you get older.

REVERSAL

It might be imagined that certain people in history—the naturally gifted, the geniuses—have either somehow bypassed the Apprenticeship Phase or have greatly shortened it because of their inherent brilliance. To support such an argument, people will bring up the classic examples of Mozart and Einstein, who seemed to have emerged as creative geniuses out of nowhere.

With the case of Mozart, however, it is generally agreed among classical music critics that he did not write an original and substantial piece of music until well after ten years of composing. In fact, a study of some seventy great classical composers determined that with only three exceptions, all of the composers had needed at least ten years to produce their first great work, and the exceptions had somehow managed to create theirs in nine years.

Einstein began his serious thought experiments at the age of sixteen. Ten years later he came up with his first revolutionary theory of relativity. It is impossible to quantify the time he spent honing his theoretical skills in those ten years, but is not hard to imagine him working three hours a day on this particular problem, which would yield more than 10,000 hours after a decade. What in fact separates Mozart and Einstein from others is the extreme youth with which they began their apprenticeships and the intensity with which they practiced, stemming from their total immersion in the subject. It is often the case that in our younger years we learn faster, absorb more deeply, and yet retain a kind of creative verve that tends to fade as we get older.

There are no shortcuts or ways to bypass the Apprenticeship Phase. It is the nature of the human brain to require such lengthy exposure to a field, which allows for complex skills to become deeply embedded and frees the mind up for real creative activity. The very desire to find shortcuts makes you eminently unsuited for any kind of mastery. There is no possible reversal to this process.

It's like chopping down a huge tree of immense girth. You won't accomplish it with one swing of your axe. If you keep chopping away at it, though, and do not let up, eventually, whether it wants to or not, it will suddenly topple down. When that time comes, you could round up everyone you could find and pay them to hold the tree up, but they wouldn't be able to do it. It would still come crashing to the ground. . . . But if the woodcutter stopped after one or two strokes of his axe to ask the third son of Mr. Chang, "Why doesn't this tree fall?" And after three or four more strokes stopped again to ask the fourth son of Mr. Li, "Why doesn't this tree fall?" he would never succeed in felling the tree. It is no different for someone who is practicing the Way.

—ZEN MASTER HAKUIN

III

ABSORB THE MASTER'S POWER: THE MENTOR DYNAMIC

Life is short, and your time for learning and creativity is limited. Without any guidance, you can waste valuable years trying to gain knowledge and practice from various sources. Instead, you must follow the example set by Masters throughout the ages and find the proper mentor. The mentor-protégé relationship is the most efficient and productive form of learning. The right mentors know where to focus your attention and how to challenge you. Their knowledge and experience become yours. They provide immediate and realistic feedback on your work, so you can improve more rapidly. Through an intense person-to-person interaction, you absorb a way of thinking that contains great power and can be adapted to your individual spirit. Choose the mentor who best fits your needs and connects to your Life's Task. Once you have internalized their knowledge, you must move on and never remain in their shadow. Your goal is always to surpass your mentors in mastery and brilliance.

THE ALCHEMY OF KNOWLEDGE

Growing up amid poverty in London, it seemed that the fate of Michael Faraday (1791–1867) was pretty much sealed for him at birth—he would either follow in his father's footsteps and become a blacksmith, or he would pursue some other manual trade. His options were severely limited by his circumstances. His parents had ten children to feed and support. The father worked sporadically because of illness, and the family needed additional income. The parents waited anxiously for the day when young Faraday would turn twelve and could get a job, or begin some kind of apprenticeship.

There was one trait, however, that marked him as different and was potentially troubling—he had an extremely active mind, one that was perhaps unsuited for a career that would entail mostly physical labor. Some of his mental restlessness was inspired by the peculiar religion his family belonged to—they were Sandemanians, a sect of Christianity. Its adherents believed that God's presence was manifested in every living thing and every natural phenomenon. By communing with God on a daily basis and getting as inwardly close to him as possible, they could see and feel his presence everywhere in the world.

Young Faraday was steeped in this philosophy. When he was not doing errands and chores for his mother, he would wander the streets of central London, observing the world around him with utmost intensity. Nature, it seemed to him, was full of secrets that he wanted to ponder and unravel. Because he was taught that the divine presence was everywhere, everything interested him, and his curiosity was limitless. He would ask endless questions of his parents, or anyone he could find, about plants or minerals or any seemingly inexplicable occurrence in nature. He seemed hungry for knowledge and frustrated by his lack of means to get it.

One day he wandered into a nearby shop that bound and sold books. The sight of so many shiny books on the shelves astounded him. His own schooling had been minimal, and he had really only known one book in his life, the Bible. The Sandemanians believed that the Scripture was the living embodiment of the Lord's will, and contained something of his presence. To Faraday this meant that the printed words of the Bible had a kind of magical power. He imagined that each of the books in this shop opened up different worlds of knowledge, a form of magic in its own right.

The owner of the shop, George Riebau, was instantly charmed by the young man's reverence for his books. He had never met someone quite so intense at such a young age. He encouraged him to return, and soon Faraday began to frequent the shop. To help Faraday's family, Riebau gave him a job as a delivery boy. Impressed with his work ethic, he invited him to join the shop itself as an apprentice bookbinder. Faraday happily accepted, and in 1805 he began his seven-year apprenticeship.

In the initial months of the job, surrounded by all these books, the young man could hardly believe his good fortune—new books were rare commodities in those days, luxury items for the well-to-do. Not even a public library contained what could be found in Riebau's shop. The owner encouraged him to read whatever he liked in his off-hours, and Faraday obliged by devouring almost every single book that passed through his hands. One evening he read an encyclopedia passage on the most recent discoveries in electricity, and he suddenly felt as if he had found his calling in life. Here was a phenomenon that was invisible to the eye, but that could be revealed and measured through experiments. This process of uncovering nature's secrets through experiment enthralled him. Science, it seemed to him, was a great quest to unravel the mysteries of Creation itself. Somehow, he would transform himself into a scientist.

This was not a realistic goal on his part and he knew it. In England at the time, access to laboratories and to science as a career was only open to those with a university education, which meant those from the upper classes. How could a bookbinder's apprentice even dream of overcoming such odds? Even if he had the energy and desire to attempt it, he had no teachers, no guidance, no structure or method to his studies. Then in 1809 a book came into the shop that finally gave him some hope. It was called *Improvement of the Mind*—a self-help guide written by Reverend Isaac Watts, first published in 1741. The book revealed a system of learning and improving your lot in life, no matter your social class. It prescribed courses of action that anyone could follow, and it promised results. Faraday read it over and over, carrying it with him wherever he went.

He followed the book's advice to the letter. For Watts, learning had to be an active process. He recommended not just reading about scientific discoveries, but actually re-creating the experiments that led to them. And so, with Riebau's blessing, Faraday began a series of basic experiments in electricity and chemistry in the back room of the shop. Watts advocated the importance of having teachers and not just learning from books. Faraday dutifully began to attend the numerous lectures on science that were popular in London at the time. Watts advocated not just listening to lectures but taking detailed notes, then reworking the notes themselves—all of this imprinting the knowledge deeper in the brain. Faraday would take this even further.

Attending the lectures of the popular scientist John Tatum, each week on a different subject, he would note down the most important words and concepts, quickly sketch out the various instruments Tatum used, and diagram the experiments. Over the next few days he would expand the notes into sentences, and then into an entire chapter on the subject, elaborately sketched and narrated. In the course of a year this added up to a thick scientific encyclopedia he had created on his own. His knowledge of science had grown by leaps and bounds, and had assumed a kind of organizational shape modeled on his notes.

One day, Monsieur Riebau showed this rather impressive collection of notes to a customer named William Dance, a member of the prestigious Royal Institution, an organization that sought to promote the latest advances in science. Thumbing through Faraday's chapters, Dance was astounded at how clearly and concisely he had summarized complicated topics. He decided to invite the young man to attend a series of lectures by the renowned and recently knighted chemist Humphry Davy, to be given at the Royal Institution where Davy was director of the chemistry laboratory.

The lectures had been sold out well in advance and this was a rare privilege for a young man of Faraday's background, but for him it was much more fateful than that. Davy was the preeminent chemist of his time; he had made numerous discoveries and was advancing the new field of electrochemistry. His experiments with various gases and chemicals were highly dangerous and had led to numerous accidents. This only added to his reputation as a fearless warrior for science. His lectures were events—he had a flair for the dramatic, performing clever experiments before a dazzled audience. He came from a modest background and had raised himself to the heights of science, having gained the attention of some valuable mentors. To Faraday, Davy was the only living scientist he could model himself after, considering Davy's lack of any solid formal education.

Arriving early each time and gaining the closest seat he could find, he soaked up every aspect of Davy's lectures, taking the most detailed notes he had ever attempted. These lectures had a different effect upon Faraday than others he had attended. He was inspired and yet he also could not help but feel somewhat dejected. After all of these years of studying on his own, he had managed to expand his knowledge of science and of the natural world. But science does not consist of the accumulation of information. It is a way of thinking, of approaching problems. The scientific spirit is creative—Faraday could feel it in Davy's presence. As an amateur scientist looking at the field from the outside, his knowledge was one-dimensional and would lead nowhere. He needed to move to the inside, where he could gain practical, hands-on experience, become part of the community and learn how to *think* like a scientist. And to move closer to this scientific spirit and absorb its essence, he would need a mentor.

This seemed like an impossible quest, but with his apprenticeship coming to an end, and facing the prospect of being a bookbinder for life, Faraday went into desperation mode. He wrote letters to the president of the Royal Society and applied for the most menial jobs in any kind of laboratory. He was relentless, and yet months went by with no results. Then one day, out of the blue, he received a message from Humphry Davy's office. The chemist had been blinded by yet another explosion in his laboratory at the Royal Institution, and the condition would last for several days. During this time he needed a personal assistant to take notes and organize his materials. Mr. Dance, a good friend of Davy's, had recommended young Faraday for the job.

There seemed something fateful, even magical, in this occurrence. Faraday would have to make the most of it, do whatever he could to impress the great chemist. Awestruck to be in Davy's presence, Faraday listened with utmost intensity to every one of his instructions and did more than was asked for. When Davy, however, had recovered his sight, he thanked Faraday for his work but made it clear that the Royal Institution already had a laboratory assistant and there were simply no openings for him on any level.

Faraday felt despondent, but he was not ready to give up; he would not let this be the end. Only a few days in Davy's presence had revealed so many learning possibilities. Davy liked to talk about his ideas as they occurred to him and gain feedback from anyone around him. Discussing with Faraday one experiment he was planning afforded the young man a glimpse into how his mind worked, and it was fascinating. Davy would be the ultimate mentor, and Faraday determined that he would have to make this happen. He went back to the notes he had taken on Davy's lectures. He worked them into a beautifully organized booklet, carefully handwritten, and full of sketches and diagrams. He sent this off to Davy as a gift. He then wrote to him a few weeks later, reminding Davy about the experiment he had mentioned but had probably forgotten about—Davy was notoriously absent-minded. Faraday heard nothing. But then one day, in February 1813, he was suddenly summoned to the Royal Institution.

That same morning the Institution's laboratory assistant had been fired for insubordination. They needed to replace him immediately, and Davy had recommended young Faraday. The job mostly involved cleaning bottles and equipment, sweeping, and lighting fireplaces. The pay was low, considerably lower than what he could gain as a bookbinder, but Faraday, hardly believing his good fortune, accepted on the spot.

His education was so rapid it shocked him; it was nothing like the progress he had made on his own. Under his mentor's supervision, he learned how to prepare Davy's chemical mixtures, including some of the more explosive varieties. He was taught the rudiments of chemical analysis from perhaps the greatest living practitioner of the art. His responsibilities began to grow, and he was given access to the lab for his own experiments. He worked night and day to bring a much-needed order to the laboratory and its shelves. And slowly, their relationship deepened—clearly Davy saw him as a younger version of himself.

That summer Davy prepared to go on an extended tour of Europe, and invited Faraday to come along as his laboratory assistant and valet. Although Faraday did not relish the thought of acting as a personal servant, the chance to meet some of Europe's most preeminent scientists and work so closely with Davy on his experiments (he traveled with a kind of portable laboratory) was too much to pass up. It was best to be around him as much as possible and soak up his knowledge, his whole way of thinking.

During the trip, Faraday assisted Davy on a particular experiment that would leave a lasting impression on him. The exact chemical composition of diamonds had long been in dispute. They appeared to be composed of carbon. But how could something so beautiful be made of exactly the same substance as charcoal? There had to be more to its chemical composition, but there was no known way to divide a diamond into its constituent elements. It was a problem that had baffled many scientists. Davy had long entertained the radical idea that it was not the elements themselves that determined the properties of things. Perhaps charcoal and diamonds had precisely the same chemical composition, but it was changes in their underlying molecular structure that determined their form. This was a much more dynamic view of nature, but Davy had no way to prove this until suddenly, traveling through France, an idea for the perfect experiment came to him.

After being reminded that one of the most powerful lenses of the time resided at the Accademia del Cimento in Florence, Davy made a detour there. Gaining permission to use the lens, he placed a diamond in a tiny glass globe containing pure oxygen and used the lens to focus intense sunlight on the globe until the diamond completely evaporated. Inside the globe, all that remained of the diamond was carbon dioxide gas, proving that it was indeed composed of pure carbon. Therefore, what turned carbon into either charcoal or a diamond *must* involve a change in the underlying molecular structure. Nothing else could explain the results of his experiment. What impressed Faraday was the thought process that went into this. From a simple speculation, Davy found his way to the one experiment that would *physically* demonstrate his idea by excluding all other possible explanations. This was a highly creative way of thinking, and it was the source of Davy's power as a chemist.

On his return to the Royal Institution, Faraday was given a pay increase and a new title—Assistant and Superintendent of the Apparatus and Mineralogical Collection. And soon a pattern developed. Davy liked to spend most of his time on the road. Trusting Faraday's growing skills, he would send back to him all kinds of mineral samples to analyze. Davy had slowly grown dependent on his assistant; in letters to Faraday he praised him as one of the best analytic chemists he knew—he had trained him well. But by the year 1821, Faraday had to confront an unpleasant reality: Davy was keeping him under his thumb. After eight years of an intense apprenticeship, he was now an accomplished chemist in his own right, with expanding knowledge of other sciences. He was doing independent research, but Davy was still treating him as an assistant, making him send packets of dead flies for his fishing lures and assigning him other menial tasks.

It was Davy who had rescued him from the drudgery of the bookbinding business. He owed him everything. But Faraday was now thirty years old, and if he were not allowed soon enough to declare his independence, his most creative years would be wasted as a laboratory assistant. To leave on bad terms, however, would ruin his name in the scientific community, especially considering his own lack of reputation. Then, finally, Faraday found a chance to separate himself from his overbearing mentor, and he exploited this opportunity to the maximum.

Scientists throughout Europe were making discoveries about the relationship between electricity and magnetism, but the effect they had on each other was strange—creating a movement that was not linear and direct, but apparently more circular. Nothing in nature was quite like this. How to reveal the exact shape of this effect or movement in an experiment became the rage, and soon Davy got involved. Working with a fellow scientist named William Hyde Wollaston, they proposed the idea that the movement created by electromagnetism was more like a spiral. Involving Faraday in their experiments, they devised a way to break up the movement into small increments that could be measured. Once this was all added up, it would show the spiral motion.

At about the same time, Faraday was asked by a close friend to write a review of all that was known about electromagnetism for an established journal, and so he began a rigorous study of the field. Thinking like his mentor, he speculated that there must be a way to physically demonstrate the motion created by electromagnetism in a continual fashion, so that no one could dispute the results. One night in September 1821 he had a vision of just such an experiment, and he put it into practice. With a bar magnet secured upright in a cup of liquid mercury (a metal that conducts electricity), Faraday placed a suspended wire, buoyed by a cork, in the mercury. When the wire was charged with electricity, the cork moved around the magnet in a precise conical path. The reverse experiment (with the wire secured in the water) revealed the same pattern.

This was the first time in history that electricity had been used to generate continual motion, the precursor to all electric motors. The experiment was so simple and yet only Faraday had seen it so clearly. It revealed a way of thinking that was very much the product of Davy's tutelage. Feeling the weight of years of poverty, crushed expectations, and servitude lifting off of him, he danced around the laboratory. This would be the discovery that would free him at last. Excited about what he had done, he rushed to have his results published.

In his haste to get his report out, however, Faraday had forgotten to mention the research done by Wollaston and Davy. Soon enough, the rumor spread that Faraday had actually plagiarized their work. Realizing his mistake, Faraday met with Wollaston and showed him how he had reached his results independent of anyone else's work. Wollaston agreed and let the matter drop. But the rumors continued, and soon it became clear that the source of them was Davy himself. He refused to accept Faraday's explanation and no one knew quite why. When Faraday was nominated to the Royal Society because of his discovery, it was Davy, as president, who tried to block it. A year later, when Faraday made yet another important discovery, Davy claimed partial credit for it. He seemed to believe that he had created Faraday from nothing and so was responsible for everything he did.

Faraday had seen enough—their relationship was essentially over. He would never correspond with or see him again. Now having authority within the scientific community, Faraday could do as he pleased. His coming experiments would soon pave the way for all of the most important advances in electrical energy, and for the field theories that would revolutionize science in the twentieth century. He would go on to become one of history's greatest practitioners of experimental science, far outshining the fame of his one-time mentor.

KEYS TO MASTERY

At table, the ladies praised a portrait by a young painter. "What is most surprising," they added, "he has learned everything by himself." This could be seen particularly in the hands, which were not correctly and artistically drawn. "We see," said Goethe, "that the young man has talent; however, you should not praise, but rather blame him, for learning everything by himself. A man of talent is not born to be left to himself, but to devote himself to art and good masters who will make something of him."

—Johann Peter Eckermann, *Conversations with Goethe*

In the past, people of power had an aura of authority that was very real. Some of this aura emanated from their accomplishments, and some of it from the position they occupied—being a member of the aristocracy or a religious elite. This aura had a definite effect and could be felt; it caused people to respect and worship those who possessed it. Over the centuries, however, the slow process of democratization has worn away this aura of authority in all of its guises, to the point today of almost nonexistence.

We feel, rightly so, that no one should be admired or worshipped merely for the position they occupy, particularly if it comes from connections or a privileged background. But this attitude carries over to people who have reached their position mostly through their own accomplishments. We live in a culture that likes to criticize and debunk any form of authority, to point out the weaknesses of those in power. If we feel any aura, it is in the presence of celebrities and their seductive personalities. Some of this skeptical spirit toward authority is healthy, particularly in relation to politics, but when it comes to learning and the Apprenticeship Phase, it presents a problem.

To learn requires a sense of humility. We must admit that there are people out there who know our field much more deeply than we do. Their superiority is not a function of natural talent or privilege, but rather of time and experience. Their authority in the field is not based on politics or trickery. It is very real. But if we are not comfortable with this fact, if we feel in general mistrustful of any kind of authority, we will succumb to the belief that we can just as easily learn something on our own, that being self-taught is more authentic. We might justify this attitude as a sign of our independence, but in fact it stems from basic insecurity. We feel, perhaps unconsciously, that learning from Masters and submitting to their authority is somehow an indictment of our own natural ability. Even if we have teachers in our lives, we tend not to pay full attention to their advice, often preferring to do things our own way. In fact, we come to believe that being critical of Masters or teachers is somehow a sign of our intelligence, and that being a submissive pupil is a sign of weakness.

Understand: all that should concern you in the early stages of your career is acquiring practical knowledge in the most efficient manner possible. For this purpose, during the Apprenticeship Phase you will need mentors whose authority you recognize and to whom you submit. Your admission of need does not say anything essential about you, but only about your temporary condition of weakness, which your mentor will help you overcome.

The reason you require a mentor is simple: Life is short; you have only so much time and so much energy to expend. Your most creative years are generally in your late twenties and on into your forties. You can learn what you need through books, your own practice, and occasional advice from others, but the process is hit-and-miss. The information in books is not tailored to your circumstances and individuality; it tends to be somewhat abstract. When you are young and have less experience of the world, this abstract knowledge is hard to put into practice. You can learn from your experiences, but it can often take years to fully understand the meaning of what has happened. It is always possible to practice on your own, but you will not receive enough focused feedback. You can often gain a self-directed apprenticeship in many fields, but this could take ten years, maybe more.

Mentors do not give you a shortcut, but they streamline the process. They invariably had their own great mentors, giving them a richer and deeper knowledge of their field. Their ensuing years of experience taught them invaluable lessons and strategies for learning. Their knowledge and experience become yours; they can direct you away from unnecessary side paths or errors. They observe you at work and provide real-time feedback, making your practice more time efficient. Their advice is tailored to your circumstances and your needs. Working closely with them, you absorb the essence of their creative spirit, which you can now adapt in your own way. What took you ten years on your own could have been done in five with proper direction.

There is more to this than just time saved. When we learn something in a concentrated manner it has added value. We experience fewer distractions. What we learn is internalized more deeply because of the intensity of our focus and practice. Our own ideas and development flourish more naturally in this shortened time frame. Having an efficient apprenticeship, we can make the most of our youthful energy and our creative potential.

What makes the mentor-protégé dynamic so intense and so productive is the emotional quality of the relationship. By nature, mentors feel emotionally invested in your education. This can be for several reasons: perhaps they like you, or see in you a younger version of themselves, and can relive their own youth through you; perhaps they recognize in you a special talent that will give them pleasure to cultivate; perhaps you have something important to offer them, mostly your youthful energy and willingness to work hard. Being useful to them can build a powerful emotional connection to you over time. On your part, you also feel emotionally drawn to them—admiration for their achievements, a desire to model yourself after them, and so on. Mentors find this immensely flattering.

With this two-way emotional connection you both open up to each other in a way that goes beyond the usual teacher-student dynamic. When you admire people, you become more susceptible to absorbing and imitating everything they do. You pay deeper attention. Your mirror neurons are more engaged, allowing for learning that involves more than the superficial transmission of knowledge, but also includes a style and way of thinking that is often powerful. On the other side, because of the emotional bond, mentors will tend to divulge more of their secrets than they would to others. You must not be afraid of this emotional component to the relationship. It is precisely what makes you learn more deeply and efficiently.

Think of it this way: the process of learning resembles the medieval practice of alchemy. In alchemy, the goal was to find a way to transform base metals or stones into gold. To effect this, alchemists searched for what was known as the philosopher's stone—a substance that would make dead stones or metals come alive and organically change their chemical composition into gold. Although the philosopher's stone was never discovered, it has profound relevance as a metaphor. The knowledge that you need to become a Master exists out there in the world—it is like a base metal or dead stone. This knowledge needs to be heated up and come alive within you, transforming itself into something active and relevant to your circumstances. The mentor is like the philosopher's stone—through direct interaction with someone of experience, you are able to quickly and efficiently heat up and animate this knowledge, turning it into something like gold.

The story of Michael Faraday is the ultimate illustration of this alchemical process. His life seemed to progress almost through magic—falling into the one job where he could read books, learn about science, and impress exactly the right person with his notes, leading to a connection to the ultimate mentor, Humphry Davy. But there was a logic behind all of this apparent magic and good fortune. As a young man he possessed an intense energy and hunger for knowledge. A kind of inner radar directed him to the one bookshop in the area. Although it was pure luck that the book *Improvement of the Mind* fell into his hands, it took someone with such focus to recognize immediately its worth and exploit it fully. Under Watt's guidance, his knowledge became more practical. But that same radar that directed him to the shop and to this book now pointed him somewhere else. The knowledge he had gained was still too diffused and disconnected. He intuited that the only way to transform it into something useful was to find a living mentor.

Once he secured Davy as his man, he threw himself into the relationship with the same focus that he had brought to everything else. Serving under Davy, Faraday learned all of the secrets of chemistry and electricity that the Master had gleaned throughout his life. He practiced with these ideas in the laboratory—mixing chemicals for Davy and doing his own experiments. In the process, he absorbed Davy's patterns of thinking, of approaching chemical analysis and experimentation. His knowledge became increasingly active.

After eight years, this interactive dynamic yielded one of the great discoveries of science—the uncovering of the secret of electromagnetism. Faraday's own studies and what he had learned from Davy became transformed into creative energy, a form of gold. If he had stayed on the path of self-apprenticeship out of fear or insecurity, he would have remained a bookbinder—miserable and unfulfilled. Through the alchemy of intense mentorship he transformed himself into one of the most creative scientists in history.

Certainly religion played an important role in Faraday's education. Because he believed that everything in the universe was alive with God's presence, he tended to animate whatever he encountered, including the books he read and the phenomenon of electricity itself. Since he saw these things as alive, he engaged with them on a deeper level, which intensified the learning process. This way of looking at the world, however, transcends religion and contains great power for all of us in our apprenticeships. We too can see the subjects that we study as possessing a kind of vital spirit with which we must interact, and which we must understand from the inside out. As with Faraday, this attitude will intensify our level of engagement with what we are learning.

To initially entice the right Master to serve as your mentor, you will want to mix in a strong element of self-interest. You have something tangible and practical to offer them, in addition to your youth and energy. Before he had ever met him, Davy was aware of Faraday's work ethic and organizational skills. That alone made him a desirable assistant. Considering this, you may not want to go in search of mentors until you have acquired some elementary skills and discipline that you can rely upon to interest them.

Almost all Masters and people of power suffer from too many demands on their time and too much information to absorb. If you can demonstrate the ability to help them organize themselves on these fronts to a degree that others cannot, it will be much easier to get their attention and interest them in the relationship. Do not shy away from anything menial or secretarial. You want person-to-person access, however you can get it. Once you establish a relationship, you will find other ways to continually hook them through their self-interest. Try to see the world through their eyes and ask the simple question of what it is they need most. Keeping their self-interest involved will only enhance any emotional connection they feel toward you.

If you work on yourself first, as Faraday did, developing a solid work ethic and organizational skills, eventually the right teacher will appear in your life. Word will spread through the proper channels of your efficiency and your hunger to learn, and opportunities will come your way. In any event, you should not feel timid in approaching Masters, no matter how elevated their position. You will be frequently surprised at how open they can be to serving as a mentor, if the fit is right and you have something to offer. The ability to transfer their experience and knowledge to someone younger often provides them with a great pleasure, akin to parenting.

The best mentors are often those who have wide knowledge and experience, and are not overly specialized in their field—they can train you to think on a higher level, and to make connections between different forms of knowledge. The paradigm for this is the Aristotle–Alexander the Great relationship. Philip II, Alexander's father and king of Macedonia, chose Aristotle to mentor his thirteen-year-old son because the philosopher had learned and mastered so many different fields. He could thus impart to Alexander an overall love of learning, and teach him how to think and reason in any kind of situation—the greatest skill of all. This ended up working to perfection. Alexander was able to effectively apply the reasoning skills he had gained from Aristotle to politics and warfare. To the end of his life he maintained an intense curiosity for any field of knowledge, and would always gather about him experts he could learn from. Aristotle had imparted a form of wisdom that played a key role in Alexander's success.

You will want as much personal interaction with the mentor as possible. A virtual relationship is never enough. There are cues and subtle aspects you can only pick up through a person-to-person interaction—such as a way of doing things that has evolved through much experience. These patterns of action are hard to put into words, and can only be absorbed through much personal exposure. In crafts or in sports this is more obvious. Tennis instructors, for example, can only reveal many secrets of their skills by demonstrating things before their pupils' eyes. Instructors may not in fact be completely conscious of what makes their backhand so effective, but in watching them in action pupils can pick up the pattern and motion, exploiting the power of mirror neurons. But this process of absorption is also relevant to nonmanual skills. It was only through constant exposure to Davy's thought process that Faraday understood the power of finding the crucial experiment to demonstrate an idea, something he would adapt later on with great success.

As the relationship progresses you can make this absorption process more conscious and direct, questioning them about the principles underlying their way of doing things. If you are clever, you can be a kind of midwife, getting them to analyze their own creativity for you, and mining all kinds of rich ideas in the process. They are often grateful for the opportunity to reveal the inner workings of their power, particularly to someone they do not perceive as a threat.

Although one mentor at a time is best, it is not always possible to find the perfect one. In such a case, an alternate strategy is to find several mentors in your immediate environment, each one filling strategic gaps in your knowledge and experience. Having more than one mentor has side benefits, giving you several connections and important allies to rely upon later on. Similarly, if your circumstances limit your contacts, books can serve as temporary mentors, as *The Improvement of the Mind* did for Faraday. In such a case you will want to convert such books and writers into living mentors as much as possible. You personalize their voice, interact with the material, taking notes or writing in the margins. You analyze what they write and try to make it come alive—the spirit and not just the letter of their work.

In a looser sense, a figure from the past or present can serve as an ideal, someone to model yourself after. Through much research and some imagination on your part, you turn them into a living presence. You ask yourself—what would they do in this situation or that? Countless generals have used Napoleon Bonaparte for just such a purpose.

Mentors have their own strengths and weaknesses. The good ones allow you to develop your own style and then to leave them when the time is right. Such types can remain lifelong friends and allies. But often the opposite will occur. They grow dependent on your services and want to keep you indentured. They envy your youth and unconsciously hinder you, or become overcritical. You must be aware of this as it develops. Your goal is to get as much out of them as possible, but at a certain point you may pay a price if you stay too long and let them subvert your confidence. Your submitting to their authority is by no means unconditional, and in fact your goal all along is eventually to find your way to independence, having internalized and adapted their wisdom.

In this respect, the mentor relationship often replays elements from our childhood. Although a mentor can be a man or a woman, he or she often assumes the form of a father figure—there to guide and help us, but sometimes trying to control too much and plot our life for us. He may take any attempt at independence, even later in the relationship, as a personal assault on his authority. You must not allow yourself to feel any guilt when the time comes to assert yourself. Instead, as Faraday did, you should feel resentful and even angry about his desire to hold you back, using such emotions to help you leave him. It is often best to set up this move earlier on so that you are emotionally prepared to make it. As the relationship progresses, you can begin to slightly distance yourself from the mentor, perhaps taking note of some of his weaknesses or character flaws, or even finding fault with his most cherished beliefs. Establishing your differences with the mentor is an important part of your self-development, whether he is of the good or bad parent type.

In Spanish they say *al maestro cuchillada*—to the Master goes the knife. It is a fencing expression, referring to the moment when the young and agile pupil becomes skillful enough to cut his Master. But this also refers to the fate of most mentors who inevitably experience the rebellion of their protégés, like the cut from a sword. In our culture, we tend to venerate those who seem rebellious or at least strike the pose. But rebellion has no meaning or power if it occurs without something solid and real to rebel against. The mentor, or father figure, gives you just such a standard from which you can deviate and establish your own identity. You internalize the important and relevant parts of their knowledge, and you apply the knife to what has no bearing on your life. It is the dynamic of changing generations, and sometimes the father figure has to be killed in order for the sons and daughters to have space to discover themselves.

In any event, you will probably have several mentors in your life, like stepping-stones along the way to mastery. At each phase of life you must find the appropriate teachers, getting what you want out of them, moving on, and feeling no shame for this. It is the path your own mentor probably took and it is the way of the world.

STRATEGIES FOR DEEPENING THE MENTOR DYNAMIC

One repays a teacher badly if one remains only a pupil.

—Friedrich Nietzsche

Although you must submit to the authority of mentors in order to learn from and absorb their power to the highest degree, this does not mean you remain passive in the process. At certain critical points, you can set and determine the dynamic, personalize it to suit your purposes. The following four strategies are designed to help you exploit the relationship to the fullest and transform the knowledge you gain into creative energy.

1. Choose the mentor according to your needs and inclinations

In 1888 the twenty-year-old Frank Lloyd Wright was an apprentice drafts-man at the prestigious Chicago firm of Joseph Lyman Silsbee. He had been there a year and was learning much about the business, but he was getting restless. In his mind he could already envision a totally new style of architecture that would revolutionize the field, but he lacked the experience to set up his own practice. Silsbee was a shrewd businessman who saw that his fortune was tied to staying true to the Victorian style of design that was popular with his clients. Wright cringed at what he was being asked to draw; he was learning antiquated design principles that offended him.

Then, out of the blue, he heard that the great Chicago architect Louis Sullivan was looking for a draftsman to help finish the drawings for a par-ticular building. It would be dangerous to leave Silsbee after such a short time and burn his bridge there, but working for Sullivan would be infinitely more stimulating for his personal development as an architect. Sullivan's firm was at the forefront of designing skyscrapers, utilizing the latest ad-vances in materials and technology.

Wright went on a charm offensive to secure the position. He managed to get a personal interview and showed Sullivan some of the more inter-esting drawings he had done on his own; he engaged him in a conversa-tion about art and philosophy, knowing Sullivan's own aesthetic predilections. Sullivan hired him for the job, and a few months later made him an apprentice draftsman in his firm. Wright cultivated a personal relationship with him, eagerly playing the role of the son that Sullivan had never had. With his talent and Sullivan's blessing, he quickly rose to the position of head draftsman in the firm. Wright became, as he put it, "the pencil in Sullivan's hand." In 1893 Sullivan fired him for moonlighting, but by then Wright had learned everything he could and was more than prepared to step out on his own. Sullivan had given him in those five years an education in modern architecture that no one else could have pro-vided.

In 1906 Carl Jung was a promising thirty-one-year-old psychiatrist, re-nowned for his work in experimental psychology and holding an important position at the famous Burghölzli Psychiatric Hospital in Zurich. But de-spite the apparent success in his life, he felt insecure. He believed that his interest in the occult and strange psychic phenomena was a weakness he needed to work through. He was frustrated that his treatment of patients was often not effective. He worried that his work had no legitimacy and that he lacked a certain rigor. He began to correspond with the founder of the psychoanalytic field, Sigmund Freud, fifty-one years old at the time. Jung was ambivalent about Freud—he admired, even worshipped him as a pioneer in the field, but he did not like his emphasis on sex as the determining factor in neurosis. Perhaps his aversion to this aspect of Freudian psychology stemmed from his own prejudices or ignorance, and needed to be overcome by talking it out. In their correspondence they quickly developed a good rapport, and Jung was able to question the Master about matters of psychology he did not fully understand.

A year later they finally met in Vienna, and talked nonstop for thirteen hours. The younger man charmed Freud—he was so much more creative than his other acolytes. He could serve as his successor in the psychoanalytic movement. For Jung, Freud could be the father figure and mentor he so desperately needed—a grounding influence. They traveled together to the United States, saw each other on frequent visits, and corresponded incessantly. But some five years into the relationship, Jung's initial ambivalence returned. He began to find Freud rather dictatorial. He chafed at the idea of having to follow Freudian dogma. He now clearly understood why he had initially disagreed with the emphasis on sexuality as the root of all neuroses.

By 1913 they had a definitive break, Jung forever banished from Freud's inner circle. But through this relationship, Jung had worked out all of his doubts and sharpened certain core ideas about human psychology. In the end, the struggle had strengthened his sense of identity. Without this mentorship, he would have never come to such a clear resolution and been capable of starting his own rival school of psychoanalysis.

Sometime in the late 1960s, V. S. Ramachandran, a medical student at a college in Madras, came upon a book called *Eye and Brain,* written by an eminent professor of neuropsychology, Richard Gregory. (For more on Ramachandran's early years, see page 32.) The book excited him—the style of writing, the anecdotes, the provocative experiments he recounted. Inspired by the book, Ramachandran did his own experiments on optics, and soon realized that he was better suited for the field than medicine. In 1974 he was admitted into the PhD Program at Cambridge University, in visual perception.

Ramachandran had been raised on stories of the great English scientists of the nineteenth century, and the almost romantic quest for truth that science seemed to represent. He loved the part that speculation played in the great theories and discoveries of men such as Faraday and Darwin. He imagined it would be somewhat similar at Cambridge, but to his surprise the students and professors tended to treat science as a kind of nine-to-five job; it was a competitive, cutthroat, almost corporate environment. He began to feel gloomy and alone in a strange country.

Then one day Richard Gregory himself, a professor at Bristol University, came to Cambridge to give a lecture. Ramachandran was mesmerized—it was like something right out of the pages of Humphry Davy. Gregory performed thought-provoking demonstrations of his ideas on stage; he had a flair for drama and a great sense of humor. This is what science should be like, Ramachandran thought. He went up after the talk and introduced himself. They had an instant rapport. He mentioned to Gregory an optical experiment he had been pondering, and the professor was intrigued. He invited Ramachandran to visit Bristol and to stay in his home, where they could try out his idea together. Ramachandran took up the offer, and from the moment he saw Gregory's house he knew he had found his mentor—it was like something out of Sherlock Holmes, full of Victorian instruments, fossils, and skeletons. Gregory was precisely the kind of eccentric Ramachandran could identify with. Soon he was commuting to Bristol regularly experiments. He had found a lifelong mentor to inspire and guide him, and over the years he would come to adapt much of Gregory's style of speculation and experiment.

Growing up in Japan in the late 1970s, Yoky Matsuoka felt like an outsider. As discussed in chapter 1 (pages 33–34), she liked to do things her own way in a country that esteemed social cohesion and conformity above everything else. When she decided to take up tennis seriously at the age of eleven, she used the players John McEnroe and Andre Agassi as her role models, consummate rebels in what had been a very genteel sport. Later, when she moved to the United States and began attending university, she brought with her the same need to go her own way in whatever she did. If there was a field no one was studying, it excited her. Following this instinct she got into the then-esoteric field of robotics, and was admitted to the PhD program at MIT.

There, for the first time in her life, she met someone of her own temperament—Rodney Brooks, professor of robotics at MIT, and the bad boy of the department. He was bold, taking on the higher-ups in the department and arguing against some of the most entrenched ideas in the field of artificial intelligence. He had developed a completely novel approach to robotics. It excited her that a professor could get away with such an unconventional attitude. She began to spend as much time around him as possible, soaking up his style of thinking, and turning him into her de facto mentor. He was not a teacher who told you what to do; he let you find your own way, including your own mistakes, but would lend you support when you needed it. This style suited her need for independence. It was only later that she realized how much his ideas had gotten under her skin. Unconsciously following his lead, she would eventually create her own approach to robotics and pioneer a totally new field, known as neurobotics.

The choice of the right mentor is more important than you might imagine. Because so much of her future influence upon you can be deeper than you are consciously aware of, the wrong choice can have a net negative effect upon your journey to mastery. You could end up absorbing conventions and styles that don't fit you and that will confuse you later on. If she is too domineering, you could end up becoming a lifelong imitation of the mentor, instead of a Master in your own right. People often err in this process when they choose someone who seems the most knowledgeable, has a charming personality, or has the most stature in the field—all superficial reasons. Do not simply choose the first possible mentor who crosses your path. Be prepared to put as much thought into it as possible.

In selecting a mentor, you will want to keep in mind your inclinations and Life's Task, the future position you envision for yourself. The mentor you choose should be strategically aligned with this. If your path is in a more revolutionary direction, you will want a mentor who is open, progressive, and not domineering. If your ideal aligns more with a style that is somewhat idiosyncratic, you will want a mentor who will make you feel comfortable with this and help you transform your peculiarities into mastery, instead of trying to squelch them. If, like Jung, you are somewhat confused and ambivalent about your direction, it can be useful to choose someone who can help you gain some clarity about what you want, someone important in the field who might not fit perfectly with your tastes. Sometimes part of what a mentor shows us is something we will want to avoid or actively rebel against. In this latter case, you might initially want to maintain a little more emotional distance than normally recommended, particularly if she is the domineering type. Over time you will see what to absorb and what to reject.

Remember: the Mentor Dynamic replays something of the parental or father-figure dynamic. It is a cliché that you do not get to choose the family you are born into, but you are happily free to choose your mentors. In this case, the right choice can perhaps provide what your parents didn't give you—support, confidence, direction, space to discover things on your own. Look for mentors who can do that, and beware of falling into the opposite trap—opting for a mentor who resembles one of your parents, including all of his negative traits. You will merely repeat what hampered you in the first place.

2. Gaze deep into the mentor's mirror

Hakuin Zenji (1685–1769) was born in a village near the town of Hara in Japan, his family on his father's side coming from an illustrious line of samurai warriors. As a child, Hakuin had the kind of relentless energy that would seem to mark him for a life dedicated to the martial arts. But at around the age of eleven, he heard a priest deliver a sermon about the torments of hell for those who were not careful, and this talk filled the young boy with an intense anguish that nothing could extinguish. All of his tenacious energy was now directed toward doubts about his own worth, and by the age of fourteen he decided that the only way to quell his anxiety was to pursue the religious path and become a priest. He was particularly attracted to Zen Buddhism, having read stories of great Masters in China and Japan overcoming endless obstacles and suffering to reach enlightenment. The idea of passing through a phase of suffering accorded well with his innermost doubts about himself.

At the age of eighteen he was sent to a training center to prepare him for his life as a priest. The method of teaching, however, disappointed him. He had imagined twenty-four-hour sessions of meditation and other ordeals. Instead, he was made to study all kinds of Chinese and Japanese texts. What he read and heard from his instructors did not change him at all. It was merely intellectual knowledge that had little connection to his daily life. His anxieties only increased. He left this temple and began to wander, looking for the mentor who could guide him.

He entered one Zen school after another, in every corner of Japan, and he began to get a clear idea of the state of Zen instruction at that time. It revolved around simple sessions of seated meditation, with little instruction, until finally a giant bell would sound and the monks would hurry to eat or sleep. In their spare time, they would chant for happiness and peace. Zen had turned into one large soporific, designed to lull students into a state of rest and lethargy. It was deemed too invasive and too overbearing to give students any direction; they were supposed to find their own way to enlightenment. Naturally, when given such free rein, they would opt for the easiest path—doing nothing. This trend had spread throughout Japan; monks everywhere had convinced themselves that Zen was easy and simple, and that whatever felt right was right.

Occasionally Hakuin would hear of some school or priest that was creating a stir somewhere, and he would travel to see for himself. In 1708, he spent weeks traveling to reach a temple at a coastal town where just such a provocative priest was making an appearance, but after hearing a few sentences from his lips, Hakuin felt the same profound boredom and disappointment—quotes from texts, clever stories, all to cover up the deadness of the words. He began to wonder if it was time to give up, if true enlightenment no longer existed. At the temple he met another young monk who was equally disappointed with the talk of the priest. They became friends, and one day the monk mentioned that he had studied for a few days under a strange and completely reclusive Master named Shoju Rojin, who was not like any other teacher he had encountered. He lived in a hard-to-reach village, accepted only a handful of students, and was very demanding. This was all Hakuin needed to hear. He asked the young monk to guide him right away to Shoju.

When he met the Master, he could see something in his eyes that was different from any other priest or teacher. He radiated power and self-mastery; you could read in his expression the pain he had endured to reach his current state. This man had lived and suffered. Hakuin was delighted when Shoju said he would accept him as a pupil, but his excitement soon turned to fear. During their first personal interview, Shoju asked him, "How do you understand the koan (a Zen anecdote designed for instruction) about the Dog and the Buddha-Nature?" "No way to lay a hand or foot on that," Hakuin replied, imagining that was a clever response, at which point Shoju reached out and grabbed his nose, pushing it with a harsh twist and yelling in his face, "Got a pretty good hand on it there!" He held on tightly for several minutes, giving Hakuin a feeling of utter paralysis.

Over the course of the next few days he endured more and more abuse. Shoju made him feel that all of his studies and traveling had taught him nothing. He could not say or do one right thing. Out of nowhere he would receive a blow or a gob of spit in his face. He began to doubt every element of his previous knowledge, and he lived in complete terror of what Shoju would do next.

Shoju gave him a series of the most difficult koans Hakuin had ever heard to ponder and discuss. He could not make heads or tails of them. His feelings of dejection and demoralization were reaching a breaking point, but knowing that persistence was important, he kept at it night and day. Soon he had doubts about Shoju himself, and entertained thoughts of leaving him in the near future.

One day, feeling particularly agitated, he wandered into a nearby village, and without knowing why or how, he began to contemplate one of the thorniest koans Shoju had given him. Deep in thought, he strayed into the garden of a private house. The woman who lived there yelled at him to leave, but Hakuin seemed oblivious. Thinking he was a madman or a bandit she attacked him with a stick, knocking him hard to the ground. When he came to, minutes later, he suddenly felt different—he had finally penetrated to the core of Shoju's koan! He understood it from the inside out! It was alive within him! Everything fell into place and he was certain that he had finally reached enlightenment, the world appearing to him in a totally new guise. He began clapping his hands and screaming with delight. For the first time he felt the weight of all of his anxieties lifted from him.

He ran all the way back to Shoju, who recognized right away what had happened to his pupil. This time the Master was gentle with him, stroking Hakuin's back with his fan. He finally revealed to his pupil his thoughts—from the first time they had met, he had recognized in Hakuin the necessary ingredients for true learning. He was fierce, determined, and hungry for enlightenment. The problem with all students, he said, is that they inevitably *stop* somewhere. They hear an idea and they hold on to it until it becomes dead; they want to flatter themselves that they know the truth. But true Zen never stops, never congeals into such truths. That is why everyone must constantly be pushed to the abyss, starting over and feeling their utter worthlessness as a student. Without suffering and doubts, the mind will come to rest on clichés and stay there, until the spirit dies as well. Not even enlightenment is enough. You must continually start over and challenge yourself.

Shoju had faith that Hakuin would continue in this process because he was tenacious. Zen was dying throughout Japan. He wanted Hakuin to stay with him and serve as his successor. He believed the young man would someday be responsible for reviving the religion. In the end, however, Hakuin could not tame his restlessness. After eight months he left Shoju, certain he would return as soon as he could. But the years went by, and once again he fell into new doubts and anxieties. He wandered from temple to temple, experiencing continual highs and lows.

At the age of forty-one, he finally had his ultimate and deepest moment of enlightenment, bringing with it a mind-set that would not leave him for the rest of his life. At this point, all of the ideas and teachings of Shoju came back to him as if he had heard them yesterday, and he realized that Shoju was the only true Master he had ever known. He wanted to return to thank him, but the Master had died some five years earlier. His way to repay him was to become a teacher himself, keeping alive his Master's teachings. In the end, it was indeed Hakuin who rescued Zen practice from the decay it had fallen into, just as Shoju had predicted.

To reach mastery requires some toughness and a constant connection to reality. As an apprentice, it can be hard for us to challenge ourselves on our own in the proper way, and to get a clear sense of our own weaknesses. The times that we live in make this even harder. Developing discipline through challenging situations and perhaps suffering along the way are no longer values that are promoted in our culture. People are increasingly reluctant to tell each other the truth about themselves—their weaknesses, their inadequacies, flaws in their work. Even the self-help books designed to set us straight tend to be soft and flattering, telling us what we want to hear—that we are basically good and can get what we want by following a few simple steps. It seems abusive or damaging to people's self-esteem to offer them stern, realistic criticism, to set them tasks that will make them aware of how far they have to go. In fact, this indulgence and fear of hurting people's feelings is far more abusive in the long run. It makes it hard for people to gauge where they are or to develop self-discipline. It makes them unsuited for the rigors of the journey to mastery. It weakens people's will.

Masters are those who by nature have suffered to get to where they are. They have experienced endless criticisms of their work, doubts about their progress, setbacks along the way. They know deep in their bones what is required to get to the creative phase and beyond. As mentors, they alone can gauge the extent of our progress, the weaknesses in our character, the ordeals we must go through to advance. In this day and age, you must get the sharpest dose of reality that is possible from your mentor. You must go in search of it and welcome it. If possible, choose a mentor who is known for supplying this form of tough love. If they shy away from giving it, force them to hold up the mirror that will reflect you as you are. Get them to give you the proper challenges that will reveal your strengths and weaknesses and allow you to gain as much feedback as possible, no matter how hard it might be to take. Accustom yourself to criticism. Confidence is important, but if it is not based on a realistic appraisal of who you are, it is mere grandiosity and smugness. Through the realistic feedback of your mentor you will eventually develop a confidence that is much more substantial and worth possessing.

3. Transfigure their ideas

In 1943 the eminent pianist and teacher Alberto Guerrero accepted a new pupil, a precocious eleven-year-old named Glenn Gould who was unlike any other student he had ever encountered. Glenn had been playing since he was four years old, having been taught by his mother, who was an accomplished piano player in her own right. After a few years under her tutelage, Glenn had surpassed his mother in skill on many levels; he began to argue and correct her; he wanted more challenging work. Guerrero was well known in Toronto, Canada, where the Goulds lived; he was reputed to be very patient, yet also demanding—traits that could serve him well as a teacher for the young Gould, which is why the parents chose him. From the very first session, Guerrero could sense an unusual seriousness and intensity in someone so young. Gould listened with complete attention and could absorb Guerrero's style of playing in a way he had never seen in a pupil. He was a consummate mimic.

Soon, however, Guerrero began to notice some strange traits in his pupil. On one occasion he decided to expand Gould's repertoire, introducing him to the music of Arnold Schoenberg—the great composer of atonal music whose work Guerrero liked to champion. Expecting his pupil to be excited by the newness of the sound, he was surprised instead to see an expression of complete disgust. Gould took the sheet music home with him, but apparently he never practiced the pieces, and Guerrero let the matter drop. Then, a few weeks later, he shared with his teacher some of his own recent compositions—interesting work that was clearly inspired by Schoenberg. Soon after that, he brought in sheet music that he wanted to practice with Guerrero—all atonal music from various composers, including Schoenberg, but not the pieces Guerrero had originally given him. He had obviously been studying the music on his own and had decided he liked it.

It became almost impossible for Guerrero to gauge how Gould would respond to his ideas. For instance, he recommended to his pupils that they learn and memorize a piece by studying it on paper, before ever trying to play it. In this way, it would come alive first in their minds and they would be able to envision it as a whole, instead of merely playing the notes. Gould dutifully followed this advice with a particular composition of Bach's, but when they discussed the structure and concept behind the piece, the young man had his own notions that were rather strange and quite contrary to Guerrero's, which Gould found romantic and quaint. On another occasion Guerrero revealed his idea that it was often best to imagine you were playing a piano piece by Bach as if it were on a harpsichord. Gould warmed to this idea, then a few months later said that he preferred imagining a different instrument with Bach.

Guerrero's most important ideas revolved around the physical aspects of playing the piano. He had spent years studying human physiology, particularly anything related to the hands and fingers. His goal was to impart in his pupils a relaxed yet powerful style, in which they would gain complete command of the keyboard with fingers that had a lightning touch. He spent hours indoctrinating Gould in his approach, working on the peculiar posture he advocated—a kind of slump or hunch over the keyboard, with all of the action coming from the lower back and hands, the shoulders and arms completely still. He demonstrated this technique endlessly to his pupil. He gave Gould all kinds of unusual exercises he had developed to strengthen the fingers. Gould seemed interested enough, but as with everything, Guerrero had the impression he would soon forget it all and go his own way.

As the years went by, Gould began to argue with his teacher more and more. He found Guerrero's ideas and approach to music too Latin, too mired in another era. Finally, at the age of nineteen, Gould announced that he was going to proceed on his own. He had no more need for a mentor, a fact that Guerrero graciously accepted. It was clear that by now the young man needed to work through his own ideas about music and performing.

Over the years, however, as Gould slowly established himself as one of the greatest pianists who has ever lived, Guerrero began to realize how deeply his former pupil had absorbed all of his ideas. He would read reviews of Gould's performances in which the critic would note how he seemed to play Bach as if it were on the harpsichord, something soon echoed by others. His posture, his way of crouching and leaning over the instrument made him look like an uncanny double of the younger Guerrero; his finger work was so unusually powerful, it was clear he had spent years using the exercises Guerrero had taught him. In interviews, Gould would talk about the importance of learning a piece of music on paper before performing it, but he would say it all as if it were his own idea. Strangest of all, Gould played particular pieces of music as Guerrero had always imagined them in his mind, but with a verve and style that he could never have matched. It was as if his former protégé had internalized the essence of his style and transfigured it into something greater.

As a child, Glenn Gould intuited his great dilemma. He had an uncanny ear for music; he was so responsive that he could pick up the nuances of another piano player and reproduce them after a single hearing. At the same time, he knew that he was a peculiar young man with very distinct tastes. He had the ambition to become a master performer. If he listened too closely to teachers and other performers and picked up their ideas or styles, he would lose his sense of identity in the process. But he also needed knowledge and mentorship. This dilemma became particularly acute with Alberto Guerrero, who was a charismatic teacher. It is often a curse to learn under someone so brilliant and accomplished—your own confidence becomes crushed as you struggle to follow all of their great ideas. Many pianists become lost in the shadow of their illustrious mentors and never amount to anything.

Because of his ambition, Gould found his way to the only real solution to this dilemma. He would listen to all of Guerrero's ideas about music and try them out. In the course of playing, he would subtly alter these ideas to suit his inclinations. This would make him feel that he had his own voice. As the years went by, he made this differentiation between himself and his instructor more pronounced. Because he was so impressionable, over the course of the apprenticeship he had unconsciously internalized all of the important ideas of his mentor, but through his own active engagement he had managed to adapt them to his individuality. In this way, he could learn and yet incubate a creative spirit that would help set him apart from everyone else once he left Guerrero.

As apprentices, we all share in this dilemma. To learn from mentors, we must be open and completely receptive to their ideas. We must fall under their spell. But if we take this too far, we become so marked by their influence that we have no internal space to incubate and develop our own voice, and we spend our lives tied to ideas that are not our own. The solution, as Gould discovered, is subtle: Even as we listen and incorporate the ideas of our mentors, we must slowly cultivate some distance from them. We begin by gently adapting their ideas to our circumstances, altering them to fit our style and inclinations. As we progress we can become bolder, even focusing on faults or weaknesses in some of their ideas. We slowly mold their knowledge into our own shape. As we grow in confidence and contemplate our independence, we can even grow competitive with the mentor we once worshipped. As Leonardo da Vinci said, "Poor is the apprentice who does not surpass his Master."

4. Create a back-and-forth dynamic

In 1978, a promising lightweight boxer named Freddie Roach traveled to Las Vegas with his father in search of a trainer that could elevate him to the next level. And as previously narrated in chapter 1 (see page 38), Freddie and his father quickly settled on Eddie Futch, one of the most legendary boxing coaches in the field.

Futch had a magnificent résumé. As a young man he had sparred with Joe Louis. Barred from turning professional because of a heart murmur, he became a trainer, working later with some of the most illustrious heavyweights, including Joe Frazier. He was a quiet, patient man who knew how to give precise instructions; he was a master at improving a fighter's technique. Under his guidance, Roach advanced quickly, winning his first ten bouts.

Soon, however, Roach began to notice a problem: in training he listened intently to what Futch had to say, and put it into practice with relative ease. But in actual bouts, the moment he exchanged blows with his opponent, he would suddenly throw out all the technique he had learned and fight on pure emotion. Sometimes this worked, but he took a lot of blows, and his career started to sputter. What surprised him several years into the process was that Futch did not really seem to notice this problem of his. With so many fighters in his stable, he tended to keep his distance; he did not give much personalized attention.

Finally, in 1986, Roach retired. Living in Vegas and moving from one bad job to another, in his off-hours he began to frequent the gym where he had trained. Soon he was giving advice to fighters and helping out. Without getting paid, he became a de facto assistant to Futch, even directly training a few of the fighters himself. He knew Futch's system well and had internalized many of the techniques he taught. He added his own wrinkle to the training sessions. He took the mitt work—the large padded gloves that a trainer uses in the ring to practice various punches and combinations with his fighter—to a higher level, creating a longer and more fluid practice session. It also gave Roach a chance to be more involved in the action, something he missed. After several years he realized he was good at this and so left Futch to begin his own career as a trainer.

To Roach, the sport was changing. Fighters had become faster, but trainers such as Futch still promoted a rather static style of boxing that did not exploit these changes. Slowly, Roach began to experiment with the whole training dynamic. He expanded the mitt work into something larger, a simulation of a fight that could go on for several rounds. This allowed him to get closer to his fighters, to literally feel their full arsenal of punches over time, to see how they moved in the ring. He began to study tapes of opponents, looking for any kind of pattern or weakness in their style. He would devise a strategy around this weakness and go over it with his boxers in the mitt work. Interacting so closely with his fighters, he would develop a different kind of rapport than what he had with Futch—more visceral and connected. But no matter the boxer, these moments of connection would inevitably fade in and out. As they improved, the fighters would begin to tune him out, feeling like they already knew enough. Their egos would get in the way and they would stop learning.

Then, in 2001, an entirely different kind of fighter came through the doors of Roach's gym in Hollywood, California. His name was Manny Pacquiao, a 122-pound left-handed featherweight fighter, who had had some success in his native Philippines but was looking for a trainer in the States, someone who could elevate his game to another level. Many trainers had already passed on Pacquiao—they watched him work out and spar, and he was impressive, but there was no money to be made from someone in such a lightweight division.

Roach, however, was a different breed of trainer—he immediately went to mitt work with Pacquiao, and from the first punch he knew something was different about this fighter. It had an explosive, intense quality, a snap unlike any another fighter's. The other trainers had only watched and could not feel what he now felt. After one round Roach was certain he had found the boxer he had always been looking to train, one who could help initiate the new style of boxing he wanted to introduce. Pacquiao was equally impressed.

To Roach, Pacquiao had the material to be an unbeatable fighter, but he was somewhat one-dimensional: he had a great left hand and not much else. He was constantly looking for the knockout blow, to the exclusion of everything else. Roach's goal was to transform Pacquiao into a multidimensional beast in the ring. He began with heavy mitt practice, trying to develop a powerful right hand and more fluid footwork. What immediately struck him was the intensity with which Pacquiao focused on his instructions and how quickly he caught on. He was eminently teachable, and so the progress was more rapid than it had ever been with any other fighter. Pacquiao seemed to never tire of training or to worry about overdoing it. Roach kept waiting for the inevitable dynamic in which the fighter would begin to tune him out, but this never came. This was a boxer he could work harder and harder. Soon, Pacquiao had developed a devastating right hand, and his footwork could match the speed of his hands. He began to win fight after fight, in impressive fashion.

As the years went by, the relationship began to evolve. In their mitt work, Pacquiao would adjust or improve upon the maneuvers Roach had been developing for the next bout. He gave input on Roach's strategy, altering it on occasion. Pacquiao had gained a sixth sense for what Roach was getting at and could take his thinking further. On one occasion Roach watched Pacquiao improvise a maneuver on the ropes in which he ducked out and attacked a fighter from an angle instead of head-on. To Roach, this was a move that made instant sense. He wanted to develop this further into a whole new possible style of fighting. He was now learning almost as much from Pacquiao. The previous trainer-fighter relationship had now morphed into something interactive and alive. To Roach, this meant that they could move past the seemingly inevitable plateau for fighters in which it all became stale and opponents would catch on to their weaknesses.

Working together in this way, Roach was able to transform this one-dimensional, relatively unknown fighter into perhaps the greatest boxer of his generation.

In theory, there should be no limit to what we can learn from mentors who have wide experience. But in practice, this is rarely the case. The reasons are several: at some point the relationship can become flat; it is difficult for us to maintain the same level of attention that we had in the beginning. We might come to resent their authority a little, especially as we gain in skill and the difference between us becomes somewhat less. Also, they come from a different generation, with a different worldview. At a certain point, some of their cherished principles might seem a bit out of touch or irrelevant, and we unconsciously tune them out. The only solution is to evolve a more interactive dynamic with the mentor. If they can adapt to some of your ideas, the relationship becomes more animated. Feeling a growing openness on their part to your input, you are less resentful. You are revealing to them your own experiences and ideas, perhaps loosening them up so their principles don't harden into dogma.

Such a style of interaction is more in tune with our democratic times and can serve as something of an ideal. But it should not go along with a rebellious attitude or a lessening in respect. The dynamic sketched out earlier in this chapter remains the same. Like Pacquiao, you bring to the relationship the utmost in admiration and your total attention. You are completely open to their instruction. Gaining *their* respect for how teachable you are, they will fall a bit under your spell, as Roach did with Pacquiao. With your intense focus, you improve in your skill levels, giving you the power to introduce more of yourself and your needs. You give them feedback to their instruction, perhaps adjust some of their ideas. This must begin with you, as you set the tone with your hunger to learn. Once a back-and-forth dynamic is sparked, the relationship has almost limitless potential for learning and absorbing power.

REVERSAL

It is never wise to purposefully do without the benefits of having a mentor in your life. You will waste valuable time in finding and shaping what you need to know. But sometimes you have no choice. There is simply no one around who can fill the role, and you are left to your own devices. In such a case, you must make a virtue of necessity. That was the path taken by perhaps the greatest historical figure to ever attain mastery alone—Thomas Alva Edison (1847–1931).

From a very early age Edison became used to doing things for himself, by necessity. His family was poor, and by the age of twelve he had to earn money to help his parents. He sold newspapers on trains, and traveling around his native Michigan for his job, he developed an ardent curiosity about everything he saw. He wanted to know how things worked—machines, gadgets, anything with moving parts. With no schools or teachers in his life, he turned to books, particularly anything he could find on science. He began to conduct his own experiments in the basement of his family home, and he taught himself how to take apart and fix any kind of watch. At the age of fifteen he apprenticed as a telegraph operator, then spent years traveling across the country plying his trade. He had no chance for a formal education, and nobody crossed his path who could serve as a teacher or mentor. And so in lieu of that, in every city he spent time in, he frequented the public library.

One book that crossed his path played a decisive role in his life: Michael Faraday's two-volume *Experimental Researches in Electricity*. This book became for Edison what *The Improvement of the Mind* had been for Faraday. It gave him a systematic approach to science and a program for how to educate himself in the field that now obsessed him—electricity. He could follow the experiments laid out by the great Master of the field and absorb as well his philosophical approach to science. For the rest of his life, Faraday would remain his role model.

Through books, experiments, and practical experience at various jobs, Edison gave himself a rigorous education that lasted about ten years, up until the time he became an inventor. What made this successful was his relentless desire to learn through whatever crossed his path, as well as his self-discipline. He had developed the habit of overcoming his lack of an organized education by sheer determination and persistence. He worked harder than anyone else. Because he was a consummate outsider and his mind had not been indoctrinated in any school of thought, he brought a fresh perspective to every problem he tackled. He turned his lack of formal direction into an advantage.

If you are forced onto this path, you must follow Edison's example by developing extreme self-reliance. Under these circumstances, you become your own teacher and mentor. You push yourself to learn from every possible source. You read more books than those who have a formal education, developing this into a lifelong habit. As much as possible, you try to apply your knowledge in some form of experiment or practice. You find for yourself second-degree mentors in the form of public figures who can serve as role models. Reading and reflecting on their experiences, you can gain some guidance. You try to make their ideas come to life, internalizing their voice. As someone self-taught, you will maintain a pristine vision, completely distilled through your own experiences—giving you a distinctive power and path to mastery.

To learn by example is to submit to authority. You follow your master because you trust his manner of doing things even when you cannot analyze and account in detail for its effectiveness. By watching the master and emulating his efforts . . . the apprentice unconsciously picks up the rules of the art, including those which are not explicitly known to the master himself.

—MICHAEL POLANYI

IV

SEE PEOPLE AS THEY ARE: SOCIAL INTELLIGENCE

Often the greatest obstacle to our pursuit of mastery comes from the emotional drain we experience in dealing with the resistance and manipulations of the people around us. If we are not careful, our minds become absorbed in endless political intrigues and battles. The principal problem we face in the social arena is our naïve tendency to project onto people our emotional needs and desires of the moment. We misread their intentions and react in ways that cause confusion or conflict. Social intelligence is the ability to see people in the most realistic light possible. By moving past our usual self-absorption, we can learn to focus deeply on others, reading their behavior in the moment, seeing what motivates them, and discerning any possible manipulative tendencies. Navigating smoothly the social environment, we have more time and energy to focus on learning and acquiring skills. Success attained without this intelligence is not true mastery, and will not last.

THINKING INSIDE

In 1718, Benjamin Franklin (1706–90) went to work as an apprentice in his brother James's printing shop in Boston. His dream was to transform himself into a great writer. At the printing shop he would not only be taught how to handle the machines, but also how to edit manuscripts. Surrounded by books and newspapers, he would have plenty of examples of good writing to study and learn from. It would be the perfect position for him.

As the apprenticeship progressed, the literary education he had imagined for himself came to pass, and his writing skills improved immensely. Then, in 1722, it seemed that he would finally have the perfect opportunity to prove himself as a writer—his brother was about to launch his own large-scale newspaper called *The New-England Courant*. Benjamin approached James with several interesting ideas for stories he could write, but to his great disappointment, his brother was not interested in his contributing to the new paper. This was a serious venture, and Benjamin's work was too immature for *The Courant*.

Benjamin knew it was pointless to argue with James; he was a very stubborn young man. But as he thought about the situation, an idea suddenly came to him: what if he were to create a fictional character who would write letters to *The Courant*? If he wrote them well enough, James would never suspect they were from Benjamin, and he would print them. In this way, he would have the last laugh. After much thinking, he decided upon the perfect character to create: a young female widow named Silence Dogood who had lots of strong opinions about life in Boston, many of them rather absurd. To make this believable, Benjamin spent long hours imagining a detailed past for her. He thought so deeply into the character that she began to come alive within him. He could hear her way of thinking, and soon there emerged a very realistic writing voice all her own.

He sent the first, rather lengthy letter to *The Courant* and watched with amusement as his brother published it and added a note in the newspaper asking for more letters from her. James probably suspected it was the work of some established writer in town using a pseudonym—the letter was so witty and satirical—but he clearly had no idea it was from Benjamin. James continued publishing the subsequent letters, and they quickly became the most popular part of *The Courant*.

Benjamin's responsibilities at the shop began to grow, and he proved to be quite an adept editor for the newspaper as well. Feeling proud of all his precocious achievements, one day he could not help himself—he confessed to James that he was the author of the Dogood letters. Expecting some praise for this, he was surprised by James's vitriolic response—his brother did not like being lied to. To make matters worse, over the next few months he turned increasingly cold and even abusive to Benjamin. It soon became impossible to work for him, and by the fall of 1723, feeling somewhat desperate, Benjamin decided to flee Boston, turning his back on brother and family.

After several weeks of wandering he ended up in Philadelphia, determined to settle there. He was only seventeen, with virtually no money and no contacts, but for some reason he felt full of hope. In the five years working for his brother he had learned more about the business than men twice his age. He was fiercely disciplined and ambitious. And he was a talented and successful writer to boot. With no more limitations on his freedom, Philadelphia would be his to conquer. Surveying the scene in his first few days there, his confidence only increased. The two printing shops in town at the time were well below the level of anything in Boston, and the writing in the local papers was abysmal. This meant endless opportunities to fill a void and make his way.

Sure enough, within a few weeks he managed to secure a position at one of the two printing shops in town, owned by a man named Samuel Keimer. Philadelphia was still relatively small and provincial at the time— word spread quickly of the newcomer and his literary skills.

The governor of the colony of Pennsylvania, William Keith, had ambitions of transforming Philadelphia into a cultural center, and was not happy with the two established printing businesses. Hearing of Benjamin Franklin and of his writing talent, he sought him out. Clearly impressed with the young man's intelligence, he urged him to start his own printing shop, promising to lend him the initial amount that was needed to get the business going. The machines and materials would have to come from London, and Keith advised him to go there personally to supervise the acquisition. He had contacts there and would bankroll it all.

Franklin could hardly believe his good fortune. Only a few months earlier he was a menial apprentice to his brother. Now, thanks to the generous and enterprising governor, he would soon have his own printing business, and through it he could start a newspaper and become a leading voice in the city, all before he turned twenty. As he made his plans for London, the money Keith had promised as a loan was not forthcoming, but after writing to him a few times, word finally came from the governor's office not to worry—letters of credit would be waiting for him once he disembarked in England. And so, without explaining to Keimer what he was up to, he quit his job and bought his passage for the transatlantic journey.

When he got to England there were no letters waiting. Feeling there must have been some kind of miscommunication, he frantically looked in London for a representative of the governor to whom he could explain their agreement. In his search he came upon a wealthy merchant from Philadelphia who, hearing his story, revealed to him the truth—Governor Keith was a notorious talker. He was always promising everything to everyone, trying to impress people with his power. His enthusiasm for a scheme would rarely last more than a week. He had no money to lend, and his character was worth about as much as his promises.

As Franklin took this all in and considered his current predicament, what disturbed him was not that he now found himself in a precarious position—alone and without money, far from home. There was no place more exciting for a young man than London, and he would somehow make his way there. What bothered him was how badly he had misread Keith and how naïve he had been.

Fortunately, London was teeming with large-scale printing shops, and within a few weeks of his arrival he found a position within one of them. To forget about the Keith fiasco he threw himself into the work, quickly impressing his employer with his dexterity with the various machines and with his editing skills. He got along well enough with his colleagues, but soon he encountered a strange British custom: five times a day his fellow printers would take a break to drink a pint of beer. It fortified them for the work, or so they said. Every week Franklin was expected to contribute to the beer fund for those in the room, including himself, but he refused to pay up—he did not like to drink during working hours, and the idea that he should give up a part of his hard-earned wages for others to ruin their health made him angry. He spoke honestly about his principles, and they politely accepted his decision.

Over the ensuing weeks, however, strange things began to happen: mistakes kept popping up in texts he had already proofread, and almost every day he noticed some new error for which he was blamed. He started to feel like he was losing his mind. If this continued any longer he would be fired. Clearly, somebody was sabotaging his work, and when he complained to his fellow printers, they attributed it all to a mischievous ghost who was known to haunt the room. Finally figuring out what this meant, he let go of his principles and contributed to the beer fund; the mistakes suddenly disappearing along with the ghost.

After this incident and several other indiscretions in London, Franklin began to seriously wonder about himself. He seemed hopelessly naïve, constantly misreading the intentions of the people around him. Thinking about this problem, he was struck by an apparent paradox: when it came to his work, he was supremely rational and realistic, always looking to improve himself. With his writing, for instance, he could see his weaknesses clearly and practiced hard to overcome them. But with people it was virtually the opposite: he would inevitably become swept up in his emotions and lose all contact with reality. With his brother, he wanted to impress him by revealing his authorship of the letters, totally unaware of the envy and malevolence he would unleash; with Keith, he was so wrapped up in his dreams that he paid no attention to obvious signs that the governor was all talk; with the printers, his anger blinded him to the fact that they would obviously resent his attempts at reform. What was worse, he seemed incapable of changing this self-absorbed dynamic.

Determined to break this pattern and change his ways, he decided there was only one solution: in all of his future interactions with people, he would force himself to take an initial step backward and not get emotional. From this more detached position, he would focus completely on the people he was dealing with, cutting off his own insecurities and desires from the equation. Exercising his mind this way every time, it would turn into a habit. In imagining how this would work, he had a strange sensation. It reminded him of the process he went through in creating the Dogood letters—thinking inside the character he had created, entering her world, and making her come alive in his mind. In essence, he would be applying this literary skill to everyday life. Gaining position inside people's minds, he could see how to melt their resistance or thwart their malevolent plans.

To make this process foolproof, he decided he would also have to adopt a new philosophy: complete and radical acceptance of human nature. People possess ingrained qualities and characters. Some are frivolous like Keith, or vindictive like his brother, or rigid like the printers. There are people like this everywhere; it has been that way since the dawn of civilization. To get upset or try to alter them is futile—it will only make them bitter and resentful. Better to accept such people as one accepts the thorns on a rose. Better to observe and accumulate knowledge on human nature, as one accumulates knowledge in the sciences. If he could follow this new path in life, he would rid himself of his terrible naïveté and bring some rationality to his social relations.

After more than a year and a half of work in London, Franklin finally saved enough money for his return journey to the colonies, and in 1727 he found himself back in Philadelphia, looking once more for work. In the midst of his search, his former employer, Samuel Keimer, surprised him by offering Franklin a nice position in the printing shop—he would be in charge of the staff and training the others Keimer had recently hired as part of his expanding business. For this he would receive a nice yearly salary. Franklin accepted, but almost from the beginning he could sense something was not right. And so, as he had promised himself, he took a step back and calmly reviewed the facts.

He had five men to train, but once he accomplished this task there would be little work left over for him. Keimer himself had been acting strangely—much friendlier than usual. He was an insecure and prickly gentleman, and this friendly front did not fit him. Imagining the situation from Keimer's perspective, he could sense that he must have greatly resented Franklin's sudden departure for London, leaving him in the lurch. He must have seen Franklin as a young whippersnapper who needed his comeuppance. He was not the type to discuss this with anyone, but would seethe from within and scheme on his own. Thinking in this way, Keimer's intentions became clear to him: he was planning to get Franklin to impart his extensive knowledge of the business to the new employees, then fire him. This would be his revenge.

Certain he had read this correctly, he decided to quietly turn the tables. He used his new managerial position to build relationships with customers and to connect with successful merchants in the area. He experimented with some new manufacturing methods he had learned in England. When Keimer was away from the shop, he taught himself new skills such as engraving and ink-making. He paid close attention to his pupils, and carefully cultivated one of them to be a first-rate assistant. And just when he suspected that Keimer was about to fire him, he left and set up his own shop—with financial backing, greater knowledge of the business, a solid base of customers who would follow him everywhere, and a first-rate assistant whom he had trained. In executing this strategy, Franklin noticed how free he was from any feelings of bitterness or anger toward Keimer. It was all maneuvers on a chessboard, and by thinking inside Keimer he was able to play the game to perfection, with a clear and level head.

Over the ensuing years, Franklin's printing business prospered. He became a highly successful newspaper publisher, a best-selling writer, a scientist renowned for his experiments with electricity, and an inventor of such things as the Franklin stove (and later in his life that of the lightning rod, bifocal glasses, and so on). As an increasingly prominent member of the Philadelphia community, in 1736 he decided it was time to take his career further and enter politics, becoming a delegate to Pennsylvania's colonial legislature. Within a few months he was chosen unanimously by fellow members to serve as the clerk to the legislature, a position of some influence. But when it was time to renew the appointment, a new member of the legislature, Isaac Norris, suddenly voiced his vehement opposition, supporting another candidate. After much heated debate Franklin won the vote, but in contemplating the situation, he saw danger on the horizon.

Norris was a wealthy, well-educated, and charismatic businessman. He was also ambitious and certain to rise within the ranks. If Franklin became antagonistic toward him, as would be expected after what had happened with the battle over the clerk position, he would confirm any unpleasant notions Norris had entertained of him and convert him into an implacable foe. On the other hand, if he ignored him, Norris might read this as an example of Franklin's haughtiness and hate him all the more. To some it might seem to be the strong and manly thing to go on the attack and fight back, proving he was not someone to mess with. But would it not be infinitely more powerful to work against Norris's expectations and subtly convert him into an implacable ally?

And so Franklin went to work. He observed the man closely in the legislature, gathered information from insiders, and thought himself deeply into Norris's mind. He came to the conclusion that Norris was a proud and somewhat emotional young man who harbored a few insecurities as well. He seemed impatient for attention, for being liked and admired by others; perhaps he envied Franklin's popularity and achievements. Through his insiders, he learned that Norris had one rather odd obsession—an extensive personal library containing many rare books, including one that was particularly rare and that he prized above all others. These books seemed to represent to him his own feelings of distinction and nobility.

Knowing all of this, Franklin decided upon the following course of action: he wrote to Norris a very polite note, expressing admiration for his collection. He was an avid book lover himself, and hearing so much about that one rare book in Norris's collection, he would be excited beyond belief if he could somehow peruse it at his leisure. If Norris would lend it to him for a few days, he would take great care of it and return it promptly.

Clearly pleased by this attention, Norris sent the book over right away and Franklin returned it as promised, with another note expressing his gratitude for the favor. At the next meeting of the legislature, Norris came up to Franklin and engaged him in friendly conversation, something he had never done before. As he had predicted, he had created doubt in Norris's mind. Instead of his suspicions being confirmed about Franklin, he was confronted with the fact that the man behaved as a true gentleman, shared his interest in rare books, and kept to his word. How could he continue to harbor bad feelings without wondering about himself and why he had sent the book? Playing on Norris's emotional nature, Franklin shifted his feelings from antagonism to warmth. They became close friends and then staunch political allies to the end of their careers. (Franklin would go on to practice similar magic on many of his future political foes.)

In Philadelphia, Benjamin Franklin was thought of as the quintessence of the trustworthy merchant and citizen. Like his fellow townsfolk, he dressed plainly; he worked harder than anyone they knew; he never frequented bars or gambling houses; and he had a folksy and even humble manner. His popularity was almost universal. But in the last public chapter of his life, he acted in a way that seemed to indicate that he had changed and lost his common touch.

In 1776, a year after the outbreak of the War of Independence, Benjamin Franklin—now a distinguished political figure—was dispatched to France as a special commissioner to obtain arms, financing and an alliance. Soon stories spread throughout the colonies of his various intrigues with French women and courtesans, and of his attendance at lavish parties and dinners—much of which was true. Prominent politicians such as John Adams accused him of becoming corrupted by the Parisians. His popularity among Americans plummeted. But what the critics and public did not realize was that wherever he went he assumed the look, the outward morals, and the behavior of the culture at hand, so that he could better make his way. Desperate to win the French over to the American cause and understanding their nature quite well, he had transformed himself into what they had wanted to see in him—the American version of the French spirit and way of life. He was appealing to their notorious narcissism.

All of this worked to perfection—Franklin became a beloved figure to the French, and a man of influence with their government. In the end, he brokered an important military alliance and gained the kind of financing nobody else could have wrested from the stingy French king. This final public act in his life was not an aberration, but the ultimate application of his social rationality.

KEYS TO MASTERY

You must allow everyone the right to exist in accordance with the character he has, whatever it turns out to be: and all you should strive to do is to make use of this character in such a way as its kind of nature permits, rather than to hope for any alteration in it, or to condemn it offhand for what it is. This is the true sense of the maxim–Live and let live. . . . To become indignant at [people's] conduct is as foolish as to be angry with a stone because it rolls into your path. And with many people the wisest thing you can do, is to resolve to make use of those whom you cannot alter.

—Arthur Schopenhauer

We humans are the preeminent social animal. Hundreds of thousands of years ago, our primitive ancestors developed complex social groupings. To adapt to this, they evolved mirror neurons (see introduction, page 7), which were more refined and sensitive than those of other primates. This meant that they could use these mirror neurons not only to imitate those around them, but also to imagine what others might be thinking and feeling, all on a preverbal level. Such empathy allowed for a higher degree of cooperation.

With the invention of language and the reasoning powers it brought them, our ancestors could take this empathic ability further—seeing patterns in people's behavior and deducing their motivations. Over the years, these reasoning skills have become infinitely more powerful and refined. In theory, all of us today possess the natural tools—empathy, rational thinking— to have a supreme understanding of our fellow humans. In practice, however, these tools remain mostly undeveloped, and the explanation for this can be found in the peculiar nature of our childhood, and our extended period of dependency.

Compared to other animals, we humans enter the world remarkably weak and helpless. We remain relatively weak for many years before we can truly operate on our own. This extended period of immaturity, lasting some twelve to eighteen years, serves a valuable function: it gives us a chance to focus on developing our brain—by far the most important weapon in the human arsenal. But this prolonged childhood comes with a price. During this time of weakness and dependency, we experience the need to idealize our parents. Our survival depends on their strength and reliability. To think of them as having their own frailties would fill us with unbearable anxiety. And so we inevitably see them as stronger, more capable, and more selfless than they are in reality. We come to view their actions through the lens of our needs, and so they become extensions of ourselves.

During this long period of immaturity, we often transfer these idealizations and distortions to teachers and friends, projecting onto them what we want and need to see. Our view of people becomes saturated with various emotions—worship, admiration, love, need, anger. Then inevitably, often in adolescence, we start to glimpse a less-than-noble side to many people, including our parents, and we cannot help but feel upset at the disparity between what we had imagined and the reality. In our disappointment, we tend to exaggerate their negative qualities, much as we once had exaggerated the positive ones. If we had been forced earlier on in life to make it on our own, practical needs would have come to dominate our thinking, and we would have become more detached and realistic. But as it is, the many years of viewing people through the lens of our emotional needs turns into a habit that we can hardly control.

Let us call this the *Naïve Perspective*. Although it is natural to have such a perspective because of the unique character of our childhood, it is also dangerous because it envelops us in childish illusions about people, distorting our view of them. We carry this perspective with us into the adult world, into the Apprenticeship Phase. In the work environment the stakes are suddenly raised. People are no longer struggling for good grades or social approval, but for survival. Under such pressure, they reveal qualities of their characters that they normally try to conceal. They manipulate, compete, and think of themselves first. We are blindsided by this behavior and our emotions are churned up even more than before, locking us into the Naïve Perspective.

The Naïve Perspective makes us feel sensitive and vulnerable. Looking inward as to how the words and actions of others implicate us in some way, we continually misread their intentions. We project our own feelings onto them. We have no real sense of what they are thinking or what motivates them. With colleagues in the work environment, we fail to see the source of their envy or the reason for their manipulations; our attempts at influencing them are based on the assumptions that they want the same things as ourselves. With mentors and bosses, we project onto them our childhood fantasies, becoming unnecessarily adoring or fearful of authority figures and creating stormy and brittle relationships in the process. We think we understand people, but we are viewing them through a distorted lens. In this state, all of our empathic powers are rendered useless.

With the inevitable mistakes we make, we become entangled in battles and dramas that consume our minds and distract us from learning. Our sense of priorities becomes warped—we end up giving far too much importance to social and political issues because we are not handling them well. If we are not careful, we carry these patterns over to the next phase in life, the Creative-Active Phase, in which we are in a more public position. At this level, being socially inept can prove particularly embarrassing, even fatal to our careers. People who retain their childish attitudes will rarely be able to hold on to the success they may achieve through their talent.

Social intelligence is nothing more than the process of discarding the Naïve Perspective and approaching something more realistic. It involves focusing our attention outward instead of inward, honing the observational and empathic skills that we naturally possess. It means moving past our tendency to idealize and demonize people, and seeing and accepting them as they are. It is a way of thinking that must be cultivated as early as possible, during the Apprenticeship Phase. But before we can begin to acquire this intelligence we must first come to grips with the Naïve Perspective itself.

Look at the case of Benjamin Franklin, the icon of social intelligence and the clearest example of the role it plays in mastery. As the second youngest of a large extended family, he learned to get his way through charm. As he got older he came to believe, as many young people do, that getting along with others is a function of behaving charmingly and winning them over with a friendly manner. But as he engaged with the real world, he began to see his charm as the actual source of his problem. Being charming was a strategy he had developed out of childish need; it was a reflection of his narcissism, of the love he had of his own words and wit. It had no relation to other people and their needs. It did not prevent them from exploiting or attacking him. To be truly charming and socially effective you have to understand people, and to understand them you have to get outside yourself and immerse your mind in *their* world.

Only when he realized how deeply naïve he had been could he take the necessary steps to move past this naïveté. His focus on gaining social intelligence was the turning point of his career—it transformed him into the preeminent observer of human nature, a man with a magical ability to see into people. It also made him the perfect social companion—men and women everywhere fell under his spell because of his ability to attune himself to their energies. With tranquil and productive social relations, he could focus more of his time and attention to writing, to questions of science, to his endless inventions—to mastery.

It might be deduced from Benjamin Franklin's story that social intelligence requires a detached, emotionless approach to people, making life rather dull in the process, but this is hardly the case. Franklin himself was by nature a very emotional man. He did not repress this nature, but rather turned his emotions in the opposite direction. Instead of obsessing over himself and what other people were not giving him, he thought deeply of how they were experiencing the world, what they were feeling and missing. Emotions seen inside other people create empathy and bring a deep understanding of what makes them tick. For Franklin, this outward focus gave him a pleasant feeling of lightness and ease; his life was hardly dull, but simply free of unnecessary battles.

Understand: you will continue to have problems in attaining social intelligence until you come to the realization that your view of people is dominated by the Naïve Perspective. Following Franklin's example, you can reach this awareness by reviewing your past, paying particular attention to any battles, mistakes, tensions, or disappointments on the social front. If you look at these events through the lens of the Naïve Perspective, you will focus only on what *other people* have done to you—the mistreatments you endured from them, the slights or injuries you felt. Instead, you must turn this around and begin with yourself—how *you* saw in others qualities they did not possess, or how *you* ignored signs of a dark side to their nature. In doing this, you will be able to clearly see the discrepancy between your illusions about who they are and the reality, and the role you played in creating this discrepancy. If you look closely enough, you can often perceive in your relationships with bosses or superiors reenactments of the childhood family dynamic—the idealizing or demonizing that has become habitual.

By making yourself aware of the distorting process of the Naïve Perspective, you will naturally grow less comfortable with it. You will realize that you are operating in the dark, blind to people's motivations and intentions, vulnerable to the same mistakes and patterns that occurred in the past. You will *feel* your lack of real connection to other people. The desire will naturally arise from within to change this dynamic—to start looking outward instead of focusing only on your own feelings, to observe before you react.

This new clarity about your perspective should be accompanied by an adjustment of your attitude. You must avoid the temptation to become cynical in your approach as an overreaction to your prior naïveté. The most effective attitude to adopt is one of supreme acceptance. The world is full of people with different characters and temperaments. We all have a dark side, a tendency to manipulate, and aggressive desires. The most dangerous types are those who repress their desires or deny the existence of them, often acting them out in the most underhanded ways. Some people have dark qualities that are especially pronounced. You cannot change such people at their core, but must merely avoid becoming their victim. You are an observer of the human comedy, and by being as tolerant as possible, you gain a much greater ability to understand people and to influence their behavior when necessary.

With this new awareness and attitude in place, you can begin to advance in your apprenticeship in social intelligence. This intelligence consists of two components, both equally important to master. First, there is what we shall call *specific knowledge of human nature*—namely the ability to read people, to get a feel for how they see the world, and to understand their individuality. Second, there is the *general knowledge of human nature*, which means accumulating an understanding of the overall patterns of human behavior that transcend us as individuals, including some of the darker qualities we often disregard. Because we are all a mix of unique qualities and traits common to our species, only the possession of both forms of knowledge can give you a complete picture of the people around you. Practice both forms of knowledge and they will yield invaluable skills that are essential in the quest for mastery.

Specific Knowledge—Reading People

Most of us have had the sensation at some point in our lives of experiencing an uncanny connection with another person. In such moments we have an understanding that is hard to put into words; we even feel that we can anticipate the thoughts of the other person. Such communication generally occurs with close friends and partners, people whom we trust and feel attuned to on many levels. Because we trust them, we open up to their influence and vice versa. In our normal state we are often nervous, defensive, and self-absorbed, and our minds are turned inward. But in these moments of connection, the internal monologue is shut off, and we pick up more cues and signals from the other person than usual.

What this means is that when we are not inward-directed but attending more deeply to another person, we gain access to forms of communication that are largely nonverbal in nature, and quite effective in their own way. We can imagine that our primitive ancestors, needing to cooperate on a high level yet not experiencing the kind of interior monologue that comes with words, possessed an incredibly powerful sensitivity to the moods and feelings of others within the group, bordering on telepathy. This would be similar to what other social animals possess, but in this case this sensitivity would have been heightened by our ancestor's ability to place themselves in the minds of others.

The intense nonverbal connection we experience with those we are close to is clearly not appropriate in a work environment, but to the degree we open ourselves up and direct our attention outward to other people, we can access a part of the sensitivity that our ancestors had, and become much more effective at reading people.

To begin this process, you need to train yourself to pay less attention to the words that people say and greater attention to their tone of voice, the look in their eye, their body language—all signals that might reveal a nervousness or excitement that is not expressed verbally. If you can get people to become emotional, they will reveal a lot more. Cutting off your interior monologue and paying deep attention, you will pick up cues from them that will register with you as feelings or sensations. Trust these sensations—they are telling you something that you will often tend to ignore because it is not easy to verbalize. Later you can try to find a pattern to these signals and attempt to analyze what they mean.

On this nonverbal level, it is interesting to observe how people behave around those in positions of power and authority. They will tend to reveal an anxiety, a resentment, or a sycophantic falseness that betrays something essential about their psychological makeup, something that goes back to their childhoods and that can be read in their body language.

When you drop your defense mechanisms and pay deep attention to others, you will need to lower your guard and open yourself up to their influence as well. But as long as your emotions and empathy are directed outward, you will be able to detach yourself when necessary and analyze what you have gleaned. Resist the temptation to interpret what they say or do as somehow implicitly involving you—this will cause you to turn your thoughts inward and close off the immediacy of the connection.

As an exercise, after you have known people for a while, try to imagine that you are experiencing the world from their point of view, placing yourself in their circumstances and feeling what they feel. Look for any common emotional experiences—a trauma or difficulty you've had, for instance, that resembles in some way what they are going through. Reliving a part of that emotion can help you begin the identifying process. The goal is not to literally inhabit their mind, which is impossible, but to practice your empathic powers and gain a more realistic appraisal of their worldview. Being able to place yourself to any degree in the mind-set of others is a brilliant means of loosening up your own thought process, which will tend to get locked into certain ways of seeing things. Your ability to empathize with others is related to the creative process of feeling your way into the subject you are studying.

This intuitive form of reading people becomes more effective and accurate the more you use it, but it is best to combine it with other, more conscious forms of observation. For instance, you should take particular note of people's actions and decisions. Your goal is to figure out the hidden motives behind them, which will often revolve around power. People will say all kinds of things about their motives and intentions; they are used to dressing things up with words. Their actions, however, say much more about their character, about what is going on underneath the surface. If they present a harmless front but have acted aggressively on several occasions, give the knowledge of that aggression much greater weight than the surface they present. In a similar vein, you should take special note of how people respond to stressful situations—often the mask they wear in public falls off in the heat of the moment.

When looking for cues to observe, you should be sensitive to any kind of extreme behavior on their part—for instance, a blustery front, an overly friendly manner, a constant penchant for jokes. You will often notice that they wear this like a mask to hide the opposite, to distract others from the truth. They are blustery because they are inwardly very insecure; they are overly friendly because they are secretly ambitious and aggressive; or they joke to hide a mean-spiritedness.

In general, you are reading and decoding every possible sign—including the clothes they wear and the organized or disorganized nature of their workspace. The choice of mate or partner can be quite eloquent too, particularly if it seems slightly inconsistent with the character they try to project. In this choice they can reveal unmet needs from childhood, a desire for power and control, a low self-image, and other qualities they normally seek to disguise. What might seem like small issues—chronically being late, insufficient attention to detail, not returning any favors on your part—are signs of something deeper about their character. These are patterns you must pay attention to. Nothing is too small to notice.

You must avoid the common mistake of making judgments based on your initial impressions of people. Such impressions can sometimes tell you something, but more often they are misleading. There are several reasons for this. In your initial encounter you tend to be nervous, less open, and more inward. You are not really paying attention. Furthermore, people have trained themselves to appear a certain way; they have a persona they use in public that acts like a second skin to protect them. Unless you are incredibly perceptive, you will tend to mistake the mask for the reality. For instance, the man you judged to be so powerful and assertive may be merely masking his fears and may have far less power than you first imagined. Often it is the quiet ones, those who give out less at first glance, who hide greater depths, and who secretly wield greater power.

What you want is a picture of a person's character over time, which will give you a far more accurate sense of their true character than any first impression could. So restrain yourself from the natural tendency to judge right away, and let the passing months reveal more and more about who people are, as you get better at reading them.

In the end, your goal is to identify and pierce through to what makes people unique, to understand the character and values that lie at their cores. The more you can fathom about people's pasts and their way of thinking about things, the more deeply you can enter into their spirit. In this way you will be able to understand their motivations, foresee their actions, and recognize how best to win them to your side. You will no longer be operating in the dark.

You will encounter thousands of various individuals in your life, and the ability to see them as they are will prove invaluable. Keep in mind, however, that people are in a state of continual flux. You must not let your ideas about them harden into a set impression. You are continually observing them and bringing your readings of them up to date.

General Knowledge—The Seven Deadly Realities

Throughout recorded history we can detect patterns of human behavior that transcend culture and time, indicating certain universal features that belong to us as a species. Some of these traits are quite positive—for instance, our ability to cooperate with one another in a group—while some of them are negative and can prove destructive. Most of us have these negative qualities—*Envy, Conformism, Rigidity, Self-obsessiveness, Laziness, Flightiness,* and *Passive Aggression*—in relatively mild doses. But in a group setting, there will inevitably be people who have one or more of these qualities to a high enough degree that they can become very destructive. We shall call these negative qualities the *Seven Deadly Realities.*

The problem for us is that people do not like to display these traits publicly because they are seen as ugly and undesirable. They tend to disguise them from view, finally revealing their reality through some action that blindsides and harms us. In our surprise, we tend to react emotionally, increasing the damage, the effects of which we can carry with us the rest of our lives. Through study and observation, we must understand the nature of these Seven Deadly Realities so that we can detect their presence and avoid triggering them in the first place. Consider the following as essential knowledge in acquiring social intelligence.

Envy: It is our nature to constantly compare ourselves to others—in terms of money, looks, coolness, intelligence, popularity, or any number of categories. If we are upset that someone we know is more successful than we are, we will naturally experience some envy, but often we will find a way to minimize it because it is an unpleasant emotion. We tell ourselves that the success of another person is a matter of luck or came through their connections, or that it won't last. But for some people it goes much deeper than this, usually because of the level of their insecurities. Seething with envy, the only way to discharge it is to find a way to obstruct or sabotage the person who elicited the emotion. If they take such action they will *never* say it is because of envy, but will find some other, more socially acceptable excuse. They often won't even admit their envy to themselves. This makes it a quality very hard to recognize in people. There are, however, a few indications you can look for. People who praise you too much or who become overly friendly in the first stages of knowing you are often envious and are getting closer in order to hurt you. You should be wary of such behavior. Also, if you detect unusual levels of insecurity in a person, he or she will certainly be more prone to envy.

In general, however, envy is very difficult to discern, and the most prudent course of action is to make sure your own behavior does not inadvertently trigger it. If you have a gift for a certain skill, you should make a point of occasionally displaying some weakness in another area, avoiding the great danger of appearing too perfect, too talented. If you are dealing with insecure types, you can display great interest in *their* work and even turn to them for advice. You must be careful not to boast of any success, and if necessary, to ascribe it to just good luck on your part. It is always wise to occasionally reveal your own insecurities, which will humanize you in other people's eyes. Self-deprecating humor will work wonders as well. You must be particularly careful to never make people feel stupid in your presence. Intelligence is the most sensitive trigger point for envy. In general, it is by standing out too much that you will spark this ugly emotion, and so it is best to maintain a nonthreatening exterior and to blend in well with the group, at least until you are so successful it no longer matters.

Conformism: When people form groups of any type, a kind of organizational mind-set inevitably sets in. Although members of the group might trumpet their tolerance and celebration of people's differences, the reality is that those who are markedly different make them feel uncomfortable and insecure, calling the values of the dominant culture into question. This culture will have unwritten standards of correctness that shift with the times we live in. In some environments, physical appearance is important. But generally, the spirit of correctness runs deeper than that. Often unconsciously conforming to the spirit of the man or woman on top, members will share the same values about morals or politics. You can become aware of this group spirit by observing how much people feel the need to *display* certain opinions or ideas that conform to the standards. There will always be a few within the group who are the overseers of correctness and who can be quite dangerous.

If you have a rebellious or naturally eccentric streak, as is often the case with those who are aiming for mastery, you must be careful in displaying your difference too overtly, particularly in the Apprenticeship Phase. Let your work subtly demonstrate your individual spirit, but when it comes to matters of politics, morals, and values, make a show of adhering to the accepted standards of your environment. Think of the workplace as a kind of theater in which you are always wearing a mask. (Reserve your most interesting and colorful thoughts for your friends, and for those whom you can trust outside work.) Be careful in what you say—it is not worth the bother of freely expressing your opinions. If you sin against this Deadly Reality, people will not acknowledge the cause of their disaffection, because they do not want to think of themselves as conformists. They will find some other reason to ostracize or sabotage you. Do not give them material for this kind of attack. Later, as you gain mastery, you will have ample opportunity to let your individuality shine through and to reveal your contempt for people's correctness.

Rigidity: The world has become increasingly complex in many ways, and whenever we humans face a situation that seems complicated our response is to resort to a kind of artificial simplicity, to create habits and routines that give us a sense of control. We prefer what is familiar—ideas, faces, procedures—because they are comforting. This extends to the group at large. People follow procedures without really knowing why, simply because these procedures may have worked in the past, and they become highly defensive if their ways are brought into question. They become hooked on a certain idea and they hold on to it, even if that idea has been proven repeatedly to be wrong. Look at the history of science: whenever a new idea or way of looking at the world is introduced, despite all of the proofs behind it, those who are entrenched in the old ways will fight to the death to preserve them. It is often against human nature, particularly as we get older, to consider alternative ways of thinking or doing things.

People do not advertise their rigidity. You will only trip up against it if you try to introduce a new idea or procedure. Some in the group—the hyper-rigid—will become irritable, even panicky at the thought of any kind of change. If you press your case with logic and reason, you will tend to make them even more defensive and resistant. If you are an adventurous, open-minded type, your very spirit will prove disruptive and upsetting. If you are not aware of the dangers of butting up against this fear of the new, you will create all sorts of hidden enemies, who will resort to anything to conserve the old order. It is useless to fight against people's rigid ways, or to argue against their irrational concepts. You will only waste time and make yourself rigid in the process. The best strategy is to simply accept rigidity in others, outwardly displaying deference to their need for order. On your own, however, you must work to maintain your open spirit, letting go of bad habits and deliberately cultivating new ideas.

Self-obsessiveness: In the work environment, we almost inevitably think first and foremost of ourselves. The world is a harsh and competitive place, and we must look after our own interests. Even when we act for the greater good, we are often unconsciously motivated by the desire to be liked by others and to have our image enhanced in the process. There is no shame in this. But because being self-interested does not make us feel or appear noble, many people go out of their way to disguise their self-interest. Often those who are the most self-absorbed will surround their actions with a moral or saintly aura, or will make a show of supporting all of the right causes. Confused by these appearances, when it is time to ask such people for assistance, you will often appeal to their sense of gratitude, their seemingly charitable nature, or their friendly feelings. You are then frustrated and disappointed when they politely decline to help you, or put you off long enough that you give up. Of course, they never reveal the real reason for this behavior—that there is nothing in it for themselves.

Instead of putting yourself in this position, you must understand and accept this Deadly Reality. When it is time to ask for a favor or help, you must think first of appealing to people's self-interest in some way. (You should apply this to everyone, no matter their level of self-obsessiveness.) You must look at the world through their eyes, getting a sense of their needs. You must give them something valuable in exchange for helping you— a return favor that will save them time, a contact they need, and so on. Sometimes the chance to look good in doing you a favor or supporting a cause will suffice, but it is generally better to find something stronger than that—some concrete benefit they can foresee coming from you in the future. In general, in your interactions with people, find a way to make the conversations revolve around them and their interests, all of which will go far to winning them to your side.

Laziness: We all have the tendency to want to take the quickest, easiest path to our goals, but we generally manage to control our impatience; we understand the superior value of getting what we want through hard work. For some people, however, this inveterate lazy streak is far too powerful. Discouraged by the thought that it might take months or years to get somewhere, they are constantly on the lookout for shortcuts. Their laziness will assume many insidious forms. For example, if you are not careful and talk too much, they will steal your best ideas and make them their own, saving themselves all of the mental effort that went into conceiving them. They will swoop in during the middle of your project and put their name on it, gaining partial credit for your work. They will engage you in a "collaboration" in which you do the bulk of the hard work but they share equally in the rewards.

Your best defense is your prudence. Keep your ideas to yourself, or conceal enough of the details so that it is not possible to steal them. If you are doing work for a superior, be prepared for them to take full credit and leave your name out (this is a part of everyone's apprenticeship and must be accepted as such), but do not let this happen with colleagues. Secure your credit in advance as part of the terms of working together. If people want you to do work for them, then pass it off as a "collaborative" effort, always gauge whether such work will add to your skill base, and examine their past record to measure the intensity of their work ethic. In general, be wary of people who want to collaborate—they are often trying to find someone who will do the heavier lifting for them.

Flightiness: We like to make a show of how much our decisions are based on rational considerations, but the truth is that we are largely governed by our emotions, which continually color our perceptions. What this means is that the people around you, constantly under the pull of their emotions, change their ideas by the day or by the hour, depending on their mood.

You must never assume that what people say or do in a particular moment is a statement of their permanent desires. Yesterday they were in love with your idea; today they seem lukewarm. This will confuse you and if you are not careful, you will waste valuable mental space trying to figure out their real feelings, their mood of the moment, their fleeting motivations.

It is best to cultivate both distance and a degree of detachment from other people's shifting emotions so that you are not caught up in the process. Focus on their actions, which are generally more consistent, and not on their words. Do not take so seriously people's promises or their ardor in wanting to help you. If they come through, so much the better, but be prepared for the more frequent change of heart. Rely upon yourself to get things done and you will not be disappointed.

Passive Aggression: The root cause of all passive aggression is the human fear of direct confrontation—the emotions that a conflict can churn up and the loss of control that ensues. And so because of this fear some people look for indirect means for getting their way, making their attacks subtle enough so that it is hard to figure out what is going on, while giving them control of the dynamic. We are all passive-aggressive to some extent. Procrastinating on a project, showing up late, or making offhand comments designed to upset people are common forms of low-level passive aggression. When dealing with this low-level variety in others, you can call them on their behavior and make them aware of it, which can often work. Or, if it is truly harmless, simply ignore it. But there are people out there seething with insecurities who are veritable passive-aggressive warriors and can literally ruin your life.

Your best defense is to recognize such types before you become embroiled in a battle, and avoid them like the plague. The most obvious clues come from their track record—they have a reputation, you hear stories of past skirmishes, and so on. Take a look at the people around them, such as assistants—do they act with unusual caution and terror in their presence? Sometimes you are confused because you suspect sabotage or obstruction, but they present such a friendly or benign exterior. Discard the exterior and focus only on their actions and you will have a clearer picture. If they evade you and delay necessary action on something important to you, or make you feel guilty and leave you unsure why, or if they act harmfully but make it seem like an accident, you are most likely under a passive-aggressive attack. You have one of two options: either get out of their way and leave their presence, or return the attack with something equally indirect, signaling in some subtle way that messing with you will come with a price. This will often discourage them and make them find another victim. At all cost, avoid entangling yourself emotionally in their dramas and battles. They are masters at controlling the dynamic, and you will almost always lose in the end.

Developing social intelligence will not simply help you manage your relations with other people—acquiring it will also have an immensely beneficial effect on your ways of thinking and on your creativity in general. Look at the example of Benjamin Franklin. With people, he cultivated the ability to home in on the details that made them unique and to connect to *their* experience and motivations. He built up a high degree of sensitivity to the subtleties of human nature, avoiding the common tendency to lump people together. He made himself uncommonly patient and open-minded in his dealings with people from many different cultures and backgrounds. And this social intelligence of his became completely integrated into his intellectual labors—his sharp eye for detail in scientific work, his fluid manner of thinking and patient approach to tackling problems, and his uncanny way of getting into the minds and voices of the various characters he created in his writing.

Understand: the human brain is an interconnected organ, which is in turn interconnected with our bodies. Our brains developed in tandem with our expanding powers as social primates. The refinement of mirror neurons for the purpose of better communication with people became equally applied to other forms of reasoning. The ability to think inside objects and phenomena is an integral part of scientific creativity—from Faraday's feeling for electricity to the thought experiments of Einstein.

In general, the greatest Masters in history—Leonardo, Mozart, Darwin, and others—displayed a fluid, sensitive way of thinking that developed along with their expanding social intelligence. Those who are more rigidly intellectual and inward can go far in their fields, but their work often ends up lacking a creativity, an openness, and a sensitivity to detail that becomes more pronounced with time. In the end, the ability to think inside other people is no different from the intuitive feel Masters gain in relation to their field of study. To develop your intellectual powers at the expense of the social is to retard your own progress to mastery, and limit the full range of your creative powers.

STRATEGIES FOR ACQUIRING SOCIAL INTELLIGENCE

We must, however, acknowledge . . . that man with all his noble qualities, with sympathy which feels for the most debased, with benevolence which extends not only to other men but to the humblest living creature, with his god-like intellect which has penetrated into the movements and constitution of the solar system—with all these exalted powers—Man still bears in his bodily frame the indelible stamp of his lowly origin.

—CHARLES DARWIN

In dealing with people, you will often encounter particular problems that will tend to make you emotional and lock you into the Naïve Perspective. Such problems include unexpected political battles, superficial judgments of your character based on appearances, or petty-minded criticisms of your work. The following four essential strategies, developed by Masters past and present, will help you to meet these inevitable challenges and maintain the rational mind-set necessary for social intelligence.

1. Speak through your work

A. In 1846, a twenty-eight-year-old Hungarian doctor named Ignaz Semmelweis began work as an assistant in the obstetrics department of the University of Vienna, and almost from the beginning he was a man obsessed. The great disease that plagued the maternity wards in Europe at the time was that of childbed fever. At the hospital where young Semmelweis worked, one in six mothers died of the disease shortly after giving birth. When their bodies were dissected, doctors would discover the same whitish pus that smelled horrifically, and an unusual amount of putrid flesh. Seeing the effects of the disease on almost a daily basis, Semmelweis could think of nothing else. He would devote his time to solving the riddle of its origins.

At the time, the most common explanation for the cause of the disease revolved around the idea that airborne particles, ingested through the lungs, brought on the fever. But to Semmelweis, this made no sense. The epidemics of childbed fever did not seem to depend on weather, atmospheric conditions, or anything in the air. He noted, as did a few others, that the incidence was much higher among women who had had their babies delivered by a doctor as opposed to a midwife. Nobody could explain the reason for such a difference, and few seemed perturbed by this.

After much thinking and studying of the literature on the subject, Semmelweis came to the startling conclusion that it was the direct, hand-to-hand contact between doctor and patient that caused the disease—a revolutionary concept at the time. As he was formulating this theory, an event occurred that seemed to prove it conclusively: A leading doctor in the department had been accidently pricked in the finger by a knife while conducting an autopsy on a woman who had had childbed fever, and the doctor died within a few days of a massive infection. When they dissected his body, he had the same white pus and putrid flesh as the woman.

It now seemed clear to Semmelweis that in the autopsy room the physicians' hands became infected, and in examining the women and delivering the babies, they passed the disease into the women's blood through various open wounds. The physicians were literally poisoning their patients with childbed fever. If this was the cause, it would be simple to solve—doctors would have to wash and disinfect their hands before handling any patients, a practice no one followed in any hospital at the time. He instituted this practice in his ward, and the number of mortalities was instantly halved.

On the brink of perhaps a major discovery in science—the connection between germs and contagious disease—Semmelweis seemed to be on his way to an illustrious career. But there was one problem. The head of the department, Johann Klein, was a most conservative gentleman who wanted his doctors to adhere to strict medical orthodoxies established by previous practice. He believed that Semmelweis was an inexperienced doctor turned radical, who wanted to overturn the establishment and make a name for himself in the process.

Semmelweis argued with him incessantly over the subject of childbed fever, and when the young man finally promulgated his theory, Klein became furious. The implication was that doctors, including Klein himself, had been murdering their patients, and this was too much to take. (Klein himself ascribed the lower number of mortalities in Semmelweis's ward to a new ventilation system he had installed.) When in 1849 Semmelweis's assistantship was nearing its end, Klein refused to renew it, essentially leaving the young man without a job.

By now, however, Semmelweis had gained several key allies within the medical department, particularly among the younger set. They urged him to conduct some controlled experiments to strengthen his case, and then to write up his findings in a book that would spread his theory throughout Europe. Semmelweis, however, could not turn his attention away from the battle with Klein. Day by day his anger rose. Klein's adherence to a ridiculous and disproven theory about the fever was criminal. Such blindness to the truth made his blood boil. How could one man have such power in his field? Why should Semmelweis have to take so much of his time to do experiments and write books, when the truth was already so apparent? He decided instead to give a series of lectures on the subject, in which he could also express his scorn toward the closed-mindedness of so many in the profession.

Doctors from all over Europe attended Semmelweis's lectures. Although some remained skeptical, he won over more converts to his cause. His allies at the university pressed him to continue the momentum by doing more research and by writing a book on his theory. But within a few months of the lectures, and for reasons no one could understand, Semmelweis suddenly left town and returned to his native Budapest, where he found the university and medical position that had eluded him in Vienna. It seemed he could not endure another moment in the same city as Klein, and required complete freedom to operate on his own—even though Budapest was somewhat of a medical backwater at the time. His friends felt completely betrayed. They had staked their reputations on supporting him, and now he had left them in the lurch.

In the Budapest hospitals where he now worked, Semmelweis instituted his disinfection policies with such a rigor and tyrannical intensity that he cut the mortality rates but alienated almost all of the doctors and nurses he worked with. More and more people were turning against him. He had forced upon everyone his novel ideas on disinfection, but without books or the proper experiments to back them up it seemed that he was merely promoting himself, or obsessed with some fanciful idea of his own creation. The vehemence with which he insisted on its truth only called more attention to the lack of scholarly rigor to back it up. Doctors speculated about other possible causes for his success in cutting the incidence of childbed fever.

Finally in 1860, under pressure from colleagues yet again, he decided to write the book that would explain his theory in full. When he was finished with it, what should have been a relatively small volume had ballooned into a 600-page diatribe that was nearly impossible to read. It was hopelessly repetitive and convoluted. His arguments would turn into polemics as he enumerated the doctors who had opposed him and who were therefore murderers. During such passages his writing became almost apocalyptic.

Now his opponents came out of the woodwork. He had committed himself to writing but had done such a bad job that they could poke holes through his arguments, or merely call attention to his violent tone, which was self-damning enough. His former allies did not rally to his cause. They had come to hate him. His behavior became increasingly grandiose and erratic, until his employers at the hospital had to dismiss him. Virtually penniless and abandoned by almost everyone, he fell ill and died in 1865 at the age of forty-seven.

B. As a medical student at the University of Padua in Italy in 1602, the Englishman William Harvey (1578–1657) began to entertain doubts about the whole conception of the heart and its function as an organ. What he had been taught in school was based on the theories of the second-century Greek physician Galen, which stated that some blood was manufactured in the liver and some in the heart, and was transported by veins and absorbed by the body, supplying it with nutrition. According to the theory, this blood flowed ever so slowly from the liver and heart to the various parts of the body that needed it, but did not flow back—it was merely consumed. What troubled

Harvey was how much blood the body contained. How could it possibly produce and consume so much liquid?

Over the ensuing years his career prospered, culminating in his appointment as Royal Physician to King James I. During these years, he continued to ponder the same questions about blood and the role of the heart. And by the year 1618 he had come up with a theory: blood flows through the body not slowly but rapidly, the heart acting as a pump. Blood is not produced and consumed; instead it circulates continually.

The problem with this theory was that he had no direct means of verifying it. At the time, to open the heart of a human to study it would spell instant death. The only means available for research was vivisection of animals and the dissection of human corpses. Once the heart was opened in animals, however, it would behave erratically and pump far too rapidly. The mechanics of the heart were complex, and for Harvey they could only be deduced through controlled experiments—such as using elaborate tourniquets on human veins—and could never be observed directly with the eyes.

After many such controlled experiments Harvey felt certain he was correct, but he knew he would have to carefully strategize his next step. His theory was radical. It would overturn many concepts about anatomy that had been accepted as fact for centuries. He knew that to publish his results so far would only stir up enmity and create many enemies for himself. And so, thinking deeply about people's natural reluctance to accept new ideas, he decided to do the following: he delayed publishing the results of his findings, waiting until he had firmed up his theory and amassed more evidence. In the meantime, he involved his colleagues in further experiments and dissections, always eliciting their opinions. Increasing numbers of them were impressed and supported his new theory. Slowly winning most of them to his side, in 1627 he was appointed to the highest position within the College of Physicians, virtually ensuring him of employment for the rest of his life and freeing him from the worry that his theory would jeopardize his livelihood.

As the court physician, first to James I and then to Charles I who ascended the throne in 1625, Harvey worked diligently to gain royal favor. He played the court diplomat, and avoided aligning himself with any faction or becoming involved in any intrigues. He behaved humbly and with self-deprecation. He confided his discoveries to the king early on to gain his trust and support. In the country, there was a young man who had severely broken ribs on the left side of his chest, leaving a cavity through which one could see and touch the heart. He brought the young man to the king's court and used him to demonstrate to Charles the nature of the heart's contractions and expansions, and how the heart worked as a pump for the blood.

Finally, in 1628 he published the results of his years of work, opening the book with a very clever dedication to Charles I: "Most serene King! The animal's heart is the basis of its life, its chief member, the sun of its microcosm; on the heart all its activity depends, from the heart all its liveliness and strength arise. Equally is the King the basis of his kingdom, the sun of his microcosm, the heart of the state; from him all power arises and all grace stems."

The book naturally created a stir, particularly on the Continent, where Harvey was less known. Opposition primarily came from older physicians who could not reconcile themselves with a theory that so completely overturned their idea of anatomy. To the numerous publications that came out to discredit his ideas, Harvey remained mostly silent. An occasional attack from eminent physicians would cause him to write personal letters in which he very politely and yet thoroughly refuted their ideas.

As he had foreseen, with the strength of his position within the medical profession and the court, and with the great amount of evidence he had accumulated over the years, which was clearly outlined in his book, his theory slowly gained acceptance. By the time of Harvey's death in 1657, his work had become an accepted part of medical doctrine and practice. As his friend Thomas Hobbes would write: "[Harvey was] the only man I know, who, conquering envy, hath established a new doctrine in his life-time."

The common historical accounts of Semmelweis and Harvey reveal our tendency to ignore the critical role of social intelligence in all fields, including the sciences. For instance, most versions of the Semmelweis story emphasize the tragic shortsightedness of men like Klein who pushed the noble-minded young Hungarian over the edge. With Harvey, they emphasize his theoretical brilliance as the singular cause of his success. But in both cases, social intelligence played a key role. Semmelweis completely ignored its necessity; such considerations annoyed him; all that mattered was the truth. But in his zeal, he unnecessarily alienated Klein, who had faced other disagreements with students before but never to such a degree. Through constant arguing, Semmelweis had pushed Klein to the point of having to fire him, and thus lost an important position within the university from which he could spread his ideas. Consumed with his battle with Klein, he failed to express his theory in a clear and reasonable form, displaying a monumental disregard for the importance of persuading others. If he had merely devoted his time to making his case in writing, he would have saved far more lives in the long run.

Harvey's success, on the other hand, was greatly due to his social agility. He understood that even a scientist must play the courtier. He involved others in his work, making them emotionally attached to his theory. He published his results in a thoughtful, well-reasoned, and easy-to-read book. And then he quietly allowed his book to speak for itself, knowing that by asserting himself after its publication, he would merely call attention to the person and not the work. He did not give fuel to the foolishness of others by engaging in petty battles, and any opposition to his theories withered away on its own.

Understand: your work is the single greatest means at your disposal for expressing your social intelligence. By being efficient and detail oriented in what you do, you *demonstrate* that you are thinking of the group at large and advancing its cause. By making what you write or present clear and easy to follow, you *show* your care for the audience or public at large. By involving other people in your projects and gracefully accepting their feedback, you *reveal* your comfort with the group dynamic. Work that is solid also protects you from the political conniving and malevolence of others—it is hard to argue with the results you produce. If you are experiencing the pressures of political maneuvering within the group, do not lose your head and become consumed with all of the pettiness. By remaining focused and speaking socially through your work, you will both continue to raise your skill level *and* stand out among all the others who make a lot of noise but produce nothing.

2. Craft the appropriate persona

From early on in life, Teresita Fernández (b. 1968) had the feeling that she was watching the world around her from a distance, like a voyeur. As a young girl growing up in Miami, Florida, she would observe the adults around her, eavesdropping on their conversations, trying to decode the secrets of their strange world. As she got older, she applied her observational skills to her classmates. In high school, people were expected to fit into one of the various cliques. She could see clearly the rules and conventions that went into being a part of these groups, and the kinds of behavior that were considered correct. She felt alienated from all of these different cliques, and so she remained on the outside.

She had a similar experience in relation to Miami itself. Although she had an affinity with the Cuban culture that was part of her own background as a first generation Cuban-American, she could not identify with the happy beach lifestyle that prevailed there. There was something more somber and edgier to her spirit. All of this accentuated her sense of being an outsider, a floater that did not fit in anywhere. There were other floaters in school, and they tended to drift into theater or the art scene—places where it was safer to be unconventional. Teresita had always liked making things with her hands, and so she began to take art classes. But the art she produced in high school did not seem to connect to that grittier side of her character. It came too easily; her work was too glib and superficial; something was lacking.

In 1986, still uncertain of her direction in life, she entered Florida International University, in Miami. Following her high school inclinations, she took a sculpture class. But working in clay, with its softness and ease of manipulation, gave her the same feeling she'd had in high school of making things that were merely artificial and pretty. Then one day, spending time in the sculpture building, she noticed some artists working in metal, crafting large-scale pieces. These sheets of steel had a visceral effect upon her unlike any other artwork she had seen, and she felt in some way that this was the material that had been meant for her all along. It was gray and heavy and resistant, requiring great effort to shape it. The properties of steel corresponded to the sense of resiliency and power that she had always felt inside herself, despite her petite size, and that she had always wanted to express.

And so she began to apply herself feverishly to her newfound medium. To work in metal required firing up the foundry and using acetylene torches. The tropical heat of Miami could make such labor intensely uncomfortable during the daytime hours, so she began to work on her sculptures exclusively at night. This led to an unusual schedule—starting at nine, working until two or three in the morning, then sleeping through a good part of the next day. Besides the cooler air, working at night had other advantages—with few people around, the studio was quite peaceful and conducive to serious work. She could focus deeply. She could experiment with her pieces, make mistakes that no one would see. She could be fearless and take chances.

Slowly Fernández began to take command of the medium, and in making her sculptures, she felt like she was forging and transforming herself. She was interested in creating pieces that were large and impressive, but to make such work she had to devise her own method. She would design the pieces on paper, but would work on them in smaller sections that she could manage by herself. Then, in the quiet of her studio, she would assemble the sculptures. Soon her pieces began to be displayed within the department and on campus.

Almost everyone was quite impressed by her work. Standing in the bright Miami sunshine, her enormous steel sculptures conveyed that sense of power she had always felt within her. But there was another response to her pieces that surprised her. Because few people had seen her at work, it appeared that these sculptures flowed out of her effortlessly—as if she had some unusual gift. This drew attention to her personality. Sculpture was a largely male domain that tended to attract the most macho male artists. As she was one of the few female artists working in heavy steel, people naturally projected onto her all kinds of preconceptions and fantasies. The discrepancy between her slight, feminine appearance and her large-scale, imposing works was quite glaring, and people would wonder how she managed to make such work, and who she really was. Intrigued by her character, and also by the way her beautifully crafted sculptures seemed to appear out of nowhere, they saw her as alluringly mysterious, a mix of hard and soft qualities, an anomaly, a magician with metal.

With all of this scrutiny, Fernández suddenly became aware that she was no longer a voyeur, watching others from a distance, but was at the center of attention. The art world felt right to her. For the first time in her life she had the sensation of fitting in, and she wanted to hold on to this interest that others had in her work. Now that she was thrust into a more public position, it would be natural for her to want to talk about herself and her experiences, but she intuited that it would be a mistake to deflate the powerful effect her work had on others by suddenly revealing to everyone how many hours she had applied herself to these sculptures, and how they were really the product of intense labor and discipline. Sometimes, she reasoned, what you do not reveal to people is all the more eloquent and powerful. She decided to go along with the image that others had of her and her work. She would create an air of mystery around her, making sure not to talk about her process, keeping details of her life hidden, and allowing people to project onto her their own fantasies.

As she progressed in her career, however, something about the persona she had created in her university years no longer felt appropriate. She noted an element in her public personality that could play against her—if she were not careful, people would judge her based on her physical appearance as an attractive young woman. They would not see her as a serious artist. Her elusiveness might seem like a cover for a lack of intelligence, as if she were merely feeling her way through things, and not on a par with the heavy-hitting intellectuals in the field. It was a prejudice female artists had to deal with. Any hint of being wishy-washy or inarticulate when it came to talking about her work carried the danger of feeding the preconception that she was frivolous, merely dabbling in the arts. And so she slowly developed a new style that suited her well—she would be assertive and speak with authority about the content of her work, while still enveloping her work process in mystery. She was not weak or vulnerable, but in clear command of the subject. If male artists needed to seem serious and articulate, as a woman she would have to appear even more so. Her assertive tone was always dignified and respectful, but she made it clear she was no lightweight.

Over the years, as Teresita Fernández became a world-renowned conceptual artist working in all types of materials, she continued to play with her appearance and make it fit her changing circumstances. The stereotype for artists is that they are disorganized and only interested in what is happening in the art world. She would play against these expectations. She transformed herself into an eloquent lecturer, exposing her work and ideas to the public at large. Audiences would ponder and be intrigued by the discrepancy between her pleasant, composed surface and the complex, challenging content of her discourse. She became versed in many fields outside art, combining these interests in her work, and in the process exposed herself to a wide range of people outside the art world. She taught herself to mingle equally well with the workers mining the graphite for her pieces as with gallery dealers—a kind of courtier flexibility that made her life as an artist much easier and made it impossible for her to be typecast. In essence, her public persona became another form of art—a material she could cast and transform according to her needs and desires.

It is not generally acknowledged or discussed, but the personality we project to the world plays a substantial role in our success and in our ascension to mastery. Look at the case of Teresita Fernández. If she had merely kept to herself and focused exclusively on her work, she would have found herself defined by others in a way that would have hindered her progress. If, after her initial success, she had boasted about all the hours of practice that went into training herself in metalwork, people would have seen her as a mere laborer and craftsman. They would have inevitably pegged her as the female artist who was using metal as a gimmick to promote herself and get attention. They would have found weaknesses in her character to exploit. The public arena, in art or any endeavor, can be ruthless that way. Able to look at herself and at the art world with a level of detachment, Fernández intuited the power she could possess by being conscious of her persona and taking control of the appearance dynamic.

Understand: people will tend to judge you based on your outward appearance. If you are not careful and simply assume that it is best to be yourself, they will begin to ascribe to you all kinds of qualities that have little to do with who you are but correspond to what they want to see. All of this can confuse you, make you feel insecure, and consume your attention. Internalizing their judgments, you will find it hard to focus on your work. Your only protection is to turn this dynamic around by consciously molding these appearances, creating the image that suits you, and controlling people's judgments. At times you will find it appropriate to stand back and create some mystery around you, heightening your presence. At other times you will want to be more direct and impose a more specific appearance. In general, you never settle on one image or give people the power to completely figure you out. You are always one step ahead of the public.

You must see the creation of a persona as a key element in social intelligence, not something evil or demonic. We all wear masks in the social arena, playing different roles to suit the different environments we pass through. You are simply becoming more conscious of the process. Think of it as theater. By creating a persona that is mysterious, intriguing, and masterful, you are playing to the public, giving them something compelling and pleasurable to witness. You are allowing them to project their fantasies onto you, or directing their attention to other theatrical qualities. In your private life, you can let the mask fall. In this diverse, multicultural world, it is best that you learn how to mingle and blend into all types of environments, giving yourself maximum flexibility. You must take pleasure in creating these personas—it will make you a better performer on the public stage.

3. See yourself as others see you

Growing up with autism, Temple Grandin (see chapter 1, pages 43–45, for more on this) had much to overcome in life, but by the end of high school she had managed to transform herself—through keen desire and discipline—into a gifted student with a promising future in the sciences. She understood that her greatest weakness was in the social arena. With animals, she had almost telepathic powers to read their moods and desires, but with humans it was the opposite. People were too tricky for her; they often seemed to communicate with one another through subtle, nonverbal cues—for instance, falling into patterns of laughter in a group, according to some interpersonal rhythm she could not fathom. She felt as if she were an alien, watching these strange creatures interact.

It seemed to her that there was nothing she could do about her awkwardness with people. What she could control, however, was her own work. She decided she would make herself so efficient in whatever job she had that her social handicap would not matter. But after graduating college with a degree in animal behavior and entering the work world as a consultant in the design of feedlots and cattle handling facilities, she realized, through a series of mistakes on her part, that this was completely unrealistic.

On one occasion, Grandin had been hired by the manager of a plant to improve its overall design. She did an excellent job, but soon she began to notice that the machinery was constantly breaking down, as if it were the fault of her design. She knew that the malfunctioning could not be because of any flaws in her work, and with further investigation she discovered that the machinery had problems only when a certain man was working in the room. The only possible conclusion was that he was sabotaging the equipment to make her look bad. This made no sense to her—why would he deliberately work against the interests of the company that employed him? This was not a design problem she could solve intellectually. She simply had to give up and leave the job.

On another occasion, a plant engineer had hired her to fix a particular problem, but after a few weeks on the job she noticed that there were other parts of the factory that were very poorly designed and clearly dangerous. She wrote to the president of the company to point this out. Her tone in the letter was a bit brusque, but she was annoyed that people could be so blind to such design issues. A few days later she was fired. Although no explanation was given, it was clear that her letter to the president must have been the cause.

As she mulled over these incidents, and other similar ones that had marred her career, she felt that the source of the problem had to be herself. She had known for years that she often did things that rubbed people the wrong way, and that they avoided her for that reason. In the past she had tried to go about her life ignoring this painful reality, but now her social deficiencies were threatening her ability to make a living.

Ever since she was a child, Grandin had the peculiar ability to see herself from the outside, as if she were looking at another person. It was more of a sensation that would come and go, but as an adult she realized she could use this gift for practical effect, by looking at her past mistakes as if watching another person in action.

For instance, in the case of the man who had sabotaged the machinery, she could clearly recall how she had barely interacted with him and the other engineers, and how she had made a point of doing everything herself. She could see in her mind the meetings in which she had presented her design ideas with rigorous logic and not opened them up for discussion. In the case of the letter to the president, she could recall how she had bluntly criticized people in front of their peers and had made no attempt to interact with the man who had hired her. Visualizing these moments with such clarity, she could finally understand the problem—she was making her coworkers feel insecure, useless, and inferior. She had injured their male egos and had paid a price.

Her realization of what had gone wrong did not stem from empathy as it might have for other people—it was an intellectual exercise, like solving a puzzle or a design problem. But because her emotions were not so deeply involved, it was easier to go through the process and make the necessary corrections. In the future, she would discuss her ideas with engineers, involve them as much as possible in her work, and never directly criticize people for anything. She would practice this in every subsequent job until it became second nature.

Slowly, developing social intelligence in her own way, Temple ironed out much of her awkwardness and her career prospered. In the 1990s, as she grew famous, she was increasingly invited to give talks—initially about her experiences as a professional who had overcome autism, and later as an expert on animal behavior.

In giving these talks, she had imagined that they had gone quite well. They were full of information and appropriate slides to illustrate her ideas.

But after a few such lectures she was handed the evaluations from the audience, and what she read was shocking. People complained that she made no eye contact, read her talk mechanically from her notes, and did not engage with the audience, to the point of rudeness. The audience had the impression that she was simply repeating the same talk over and over, with the same slides, as if she were a machine.

Strangely enough, none of this bothered Temple. In fact, the idea of these evaluations excited her. They gave her a clear and realistic picture of herself as others saw her, and that is all she ever needed for self-correction. She pursued this process with great zeal, determined to transform herself into a skilled lecturer. As enough evaluations came in, she pored over them, looking for patterns and criticisms that made sense. Working from this feedback, she taught herself to mix in anecdotes and even jokes, and to make her slides not so logical and tight. She shortened the length of her talks, trained herself to speak without notes, and made sure to take as many questions as the audience wanted to ask at the end.

For those who had seen her initial efforts and then attended her lectures years later, it was hard to believe she was the same person. She was now an entertaining and engaging speaker, one who could hold the attention of an audience better than most. They could not imagine how this had come about, which made her transformation seem all the more miraculous.

Almost all of us have social flaws of some sort, ranging from the relatively harmless to those that can get us in trouble. Perhaps it could be that we talk too much, or are too honest in our criticisms of people, or take offense too easily when others do not respond positively to our ideas. If we repeat instances of such behavior often enough, we tend to offend people without ever really knowing why. The reason for this is twofold: first, we are quick to discern the mistakes and defects of others, but when it comes to ourselves we are generally too emotional and insecure to look squarely at our own. Second, people rarely tell us the truth about what it is that we do wrong. They are afraid to cause conflict or to be viewed as mean-spirited. And so it becomes very difficult for us to perceive our flaws, let alone correct them.

We sometimes have the experience of doing work that we consider to be quite brilliant, and then are rather shocked when we receive feedback from others who do not see it the same way at all. In such moments we are made aware of the discrepancy between our emotional and subjective relationship to our own work, and the response of others who view it with complete detachment, capable of pointing out flaws we could never see. The same discrepancy, however, exists on the social level. People see our behavior from the outside, and their view of us is never what we imagine it to be. To have the power to see ourselves through the eyes of others would be of immense benefit to our social intelligence. We could begin to correct the flaws that offend, to see the role that we play in creating any kind of negative dynamic, and to have a more realistic assessment of who we are.

To see ourselves objectively, we must follow the example of Temple Grandin. We can begin this process by looking at negative events in our past—people sabotaging our work, bosses firing us for no logical reason, nasty personal battles with colleagues. It is best to start with events that are at least several months old, and thus not so emotionally charged. In dissecting these occurrences, we must focus on what *we* did that either triggered or worsened the dynamic. In looking at several such incidents, we might begin to see a pattern that indicates a particular flaw in our character. Seeing these events from the perspective of the other people involved will loosen the lock our emotions have on our self-image, and help us understand the role we play in our own mistakes. We can also elicit opinions from those we trust about our behavior, making certain to first reassure them that we want their criticisms. Slowly, in this way, we can develop increasing self-detachment, which will yield us the other half of social intelligence—the ability to see ourselves as we really are.

4. Suffer fools gladly

In 1775, the twenty-six-year-old German poet and novelist Johann Wolfgang Goethe (later von Goethe) was invited to spend some time at the court of Weimar by its eighteen-year-old Duke Karl August. The duke's family had been trying to transform the isolated and less renowned duchy of Weimar into a literary center, and the addition of Goethe to their court would be a great coup. Shortly after his arrival, the duke offered him a prominent position in his cabinet and the role of personal adviser, and so Goethe decided to stay. The poet saw this as a way to broaden his experience in the world and perhaps apply some enlightened ideas to the government of Weimar.

Goethe came from a solid middle-class background, and had never really spent much time around nobility. Now, as a prized member of the duke's court, he was to have his apprenticeship in aristocratic manners. After only a few short months, however, he found court life quite unbearable. The lives of the courtiers revolved around rituals of card games, shooting parties, and the exchanging of endless bits of gossip. A passing remark by Herr X, or the failure of Frau Y to show up at a soirée, would be blown up into something of great importance, and courtiers would strain to interpret the meaning of it. After attending the theater they would chat endlessly about who had shown up accompanied by whom, or dissect the look of the new actress on the scene, but they would never discuss the play itself.

In conversation, if Goethe dared to discuss some reform he was considering, suddenly a courtier would get all up in arms about what this might mean for a particular minister, and how it could jeopardize his position within the court, and Goethe's idea would get lost in the ensuing heated dialog. Even though he was the author of the most famous novel of the day, *The Sorrows of Young Werther*, nobody seemed particularly interested in his opinions. They found it more interesting to tell the celebrated novelist their own ideas and to see his reaction. In the end, their interests seemed constricted to the claustrophobic court and its intrigues.

Goethe felt trapped—he had accepted a position with the duke and took it most seriously, but he found it hard to tolerate the social life to which he was now condemned. As a confirmed realist in life, however, he found it useless to complain about what he could not change. And so, accepting his fellow courtiers as his companions for the next few years, Goethe devised a strategy, making a virtue out of necessity: He would talk very little, rarely venturing an opinion on anything. He would get his interlocutors to go on and on and about this or that subject. He would wear a pleasant mask as he listened, but inwardly he would observe them as if they were figures in a stage play. They would reveal to him their secrets, their petty dramas, and their inane ideas, and all the while he would smile and always take their side.

What the courtiers did not realize was that they were supplying him with endless material—for characters, bits of dialogue, and stories of folly that would fill the plays and novels he was to write in the future. In this way he transformed his social frustrations into a most productive and pleasant game.

The great Austrian-American film director Josef von Sternberg (1894–1969) had risen from studio errand boy to become one of the most successful directors in Hollywood during the 1920s and '30s. He developed along the way a particular philosophy that would serve him well throughout his directorial career, which would last into the 1950s: all that mattered was the final product. His role was to get everyone on the same page and guide the production according to the vision he had, employing whatever means necessary to get the results he wanted. And the greatest impediment to realizing his vision came inevitably from the actors. They thought first and foremost of their careers. The film as a whole mattered less than the attention they received for their part. This would make them try to steal the limelight, and in the process they would alter the quality of the film. With such actors, von Sternberg would have to find a way to trick or beguile them into doing his bidding.

In 1930, von Sternberg was invited to Berlin to direct what would be his most famous film, *The Blue Angel*, which would feature the world-renowned actor Emil Jannings. In looking for the female lead for the film, von Sternberg discovered a relatively unknown German actress named Marlene Dietrich, whom he would go on to direct in seven feature films, singlehandedly transforming her into a star. Von Sternberg had worked with Jannings before and knew that the actor was an impossibly foolish person. Jannings did everything he could to disrupt the flow of the production. He took as a personal affront any attempt by the director to direct him. His whole method was to goad the director into useless battles and wear him down until he relented and let Jannings do as he wished.

Von Sternberg was prepared for all of this and went to war in his own way. He steeled himself against Jannings's childish games. Jannings demanded that the director show up every morning in his dressing room to reassure the actor of his undying love and admiration for his work—von Sternberg did this without complaint. He asked that the director take him to lunch every day and listen to his ideas about the film—von Sternberg indulged him in this, listening patiently to Jannings's horrible suggestions. If von Sternberg showed attention to any other actor, Jannings would throw a jealous fit, and von Sternberg would have to act the role of the contrite spouse. Letting him have his way on these petty matters, he took much of the bite out of Jannings's strategy. On the set, he would not become entangled in any battles. But since time was of the essence, he would inevitably have to trick the actor into doing what he wanted.

When for some unknown reason Jannings refused to pass through a doorway and make his entrance into a scene, von Sternberg set up the hottest light available to boil the back of his neck every time Jannings stood there, forcing him to pass through. When Jannings declaimed his first scene in the most ridiculously elevated German, von Sternberg congratulated him for his fine tone and said he would be the only person in the film to talk like that, which would make him stand out and look bad, but so be it. Jannings quickly dropped the haughty accent. Whenever he went into a pout and remained in his room, von Sternberg would get the word passed to him that the director was lavishing attention on Marlene Dietrich, which would promptly make the jealous actor hurry to the set to compete for attention. Scene by scene, von Sternberg maneuvered him into the position he desired, managing to extract out of Jannings perhaps the greatest performance of his career.

As previously discussed in chapter 2 (page 72), Daniel Everett and his family moved to the heart of the Amazon in 1977, to live among people known as the Pirahã. Everett and his wife were missionaries, and their task was to learn the Pirahã language—which was then considered the hardest in the world to decipher—and to translate the Bible into their indigenous tongue.

Slowly, Everett made progress, using the various devices he had been taught in his training in linguistics.

He had studied in depth the works of the great MIT linguist Noam Chomsky, who advocated the idea that all languages are essentially related because grammar itself is hardwired into the human brain, and is part of our genetic code. This would mean that by their nature all languages share the same features. Convinced that Chomsky was correct, Everett worked hard to find these universal features in Pirahã. Over the years of studying it, however, he began to find many exceptions to Chomsky's theory, and this troubled him.

After much thought, Everett came to the conclusion that the Pirahã language reflected many peculiarities of their life in the jungle. He determined, for instance, that their culture placed a supreme value on "immediacy of experience"—what was not before their eyes did not exist, and therefore there were almost no words or concepts for things outside immediate experience. In elaborating this concept, he theorized that the basic features of all languages are not simply genetic in origin and universal, but that each language has elements that reflect the uniqueness of its culture. Culture plays a larger role than we might imagine in how we think and communicate.

In 2005 he finally felt ready to make all of this public, and had an article published in an anthropology journal that expressed these revolutionary ideas. He expected that his findings might stir up some animated discussion, but he was not prepared at all for what would ensue.

People at MIT (linguists and graduate students) associated with Chomsky began to hound Everett. When he gave a talk at an important symposium at the University of Cambridge about his findings, some of these linguists flew over to attend it. They peppered him with questions meant to poke holes in his ideas and publicly embarrass him. Not ready for this, Everett fumbled and did not handle it well. This continue with subsequent lectures. They zeroed in on any kind of inconsistency in his talk or his writings, and used these inconsistencies to discredit his overall idea. Some of their attacks on him became personal—they publicly called him a charlatan, and questioned his motives. Even Chomsky himself implied that Everett was out for fame and money.

When Everett published his first book, *Don't Sleep, There are Snakes*, some of these linguists wrote letters to critics who were going to review it, trying to dissuade them from even discussing his material—it was too far below academic standards, they claimed. They went so far as to put pressure on National Public Radio, which was about to do a large segment on Everett. The show was canceled.

At first Everett could not help but become emotional. What his detractors were bringing up in their arguments did not discredit his theory, but merely revealed some possible weak points. They seemed less interested in the truth and more concerned with making him look bad. Quickly, however, he moved past this emotional stage and began to use these attacks for his own purpose—they forced him to make sure everything he wrote was airtight; they made him rethink and strengthen his arguments. He could hear their possible criticisms in his head, and he addressed them one by one in his subsequent writings. This made him a better writer and thinker, and the controversy they stirred up only increased the sales of *Don't Sleep, There are Snakes*, winning many converts to his argument in the process. In the end, he came to welcome the attacks of his enemies for how much they had improved his work and toughened him up.

In the course of your life you will be continually encountering fools. There are simply too many to avoid. We can classify people as fools by the following rubric: when it comes to practical life, what should matter is getting long-term results, and getting the work done in as efficient and creative a manner as possible. That should be the supreme value that guides people's actions. But fools carry with them a different scale of values. They place more importance on short-term matters—grabbing immediate money, getting attention from the public or media, and looking good. They are ruled by their ego and insecurities. They tend to enjoy drama and political intrigue for their own sake. When they criticize, they always emphasize matters that are irrelevant to the overall picture or argument. They are more interested in their career and position than in the truth. You can distinguish them by how little they get done, or by how hard they make it for others to get results. They lack a certain common sense, getting worked up about things that are not really important while ignoring problems that will spell doom in the long term.

The natural tendency with fools is to lower yourself to their level. They annoy you, get under your skin, and draw you into a battle. In the process, you feel petty and confused. You lose a sense of what is really important. You can't win an argument or get them to see your side or change their behavior, because rationality and results don't matter to them. You simply waste valuable time and emotional energy.

In dealing with fools you must adopt the following philosophy: they are simply a part of life, like rocks or furniture. All of us have foolish sides, moments in which we lose our heads and think more of our ego or short-term goals. It is human nature. Seeing this foolishness within you, you can then accept it in others. This will allow you to smile at their antics, to tolerate their presence as you would a silly child, and to avoid the madness of trying to change them. It is all part of the human comedy, and it is nothing to get upset about or lose sleep over. This attitude—"Suffer Fools Gladly"—should be forged in your Apprenticeship Phase, during which you are almost certainly going to encounter this type. If they are causing you trouble, you must neutralize the harm they do by keeping a steady eye on your goals and what is important, and ignoring them if you can. The height of wisdom, however, is to take this even further and to actually exploit their foolishness—using them for material for your work, as examples of things to avoid, or by looking for ways to turn their actions to your advantage. In this way, their foolishness plays into your hands, helping you achieve the kind of practical results they seem to disdain.

REVERSAL

While studying for his PhD at Harvard University in Computer Science, Paul Graham (b. 1964) discovered something about himself: he had a profound distaste for any kind of politicking or social maneuvering. (For more on Graham, see pages 87–89.) He was not good at it, and it irritated him to no end to be dragged into situations in which others behaved manipulatively. His brief encounter with politics within the department convinced him he was not cut out for a life in academia. This lesson became strengthened a few years later when he went to work for a software company. Almost everything they did was irrational—firing the original tech people, making a salesperson the head of the company, creating too long a time between releases of new products. All of these bad choices came about because in a group, politics and ego often trump sound decision making.

Unable to tolerate this, he came up with his own solution: as much as possible, he would avoid any environment that involved politicking. This meant sticking to doing startups on the smallest scale—a constraint that made him disciplined and creative. Later, when he founded *Y Combinator*, a kind of apprenticeship system for tech startups, he could not prevent the company from growing in size—it was too successful. His solution was twofold: One, he had his wife and partner in the company, Jessica Livingston, handle all of the tricky social situations, since she possessed a high level of social intelligence. Two, he maintained a very loose, non-bureaucratic structure to the company.

If, like Graham, you simply do not have the patience that is required for managing and mastering the more subtle and manipulative sides of human nature, then your best answer is to keep yourself away from those situations as best as possible. This will rule out working in groups larger than a handful of people—above a certain number, political considerations inevitably rise to the surface. This means working for yourself or on very small startups.

Even still, it is generally wise to try to gain the rudiments of social intelligence—to be able to read and recognize the sharks, and to charm and disarm difficult people. The reason is that no matter how hard you might try to avoid situations that call for such knowledge, the world is one large teeming court of intrigue, and it will inevitably pull you in. Your conscious attempt to opt out of the system will retard your apprenticeship in social intelligence and can make you vulnerable to the worst forms of naïveté, with all of the disasters that are likely to ensue.

It is a great folly to hope that other men will harmonize with us; I have never hoped this. I have always regarded each man as an independent individual, whom I endeavored to understand with all his peculiarities, but from whom I desired no further sympathy. In this way have I been enabled to converse with every man, and thus alone is produced the knowledge of various characters and the dexterity necessary for the conduct of life.

—JOHANN WOLFGANG VON GOETHE

V

AWAKEN THE DIMENSIONAL MIND: THE CREATIVE-ACTIVE

As you accumulate more skills and internalize the rules that govern your field, your mind will want to become more active, seeking to use this knowledge in ways that are more suited to your inclinations. What will impede this natural creative dynamic from flourishing is not a lack of talent, but your attitude. Feeling anxious and insecure, you will tend to turn conservative with your knowledge, preferring to fit into the group and sticking to the procedures you have learned. Instead, you must force yourself in the opposite direction. As you emerge from your apprenticeship, you must become increasingly bold. Instead of feeling complacent about what you know, you must expand your knowledge to related fields, giving your mind fuel to make new associations between different ideas. You must experiment and look at problems from all possible angles. As your thinking grows more fluid your mind will become increasingly dimensional, seeing more and more aspects of reality. In the end, you will turn against the very rules you have internalized, shaping and reforming them to suit your spirit. Such originality will bring you to the heights of power.

THE SECOND TRANSFORMATION

From the moment he was born, Wolfgang Amadeus Mozart (1756–91) was surrounded by music. His father, Leopold, was a violinist and composer in the court of Salzburg, Austria, as well as a music instructor. All during the day, Wolfgang would hear Leopold and his students practicing in the house. In 1759, his seven-year-old sister Maria Anna began taking piano lessons from their father. She showed great promise and practiced at all hours. Wolfgang, enchanted by the simple melodies that she played, began to hum along to the music; he would sometimes sit at the family's harpsichord and try to imitate what his sister had played. Leopold could soon detect something unusual in his son. For a three-year-old, the child had a remarkable memory for melody and an impeccable sense of rhythm, all without having had any instruction.

Although he had never attempted to teach someone so young, Leopold decided to begin teaching piano to Wolfgang when he turned four, and after only a few sessions he realized the boy had other interesting qualities. Wolfgang listened more deeply than other students, his mind and body completely absorbed in the music. With such intensity of focus, he learned more quickly than other children. Once when he was five years old, he stole a rather complicated exercise meant for Maria Anna, and within thirty minutes he could play it with ease. He had heard Maria Anna practice the piece, and remembering it vividly, the moment he saw the notes on the page he could rapidly reproduce the music.

This remarkable focus had its roots in something that Leopold saw almost from the beginning—the boy had an intense love of music itself. His eyes would light up with excitement the moment Leopold laid out a new

challenging piece for him to conquer. If the piece was new and hard to figure out, he would attack it day and night with such tenacity that it would
soon become part of his repertoire. At night, his parents would have to force
him to stop practicing and send him to bed. This love of practice only seemed
to increase with the years. When it came time to play with other children, he
would find a way to transform a simple game into something that involved
music. His favorite game, however, was to take some piece he had been playing and improvise on it, giving it a personal flair that was quite charming
and inventive.

From his earliest years, Wolfgang was exceptionally emotional and sensitive. His moods would swing wildly—he would be petulant one moment,
highly affectionate the next. He had a perpetually anxious look on his face
that would only disappear when he sat down at the piano; then he was in
his element, losing himself in the music.

One day in 1762, as Leopold Mozart heard his two children playing a
piece for two pianos, an idea came to him. His daughter Maria Anna was a
very talented piano player in her own right, and Wolfgang was a veritable
marvel. Together, they were like precious toys. They had a natural charisma,
and Wolfgang had a showman's flair. As a mere court musician, Leopold's
income was rather limited, but he could see the potential for making a fortune through his children. And so, thinking this through, he decided to take
his family on a grand tour of the capitals of Europe, playing before royal
courts and the public and charging money for the entertainment. To add to
the spectacle, he dressed the children up—Maria Anna as a princess, and
Wolfgang as a court minister, complete with wig, elaborate waistcoat, and a
sword dangling from his belt.

They began in Vienna, where the children charmed the Austrian emperor and empress. They then spent months in Paris, where they played for
the royal court and Wolfgang bounced on the knee of the delighted King
Louis XV. They continued to London where they ended up staying for over
a year, playing before all kinds of large crowds. And while the sight of the
two children in their costumes charmed audiences enough, Wolfgang's
playing astounded them. He had developed numerous parlor tricks, stage-
managed by his father. He would play a minuet on a keyboard that was
hidden from his view by a cloth, using only one finger. He would deftly
sight-read the latest composition by a famous composer. He would play his
own compositions—it was impressive to hear a sonata composed by a seven-
year-old, no matter how simple it was. Most marvelous of all, Wolfgang
could play at an incredible speed, his tiny fingers flying over the keyboard.

As the tour continued, an amusing pattern began to develop. The family would be invited to do some sightseeing, tour the countryside, or attend
a soirée, while Wolfgang would find some excuse to stay behind—a feigned

illness or complaints of exhaustion—and would devote his time instead to music. His favorite ploy in this vein was to attach himself to the most illustrious composers in the particular court they were visiting. In London, for instance, he managed to charm the great composer Johann Christian Bach, son of Johann Sebastian Bach. When the family was invited out on a jaunt, he declined to join them with the perfect excuse—he had already engaged Bach to give him lessons in composition.

The education he received in this fashion, from all of the composers he met, went far beyond anything any child could hope to receive. Although some argued that it was a waste of childhood for someone so young to be so single-minded, Wolfgang felt such an ardent love for music and the constant challenges it presented that in the end he derived much greater pleasure from his obsession than any amusement or game could provide.

The tour was a great financial success, but it nearly ended in tragedy. In Holland in 1766, as the family was beginning its return journey, Wolfgang fell ill with a powerful fever. Losing weight rapidly, he drifted in and out of consciousness, and at one point appeared near death. But miraculously, the fever passed, and over the course of several months he slowly recovered. The experience, however, altered him. From that moment on, he had a constant feeling of melancholy and a foreboding that he would die young.

The Mozart family had come now to depend on the money that the children had generated through the tour, but as the years went by the invitations began to dry up. The novelty had worn off, and the children no longer seemed so young and precious. Desperate to generate money, Leopold came up with a different scheme. His son was turning into a serious composer, with the ability to compose in different genres. What was needed was to secure for him a stable position as a court composer, and attract commissions for concertos and symphonies. With this goal in mind, in 1770 father and son embarked on series of tours of Italy, then the center of all things musical in Europe.

The trip went well. Wolfgang performed his magic on the piano before all of the major courts in Italy. He gained acclaim for his symphonies and concert pieces—they were quite impressive for a teenager. He mingled yet again with the most celebrated composers of his time, intensifying the musical knowledge he had gained on his previous tours. In addition, he rediscovered his greatest passion in music—the opera. As a child he had always had the feeling that he was destined to compose great operas. In Italy he saw the finest productions and realized the source of his fascination—it was the drama translated into pure music, the nearly limitless potential of the human voice to express the full range of emotion, and the overall spectacle. He had an almost primal attraction to any kind of theater. But despite all of the attention and inspiration he received, after nearly three years of visiting the various courts in Italy, he was not offered a position or a commission that was worthy of his talents. And so, in 1773, father and son returned to Salzburg.

After some delicate negotiation with the archbishop of Salzburg, Leopold finally managed to secure for his son a relatively lucrative position as court musician and composer. And by all appearances the arrangement was good: not having to worry about money, Wolfgang would have endless time to work on composing. But almost from the beginning Wolfgang felt uncomfortable and restless. He had spent almost half of his youth traveling throughout Europe, mingling with the leading minds in music, and listening to the most renowned orchestras, and now he was relegated to life in provincial Salzburg, isolated from the European centers of music, in a city that had no theater or opera tradition.

More troubling, however, was the mounting frustration he felt as a composer. For as long as he could remember, his head was continuously filled with music, but it was always the music of other people. He knew that his own pieces were simply clever imitations and adaptations of other composers. He had been like a young plant, passively absorbing nutrients from the environment in the form of the different styles he had learned and mastered. But he could feel stirring from deep within something more active, the desire to express his own music and to stop imitating. The soil was now rich enough. As an adolescent, he was assailed by all kinds of conflicting and powerful emotions—elation, depression, erotic desires. His great desire was to transpose these feelings into his work.

Almost without being aware of it, he began to experiment. He wrote a series of slow movements for various string quartets that were long and drawn out with strange mixes of moods, full of anxiety that would rise to great crescendos. When he showed these pieces to his father, Leopold was horrified. Their income depended on Wolfgang supplying the court with the kind of pleasant melodies that would delight people and make them smile. If they or the archbishop heard these new compositions, they would think Wolfgang had gone insane. Besides, the pieces were too complicated for the court musicians of Salzburg to perform. He begged his son to stop indulging in such strange music, or at least to wait until he had a position somewhere else.

Wolfgang acquiesced, but as time went on he grew increasingly depressed. The music he was being forced to write seemed so hopelessly dead and conventional; it had no relation to what was going on inside him. He composed fewer pieces and performed less often. For the first time in his life he was losing his love for music itself. Feeling imprisoned, he grew irritable. When he heard an operatic aria sung in public he was reminded of the kind of music he could be composing, and he would go into a funk. He began to quarrel incessantly with his father, passing from anger to begging for forgiveness for his disobedience. Slowly he resigned himself to his fate: he would die in Salzburg at an early age, without the world ever hearing the kind of music he knew existed within him.

In 1781 Wolfgang was invited to accompany the archbishop of Salzburg to Vienna, where he was planning to showcase the musical talents of his various court musicians. Suddenly, in Vienna, the nature of his status as a court musician became clear. The archbishop ordered him about as if he were simply one of his personal staff, a mere servant. Now all the resentment Wolfgang had felt for the past seven years bubbled and rose to the surface. He was twenty-five years old and losing valuable time. His father and the archbishop were actively holding him back. He loved his father and depended on his family for emotional support, but he could tolerate his circumstances no longer. When it was time to return to Salzburg, he did the unthinkable—he refused to leave. He asked to be dismissed from his position. The archbishop treated him with the utmost contempt, but finally relented. His father sided with the archbishop and ordered his son to return, promising that all would be forgiven. But Wolfgang had made up his mind: he would stay in Vienna, for what would turn out to be the rest of his life.

The rift with his father was permanent and extremely painful, but sensing that his time was short and that he had almost too much to express, he threw himself into his music with an intensity that was even greater than what he had displayed in childhood. As if all of his ideas had been pent up for too long, he exploded in a creative outburst unprecedented in the history of music.

The apprenticeship of the past twenty years had prepared him well for this moment. He had developed a prodigious memory—in his mind he could hold together all of the harmonies and melodies that he had absorbed over the years. Instead of notes or chords, he could think in terms of blocks of music and write them out as quickly as he heard them in his head. His speed of composing would now astonish those who witnessed it. For instance, the night before the premiere in Prague of the opera *Don Giovanni,* Mozart had gone out drinking. When his friends reminded him that he had not yet written the overture, he hurried home, and while his wife kept him awake by singing to him, he wrote one of his most popular and brilliantly conceived overtures in a matter of hours.

More important, the years he had spent learning how to compose in every conceivable genre now allowed him to use these genres to express something new, to stretch their boundaries and even permanently transform them through his creative powers. Feeling turmoil within himself, he searched for a way to make music something powerful and expressive, and not merely decorative.

In his time, the piano concerto and symphony had become rather light and frivolous genres, with short, simple movements, small orchestras, and an overabundance of melody. Mozart completely reworked these forms from within. He wrote for larger orchestras, expanding in particular the violin sections. Such orchestras could produce a more powerful sound than had previously been known. He expanded the length of his symphonic movements well beyond convention. In his opening movement, he would establish a mood of tension and dissonance that he would proceed to build up in the slow second movement, and which he would resolve in a grand and dramatic resolution at the finale. He gave his compositions the power to express dread, sadness, foreboding, anger, exhilaration, and ecstasy. Audiences were spellbound by this new sweeping sound that suddenly had so many new dimensions. After these innovations, it became almost impossible for composers to return to the light, frothy court music that had previously prevailed. European music had forever been altered.

These innovations did not spring from any conscious desire on his part to provoke or rebel. Rather, his transforming spirit emerged as if it were completely natural and beyond his control, like a bee secreting wax. Aided by his superior sense of music, he simply could not help but personalize every genre he worked in.

In 1786 he came upon a version of the Don Juan legend that excited him. He immediately identified with the story of the great seducer. He shared Don Juan's obsessive need and love for women, and he had the same disdain for authority figures. But more important, Mozart felt that as a composer he had the supreme ability to seduce audiences and that music itself represented the ultimate seduction, with its irresistible power to strike at our emotions. Translating this story into an opera, he could convey all of these ideas. And so the following year he began early work on his opera *Don Giovanni* (Italian for Don Juan). To make this story come alive in the way he had imagined it, he would once again apply his transformative powers—this time to the genre of opera.

At the time, operas tended to be rather static and formulaic. They consisted of recitatives (spoken dialogue accompanied by harpsichord that conveyed the story and action), arias (sung portions in which the singer would react to the information in the recitative), and choral pieces, featuring large groups of people singing together. For his opera, Mozart created something that flowed as a continuous whole. He conveyed the character of Don Giovanni not just through the words but through the music, accompanying the seducer's presence on stage with a constant twitching tremolo in the violins to represent his nervous, sensual energy. He gave the work an accelerated, almost frantic pace that no one had ever witnessed before in the theater. To push the expressive value of the music further, he invented ensembles—stirring, climactic moments in which several characters would sing, sometimes over one another, in an elaborate counterpoint, giving the opera a dreamlike feel and flow.

From beginning to end, *Don Giovanni* resonated with the demonic presence of the great seducer. Although all of the other characters condemn him, it is impossible not to admire Don Giovanni even as he remains unrepentant to the end, laughing all the way to hell and refusing to submit to authority. *Don Giovanni* was not like any opera anyone had ever seen before, either in the story or in the music, and it was perhaps too far ahead of its time. Many complained that it was all rather ugly and harsh to the ears; they found the pace too frenetic and the moral ambiguity too disturbing.

Continuing to work at a deliriously creative pace, Mozart exhausted himself and died in 1791, two months after the premier of his last opera, *The Magic Flute*, at the age of thirty-five. Several years after his death audiences caught up with the radical sound he had created in works such as *Don Giovanni*, which soon became among the five most frequently performed operas in history.

KEYS TO MASTERY

. . . Several things dovetailed in my mind, & at once it struck me, what quality went to form a Man of Achievement especially in Literature & which Shakespeare possessed so enormously—I mean Negative Capability, that is when man is capable of being in uncertainties, Mysteries, doubts, without any irritable reaching after fact & reason. . . .

—John Keats

If we think deeply about our childhood, not just about our memories of it but how it actually felt, we realize how differently we experienced the world back then. Our minds were completely open, and we entertained all kinds of surprising, original ideas. Things that we now take for granted, things as simple as the night sky or our reflection in a mirror, often caused us to wonder. Our heads teemed with questions about the world around us. Not yet having commanded language, we thought in ways that were preverbal—in images and sensations. When we attended the circus, a sporting event, or a movie, our eyes and ears took in the spectacle with utmost intensity. Colors seemed more vibrant and alive. We had a powerful desire to turn everything around us into a game, to play with circumstances.

Let us call this quality the *Original Mind*. This mind looked at the world more directly—not through words and received ideas. It was flexible and receptive to new information. Retaining a memory of this *Original Mind*, we cannot help but feel nostalgia for the intensity with which we used to experience the world. As the years pass, this intensity inevitably diminishes. We come to see the world through a screen of words and opinions; our prior experiences, layered over the present, color what we see. We no longer look at things as they are, noticing their details, or wonder why they exist. Our minds gradually tighten up. We become defensive about the world we now take for granted, and we become upset if our beliefs or assumptions are attacked.

We can call this way of thinking the *Conventional Mind*. Under pressure to make a living and conform to society, we force our minds into tighter and tighter grooves. We may seek to retain the spirit of childhood here and there, playing games or participating in forms of entertainment that release us from the *Conventional Mind*. Sometimes when we visit a different country where we cannot rely upon everything being familiar, we become childlike again, struck by the oddness and newness of what we are seeing. But because our minds are not completely engaged in these activities, because they last only a short while, they are not rewarding in a deep sense. They are not creative.

Masters and those who display a high level of creative energy are simply people who manage to retain a sizeable portion of their childhood spirit despite the pressures and demands of adulthood. This spirit manifests itself in their work and in their ways of thinking. Children are naturally creative. They actively transform everything around them, play with ideas and circumstances, and surprise us with the novel things they say or do. But the natural creativity of children is limited; it never leads to discoveries, inventions, or substantial works of art.

Masters not only retain the spirit of the *Original Mind,* but they add to it their years of apprenticeship and an ability to focus deeply on problems or ideas. This leads to high-level creativity. Although they have profound knowledge of a subject, their minds remain open to alternative ways of seeing and approaching problems. They are able to ask the kinds of simple questions that most people pass over, but they have the rigor and discipline to follow their investigations all the way to the end. They retain a childlike excitement about their field and a playful approach, all of which makes the hours of hard work alive and pleasurable. Like children, they are capable of thinking beyond words—visually, spatially, intuitively—and have greater access to preverbal and unconscious forms of mental activity, all of which can account for their surprising ideas and creations.

Some people maintain their childlike spirit and spontaneity, but their creative energy is dissipated in a thousand directions, and they never have the patience and discipline to endure an extended apprenticeship. Others have the discipline to accumulate vast amounts of knowledge and become experts in their field, but they have no flexibility of spirit, so their ideas never stray beyond the conventional and they never become truly creative. Masters manage to blend the two—discipline and a childlike spirit—together into what we shall call the *Dimensional Mind*. Such a mind is not constricted by limited experience or habits. It can branch out into all directions and make deep contact with reality. It can explore more dimensions of the world. The *Conventional Mind* is passive—it consumes information and regurgitates it in familiar forms. The *Dimensional Mind* is active, transforming everything it digests into something new and original, *creating* instead of *consuming*.

It is hard to say exactly why Masters are able to retain their childlike spirit while accumulating facts and knowledge, when such a feat has been difficult if not impossible for so many. Perhaps they found it harder to let go of childhood, or perhaps at some point they intuited the powers they could have by keeping their childhood spirit alive and bringing it to bear in their work. In any event, achieving the *Dimensional Mind* is never easy. Often, the childlike spirit of Masters lies dormant in the Apprenticeship Phase as they patiently absorb all of the details of their field. This spirit then comes back to them as they attain the freedom and opportunity to actively use the knowledge they have gained. Often it is a struggle, and Masters go through a crisis as they deal with the demands of others to conform and be more conventional. Under such pressure, they may try to repress their creative spirit, but often it comes back later with double intensity.

Understand: we all possess an inborn creative force that wants to become active. This is the gift of our *Original Mind*, which reveals such potential. The human mind is naturally creative, constantly looking to make associations and connections between things and ideas. It wants to explore, to discover new aspects of the world, and to invent. To express this creative force is our greatest desire, and the stifling of it the source of our misery. What kills the creative force is not age or a lack of talent, but our own spirit, our own attitude. We become too comfortable with the knowledge we have gained in our apprenticeships. We grow afraid of entertaining new ideas and the effort that this requires. To think more flexibly entails a risk—we could fail and be ridiculed. We prefer to live with familiar ideas and habits of thinking, but we pay a steep price for this: our minds go dead from the lack of challenge and novelty; we reach a limit in our field and lose control over our fate because we become replaceable.

What this means, however, is that we equally possess the potential to spark this innate creative force back to life, no matter how old we are. Experiencing a return of this creative force has an immensely therapeutic effect on our spirits and on our career. By understanding how the *Dimensional Mind* operates and what helps it flourish, we can consciously revive our mental elasticity and reverse the deadening process. The powers that the

Dimensional Mind can bring are nearly limitless, and within the reach of almost all of us.

Look at the case of Wolfgang Amadeus Mozart. He is generally considered the epitome of the child prodigy and the inexplicable genius, a freak of nature. How else are we to explain his uncanny abilities at such a young age, and the ten-year burst of creative activity at the end of his life that culminated in so many innovations and universally loved works? In truth, his genius and creativity is eminently explicable, which does not at all diminish his achievements.

Immersed in and enchanted by music from the very beginning of his life, he brought to his earliest studies a high level of focus and intensity. The mind of a four-year-old is even more open and impressionable than that of a child a few years older. Much of this powerful attention stemmed from his deep love of music. And so practicing the piano was not some kind of chore or duty, but an opportunity to expand his knowledge and to explore more musical possibilities. By the age of six, he had accumulated the hours of practice of someone twice his age. The years of touring exposed him to every possible trend and innovation of his time. His mind became filled with an extensive vocabulary of forms and styles.

In his adolescence Mozart experienced a typical creative crisis, one that often destroys or derails those who are less tenacious. For close to eight years, under pressure from his father, the archbishop, and the court of Salzburg, and bearing the burden of supporting his family, he had to temper his own powerful creative urges. At this critical point he could have succumbed to this dampening of his spirit and continued to write relatively tame pieces for the court. He would have then ended up among the lesser-known composers of the eighteenth century. Instead he rebelled and reconnected with his childlike spirit—that original desire of his to transform the music into his own voice, to realize his dramatic urges in opera. With all of his pent-up energy, his long apprenticeship, the deep level of his knowledge, he naturally exploded with creativity once he had freed himself from his family. The speed with which he could compose such masterpieces is not a reflection of some divine gift, but rather of how powerfully his mind had come to think in musical terms, which he could translate easily onto paper. He was not a freak, but a signpost of the outer reaches of the creative potential we all naturally possess.

The *Dimensional Mind* has two essential requirements: one, a high level of knowledge about a field or subject; and two, the openness and flexibility to use this knowledge in new and original ways. The knowledge that prepares the ground for creative activity largely comes from a rigorous apprenticeship in which we have mastered all of the basics. Once the mind is freed from having to learn these basics, it can focus on higher, more creative matters. The problem for us all is that the knowledge we gain in the Apprenticeship Phase—including numerous rules and procedures—can slowly become a prison. It locks us into certain methods and forms of thinking that are one-dimensional. Instead, the mind must be forced from its conservative positions and made active and exploratory.

To awaken the *Dimensional Mind* and move through the creative process requires three essential steps: first, choosing the proper *Creative Task*, the kind of activity that will maximize our skills and knowledge; second, loosening and opening up the mind through certain *Creative Strategies;* and third, creating the optimal mental conditions for a *Breakthrough* or *Insight*. Finally, throughout the process we must also be aware of the *Emotional Pitfalls*—complacency, boredom, grandiosity, and the like—that continually threaten to derail or block our progress. If we can move through the steps while avoiding these traps, we cannot fail to unleash powerful creative forces from within.

Step One: The Creative Task

You must begin by altering your very concept of creativity and by trying to see it from a new angle. Most often, people associate creativity with something intellectual, a particular way of thinking. The truth is that creative activity is one that involves the entire self—our emotions, our levels of energy, our characters, *and* our minds. To make a discovery, to invent something that connects with the public, to fashion a work of art that is meaningful, inevitably requires time and effort. This often entails years of experimentation, various setbacks and failures, and the need to maintain a high level of focus. You must have patience and faith that what you are doing will yield something important. You could have the most brilliant mind, teeming with knowledge and ideas, but if you choose the wrong subject or problem to attack, you can run out of energy and interest. In such a case all of your intellectual brilliance will lead to nothing.

The task that you choose to work on must have an obsessive element. Like the Life's Task, it must connect to something deep within you. (For Mozart, it wasn't simply music, but opera that fully engaged him.) You must be like Captain Ahab in Melville's *Moby-Dick*, obsessed with hunting down the Great White Whale. With such a deep-rooted interest, you can withstand the setbacks and failures, the days of drudgery, and the hard work that are always a part of any creative action. You can ignore the doubters and critics. You will then feel personally committed to solving the problem and will not rest until you do so.

Understand: it is the choice of where to direct his or her creative energy that makes the Master. When Thomas Edison saw his first demonstration of the electric arc light, he knew then and there that he had found the ultimate challenge and the perfect goal toward which to direct his creative energies. Figuring out how to make electric light not just a gimmick, but something that would eventually replace the gaslight, would require years of intense labor, but it would change the world like nothing else. It was the perfect riddle for him to solve. He had met his creative match. For the artist Rembrandt, it was not until he found particular subject matters that appealed to him—dramatic scenes from the Bible and elsewhere that conveyed the darker and more tragic aspects of life—that he rose to the occasion and invented a whole new way of painting and capturing light. The writer Marcel Proust suffered for years as he struggled to find the subject matter upon which to base a novel. Finally, when he realized that his own life and his own failed attempts to write the great novel was actually the subject he was looking for, it all poured out of him and into one of the greatest novels ever written, *In Search of Lost Time*.

This is *The Primary Law of the Creative Dynamic* that you must engrave deeply in your mind and never forget: your emotional commitment to what you are doing will be translated directly into your work. If you go at your work with half a heart, it will show in the lackluster results and in the laggard way in which you reach the end. If you are doing something primarily for money and without a real emotional commitment, it will translate into something that lacks a soul and that has no connection to you. You may not see this, but you can be sure that the public will feel it and that they will receive your work in the same lackluster spirit it was created in. If you are excited and obsessive in the hunt, it will show in the details. If your work comes from a place deep within, its authenticity will be communicated. This applies equally to science and business as to the arts. Your creative task may not rise to the same obsessive level as it did for Edison, but it must have a degree of this obsessiveness or your efforts will be doomed. You must never simply embark on any creative endeavor in your field, placing faith in your own brilliance to see it through. You must make the right, the perfect choice for your energies and your inclinations.

To aid in this process, it is often wise to choose something that appeals to your sense of unconventionality and calls up latent feelings of rebelliousness. Perhaps what you want to invent or discover is being ignored or ridiculed by others. The work that you envision will stir up controversy and ruffle some feathers. In opting for something that has deep personal appeal to you, you will naturally move in an unorthodox direction. Try to ally this with a desire to subvert conventional paradigms and go against the grain. The sense of having enemies or doubters can serve as a powerful motivating device and fill you with an added creative energy and focus.

There are two things to keep in mind: First, the task that you choose must be realistic. The knowledge and skills you have gained must be eminently suited to pulling it off. To reach your goal you may have to learn a few new things, but you must have mastered the basics and possess a solid enough grasp of the field so that your mind can focus on higher matters. On the other hand, it is always best to choose a task that is slightly above you, one that might be considered ambitious on your part. This is a corollary of the Law of the Creative Dynamic—the higher the goal, the more energy you will call up from deep within. You will rise to the challenge because you have to, and will discover creative powers in yourself that you never suspected.

Second, you must let go of your need for comfort and security. Creative endeavors are by their nature uncertain. You may know your task, but you are never exactly sure where your efforts will lead. If you need everything in your life to be simple and safe, this open-ended nature of the task will fill you with anxiety. If you are worried about what others might think and about how your position in the group might be jeopardized, then you will never really create anything. You will unconsciously tether your mind to certain conventions, and your ideas will grow stale and flat. If you are worried about failure or going through a period of mental and financial instability, then you will violate the Primary Law of the Creative Dynamic, and your worries will be reflected in the results. Think of yourself as an explorer. You cannot find anything new if you are unwilling to leave the shore.

Step Two: Creative Strategies

Think of the mind as a muscle that naturally tightens up over time unless it is consciously worked upon. What causes this tightening is twofold. First, we generally prefer to entertain the same thoughts and ways of thinking because they provide us with a sense of consistency and familiarity. Sticking with the same methods also saves us a lot of effort. We are creatures of habit. Second, whenever we work hard at a problem or idea, our minds naturally narrow their focus because of the strain and effort involved. This means that the further we progress on our creative task, the fewer alternative possibilities or viewpoints we tend to consider.

This tightening process afflicts all of us, and it is best to admit that you share in this flaw. The only antidote is to enact strategies to loosen up the mind and let in alternative ways of thinking. This is not only essential for the creative process, but is also immensely therapeutic for our psyches. The following five strategies for developing such flexibility have been distilled from the lessons and stories of the most creative Masters, past and present. It would be wise to adapt all of them at some point, stretching and loosening the mind in all directions.

A. CULTIVATE NEGATIVE CAPABILITY

In 1817 the twenty-two-year-old poet John Keats wrote a letter to his brothers in which he explained his most recent thoughts on the creative process. The world around us, he wrote, is far more complex than we can possibly imagine. With our limited senses and consciousness, we only glimpse a small portion of reality. Furthermore, everything in the universe is in a state of constant flux. Simple words and thoughts cannot capture this flux or complexity. The only solution for an enlightened person is to let the mind absorb itself in what it experiences, without having to form a judgment on what it all means. The mind must be able to feel doubt and uncertainty for as long as possible. As it remains in this state and probes deeply into the mysteries of the universe, ideas will come that are more dimensional and real than if we had jumped to conclusions and formed judgments early on.

To accomplish this, he wrote, we must be capable of negating our ego. We are by nature fearful and insecure creatures. We do not like what is unfamiliar or unknown. To compensate for this, we assert ourselves with opinions and ideas that make us seem strong and certain. Many of these opinions do not come from our own deep reflection, but are instead based on what other people think. Furthermore, once we hold these ideas, to admit they are wrong is to wound our ego and vanity. Truly creative people in all fields can temporarily suspend their ego and simply experience what they are seeing, without the need to assert a judgment, for as long as possible. They are more than ready to find their most cherished opinions contradicted by reality. This ability to endure and even embrace mysteries and uncertainties is what Keats called *negative capability*.

All Masters possess this Negative Capability, and it is the source of their creative power. This quality allows them to entertain a broader range of ideas and experiment with them, which in turn makes their work richer and more inventive. Throughout his career, Mozart never asserted any particular opinions about music. Instead, he absorbed the styles he heard around himself and incorporated them into his own voice. Late in his career, he encountered for the first time the music of Johann Sebastian Bach—a kind of music very different from his own, and in some ways more complex. Most artists would grow defensive and dismissive of something that challenged their own principles. Instead, Mozart opened his mind up to new possibilities, studying Bach's use of counterpoint for nearly a year and absorbing it into his own vocabulary. This gave his music a new and surprising quality.

At a young age, Albert Einstein found himself fascinated by the apparent paradox of two people observing the same beam of light—one pursuing it at the speed of light, the other at rest, on Earth—and how it would appear the same to both of them. Instead of using available theories to gloss this over or explain it away, for ten long years he contemplated this paradox, in a state of Negative Capability. Operating in this way, he was able to consider almost every possible solution, until finally he hit upon the one that led to his theory of relativity. (For more on this, see chapter 6, page 278.)

This might seem like some kind of poetic conceit, but in fact cultivating Negative Capability will be the single most important factor in your success as a creative thinker. In the sciences, you will tend to entertain ideas that fit your own preconceptions and that you *want* to believe in. This unconsciously colors your choices of how to verify these ideas, and is known as *confirmation bias*. With this type of bias, you will find the experiments and data that confirm what you have already come to believe in. The uncertainty of not knowing the answers beforehand is too much for most scientists. In the arts and letters, your thoughts will congeal around political dogma or predigested ways of looking at the world, and what you will often end up expressing is an opinion rather than a truthful observation about reality. To Keats, William Shakespeare was the ideal because he did not judge his characters, but instead opened himself up to their worlds and expressed the reality of even those who were considered evil. The need for certainty is the greatest disease the mind faces.

To put Negative Capability into practice, you must develop the habit of suspending the need to judge everything that crosses your path. You consider and even momentarily entertain viewpoints opposite to your own, seeing how they feel. You observe a person or event for a length of time, deliberately holding yourself back from forming an opinion. You seek out what is unfamiliar—for instance, reading books from unfamiliar writers in unrelated fields or from different schools of thought. You do anything to break up your normal train of thinking and your sense that you already know the truth.

To negate the ego you must adopt a kind of humility toward knowledge. The great scientist Michael Faraday expressed this attitude in the following way: Scientific knowledge is constantly progressing. The greatest theories of the time are eventually disproven or altered at some future point. The human mind is simply too weak to have a clear and perfect vision of reality. The idea or theory that you are currently formulating, that seems so fresh and alive and truthful, will almost certainly be shot down or ridiculed in a few decades or centuries. (We tend to laugh at people prior to the twentieth century who did not yet believe in evolution and who saw the world as only 6,000 years old, but imagine how people will be laughing at us for the naïve beliefs we hold in the twenty-first century!) And so it is best to keep this in mind and not grow too fond of your ideas or too certain of their truth.

Negative Capability should not be a permanent state of mind. In order to produce work of any sort we must create limits on what we'll consider;

we must organize our thoughts into relatively cohesive patterns, and eventually, come up with conclusions. In the end, we must make certain judgments. Negative Capability is a tool we use in the process to open the mind up temporarily to more possibilities. Once this way of thinking leads to a creative avenue of thought, we can give our ideas a clearer shape and gently let it go, returning to this attitude whenever we feel stale or blocked.

B. ALLOW FOR SERENDIPITY

The brain is an instrument developed for making connections. It operates as a dual processing system, in which every bit of information that comes in is at the same time compared to other information. The brain is constantly searching for similarities, differences, and relationships between what it processes. Your task is to feed this natural inclination, to create the optimal conditions for it to make new and original associations between ideas and experiences. And one of the best ways to accomplish this is by letting go of conscious control and allowing chance to enter into the process.

The reason for this is simple. When we are consumed with a particular project, our attention tends to become quite narrow as we focus so deeply. We grow tense. In this state, our mind responds by trying to reduce the amount of stimuli we have to deal with. We literally close ourselves off from the world in order to concentrate on what is necessary. This can have the unintended consequence of making it harder for us to see other possibilities, to be more open and creative with our ideas. When we are in a more relaxed state, our attention naturally broadens and we take in more stimuli.

Many of the most interesting and profound discoveries in science occur when the thinker is not concentrating directly on the problem but is about to drift off to sleep, or get on a bus, or hears a joke—moments of unstrained attention, when something unexpected enters the mental sphere and triggers a new and fertile connection. Such chance associations and discoveries are known as *serendipity*—the occurrence of something we are not expecting—and although by their nature you cannot force them to happen, you can invite serendipity into the creative process by taking two simple steps.

The first step is to widen your search as far as possible. In the research stage of your project, you look at more than what is generally required. You expand your search into other fields, reading and absorbing any related information. If you have a particular theory or hypothesis about a phenomenon, you examine as many examples and potential counterexamples as humanly possible. It might seem tiring and inefficient, but you must trust this process. What ensues is that the brain becomes increasingly excited and stimulated by the variety of information. As William James expressed it, the mind "transitions from one idea to another . . . the most unheard of combination of elements, the subtlest associations of analogy; in a word, we seem suddenly introduced into a seething cauldron of ideas, where everything is fizzling and bobbling about in a state of bewildering activity." A kind of mental momentum is generated, in which the slightest chance occurrence will spark a fertile idea.

The second step is to maintain an openness and looseness of spirit. In moments of great tension and searching, you allow yourself moments of release. You take walks, engage in activities outside your work (Einstein played the violin), or think about something else, no matter how trivial. When some new and unanticipated idea now enters your mind, you do not ignore it because it is irrational or does not fit the narrow frame of your previous work. You give it instead full attention and explore where it leads you.

Perhaps the greatest illustration of this would be the discovery by Louis Pasteur of immunology and how contagious diseases can be prevented by inoculation. Pasteur spent years demonstrating that various diseases are caused by microorganisms or germs, a novel concept for the time. In developing his germ theory, he expanded his knowledge into all different branches of medicine and chemistry. In 1879 he was researching chicken cholera. He had prepared cultures of this disease, but the cholera work got interrupted by other projects, and for several months the cultures remained untouched in his laboratory. When he returned to the work, he injected the cultures into chickens and was surprised when they all recovered easily from the disease. Figuring these cultures had lost their virulence because of the time factor, he ordered some new varieties, which he injected immediately into the same chickens and into some new ones as well. The new ones all died, as expected, but all of the old chickens survived.

Many doctors in the past had witnessed similar phenomena, but had not taken notice or had refused to contemplate its meaning. Pasteur had such wide and deep knowledge of the field that the survival of the chickens instantly caught his attention. In thinking deeply about what it could mean, he realized he had stumbled upon a whole new practice in medicine—the inoculation of the body against disease by injecting small doses of the actual disease. The wideness of his searches and the openness of his spirit allowed him to make this connection and "random" discovery. As Pasteur himself commented, "Chance favors only the prepared mind."

Such serendipitous discoveries are extremely common in science and in technological inventions. The list would include, among hundreds of others, the discoveries by Wilhelm Röntgen of X-rays and Alexander Fleming of penicillin, and the invention of the printing press by Johannes Gutenberg. Perhaps one of the most illuminating of all such examples occurred with the great inventor Thomas Edison. He had been working long and hard on improving the mechanics of the roll of paper as it moved through the telegraph and recorded the various dots and dashes. The work was not going well, and what particularly bothered him was the sound the machine made as the paper passed through—it gave off "a light, musical, rhythmical sound, resembling human talk heard indistinctly."

He wanted to get rid of this sound somehow, but over the course of the next few months as he let go of the work on the telegraph, the whirring noise continued to haunt him. One day, as he heard it yet again in his head, an astounding thought occurred to him—he might have inadvertently hit upon a way to record sound and the human voice. He spent the next few months immersing himself in the science of sound, which led to his first experiments on creating a phonograph that would record the human voice, using a very similar technology to the telegraph.

This discovery shows us the essence of the creative mind. In such a mind, every stimulus that enters the brain is processed, turned over, and reevaluated. Nothing is taken at face value. A whirring sound is never neutral, never merely a sound, but something to interpret, a possibility, a sign. Dozens of such possibilities lead nowhere, but to an open and fluid mind they are not only worth considering, but are a constant pleasure to investigate. Perception itself becomes a stimulating exercise in thinking.

One reason that serendipity plays such a large role in discoveries and inventions is that our minds are limited. We cannot explore all avenues and imagine every possibility. Nobody could have come upon the invention of the phonograph in Edison's time by a rational process of imagining rolls of paper that could record sound. Random external stimuli lead us to associations we cannot come by on our own. Like seeds floating in space, they require the soil of a highly prepared and open mind to take root in and sprout a meaningful idea.

Serendipity strategies can be interesting devices in the arts as well. For instance, the writer Anthony Burgess, trying to free his mind up from the same stale ideas, decided on several occasions to choose random words in a reference book and use them to guide the plot of a novel, according to the order and associations of the words. Once he had completely haphazard starting points, his conscious mind took over and he worked them into extremely well-crafted novels with surprising structures. The surrealist artist Max Ernst did something similar in a series of paintings inspired by the deep grooves in a wood floor that had been scrubbed too many times. He laid pieces of paper rubbed with black lead on the floor at odd angles, and made prints of them. Based on these prints, he proceeded to make surreal and hallucinatory drawings. In these examples, a random idea was used to force the mind to create novel associations and to loosen up the creative urge. This mix of complete chance and conscious elaboration often creates novel and exciting effects.

To help yourself to cultivate serendipity, you should keep a notebook with you at all times. The moment any idea or observation comes, you note it down. You keep the notebook by your bed, careful to record ideas that come in those moments of fringe awareness—just before falling asleep, or just upon waking. In this notebook you record any scrap of thought that occurs to you, and include drawings, quotes from other books, anything at all. In this way, you will have the freedom to try out the most absurd ideas. The juxtaposition of so many random bits will be enough to spark various associations.

In general you must adopt a more *analogical* way of thinking, taking greater advantage of the associative powers of the mind. Thinking in terms of analogies and metaphors can be extremely helpful to the creative process. For instance, an argument people used in the sixteenth and seventeenth centuries to prove that the earth does not move was to say that a rock dropped from a tower lands at its base. If the earth were moving, they argued, it would fall elsewhere. Galileo, a man who habitually thought in terms of analogies, saw the earth in his mind as a kind of sailing ship in space. As he explained to doubters of the earth's movement, a rock dropped from the mast of a moving ship still lands at its base.

These analogies can be tight and logical, such as Isaac Newton's comparison of the falling apple from a tree in his garden to the moon falling in space. Or they can be loose and somewhat irrational, such as the jazz artist John Coltrane's thinking of his own compositions as cathedrals of sound he was constructing. In any event, you must train yourself to look constantly for such analogies to reframe and expand your ideas.

C. ALTERNATE THE MIND THROUGH "THE CURRENT"

In 1832, as Charles Darwin voyaged around the coastline of South America and traveled into the interior, he began to take note of several strange phenomena—bones of animals long extinct, marine fossils near the top of mountains in Peru, and animals on islands that were similar and yet quite different from their mainland counterparts. In his notebooks, he began to speculate on what all this could mean. Clearly, the earth appeared to be much older than indicated in the Bible, and it became increasingly difficult for him to imagine that all of life was created at once. Based on these continuing speculations, he began to look more closely at the plant and animal life he was observing. In doing so, he took note of even more anomalies in nature and tried to find a pattern among them. When he visited the Galápagos Islands near the end of his voyage, he witnessed so much variety of life in such a small area that he finally saw the pattern—the idea of evolution itself.

For the next twenty years Darwin expanded upon the process that he started as a young man. He speculated on how variety within species might actually occur, and to test out his ideas he began to keep and breed different types of pigeons. The theory of evolution he was developing depended on the movement of plants and animals across wide expanses of the globe. This was easier to imagine with animals than with plants—for instance, how did such rich vegetation end up on relatively young volcanic islands? Most believed it was from an act of God. And so Darwin began a series of experiments, soaking various seeds in salt water to see how long they could survive in such an element and still germinate. The results proved they could last longer than he had imagined. Considering ocean currents, he calculated that many varieties of seeds could travel more than 1,000 miles in some forty days and still germinate.

As his ideas began to solidify, he decided to intensify his research by spending eight years studying many species of one type of crustacean, the barnacle, in order to prove or disprove his speculations. This research ended up validating his ideas and adding some new wrinkles. Certain that he had discovered something meaningful after all this work, he finally published his results on an evolutionary process that he called natural selection.

The theory of evolution as formulated by Charles Darwin represents one of the most astounding achievements of human creative thinking, and is a testament to the powers of the mind. Evolution is not something that can be seen with the eyes. It depends on a powerful use of the imagination— to imagine what could happen on Earth in the course of millions upon millions of years, a period of time that is so astoundingly long we have no way of really conceptualizing it. It also required the ability to imagine a process that could occur on its own, without the guidance of a spiritual force. Darwin's theory could only have been deduced by looking at evidence and making connections in the mind about what his findings could mean. His theory of evolution, devised in this way, has stood the test of time and has come to have profound ramifications on almost all forms of science. Through a mental process that we shall call the *Current*, Charles Darwin made visible to us all what is completely invisible to the human eye.

The Current is like a mental electrical charge that gains its power through a constant alternation. We observe something in the world that strikes our attention and makes us wonder what it might mean. In thinking about it, we devise several possible explanations. When we look at the phenomenon again we see it differently as we cycle through the various ideas we had imagined to account for it. Perhaps we conduct experiments to verify or alter our speculations. Now when we look at the phenomenon yet again, weeks or months later, we see more and more aspects of its hidden reality.

If we had failed to speculate on the meaning of what we had observed, we simply would have had an observation that led us nowhere. If we had speculated without continuing to observe and verify, then we simply would have had some random idea floating in our heads. But by continually cycling between speculation and observation/experiment, we are able to pierce deeper and deeper into reality, like a drill that penetrates a piece of wood through its motion. The Current is a constant dialogue between our thoughts and reality. If we go into this process deeply enough, we come into contact with a theory that explains something far beyond the capability of our limited senses.

The Current is merely an intensification of the most elementary powers of human consciousness. Our most primitive ancestors would take note of something unusual or out of place—broken twigs, chewed leaves, the outline of a hoof or paw. Through an act of pure imagination, they would deduce that this meant that an animal had passed by. This fact would be verified by tracking the footprints. Through this process, what was not immediately visible to the eyes (a passing animal) became visible. All that has occurred since then is an elaboration of this power to increasingly higher levels of abstraction, to the point of understanding hidden laws of nature—like evolution and relativity.

Most often in culture we see people who *short-circuit* the Current. They observe some phenomenon in culture or nature that makes them emotional and they run rampant with speculations, never taking the time to entertain possible explanations that could have been verified by further observation. They disconnect themselves from reality and can then imagine whatever they want. On the other hand, we see many people, particularly in academia or in the sciences, who accumulate mountains of information and data from studies and statistics but never venture to speculate on the larger ramifications of this information or connect it all into a theory. They are afraid to speculate because it seems unscientific and subjective, failing to understand that speculation is the heart and soul of human rationality, our way of connecting to reality and seeing the invisible. To them, it is better to stick to facts and studies, to keep a micro view, rather than possibly embarrassing themselves with a speculation that could be wrong.

Sometimes this fear of speculation masquerades as skepticism. We see this in people who delight in shooting down any theory or explanation before it gets anywhere. They are trying to pass off skepticism as a sign of high intelligence, but in fact they are taking the easy route—it is quite simple to find arguments against any idea and knock it down from the sidelines. Instead, you must follow the route of all creative thinkers and go in the opposite direction. You then not only speculate, but are bold and audacious with your ideas, all of which forces you to work hard to confirm or disconfirm your theories, piercing into reality in the process. As the great physicist Max Planck put it, scientists "must have a vivid intuitive imagination, for new ideas are not generated by deduction, but by an artistically creative imagination."

The Current has applications far beyond science. The great inventor Buckminster Fuller was constantly coming up with ideas for possible inventions and new forms of technology. Early in his career, Fuller noticed that many people have great ideas, but are afraid to put them into action in any form. They prefer to engage in discussions or critiques, writing about their fantasies but never playing them out in the real world. To set himself apart from these dreamers, he created a strategy of forging what he called "artifacts." Working off his ideas, which were sometimes quite wild, he would make models of things he imagined, and if they seemed at all feasible, he would proceed to invent prototypes of them. By actually translating his ideas into tangible objects, he could gain a sense of whether they were potentially interesting or merely ridiculous. Now his seemingly outlandish ideas were no longer speculations, but realities. He would then take his prototypes to another level, constructing artifacts for the public to see how they would respond.

One artifact he made was the Dymaxion car, which he unveiled to the public in 1933. It was meant to be much more efficient, maneuverable, and aerodynamic than any vehicle in existence, featuring three wheels and an unusual teardrop shape; in addition, it could be quickly and cheaply assembled. In making this artifact public he realized several faults in its design and reformulated it. Although it led nowhere, particularly as the auto industry put all kinds of roadblocks before him, the Dymaxion car ended up influencing future designers, and caused many to question the single-minded approach people had to the design of the automobile. Fuller would expand this artifact strategy to all of his ideas, including his most famous one—the geodesic dome.

Fuller's process of making artifacts is a great model for any kind of new invention or idea in business and commerce. Let us say you have an idea for a new product. You can design it on your own and then launch it, but often you notice a discrepancy between your own level of excitement for your product and the somewhat indifferent response of the public. You have not engaged in a dialogue with reality, which is the essence of the Current. Instead, it is better to produce a prototype—a form of speculation—and see how people respond to it. Based on the assessments you gain, you can redo the work and launch it again, cycling through this process several times until you perfect it. The responses of the public will make you think more deeply about what you are producing. Such feedback will help make visible what is generally invisible to your eyes—the objective reality of your work and its flaws, as reflected through the eyes of many people. Alternating between ideas and artifacts will help you to create something compelling and effective.

D. ALTER YOUR PERSPECTIVE

Consider thinking as an extended form of vision that allows us to see more of the world, and creativity as the ability to expand that vision beyond conventional boundaries.

When we perceive an object, our eyes relay only a portion or outline of it to our brains, leaving our mind to fill in the rest, giving us a fast and relatively accurate assessment of what we are seeing. Our eyes are not paying deep attention to all of the details, but noticing patterns. Our thought processes, modeled after visual perception, use a similar shorthand. When an event occurs or when we meet a new person, we do not stop to consider all aspects or details, but instead we see an outline or pattern that fits into our expectations and past experiences. We fit the event or person into categories. As with vision, for us to have to think deeply about every new occurrence or perceived object would exhaust the brain. Unfortunately, we transfer this mental shorthand to almost everything—it is the main characteristic of the *Conventional Mind.* We might imagine that when we are engaged in solving a problem or realizing an idea that we are being highly rational and thorough, but just as with our eyes, we are not aware of how deeply our thoughts fall into the same narrow grooves and the same categorizing shorthand.

Creative people are those who have the capacity to resist this shorthand. They can look at a phenomenon from several different angles, noticing something we miss because we only look straight on. Sometimes, after one of their discoveries or inventions is made public, we are surprised at how obvious it seems and wonder why no one else had thought of it before. This is because creative people are actually looking at what is hidden in plain sight, and not rushing to generalize and label. Whether such powers are natural or learned does not matter: the mind can be trained to loosen itself up and move outside the grooves. To do this you must become aware of the typical patterns your mind falls into and how you can break out of these patterns and alter your perspective through conscious effort. Once you engage in this process, you will be astonished at the ideas and creative powers it will unleash. The following are several of the most common patterns or shorthands, and how you can subvert them.

Looking at the "what" instead of the "how":
Let us say that something goes wrong in a project of some sort. Our conventional tendency is to look for a single cause or a simple explanation, which then reveals to us how to fix the problem. If the book we are creating is not working out, we focus on the uninspired writing or the misguided concept behind it. Or if the company we work for is not performing well, we look at the products we are designing and marketing. Although we think we are

being rational when we think in this way, most often problems are more complicated and holistic; we are simplifying them, based on the law that the mind always looks for shorthands.

To look at the "how" instead of the "what" means focusing on the structure—how the parts relate to the whole. With the book, it may not be working out because it is organized poorly, the faulty organization a reflection of ideas that have not been thought out. Our minds are a jumble, and this is reflected in the work. Thinking in this way, we are forced to go more deeply into the parts and how they relate to the overall concept; improving the structure will improve the writing. With the company, we should look deeply at the organization itself—how well people communicate with one another, how quickly and fluidly information is passed along. If people are not communicating, if they are not on the same page, no amount of changes in the product or marketing will improve performance.

Everything in nature has a structure, a way that the parts relate to one another, which is generally fluid and not so easy to conceptualize. Our minds naturally tend to separate things out, to think in terms of nouns instead of verbs. In general you want to pay greater attention to the relationships between things, because that will give you a greater feel for the picture as a whole. It was in looking at the relationship between electricity and magnetism and the relativity of their effects that scientists created a whole revolution in scientific thinking, leading from Michael Faraday to Albert Einstein and the elaboration of field theories. This is a revolution that is waiting to happen on a more mundane level, in our everyday thinking.

Rushing to generalities and ignoring details:
Our minds are always hurrying to generalize about things, often based on the most minimal amounts of information. We form opinions quickly, in conformity with our previous opinions, and we do not pay great attention to the details. To combat this pattern we must sometimes shift our focus from the *macro* to the *micro*—placing much greater emphasis on the details, the small picture. When Darwin wanted to make sure his theory was accurate, he devoted eight long years of his life to the exclusive study of barnacles. Looking at this intensely microscopic glimpse of nature, he saw a perfect corroboration of his larger theory.

When Leonardo da Vinci wanted to create a whole new style of painting, one that was more lifelike and emotional, he engaged in an obsessive study of details. He spent endless hours experimenting with forms of light hitting various geometrical solids, to test how light could alter the appearance of objects. He devoted hundreds of pages in his notebooks to exploring the various gradations of shadows in every possible combination. He gave this same attention to the folds of a gown, the patterns in hair, the various minute changes in the expression of a human face. When we look at his work we are not consciously aware of these efforts on his part, but we feel how much more alive and realistic his paintings are, as if he had captured reality.

In general, try approaching a problem or idea with a much more open mind. Let your study of the details guide your thinking and shape your theories. Think of everything in nature, or in the world, as a kind of hologram—the smallest part reflecting something essential about the whole. Immersing yourself in details will combat the generalizing tendencies of the brain and bring you closer to reality. Make sure, however, that you do not become lost in the details and lose sight of how they reflect the whole and fit into a larger idea. That is simply the other side of the same disease.

Confirming paradigms and ignoring anomalies:
In any field there are inevitable paradigms—accepted ways of explaining reality. This is necessary; without such paradigms we would not be able to make sense of the world. But sometimes these paradigms end up dominating our way of thinking. We routinely look for patterns in the world that confirm the paradigms we already believe in. The things that do not fit the paradigm—the anomalies—tend to be ignored or explained away. In truth, anomalies themselves contain the richest information. They often reveal to us the flaws in our paradigms and open up new ways of looking at the world. You must turn yourself into a detective, deliberately uncovering and looking at the very anomalies that people tend to disregard.

In the late nineteenth century several scientists noted the strange phenomenon of rare metals like uranium emitting luminescent rays of an unknown nature, without any exposure to light. But nobody paid much attention to this. It was assumed that someday a rational explanation for this phenomenon would come up, one that fit with general theories of matter. But to the scientist Marie Curie, this anomaly was precisely the subject that needed to be investigated. She intuited that it contained the potential for expanding our concept of matter. For four long years Marie, with the help of her husband, Pierre, devoted her life to studying this phenomenon, which she eventually named *radioactivity.* In the end her discovery completely altered scientists' view on matter itself, which had previously been seen as containing static and fixed elements, but now was revealed to be much more volatile and complex.

When Larry Page and Sergey Brin, the founders of Google, examined the search engines that existed in the mid-1990s, they focused exclusively on the seemingly trivial flaws in systems such as AltaVista, the anomalies. These search engines, which were the hottest startups of the time, ranked searches mostly based on the number of times the subject had been mentioned in a given article. Although this method sometimes produced results that were unhelpful or irrelevant, it was considered merely a quirk in the system that would eventually be ironed out or simply accepted. By focusing on this one anomaly, Page and Brin were able to see a glaring weakness in the whole concept and to develop a much different ranking algorithm—based on the number of times an article had been linked to—which completely transformed the effectiveness and use of the search engine.

For Charles Darwin, the crux of his theory came from looking at mutations. It is the strange and random variation in nature that often sets a species off in a new evolutionary direction. Think of anomalies as the creative form of such mutations. They often represent the future, but to our eyes they seem strange. By studying them, you can illuminate this future before anyone else.

Fixating on what is present, ignoring what is absent:
In the Arthur Conan Doyle story "Silver Blaze," Sherlock Holmes solves a crime by paying attention to what did not happen—the family dog had not barked. This meant that the murderer must have been someone the dog knew. What this story illustrates is how the average person does not generally pay attention to what we shall call *negative cues,* what should have happened but did not. It is our natural tendency to fixate on positive information, to notice only what we can see and hear. It takes a creative type such as Holmes to think more broadly and rigorously, pondering the missing information in an event, visualizing this absence as easily as we see the presence of something.

For centuries, doctors considered diseases exclusively as something stemming from outside the body attacking it—a contagious germ, a draft of cold air, miasmic vapors, and so on. Treatment depended on finding drugs of some sort that could counteract the harmful effects of these environmental agents of disease. Then, in the early twentieth century, the biochemist Frederick Gowland Hopkins, studying the effects of scurvy, had the idea to reverse this perspective. What caused the problem in this particular disease, he speculated, was not what was attacking from the outside, but what was *missing* from within the body itself—in this case what came to be known as vitamin C. Thinking creatively, he did not look at what was present but precisely at what was absent, in order to solve the problem. This led to his groundbreaking work on vitamins, and completely altered our concept of health.

In business, the natural tendency is to look at what is already out there in the marketplace and to think of how we can make it better or cheaper. The real trick—the equivalent of seeing the negative cue—is to focus our attention on some need that is not currently being met, on what is absent.

This requires more thinking and is harder to conceptualize, but the rewards can be immense if we hit upon this unfulfilled need. One interesting way to begin such a thought process is to look at new and available technology in the world and to imagine how it could be applied in a much different way, meeting a need that we sense exists but that is not overly apparent. If the need is too obvious, others will already be working on it.

In the end, the ability to alter our perspective is a function of our imagination. We have to learn how to imagine more possibilities than we generally consider, being as loose and radical with this process as we can. This pertains as much to inventors and businesspeople as it does to artists. Look at the case of Henry Ford, a highly creative thinker in his own right. In the early stages of the manufacturing of automobiles, Henry Ford imagined a whole different kind of business than existed at the time. He wanted to mass-produce the automobile, helping to create the consumer culture he felt was coming. But the men in his factories would average some twelve and a half hours to manufacture a single automobile, which was far too slow to achieve his goal.

One day, trying to think of ways to speed up production, Ford watched his men at work as they scrambled around as fast as they could to assemble an automobile as it stood still on a platform. Ford did not focus on the tools that could be improved, or how to get the men to move faster, or the need to hire more workers—the kinds of small changes that would not have altered the dynamic enough for mass-production. Instead, he *imagined* something completely different. In his mind, he suddenly saw the cars moving and the men standing still, each worker doing a small portion of the job as the car moved from position to position. Within days he tried this out and realized what he was on to. By the time it was fully instituted in 1914, the Ford factory could now produce a car in ninety minutes. Over the years, he would speed up this miraculous saving of time.

As you work to free up your mind and give it the power to alter its perspective, remember the following: the emotions we experience at any time have an inordinate influence on how we perceive the world. If we feel afraid, we tend to see more of the potential dangers in some action. If we feel particularly bold, we tend to ignore the potential risks. What you must do then is not only alter your mental perspective, but reverse your emotional one as well. For instance, if you are experiencing a lot of resistance and setbacks in your work, try to see this as in fact something that is quite positive and productive. These difficulties will make you tougher and more aware of the flaws you need to correct. In physical exercise, resistance is a way to make the body stronger, and it is the same with the mind. Play a similar reversal on good fortune—seeing the potential dangers of becoming soft, addicted to attention, and so forth. These reversals will free up the imagination to see more possibilities, which will affect what you do. If you see setbacks as opportunities, you are more likely to make that a reality.

E. REVERT TO PRIMAL FORMS OF INTELLIGENCE

As discussed in the introduction (see page 6), our most primitive ancestors developed various forms of intelligence that predated the invention of language, which aided them in the harsh struggle for survival. They thought mostly in terms of visual images, and became highly adept at noticing patterns and discerning important details in their environment. Roaming over vast spaces, they developed the ability to think spatially and learned how to orient themselves in varied landscapes, using landmarks and the position of the sun. They were able to think in mechanical terms, and became supremely skilled at coordinating the hand and eye in making things.

With the invention of language, the intellectual powers of our ancestors were vastly enhanced. Thinking in words, they could imagine more possibilities in the world around them, which they could then communicate and act on. The human brain thus developed along these evolutionary lines as a multiuse, immensely flexible instrument that is able to think on various levels, combining many forms of intelligence with all of the senses. But somewhere along the way a problem developed. We slowly lost our previous flexibility and became largely dependent on words for our thinking. In the process, we lost our connection to the senses—sight, smell, touch—that once played such a vital role in our intelligence. Language is a system largely designed for social communication. It is based on conventions that everyone can agree upon. It is somewhat rigid and stable, so that it allows us to communicate with minimum friction. But when it comes to the incredible complexity and fluidity of life, it can often fail us.

The grammar of language locks us into certain forms of logic and ways of thinking. As the writer Sidney Hook put it, "When Aristotle drew up his table of categories which to him represented the grammar of existence, he was really projecting the grammar of the Greek language on the cosmos." Linguists have enumerated the high number of concepts that have no particular word to describe them in the English language. If there are no words for certain concepts, we tend to not think of them. And so language is a tool that is often too tight and constricting, compared to the multilayered powers of intelligence we naturally possess.

In the last few hundred years, with the rapid development of the sciences, technology, and the arts, we humans have had to use our brains to solve increasingly complex problems, and those who are truly creative have developed the ability to think beyond language, to access the lower chambers of consciousness, to revert to those primal forms of intelligence that served us for millions of years.

According to the great mathematician Jacques Hadamard, most mathematicians think in terms of images, creating a visual equivalent of the theorem they are trying to work out. Michael Faraday was a powerful visual thinker. When he came up with the idea of electromagnetic lines of force, anticipating the field theories of the twentieth century, he saw them literally in his mind's eye before he wrote about them. The structure of the periodic table came to the chemist Dmitry Mendeleyev in a dream, where he literally saw the elements laid out before his eyes in a visual scheme. The list of great thinkers who relied upon images is enormous, and perhaps the greatest of them all was Albert Einstein, who once wrote, "The words of the language, as they are written or spoken, do not seem to play any role in my mechanism of thought. The psychical entities which seem to serve as elements in thought are certain signs and more or less clear images which can be voluntarily reproduced and combined."

Inventors such as Thomas Edison and Henry Ford thought not only in visual terms, but also in three-dimensional models. The great electrical and mechanical engineer Nikola Tesla could supposedly visualize in minute detail a machine and all of its working parts, which he would then proceed to invent according to what he had imagined.

The reason for this "regression" to visual forms of thinking is simple. Human working memory is limited. We can only keep in mind several pieces of information at the same time. Through an image we can simultaneously imagine many things at once, at a glance. As opposed to words, which can be impersonal and rigid, a visualization is something we create, something that serves our particular needs of the moment and can represent an idea in a way that is more fluid and real than simply words. The use of images to make sense of the world is perhaps our most primitive form of intelligence, and can help us conjure up ideas that we can later verbalize. Words also are abstract; an image or model makes our idea suddenly more concrete, which satisfies our need to see and feel things with our senses.

Even if thinking in this way is not natural to you, using diagrams and models to help further the creative process can be immensely productive. Early in his research, Charles Darwin, who was normally not a visual thinker, came up with an image to help him conceptualize evolution—an irregularly branching tree. This signified that all of life started from one seed; some branches of the tree ending, others still growing and sending off new shoots. He literally drew such a tree in a notebook. This image proved extremely helpful, and he returned to it time and again. The molecular biologists James D. Watson and Francis Crick created a large three-dimensional model of the

DNA molecule with which they could interact and alter; this model played an important role in their discovery and description of DNA.

This use of images, diagrams, and models can help reveal to you patterns in your thinking and new directions you can take that you would find hard to imagine exclusively in words. With your idea exteriorized in a relatively simple diagram or model, you can see your entire concept projected at once, which will help you organize masses of information and add new dimensions to your concept.

This conceptual image or model can be the result of hard thinking, which is how Watson and Crick devised their three-dimensional DNA model, or it can come in moments of fringe awareness—from a dream or a daydream. In the latter case, such visualizations require a degree of relaxation on your part. If you think too hard, you will come up with something too literal. Let your attention wander, play around the edges of your concept, loosen up your hold on consciousness, and allow images to come to you.

Early in his career, Michael Faraday took lessons in drawing and painting. He did this so he could recreate the experiments he had witnessed at various lectures. But he discovered that drawing helped him think in many ways. The hand-brain connection is something deeply wired within us; when we attempt to sketch something we must observe it closely, gaining a feel through our fingers of how to bring it to life. Such practice can help you think in visual terms and free your mind from its constant verbalizations. To Leonardo da Vinci, drawing and thinking were synonymous.

One day, the writer and polymath Johann Wolfgang von Goethe made a curious discovery about the creative process of his friend, the great German writer Friedrich Schiller. Paying a visit to Schiller's home, he was told that the writer was not in but would return shortly. Goethe decided to wait for him and sat down at Schiller's writing desk. He began to be assailed by a strange feeling of faintness, his head slowly spinning. If he moved to the window, the sensation went away. Suddenly, he realized that some kind of weird and nauseating smell was emanating from a drawer of the desk. When he opened it he was shocked to see that it was full of rotten apples, some in an extreme state of decay. When Schiller's wife came into the room, he asked her about the apples and the stench. She told Goethe that she herself filled the drawers with these apples on a regular basis—her husband delighted in the smell and he found he did his most creative work while inhaling the fumes.

Other artists and thinkers have devised similar peculiar aids to their creative process. When doing his deepest thinking about the theory of relativity, Albert Einstein liked to hold on to a rubber ball that he would periodically squeeze in tandem with the straining of his mind. In order to work, the writer Samuel Johnson required that he had on his desk a cat, which he would periodically stroke to make it purr, and a slice of orange. Supposedly only these various sensual cues could properly stimulate him for his work.

These examples are all related to the phenomenon of synesthesia—moments in which the stimulation of one sense provokes another. For instance, we hear a particular sound and it makes us think of a color. Studies have indicated that synesthesia is far more prevalent among artists and high-level thinkers. Some have speculated that synesthesia represents a high degree of interconnectivity in the brain, which also plays a role in intelligence. Creative people do not simply think in words, but use all of their senses, their entire bodies in the process. They find sense cues that stimulate their thoughts on many levels—whether it be the smell of something strong, or the tactile feel of a rubber ball. What this means is that they are more open to alternative ways of thinking, creating, and sensing the world. They allow themselves a broader range of sense experience. You must expand as well your notion of thinking and creativity beyond the confines of words and intellectualizations. Stimulating your brain and senses from all directions will help unlock your natural creativity and help revive your original mind.

Step Three: The Creative Breakthrough—Tension and Insight

In the creative lives of almost all Masters, we hear of the following pattern: They begin a project with an initial intuition and an excitement about its potential success. Their project is deeply connected to something personal and primal, and seems very much alive to them.

As their initial nervous excitement inspires them in certain directions, they begin to give their concept shape, narrowing down its possibilities, and channeling their energies into ideas that grow more and more distinct. They enter a phase of heightened focus. But Masters inevitably possess another quality that complicates the work process: They are not easily satisfied by what they are doing. While able to feel excitement, they also feel doubt about the worthiness of their work. They have high internal standards. As they progress, they begin to detect flaws and difficulties in their original idea that they had not foreseen.

As the process begins to become more conscious and less intuitive, that idea once so alive in them starts to seem somewhat dead or stale. This is a difficult feeling to endure and so they work even harder, trying to force a solution. The harder they try, the more inner tension and frustration they create. The sense of staleness grows. In the beginning, their mind teemed with rich associations; now it seems condemned to a narrow track of thought that does not spark the same connections. At certain points in this process, lesser types would simply give up or settle for what they have—a mediocre and half-realized project. But Masters are stronger. They have been through this before, and on an unconscious level they understand that they must plow forward, and that the frustration, or the feeling of being blocked, has a purpose.

At a particular high point of tension, they let go for a moment. This could be as simple as stopping work and going to sleep; or it could mean deciding to take a break, or to temporarily work on something else. What almost inevitably happens in such moments is that the solution, the perfect idea for completing the work *comes to them*.

After ten long years of incessant thinking on the problem of general relativity, Albert Einstein decided one evening to simply give up. He had had enough. It was beyond him. He went to bed early, and when he awoke the solution suddenly came to him. The composer Richard Wagner had worked so hard on his opera *Das Rheingold* that he became completely blocked. Beyond frustration, he took a long walk in the woods, lay down, and fell asleep. In a sort of half dream, he felt himself sinking in swiftly flowing water. The rushing sounds formed into musical chords. He awoke, terrified by a feeling of drowning. He hurried home and noted down the chords of his dream, which seemed to perfectly conjure up the sound of rushing water. These chords became the prelude of the opera, a leitmotif that runs through-out it, and one of the most astonishing pieces he had ever written.

These stories are so common as to indicate something essential about the brain and how it reaches certain peaks of creativity. We can explain this pattern in the following way: If we remained as excited as we were in the beginning of our project, maintaining that intuitive feel that sparked it all, we would never be able to take the necessary distance to look at our work objectively and improve upon it. Losing that initial verve causes us to work and rework the idea. It forces us to not settle too early on an easy solution. The mounting frustration and tightness that comes from single-minded de-votion to one problem or idea will naturally lead to a breaking point. We realize we are getting nowhere. Such moments are signals from the brain to let go, for however long a period necessary, and most creative people con-sciously or unconsciously accept this.

When we let go, we are not aware that below the surface of conscious-ness the ideas and the associations we had built up continue to bubble and incubate. With the feeling of tightness gone, the brain can momentarily return to that initial feeling of excitement and aliveness, which by now has been greatly enhanced by all of our hard work. The brain can now find the proper synthesis to the work, the one that was eluding us because we had become too tight in our approach. Perhaps the idea for the watery sounds in *Das Rheingold* had stirred before in different forms in Wagner's brain as he strained to find the right opening. Only by giving up the chase and falling asleep in the woods was he able to access his unconscious mind, and allow an idea that had been brewing there to surface by way of a dream.

The key is to be aware of this process and to encourage yourself to go as far as you can with your doubts, your reworkings, and your strained efforts, knowing the value and purpose of the frustration and creative blocks you are facing. Think of yourself as your own Zen Master. Such Masters would often beat their pupils and deliberately lead them to points of maximum doubt and inner tension, knowing such moments often precede enlightenment.

Among the thousands of stories of great insights and discoveries, perhaps the strangest one of all is that of Evariste Galois, a promising student of mathematics in France who in his teens revealed exceptional brilliance in algebra. In 1831, at the age of twenty, he became embroiled in a quarrel over a woman, which resulted in his being challenged to a duel. The night before the duel, certain he was going to die, Galois sat down and tried to summarize all of the ideas on algebraic equations that had been troubling him for several years. Suddenly, the ideas flowed, and even new ones came to him. He wrote all night at a feverish pitch. The next day, as he had foreseen, he died in the duel, but in the ensuing years his notes were read and published, leading to a complete revolution in higher algebra. Some of his scribbled notes indicated directions in mathematics that were so far ahead of his time, it is hard to fathom where they came from.

This is a somewhat extreme example, but the story reveals something elemental about the need for tension. The feeling that we have endless time to complete our work has an insidious and debilitating effect on our minds. Our attention and thoughts become diffused. Our lack of intensity makes it hard for the brain to jolt into a higher gear. The connections do not occur. For this purpose you must always try to work with deadlines, whether real or manufactured. Faced with the slenderest amount of time to reach the end, the mind rises to the level you require. Ideas crowd upon one another. You don't have the luxury of feeling frustrated. Every day represents an intense challenge, and every morning you wake up with original ideas and associations to push you along.

If you don't have such deadlines, manufacture them for yourself. The inventor Thomas Edison understood how much better he worked under pressure. He would deliberately talk to the press about an idea before it was ready. This would create some publicity and excitement in the public as to the possibilities of the proposed invention. If he dropped the ball or let too much time pass, his reputation would suffer, and so his mind would spark into high gear and he would make it happen. In such cases your mind is like the army that is now backed up against the sea or a mountain and cannot retreat. Sensing the proximity of death, it will fight harder than ever.

Emotional Pitfalls

When we arrive at the Creative-Active phase in our career, we are confronted by new challenges that are not simply mental or intellectual. The work is more demanding; we are on our own and the stakes are higher. Our work is now more public and highly scrutinized. We might have the most brilliant ideas and a mind capable of handling the greatest intellectual challenges, but if we are not careful, we will tumble into emotional pitfalls. We will grow insecure, overly anxious about people's opinions, or excessively self-confident. Or we will become bored and lose a taste for the hard work that is always necessary. Once we fall into these traps it is hard to extricate ourselves; we lose the necessary perspective to see where we have gone wrong. Better to be aware of these pitfalls in advance and never step into them. The following are the six most common pitfalls that threaten us along the way.

Complacency: In childhood, the world seemed like an enchanted place. Everything that we encountered had an intensity to it, and sparked feelings of wonder. Now, from our mature viewpoint, we see this wonderment as naïve, a quaint quality we have outgrown with our sophistication and vast experience of the real world. Such words as "enchantment" or "wonder" cause us to snicker. But imagine for an instant that the opposite is the case. The fact that life began on its own so many billions of years ago, that a conscious species such as ours ever came about and evolved into our present form, that we have visited the moon and come to understand vital laws of physics, and so on—all of this should continually fill us with awe. Our skeptical, cynical attitudes can actually cut us off from so many interesting questions, and from reality itself.

After we pass through a rigorous apprenticeship and begin to flex our creative muscles, we cannot help but feel satisfaction in what we have learned and how far we have progressed. We naturally begin to take for granted certain ideas we have learned and developed. Slowly, we stop asking the same kinds of questions that plagued us earlier on. We already know the answers. We feel ever so superior. Unknown to ourselves, the mind slowly narrows and tightens as complacency creeps into the soul, and although we may have achieved public acclaim for our past work, we stifle our own creativity and never get it back. Fight this downhill tendency as much as you can by upholding the value of active wonder. Constantly remind yourself of how little you truly know, and of how mysterious the world remains.

Conservatism: If you gain any kind of attention or success for your work in this phase, you face the great danger of creeping conservatism. This danger comes in several forms. You begin to fall in love with the ideas and strategies that worked for you in the past. Why risk changing your style in midstream, or adapting a new approach to your work? Better to stick to the tried and true. You also will have a reputation to protect—better to not say or do anything that might rock the boat. You become subtly addicted to the material comforts you have acquired and before you know it, you uphold ideas that you think you believe in, but that really are tied to your need to please the audience or your sponsors, or whomever.

Creativity is by its nature an act of boldness and rebellion. You are not accepting the status quo or conventional wisdom. You are playing with the very rules you have learned, experimenting and testing the boundaries. The world is dying for bolder ideas, for people who are not afraid to speculate and investigate. Creeping conservatism will narrow your searches, tether you to comfortable ideas, and create a downward spiral—as the creative spark leaves you, you will find yourself clutching even more forcefully to dead ideas, past successes, and the need to maintain your status. Make creativity rather than comfort your goal and you will ensure far more success for the future.

Dependency: In the Apprenticeship Phase you relied upon mentors and those above you to supply you with the necessary standards of judgment for your field. But if you are not careful, you will carry this need for approval over into the next phase. Instead of relying on the Master for evaluation of your work, you—ever insecure about your work and how it will be judged—come to rely on the opinions of the public. It is not that you must ignore these judgments, but that you must first work hard to develop internal standards and a high degree of independence. You have the capacity to see your own work with some distance; when the public reacts, you can distinguish between what is worth paying attention to and what you should ignore. What you want in the end is to internalize the voice of your Master so that you become both teacher and pupil. If you fail to do so you will have no internal gauge as to the value of your work, and you will be blown here and there by the opinions of others, never to find yourself.

Impatience: This is perhaps the single greatest pitfall of them all. This quality continually haunts you, no matter how disciplined you might think you are. You will convince yourself that your work is essentially over and well done, when really it is your impatience speaking and coloring your judgment. You tend to lose the energy you had when you were younger and hungrier. Unconsciously, you will veer toward repetition—reusing the same ideas and processes as a kind of shortcut. Unfortunately, the creative process requires continual intensity and vigor. Each exercise or problem or project is different. Hurrying to the end or warming up old ideas will ensure a mediocre result.

Leonardo da Vinci understood the dangers of such impatience. He adopted as his motto the expression *ostinato rigore,* which translates as "stubborn rigor" or "tenacious application." For every project he involved himself in—and by the end of his life they numbered in the thousands—he repeated this to himself, so he would attack each one with the same vigor and tenacity. The best way to neutralize our natural impatience is to cultivate a kind of pleasure in pain—like an athlete, you come to enjoy rigorous practice, pushing past your limits, and resisting the easy way out.

Grandiosity: Sometimes greater danger comes from success and praise than from criticism. If we learn to handle criticism well, it can strengthen us and help us become aware of flaws in our work. Praise generally does harm. Ever so slowly, the emphasis shifts from the joy of the creative process to the love of attention and to our ever-inflating ego. Without realizing it, we alter and shape our work to attract the praise that we crave. We fail to understand the element of luck that always goes into success—we often depend on being in the right place at the right time. Instead, we come to think that our brilliance has naturally drawn our success and attention, as if it were indeed fated. Once the ego inflates it will only come back to earth through some jarring failure, which will equally scar us. To avoid this fate, you must have some perspective. There are always greater geniuses out there than yourself. Luck certainly played a role, as did the help of your mentor and all those in the past who paved the way. What must ultimately motivate you is the work itself and the process. Public attention is actually a nuisance and a distraction. Such an attitude is the only defense against falling into the traps set by our ego.

Inflexibility: Being creative involves certain paradoxes. You must know your field inside and out, and yet be able to question its most entrenched assumptions. You must be somewhat naïve to entertain certain questions, and optimistic that you will solve the problem at hand; at the same time, you must regularly doubt that you have achieved your goal and subject your work to intensive self-criticism. All of this requires a great deal of flexibility, which means you must not get too hung up on any single frame of mind. You must bend to the moment and adopt the attitude appropriate to the moment.

Flexibility is not an easy or natural quality to develop. Once you spend a period of time being excited and hopeful about an idea, you will find it hard to shift to a more critical position. Once you look at your work with intensity and doubt, you will lose your optimism and your love of what you do. Avoiding these problems takes practice and often some experience—when you have pushed past the doubt before, you will find it easier the next time. In any event, you must avoid emotional extremes and find a way to feel optimism and doubt at the same time—a difficult sensation to describe in words, but something all Masters have experienced.

We are all in search of feeling more connected to reality—to other people, the times we live in, the natural world, our character, and our own uniqueness. Our culture increasingly tends to separate us from these realities in various ways. We indulge in drugs or alcohol, or engage in dangerous sports or risky behavior, just to wake ourselves up from the sleep of our daily existence and feel a heightened sense of connection to reality. In the end, however, the most satisfying and powerful way to feel this connection is through creative activity. Engaged in the creative process we feel more alive than ever, because we are making something and not merely consuming, Masters of the small reality we create. In doing this work, we are in fact creating ourselves.

Although it involves much pain, the pleasure that comes from the overall process of creativity is of an intensity that makes us want to repeat it. That is why creative people return again and again to such endeavors, despite all of the anxiety and doubt they stir up. It is nature's way of rewarding us for the effort; if we had no such rewards, people would not engage in such activity, and mankind would suffer irreparably from this loss. This pleasure will be your reward as well, to whatever degree you pursue the process.

STRATEGIES FOR THE CREATIVE-ACTIVE PHASE

Don't think about why you question, simply don't stop questioning. Don't worry about what you can't answer, and don't try to explain what you can't know. Curiosity is its own reason. Aren't you in awe when you contemplate the mysteries of eternity, of life, of the marvelous structure behind reality? And this is the miracle of the human mind—to use its constructions, concepts, and formulas as tools to explain what man sees, feels and touches. Try to comprehend a little more each day. Have holy curiosity.

—ALBERT EINSTEIN

As future Masters emerge from their apprenticeships, they all face the same dilemma: no one has ever really instructed them about the creative process, and there are no real books or teachers to turn to. Struggling on their own to become more active and imaginative with the knowledge they have gained, they evolve their own process—one that suits their temperament and the field they are working in. And in these creative evolutions we can detect some basic patterns and lessons for us all. The following stories of nine Masters reveal nine different strategic approaches to the same goal. The methods they employ may be applied to any field because they are connected to the creative powers of the brain that we all possess. Try to absorb each one of them, enriching your own knowledge of the process of mastery and widening your creative arsenal.

1. The Authentic Voice

As a boy growing up in North Carolina, John Coltrane (1926–67) took up music as a kind of hobby. He was an anxious young man who needed an outlet for all of his pent-up energy. He started with the alto horn, moved to the clarinet, and finally settled on the alto saxophone. He played for his school band, and to those who heard him play back then he was a completely insignificant member of the group.

Then in 1943 his family moved to Philadelphia. One evening shortly after the move Coltrane happened to catch a performance of the great bebop saxophonist Charlie Parker, and he was instantly transfixed. (See page 31.) He had never heard such playing, had never imagined such possibilities in music. Parker had a way of lilting and singing through his saxophone as if the instrument had melded with his own voice, and in hearing him play it seemed possible to feel what he was feeling. From that moment on, John Coltrane was a man possessed. Following in Parker's footsteps, in his own way, would now be his Life's Task.

Coltrane was not sure how he could reach such heights, but he knew that Parker was an intense student of all types of music and practiced the instrument harder than anyone. This fit in nicely with Coltrane's own inclinations—always being somewhat of a loner, he loved nothing more than to study and expand his knowledge. He started taking theory lessons at a local music school. And he began to practice night and day, with such assiduity that his reeds would become red from blood. In the time in between practicing, he went to the public library and listened to classical music, hungry to absorb every conceivable harmonic possibility. He practiced scales like a fiend, driving his family insane. He took scale-book exercises designed for the piano and used them for the saxophone, going through all of the keys in Western music. He began to get gigs in bands in Philadelphia, getting his first real break in Dizzy Gillespie's orchestra. Gillespie made him change to the tenor sax to get more of the Charlie Parker sound, and within a few months Coltrane had mastered the new instrument—through endless hours of practice.

Over the next five years Coltrane would bounce around from one band to another, each with its different style and repertoire of songs. This wandering existence suited him well—he felt as if he needed to internalize every conceivable style of music. But this also caused him some problems. When it came time for him to perform a solo, he was quite awkward and halting. He had an unusual sense of rhythm, a hopping and skipping style that was peculiar to him and not quite right for the bands he was playing for. Feeling self-conscious, when it came time for a solo he would resort to imitating someone else's way of playing. Every few months he would suddenly experiment with a new sound that he had heard. To some, it seemed like young Coltrane had gotten lost in all of his studying and roaming about.

In 1955 Miles Davis—leader of the most famous jazz quartet at the time—decided to take a chance and invite Coltrane into his group. Like everyone else, he knew that the young man was the most technically brilliant player around, the result of so many hours of practice. But he also detected in his work something strange, a new kind of voice straining to come out. He encouraged Coltrane to go his own way and never look back. In the months to come, Davis would have moments of regret—he had let loose something that was hard to integrate into his group. Coltrane had a way of starting chords in the strangest places. He would alternate fast passages with long tones, giving the impression that several voices were coming through the saxophone at once. No one had ever heard such a sound. His tone was equally peculiar; he had his own way of tightly clenching the mouthpiece, making it seem as if it were his own gravelly voice that was emerging from the instrument. His playing had an undercurrent of anxiety and aggression, which gave his music a sense of urgency.

Although many were put off by this strange new sound, some critics began to recognize something exciting in it. One writer described what came out of Coltrane's saxophone as "sheets of sound," as if he were playing groups of notes at once and sweeping the listener away with his music. Although he was now gaining recognition and attention, Coltrane continued to feel restless and uncertain. Through all of his years of practicing and playing he had been searching for something he could hardly put into words. He wanted to personalize his sound to the extreme, to make it the perfect embodiment of how he was feeling—often emotions of a spiritual and transcendental nature, and thus hard to verbalize. At moments his playing would come alive, but at other times the sensation of his own voice would elude him. Perhaps all of his knowledge was in fact cramping and inhibiting him. In 1959 he left Miles Davis to form his own quartet. From now on, he would experiment and try almost anything until he found the sound that he had been looking for.

His song "Giant Steps," on his first major album of the same name, was an exercise in unconventional music. Using peculiar chord progressions that moved in thirds, with constant key and chord changes, the music was impelled frantically forward. (Its third-related chord progressions became known as Coltrane changes, and are still used by musicians as a template for jazz improvisation.) The album was a huge success; several pieces from it went on to become jazz standards, but the experiment left Coltrane cold. He now wanted to return to melody, to something freer and more expressive, and he found himself going back to the music of his early childhood— Negro spirituals. In 1960 he created his first huge popular hit, an extended version of the song "My Favorite Things," from the smash Broadway musical *The Sound of Music*. He played it on the soprano saxophone in a style that seemed almost East Indian, blending in as well a touch of Negro spirituals, all with his strange propensity for chord changes and rapid scales. It was a weird blend of experimental and popular music, unlike anything anyone else had done.

Coltrane was now like an alchemist, involved in an almost impossible quest to discover the essence of music itself, to make it express more deeply and directly the emotions he was feeling, to connect it to the unconscious. And slowly, it seemed he was getting closer to his goal. His ballad "Alabama," written in response to the 1963 bombing by the Ku Klux Klan of a church in Birmingham, Alabama, seemed to capture something essential about the moment and the mood of the time. It seemed to be the incarnation of sadness and despair. A year later, his album *A Love Supreme* appeared. It was recorded in one day, and making the music was like a religious experience for him. It had everything he was aiming for—extended movements that went as long as it felt natural to do so (something novel in jazz), and a trance-like effect on listeners, while still containing the hard-driving sound and technical brilliance he was known for. It was an album that expressed that spiritual element he could not put into words. It became a sensation, drawing a whole new audience to his music.

People who saw his live performances in this period proclaimed the uniqueness of the experience. As the saxophonist Joe McPhee described it, "I thought I was going to die from the emotion . . . I thought I was just going to explode right in the place. The energy level kept building up, and I thought, God almighty, I can't take it." Audiences would go wild, some people screaming at the intensity of the sound. It seemed as if the music from Coltrane's saxophone was a direct translation of some deep mood or feeling of his, and that he could move the audience in whatever direction he wanted with it. No other jazz artist had such an effect on audiences.

As part of the Coltrane phenomenon, every change he introduced into jazz was suddenly adopted as the latest trend—extended songs, larger groups, tambourines and bells, Eastern sounds, and so on. The man who had spent ten long years absorbing the styles of all forms of music and jazz now had become the trendsetter for others. Coltrane's meteoric career, however, was cut short in 1967, when he died at the age of forty of liver cancer.

In Coltrane's era jazz had become a celebration of individuality. Players like Charlie Parker made the jazz solo the centerpiece of any work. In the solo, the player would pour out his own unique voice. But what is this voice that comes through so clearly in the work of the greats? It is not something we can exactly put into words. Musicians are expressing something deep about their nature, their particular psychological makeup, even their unconscious. It comes out in their style, their unique rhythms and phrasings. But this voice does not emerge from just being oneself and letting loose. A person who would take up an instrument and try to express this quality right away would only produce noise. Jazz or any other musical form is a language, with conventions and vocabulary. And so the extreme paradox is that those who impress the most with their individuality—John Coltrane at the top—are the ones who first completely submerge their character in a long apprenticeship. In Coltrane's case, this process can be broken up neatly—just over ten years of an intense apprenticeship, followed by ten years of perhaps the most amazing creative explosion in modern music, up until his death.

By spending so long learning structure, developing technique, and absorbing every possible style and way of playing, Coltrane built up a vast vocabulary. Once all of this became hardwired into his nervous system, his mind could focus on higher things. At an increasingly rapid pace, he could bend all of the techniques he had learned into something more personal. In being so open to exploring and trying things out, he could discover in a serendipitous fashion those musical ideas that suited him. With all that he had learned and mastered, he could combine ideas and styles in unique ways. By being patient and following the process, individual expression flowed out of him naturally. He personalized every genre he worked in, from blues to Broadway show tunes. His authentic voice—with its anxious, urgent tone—was a reflection of his uniqueness at birth, and came to him in a lengthy, organic process. By expressing his deepest self and his most primal emotions, he created a visceral effect on listeners.

Understand: the greatest impediment to creativity is your impatience, the almost inevitable desire to hurry up the process, express something, and make a splash. What happens in such a case is that you do not master the basics; you have no real vocabulary at your disposal. What you mistake for being creative and distinctive is more likely an imitation of other people's style, or personal rantings that do not really express anything. Audiences, however, are hard to fool. They feel the lack of rigor, the imitative quality, the urge to get attention, and they turn their backs, or give the mildest praise that quickly passes. The best route is to follow Coltrane and to love learning for its own sake. Anyone who would spend ten years absorbing the techniques and conventions of their field, trying them out, mastering them, exploring and personalizing them, would inevitably find their authentic voice and give birth to something unique and expressive.

2. The Fact of Great Yield

For as long as he can remember, V. S. Ramachandran (b. 1951) has been fascinated by any kind of strange phenomenon in nature. As narrated in chapter 1 (see page 32), at a very young age he began collecting seashells from beaches near his home in Madras. In researching the subject, his attention was drawn to the most peculiar varieties of seashells, such as the carnivorous murex. Soon he added these unusual specimens to his collection. As he got older, he transferred this interest to abnormal phenomena in chemistry, astronomy, and human anatomy. Perhaps he intuited that these anomalies fulfilled some kind of purpose in nature, that what does not fit the pattern has something interesting to tell us. Perhaps he felt that he himself—with his passion for science when other boys were attracted to sports or games—was a bit of an anomaly as well. In any event, as he matured his attraction to the bizarre and abnormal only grew.

In the 1980s, as a professor of visual psychology at the University of California at San Diego, he came upon a phenomenon that appealed to his interest in anomalies in the deepest way—the so-called phantom limb syndrome. In this case, people who have had a limb amputated continue to experience sensation and pain where the limb used to be. In his research as a visual psychologist, Ramachandran had specialized in optical illusions—instances in which the brain would incorrectly fill in information from what the eyes had processed. Phantom limbs represented an optical illusion on a much larger scale, with the brain supplying sensation where there could be none. Why would the brain send such signals? What does such a phenomenon tell us about the brain in general? And why were there so few people interested in this truly bizarre condition? He became obsessed with these questions, and read everything he could about the subject.

One day in 1991, he read about an experiment conducted by Dr. Timothy Pons of the National Institute of Health that astounded him with its possible ramifications. Pons's experiment was based on research from the 1950s in which the Canadian neurosurgeon, Wilder Penfeld, had been able to map the areas of the human brain that regulate sensation in various body parts. This map ended up being applicable to primates as well.

In Pons's experiment, he worked with monkeys whose nerve fibers from the brain to one arm had been severed. In testing out the map of their brains, Pons discovered that when he touched the hand of the dead arm, there was no activity in the corresponding part of the brain, as expected. But when he touched their faces, suddenly the cells in the brain that corresponded to the dead hand began to fire rapidly, in addition to those of the face. The nerve cells in the brain that govern sensation in the hand had somehow migrated to the area of the face. It was impossible to know for sure, but it seemed that these monkeys were experiencing sensation in the dead hand when their faces were touched.

Inspired by this discovery, Ramachandran decided to conduct an experiment that was astonishing for its simplicity. He brought into his office a young man who, because of a recent car accident, had had his left arm amputated from just above the elbow, and was now experiencing considerable sensation in his phantom limb. Using a cotton swab, Ramachandran proceeded to touch the man's legs and stomach. He reported completely normal sensations. But when Ramachandran swabbed a particular part of his cheek, the man experienced a sensation both in the cheek and in the thumb of his phantom hand. Moving around the face with the Q-tip, Ramachandran found other areas corresponding to other parts of the missing hand. The results were remarkably similar to those of Pons's experiment.

The implications of this one simple test were profound. It had been largely assumed in neuroscience that the connections in the brain are hardwired at birth or in the earliest years, and are essentially permanent. The results of this experiment contradicted this assumption. In this case, after a traumatic accident, it appeared that the brain had altered itself in a dramatic fashion, creating whole new networks of connections in a relatively short amount of time. This meant that the human brain is potentially far more plastic than had been imagined. In this case the brain had altered itself in an odd and seemingly inexplicable way. But what if this power to alter itself could be harnessed for positive, therapeutic uses?

Based on this experiment, Ramachandran decided to shift fields, moving into the neuroscience department at UCSD and devoting his time and research to anomalous neurological disorders. He decided to take his phantom limb experiment a step further. Many patients with a severed limb experience an odd kind of paralysis that is highly painful. They feel the phantom limb, they want to move it but cannot, and they feel a cramping and sometimes an excruciating ache. Ramachandran speculated that before the limb had been amputated the brain had learned to experience the arm or leg as paralyzed, and once it had been amputated it continued to feel it that way. Would it be possible, considering the plasticity of the brain, to unlearn this paralysis? And so he came up with yet another incredibly simple experiment to test out his idea.

Using a mirror that he had in his office, he proceeded to construct his own apparatus. He took a cardboard box with the lid removed, and made two armholes in the front of the box. He then positioned the upright mirror inside of it. Patients were instructed to place their good arm through one hole and their severed arm right up to the other hole. They were to maneuver the mirror until the image of their good arm was seen in the position where their other arm should be. In moving their good arm and seeing it move in the position of the severed one, almost instantly, these patients experienced an alleviation of the feeling of paralysis. Most of the patients who took the box home with them and practiced with it were able to unlearn the paralysis, much to their relief.

Once again, the meaning of this discovery was profound. Not only was the brain more plastic, but the senses were also much more interconnected than previously imagined. The brain did not consist of modules for each sense; instead they overlapped. In this case, pure visual stimuli had altered the sense of touch and sensation. But beyond that, this experiment also called into question the whole notion of pain. Pain, it seemed, was a kind of opinion the body rendered on what it was experiencing, on its own health. This opinion could be tricked or manipulated, as the mirror experiment had shown.

In further experiments, Ramachandran arranged it so that patients would see a student's arm instead of their own, superimposed over the phantom limb. They would not be aware that this had been done, and when the student moved the arm, they experienced the same relief from paralysis. It was merely the sight of the movement that created the effect. This made the sensation of pain seem increasingly more subjective and subject to alteration.

Over the ensuing years, Ramachandran would perfect this creative style of investigation into an art, transforming himself into one of the leading neuroscientists in the world. He developed certain guidelines for his strategy. He would look for any evidence of anomalies in neuroscience or in related fields, ones that brought up questions that had the potential to challenge conventional wisdom. His criteria were that he had to be able to show it was a real phenomenon (something like telepathy would not fall into this category), that it could be explained in terms of current science, and that it had important implications stretching beyond the confines of his own field. If others were ignoring it because it seemed too weird, so much the better—he would have the research field all to himself.

Furthermore, he looked for ideas that he could verify through simple experiments—no heavy or expensive equipment. He had noticed that those who got large grants for their research, which would include all of the technological gadgetry that went with it, would become embroiled in political games in order to justify the money being spent on them. They would rely on technology instead of on their own thinking. And they would become conservative, not wanting to rock the boat with their conclusions. He preferred to do his work with cotton swabs and mirrors, and by engaging in detailed conversations with his patients.

For instance, he became intrigued by the neurological disorder known as apotemnophilia—the desire of perfectly healthy people to have a limb amputated, with many of them actually going through with the surgery. Some had speculated that this well-known disorder is a cry for attention, or stems from a form of sexual perversion, or that patients had seen in childhood an amputee and the image had somehow become imprinted as an ideal to them. In all of these speculations, people seemed to doubt the reality of the actual sensation—it was all in their heads, they implied.

Through simple interviews with several such patients, Ramachandran made some discoveries that dispelled these notions. In all cases they involved the left leg, which was curious enough. In talking to them, it seemed clear to Ramachandran that they were not after attention, nor were they sexually perverse, but rather they were experiencing a very real desire, because of some very real sensation. With a pen, they all marked the exact spot where they wanted the amputation.

When he did simple galvanic skin response tests on their bodies (tests that record the registering of slight amounts of pain), he discovered that everything was normal, except when he pricked the part of the leg the patient wanted amputated. The response was through the roof. The patient was experiencing that part of the limb as if it were too present, too intense, and this overactive sensation could only be done away with through amputation.

In subsequent work he was able to locate neurological damage to the part of their brains that create and control our sense of body image. This damage had occurred at birth, or very early on. This meant that the brain could create a body image in a perfectly healthy person that was highly irrational. It seemed as well that our sense of self is far more subjective and fluid than we had thought. If our experience of our own body is something constructed in the brain and can go haywire, then perhaps our sense of self is also something of a construction or illusion, one that we create to suit our purposes, and one that can malfunction. The implications here go beyond neuroscience, and into the realm of philosophy.

The animal world can be divided into two types—specialists and opportunists. Specialists, like hawks or eagles, have one dominant skill upon which they depend for their survival. When they are not hunting, they can go into a mode of complete relaxation. Opportunists, on the other hand, have no particular specialty. They depend instead on their skill to sniff out any kind of opportunity in the environment and seize upon it. They are in states of constant tension and require continual stimulation. We humans are the ultimate opportunists in the animal world, the least specialized of all living creatures. Our entire brain and nervous system is geared toward looking for any kind of opening. Our most primitive ancestors did not begin with an idea in their heads for creating a tool to help them in scavenging and killing. Instead they came upon a rock, perhaps one that was unusually sharp or elongated (an anomaly), and saw in this a possibility. In picking it up and handling it, the idea came to them to use it as a tool. This opportunistic bent of the human mind is the source and foundation of our creative powers, and it is in going with this bent of the brain that we maximize these powers.

And yet when it comes to creative endeavors, so often we find people going at them from the wrong end. This generally afflicts those who are young and inexperienced—they begin with an ambitious goal, a business, or an invention or a problem they want to solve. This seems to promise money and attention. They then search for ways to reach that goal. Such a search could go in thousands of directions, each of which could pan out in its own way, but in which they could also easily end up exhausting themselves and never find the key to reaching their overarching goal. There are too many variables that go into success. The more experienced, wiser types, such as Ramachandran, are opportunists. Instead of beginning with some broad goal, they go in search of the fact of great yield—a bit of empirical evidence that is strange and does not fit the paradigm, and yet is intriguing. This bit of evidence sticks out and grabs their attention, like the elongated rock. They are not sure of their goal and they do not yet have in mind an application for the fact they have uncovered, but they are open to where it will lead them. Once they dig deeply, they discover something that challenges prevailing conventions and offers endless opportunities for knowledge and application.

In looking for facts of great yield, you must follow certain guidelines. Although you are beginning within a particular field that you understand deeply, you must not allow your mind to become tethered to this discipline. Instead you must read journals and books from all different fields. Sometimes you will find an interesting anomaly in an unrelated discipline that may have implications for your own. You must keep your mind completely open—no item is too small or unimportant to escape your attention. If an apparent anomaly calls into question your own beliefs or assumptions, so much the better. You must speculate on what it could mean, this speculation guiding your subsequent research but not determining your conclusions. If what you have discovered seems to have profound ramifications, you must pursue it with the utmost intensity. Better to look into ten such facts, with only one yielding a great discovery, than to look into twenty ideas that bring success but have trivial implications. You are the supreme hunter, ever alert, eyes scanning the landscape for the fact that will expose a once-hidden reality, with profound consequences.

3. Mechanical Intelligence

From their earliest years the brothers Wilbur Wright (1867–1912) and Orville Wright (1871–1948) displayed a rather unusual interest in the working parts of any kind of device, particularly the elaborate toys their father often brought home to them from his travels as a bishop in the United Brethren Church. They would take these toys apart in a state of extreme excitement, avid to figure out what made them tick. Then they would reassemble them, always with some modification.

Although the boys were reasonably good at schoolwork, neither of them received a high school diploma. They wanted to live in a world of machines, and the only knowledge that really interested them was that which related to the design and construction of some new device. They were extremely practical.

In 1888 their father needed to quickly print out a pamphlet for his work. To help him, the brothers cobbled together their own small job press, using the hinge from a folding buggy top in the backyard, rusty springs, and other pieces of scrap. The press worked brilliantly. Inspired by their success, they improved the design, using better parts, and opened their own printing shop. Those who knew the business marveled at the peculiar press the brothers had concocted, which managed to spit out 1,000 pages per hour, double the usual rate.

The brothers, however, had a restless spirit. They needed constant challenges, and in 1892 Orville discovered the perfect new outlet for them. With the invention of the safety bicycle (the first bicycle featuring two wheels of the same size), America had become seized with a biking craze. The brothers purchased their own bicycles, entered races, and became fanatics in the sport. Soon they were taking their bicycles apart and making minor adjustments. Seeing them at work in the backyard, friends and acquaintances would bring them their own bicycles for repairs. Within months they knew bicycle technology from the inside out, and decided to open their own shop in their native Dayton, Ohio, where they sold, repaired and even modified the latest models.

This seemed to be the perfect match for their skills. They could make various changes on a bicycle, take it out for a test ride, feel what worked and didn't work, and then make further improvements. They were constantly striving to make the bicycles more maneuverable and aerodynamic, changes that would qualitatively alter the experience of riding and give the rider a feeling of being in complete control. Dissatisfied with the latest designs, they decided that the next logical step was to build their own aluminum frames and design their own custom-built bicycle. This represented a steep challenge—it would require months of on-the-job learning to be able to properly build frames. The slightest flaw could cause all kinds of horrifying accidents. In the process of learning this skill, they purchased a slew of the latest tools, built their own one-cylinder engine to power them, and steadily became master bicycle craftsmen. Those who rode the Wright brothers' bicycles could feel right away the superiority of their version, which included technological improvements that would soon become industry standards.

In 1896, while convalescing from an injury, Wilbur read an article that would haunt him for years. It concerned the death of Otto Lilienthal, the leading designer of gliders and an expert in the growing field of aviation. He had died in a crash with his latest glider design. The photographs of the various gliders he had built, all in flight, astounded Wilbur—they looked like the wings of a giant prehistoric bird. As someone with a powerful sense of visualization, Wilbur could imagine the sensation of flying itself, and it thrilled him. But what surprised him in the article was that over many years of test flights, perhaps numbering in the hundreds, Lilienthal had never been able to maintain the flight long enough to get a feel for the necessary improvements, and had probably died because of this.

Several years later, newspapers were filled with stories about the latest pioneers in aviation, many of whom appeared to be getting closer to the goal of creating a motored flying machine. It was now turning into a race to be the first to succeed. His curiosity on the subject getting deeper, Wilbur decided to write to the Smithsonian Institution in Washington, D.C., requesting all of their available information on aeronautics and flying machines. For the next few months he pored over the materials, reading about the physics and mathematics behind flight, the designs of Leonardo da Vinci, and the gliders of the nineteenth century. He added to his reading list books about birds, which he now began to observe and study. And the more he read, the more he had the strange sensation that he and his brother could actually be the ones to win such a race.

At first glance this would seem an absurd idea. The men in the field were all experts with incredible technical knowledge, some with impressive college degrees. They had an enormous head start over the Wright brothers. Designing and building a flying machine was an expensive venture that could total thousands of dollars and lead to yet another crash. The favorite to win the race was Samuel Langley, the secretary of the Smithsonian Institution, who had an enormous government grant to pursue his work and had already successfully flown a steam-powered, unmanned model. The brothers came from a modest background, and the only money they had was the slender profits from their bicycle shop. But what all of these men lacked, in Wilbur's mind, was some basic common sense when it came to any kind of machine.

These aviators had begun with the premise that what mattered was to get the machine in the air using a powerful engine of some sort, figuring the rest out once flight had been achieved. Getting in the air would impress the public, gain attention, and attract financial backing. This led to many crashes, constant redesigns, the search for the perfect engine, new materials, and more crashes. They were getting nowhere, and the reason was simple. As Wilbur knew, the key to building anything right is repetition. It was only by getting their hands on bicycles, fiddling and tinkering with them, then riding them and gaining a feel for what worked, that the brothers had been able to design a superior variety of bicycle. Because the designers of the flying machines could not fly for more than a minute, they were locked into a vicious cycle—they were never airborne long enough to learn how to fly and properly test out their designs, or get a feel for what might work. They were doomed to failure.

Wilbur discovered another great flaw in their thinking that shocked him: they all overvalued the importance of stability. They thought in terms of a ship floating through the air. A ship is designed to maintain balance, and to move in as stable and straight a manner as possible; tipping from side to side is far too dangerous. Based on this analogy, they decided to design the wings of their flying machines in a slight V shape, to compensate for any sudden gusts of wind and to keep the cruising aircraft in a straight line. But Wilbur felt that thinking in terms of ships was the wrong analogy. Instead, it was far wiser to think in terms of a bicycle. A bicycle is inherently unstable. It is the rider who learns quickly enough how to keep the bike in a secure position, and to steer it properly by leaning to the side. A pilot of a flying machine, as he imagined it, should be able to safely bank and turn, or tilt up or down, and not be locked into a rigid horizontal line, like a ship. Trying to free the machine from the effects of the wind was actually quite dangerous, because it would remove the ability of the pilot to adjust.

Armed with this knowledge, it was easy enough for Wilbur to convince his brother that a flying machine should be their next and ultimate challenge. They would have to use their limited profits from the bicycle shop to fund the project. This would force them to be creative, using scrap parts and never trying anything beyond their means. Instead of beginning with a grandiose device to test out their ideas, they would have to slowly evolve the perfect design, just as they had done with the printing press and the bicycle.

They decided to begin as modestly as possible. They designed various kites to help them determine the perfect overall shape for a test glider. Then, based on what they had learned, they fashioned the glider itself. They wanted to teach themselves how to fly. The usual method of launching a glider off the crest of a hill was too dangerous. Instead, they decided to move operations to Kitty Hawk, North Carolina, the site of the strongest winds in the United States. There, on the sand dunes of the beaches at Kitty Hawk, they could get airborne from small elevations, fly close to the ground, and land in a soft bed of sand. In the year 1900 alone they were able to perform more test flights than Lilienthal had attempted over many years. They slowly perfected the design, and improved the materials and configuration—for instance, they learned to make the wings longer and thinner to improve the lift. By 1903 they had a glider they could fly for considerable distances, with remarkable control over turning and banking. It was indeed like a flying bicycle.

Now it was time to take the final step—adding the engine and propellers to their design. As before, they looked at the designs of their rivals and noticed another weakness: they had modeled their propellers on those of boats, once again opting for stability. Based on their own research, the brothers decided that the blades should be cambered, like the wings of a bird—that would give the plane more thrust. Looking to purchase the lightest engine to power the machine, they found it was far beyond their budget. So with the help of a mechanic in their shop, they built their own engine. In total, the cost of their flying apparatus would come in under $1,000—considerably less than any of the designs of their competitors.

On December 17, 1903, Wilbur piloted their flying machine at Kitty Hawk for an impressive fifty-nine seconds—the first manned, controlled, and powered flight in history. Over the years they would improve the design, and the flight times would increase. For the other competitors in the race it was a complete mystery how two men without any engineering or aeronautic experience or financial backing had managed to get there first.

The development of the airplane represents one of the greatest technological achievements in our history, with profound ramifications for the future. There simply was no real precedent or model to base the flying machine on. It was a genuine puzzle, and it required the highest degree of ingenuity to solve it. In the history of its invention, we can observe two radically different approaches. On the one side was a large group of engineers and designers with backgrounds in the sciences who saw the problem in abstract terms: how to get the plane launched and propelled, how to overcome wind resistance, and so on. They focused largely on the technology and worked to create the most efficient parts—the most powerful engines, the best-designed wings, all of this based on elaborate lab research. Money was no object. This process depended on specialization—individuals who focused on different parts and who specialized in different materials. In many cases, the designer would not end up being the pilot; someone else would do the test flights.

On the other side were two men from a completely different background. For them, the pleasure and excitement of design was in doing everything themselves. They designed the machine, built it, and flew it. Their model depended not on superior technology, but on the highest number of test runs, creating an optimal learning curve. This revealed flaws to be worked on and gave them a *feel* for the product that could never be had in the abstract. The emphasis was not on the parts, but on the overall flying experience; not on power, but on control. Since money was a factor, supreme importance was placed on ingenuity in getting the most out of the least. The differences between the two approaches can be seen in the analogies they chose to base their designs on. The abstract thinkers opted for the ship analogy, working on the similarity of navigating an alien medium (water or air), which made them place importance on stability. The Wright brothers chose the bicycle, which emphasized the rider or pilot, the user-friendliness of the machine, and its overall functionality. Focusing on the pilot instead of the medium ended up being the right answer to the puzzle, because it led to the design of something that could be maneuvered. From that starting point, a more complex airplane could be easily evolved.

Understand: mechanical intelligence is not a degraded form of thinking, as compared to abstract reasoning. It is in fact the source of many of our reasoning skills and creative powers. Our brain developed to its present size because of the complex operations of our hands. In working with resistant materials to create tools, our ancestors developed a pattern of thinking that transcends manual labor itself. The principles behind mechanical intelligence can be summarized as follows: whatever you are creating or designing, you must test and use it yourself. Separating out the work will make you lose touch with its functionality. Through intense labor on your part, you gain a feel for what you are creating. In doing this work, you see and feel the flaws in the design. You do not look at the parts separately but at how they interact, experiencing what you produce as a whole. What you are trying to create will not magically take off after a few creative bursts of inspiration, but must be slowly evolved through a step-by-step process as you correct the flaws. In the end, you win through superior craftsmanship, not marketing. This craftsmanship involves creating something with an elegant, simple structure, getting the most out of your materials—a high form of creativity. These principles work with the natural bent of your brain, and are to be violated at your own peril.

4. Natural Powers

After graduating from architecture school in Spain in 1973, Santiago Calatrava experienced some anxiety at the thought of rushing into an architecture practice. (For more on Calatrava, see pages 84–86.) He had ambitions early in life of becoming an artist, but gravitated toward architecture as a more expansive form of expression—something functional yet sculptural, something that could be realized on a large public scale. Architecture is a strange profession. It involves so many constraints when it comes to actually realizing a structure—the desires of the client, the budget, the materials available, the landscape, and even political issues. In the works of great architects in history, such as Le Corbusier, we can see a lot of their personal style in the finished product, but with many others their work becomes overwhelmed by the various constraints and interferences. Calatrava felt that he had not developed a sufficiently large vocabulary or mastered enough elements to be able to assert himself. If he went to work at a firm, his creative energies would be buried beneath all of the commercial pressures, and he would never recover.

And so he made an unusual decision: he would attend the Federal Institute of Technology in Zurich to gain a degree in civil engineering. He wanted to become an engineer so that he could understand the limits of what was possible in designing buildings and structures. He had the idea of someday attempting the construction of buildings that could move, transgressing some of the most fundamental principles of architecture. For such a purpose, he studied designs by NASA in which various devices had been made that could fold up and expand, making them practical for space missions. Such designs required mastering new engineering principles that Calatrava immersed himself in at the Institute.

After graduating in 1981 with an engineering degree, he finally began his practice as an architect and engineer. He was now well versed in the technical aspects of his job and in the basic requirements for completing a work, but no one had instructed him in the creative process itself. He would have to learn and invent such a process for himself.

His first big project came in 1983, when he was asked to design the façade of an already existing structure—an enormous warehouse for Ernsting, a well-known clothing manufacturer in Germany. He decided to cover the structure with untreated aluminum. This would tie the entire building together, but on each side the sunlight would create different, sometimes dazzling effects. To Calatrava the key part of the design was that of the three loading bay doors, each on different sides of the warehouse. Here he could experiment with his ideas of movement and foldability. And so, not certain where or how to begin the actual process, he started to sketch out various possibilities for these doors. As a child he had loved to draw, and he was constantly sketching. He had become so proficient with a pencil or brush that he could draw almost anything with great speed and accuracy. He could sketch as fast as he could think, his innermost visions translated with ease onto paper.

Without any sense of where he was headed, he began to draw in watercolors, putting everything that came to him on paper, almost in a free-associative manner. For some reason, the image of a beached whale occurred to him and so he drew it. He took it further and metamorphosed the whale into the warehouse, the teeth and mouth of the whale opening into the bay door. Now he understood the image. It was as if the warehouse had become Jonah's whale, disgorging trucks and materials from its mouth. On the margin of the drawing he wrote, "the building as a living organism." As he stared at the sketch, his attention was drawn to the rather large whale eye he had painted to the side of the mouth/bay door. It seemed like an interesting metaphor all by itself, and indicated a new direction to take.

He began to do different drawings of eyes on the sides of the warehouse, with the eyes turning into the doors. Now his drawings took on more detail and became more architectural as he began to sketch out the actual sides of the building and the doors in a more realistic rendering, but still based on the opening and closing of an enormous eye. In the end, this would turn into the actual design of the folding doors that would raise themselves up in the curved shape of an eyelid.

By the end of the design process Calatrava had generated a large number of sketches, and as he thumbed through them in sequential order, he could see a most interesting progression—from the loose imaginings of his unconscious to more and more precise renderings. Even in the most accurate sketches of the façade, however, there was still apparent some kind of artistic and playful element. To look at the drawings was almost to see the gradual development of a photograph in a chemical tray. Taking this form of attack was immensely satisfying. It gave him the feeling of creating something that was alive. Working in this way, his emotions were deeply engaged as he played upon all kinds of metaphors, both mythical and Freudian.

In the end, his design had a strange and powerful effect. Working with only the façade of the building, he had created the look of a Greek temple, the aluminum undulating like silver columns. The bay doors added a surreal touch, and when folded up, looked even more like the entranceway to a temple. All of this blended perfectly with the functionality of the structure. It was a great success, and garnered him immediate attention.

As the years went by, one important commission followed another. Working on increasingly larger projects, Calatrava could see clearly the dangers ahead of him. Completing a design could often take ten years or more, from the initial sketch to the actual construction. In that time, all kinds of problems and conflicts could arise, which could end up spoiling the initial vision. With larger budgets would come more constraints, and the need to please many different people. If he were not careful, his desire to transgress the rules and to express a personal vision would get lost in the process. And so, as his career progressed, something inside him made him return to the method he had developed for the Ernsting warehouse, and to elaborate it even further.

He would always begin with the drawings. Drawing by hand had become increasingly unusual in the era of computer graphics that had come to dominate so many aspects of architectural design in the 1980s. As a trained engineer, Calatrava knew the tremendous advantages the computer provided for running models and testing the soundness of a structure. But working exclusively on a computer, he could not create in the same way as he could with pencil or brush and paper. The intervention of the computer screen cut off the dreamlike process of sketching, the direct contact it gave him with his unconscious. His hand and his mind seemed to work together in a way that was primal and real, and that could not be duplicated through a computer.

Now his drawings for a single project would number in the hundreds. He would start out in the same loose manner, building up all kinds of associations. He would begin with a feeling or an emotion that the idea of the design sparked in him. This would lead to an image, however vague. For instance, when asked to design an elaborate addition to the Milwaukee Art Museum, what first came to mind and then to paper was the image of a bird about to take flight. This image would go through the mill of his sketching process, but in the end the roof of the building he designed featured two enormous, ribbed panels that would open and close according to the sunlight, giving the impression of an enormous prehistoric bird about to fly over Lake Michigan.

Most of these early, free associations would revolve around nature—plants, trees, human figures in various poses, skeletal ribbing—and would be intimately tied to the landscape. Slowly, the shape of the overall structure would come into focus through this process, as he would make the idea increasingly rational and architectural. As an adjunct to this process he would build models, sometimes beginning with a completely abstract sculptural shape that in subsequent versions would become the design for the structure itself. All of these drawings and sculptures were like exteriorizations of his unconscious and nonverbal thought processes.

Inevitably, as he moved closer to the construction phase, he would come up against constraints, such as the materials to be used and budgetary considerations. But working from this initial strategy, he experienced these factors merely as creative challenges: for instance, how could he incorporate certain materials into the vision he had sketched out and make it all work? If it were a train or subway station, how could he make the platforms and the movement of the trains fit into the overall vision, even enhancing their functionality? Such challenges excited him.

The greatest danger he faced was that his energy would go flat over time as the design dragged on into years, and he would lose touch with his original vision. To combat this, Calatrava would maintain an attitude of constant dissatisfaction. The drawings were never quite right. They had to be continually improved and perfected. By pushing for perfection and holding on to this constant feeling of uncertainty, the project never froze into something rigid and lifeless. It had to feel alive in the moment, as his brush touched the paper. If what he was designing began to feel dead in any way, it was time to start over. This not only required tremendous patience on his part, but a good deal of courage, as he wiped out the work of several months. Maintaining the edge and feeling of aliveness, however, was more important.

As the years went by and Calatrava was able to look back on all of his projects, he had a strange sensation. The process he had evolved felt as if it had come from outside of him. It was not something he had created through his own imagination, but rather it was nature itself that had led him to this perfectly organic and beautifully effective process. The projects would take root in his mind with some emotion or idea, and slowly grow through the drawings, always alive and as fluid as life itself, like the stages of a plant leading to a flower. Feeling such vitality during the work, he would translate this sensation into the structures themselves, evoking awe and wonder in the public that saw and used them.

Because the creative process is an elusive subject and one for which we receive no training, in our first creative endeavors we are most often left to our own devices, to sink or swim. And in these circumstances we have to evolve something that suits our individual spirit and our profession. Often, however, we can go quite wrong in evolving this process, particularly with the pressure to produce results and the fear this instills in us. In the process Calatrava developed for his work, we can discern an elemental pattern and principles that have wide application, built as they are on the natural inclinations and strengths of the human brain.

First, it is essential to build into the creative process an initial period that is open-ended. You give yourself time to dream and wander, to start out in a loose and unfocused manner. In this period, you allow the project to associate itself with certain powerful emotions, ones that naturally come out of you as you focus on your ideas. It is always easy to tighten up your ideas later on, and to make your project increasingly realistic and rational. But if you begin with a feeling of tightness and pressure, focusing on the funding, the competition, or people's opinions, you will stifle the associative powers of the brain and quickly turn the work into something without joy or life. Second, it is best to have wide knowledge of your field and other fields, giving your brain more possible associations and connections. Third, to keep this process alive, you must never settle into complacency, as if your initial vision represents the endpoint. You must cultivate profound dissatisfaction with your work and the need to constantly improve your ideas, along with a sense of uncertainty—you are not exactly sure where to go next, and this uncertainty drives the creative urge and keeps it fresh. Any kind of resistance or obstacle that crosses your path should be seen as yet another chance to improve your work.

Finally, you must come to embrace slowness as a virtue in itself. When it comes to creative endeavors, time is always relative. Whether your project takes months or years to complete, you will always experience a sense of impatience and a desire to get to the end. The single greatest action you can take for acquiring creative power is to reverse this natural impatience. You take pleasure in the laborious research process; you enjoy the slow cooking of the idea, the organic growth that naturally takes shape over time. You do not unnaturally draw out the process, which will create its own problems (we all need deadlines), but the longer you can allow the project to absorb your mental energies, the richer it will become. Imagine yourself years in the future looking back at the work you have done. From that future vantage point, the extra months and years you devoted to the process will not seem painful or laborious at all. It is an illusion of the present that will vanish. Time is your greatest ally.

5. The Open Field

Martha Graham's father, Dr. George Graham, was one of the few pioneering doctors in the 1890s to specialize in the treatment of mental illness. (For more on Martha Graham, see pages 30–31 and 66–67.) Around the family he did not talk much about his work, but one subject he would discuss openly with Martha completely fascinated her. In working with his patients, Dr. Graham had developed the ability to judge much about their states of mind from their body language. He could read their level of anxiety in how they walked or moved their arms or fixed their eyes on something. "The body does not lie," he would often tell her.

In high school in Santa Barbara, California, Martha developed an interest in theater. But one evening in 1911, Dr. Graham took his seventeen-year-old daughter to Los Angeles to see a performance of the famous dancer Ruth St. Denis, and from then on all she could think about was becoming a dancer. Influenced by her father, she was intrigued by the ability to express emotions without any words, strictly through the movement of the body. As soon as St. Denis opened up her own dance school (along with her partner, Ted Shawn) in 1916, Martha enrolled as one of its first pupils.

Much of the choreography was a kind of free-form ballet, with an emphasis on making everything seem easy and natural. There was a lot of posing and moving about with scarves, similar to the work of Isadora Duncan.

At first, Graham was not considered a promising dancer. She was shy, always staying toward the back of the class. She was not particularly built for the art (she did not have a lithe ballerina's body), and she was slow to pick up the choreography. But when she was given her first solo, St. Denis and Shawn saw something that surprised them: she exploded with an energy they had not suspected in her. She had charisma. St. Denis compared her to "a young tornado" when she took the stage. Everything they taught her she had a way of transforming into something sharper and more aggressive.

After several years she became one of their leading students, a major performer in their troupe and a teacher of the Denishawn method, as it came to be known. But soon she began to tire of this form of dancing. It did not suit her temperament. To get some distance from the school she moved to New York, and to support herself she taught classes in the Denishawn method. Then one day in 1926, perhaps upset at her leaving the troupe, Ted Shawn surprised her with an ultimatum—she would have to pay $500 for the right to teach Denishawn exercises and dance material. If not, she was strictly forbidden, under penalty of a lawsuit, ever to use any of their methods in her classes or personal work.

For Graham, this precipitated a crisis of sorts. She was now thirty-two years old, no longer young for a career in dance. She had barely $50 to her name, which meant that she could never pay Shawn even if she had wanted to. To earn extra money she had already tried working in popular dance shows on Broadway and had hated it, vowing never to go back. But as she weighed her options, one idea kept recurring to her. In her mind she had always been able to envision a kind of dance that did not exist in the world but that spoke to her innermost desires, both as a performer and a spectator. This dance was the polar opposite of the Denishawn method, which now seemed to her like empty, arty gesturing. It was more related to what she had seen of modern art—somewhat jagged and occasionally dissonant, full of power and rhythm. It was a visceral form of dance that she envisioned, and as she imagined it her thoughts kept returning to her father and their discussions about the body, about the language that all animals express through their movement.

This dance she could visualize was rigorous, based on a new kind of discipline—not at all free-floating and spontaneous like the Denishawn style. It would have its own vocabulary. She could not shake the image of the beauty of this nonexistent dance. She would never have this chance again. With age comes conservatism and the need for comfort. To create what was not out there, she would have to start her own school and dance troupe, building up the technique and discipline on her own. To support herself, she would have to give classes, teaching the new dance movements she would be in the process of creating. It would entail a tremendous risk, and money would be a constant problem, but her desperation to create what she could imagine would fuel her past any obstacles.

Within weeks of Ted Shawn's ultimatum, she made her first move. She rented out a studio, and to show her pupils that this was a new kind of dance they were going to learn, she covered the walls in burlap. Unlike other dance studios, her studio would have no mirrors. The dancers would have to focus intensely on what she was teaching and learn how to correct themselves by feeling the movement in their bodies, not becoming fixated on their images. Everything she wanted in this new form of dance was outwardly directed at the audience, without self-consciousness.

At first, it all seemed rather impossible. She had only a few students, just enough to cover rent. They would often have to wait for her as she slowly invented some new kind of movement or exercise, which they would then practice together and refine. A few early performances, although awkward, managed to attract more recruits, enough for Graham to think of creating a small troupe. From this group, she demanded the utmost discipline. They were creating a new language and would have to work hard. Week by week she built up a set of exercises that would bring the dancers more control, along with an entirely new mechanics of movement. She and her recruits would spend an entire year working on and perfecting one simple new technique, until it became second nature.

To distinguish her method from other forms of dance, she placed all of the emphasis on the torso. She called the torso "the house of the pelvic truth." She had determined that the most expressive part of the human body came from the contractions of the diaphragm and the sharp movements of the torso. This would be the center of focus, not the face and arms that made dance too romantic. She created endless exercises to build up this area, and she encouraged her dancers to feel the deep well of emotions that came from using these muscles.

Much of what stimulated her in this early phase was the desire to create something that had never been seen before on the stage. In Western dance, for instance, it was taboo for a dancer to fall—that would be a sign of a mistake and loss of control. The ground was something to resist and never surrender to. She decided to turn this around by creating a new sequence of controlled falls in which the dancer would melt into the ground and reascend, ever so slowly. This required building up a whole new series of muscles. She took this concept further, using the ground itself as a space upon which the dancer could move like a coiled snake. In her new system, suddenly the knee became a different instrument of expression—a hinge upon which the dancer could balance and move, giving the effect of weightlessness.

Slowly, as the work progressed, she could see coming to life the new form of dance that she had visualized. To add to the effect of newness, Graham decided to design and sew her own costumes. These costumes, often made out of stretch materials, would turn the dancers into almost abstract shapes, accentuating their sharp movements. Unlike the usual fairy-tale decor that was used for ballets, her sets would be minimal and stark. The dancers would wear little makeup. Everything would be designed to set them off from the stage and make their movements explode.

The response to her first series of performances was electrifying. The public had never seen anything remotely like it before. Many were disgusted and repulsed. Others found the work strangely emotional, giving dance an expressive quality they had never suspected it could possess. The work elicited extremes of reaction, a sign of its power. Over the years, what had seemed initially so harsh and ugly began to be accepted, as Martha Graham had indeed single-handedly created a new genre—modern dance as we know it today. To avoid this dance turning into yet another convention, she would constantly struggle to upset people's expectations, never going over old ground, and constantly changing the subject matter of the dances, from Greek myths to Americana and depictions from literature. For close to sixty years after the formation of her troupe, she continued to drive herself to create that feeling of newness and immediacy she had always wanted.

Perhaps the greatest impediment to human creativity is the natural decay that sets in over time in any kind of medium or profession. In the sciences or in business, a certain way of thinking or acting that once had success quickly becomes a paradigm, an established procedure. As the years go by, people forget the initial reason for this paradigm and simply follow a lifeless set of techniques. In the arts, someone establishes a style that is new and vibrant, speaking to the particular spirit of the times. It has an edge because it is so different. Soon imitators pop up everywhere. It becomes a fashion, something to conform to, even if the conformity appears to be rebellious and edgy. This can drag on for ten, twenty years; it eventually becomes a cliché, pure style without any real emotion or need. Nothing in culture escapes this deadening dynamic.

We may not be aware of it, but we suffer from the dead forms and conventions that clutter our culture. This problem, however, sets up a tremendous opportunity for creative types, one epitomized by the example of Martha Graham. The process goes as follows: You begin by looking inward. You have something you want to express that is unique to yourself and related to your inclinations. You must be sure it is not something that is sparked by some trend or fashion, but that it comes from you and is real. Perhaps it is a sound you are not hearing in music, a type of story not being told, a type of book that does not fit into the usual tidy categories. Perhaps it is even a new way of doing business. Let the idea, the sound, the image take root in you. Sensing the possibility of a new language or way of doing things, you must make the conscious decision to play against the very conventions that you find dead and want to get rid of. Martha Graham did not create her work out of a vacuum; her vision corresponded to what ballet and modern dance of the time were not giving her. She took their conventions and turned them upside down. Following this strategy will give your work a kind of reverse reference point and a way to shape it.

Like Graham, you must not mistake newness with wild spontaneity. There is nothing that becomes repetitive and boring more quickly than free expression that is not rooted in reality and discipline. You must bring to your new idea all of the knowledge you have acquired in your field, but for the purpose of reversing it, as Graham did with the Denishawn method. In essence, what you are doing is creating some space in a cluttered culture, claiming for yourself an open field in which you can finally plant something new. People are dying for the new, for what expresses the spirit of the time in an original way. By creating something new you will create your own audience, and attain the ultimate position of power in culture.

6. The High End

Yoky Matsuoka (see chapter 1, pages 33–35) always had the feeling that she was different from others. It wasn't so much how she dressed or looked, but her interests that set her apart. As a teenager in Japan in the early 1980s, she was expected to focus on a particular subject that she would transform into a career. But as she got older, her interests only widened. She had a love for physics and mathematics, but was attracted to biology and physiology as well. She was also a talented athlete with a future as a professional tennis player, until an injury cut this short. On top of it all, she loved working with her hands and tinkering with machines.

Much to her relief, when she began her undergraduate studies at the University of California at Berkeley, she fell upon a subject that seemed to open up all sorts of larger questions that would satisfy her voracious, wide-ranging interests—the relatively new field of robotics. After completing her undergraduate studies, curious to explore this subject further, she entered the masters program in robotics at MIT. As part of her work in the department, she was to help in the design of the large-scale robot they were building, and soon she chose to work exclusively on the design of the robot's hands. She had always been fascinated by the complexity and power of the human hand,

and with the chance to combine so many of her interests (mathematics, physiology, and building things), it seemed she had finally found her niche.

As she began her work on the hands, however, she realized yet again how different she was in her way of thinking. The other students in the department were mostly men, and they tended to reduce everything to questions of engineering—how to pack the robot with as many mechanical options as possible so it could move and act in reasonably human ways. They thought of their robot as intrinsically a machine. To build it meant solving a series of technical issues and creating a kind of moving computer that could mimic some basic thought patterns.

Matsuoka had a much different approach. She wanted to create something as lifelike and anatomically correct as possible. That was the real future of robotics, and to reach such a goal meant engaging in questions that were on a much higher level—what makes anything alive and organically complex? To her, it was as important to study evolution, human physiology, and neuroscience as it was to immerse oneself in engineering. Perhaps it would complicate her career path, but she would follow her own inclinations and see where they led.

In going about her design, Matsuoka made a key decision: she would begin by building a model of a robotic hand that would replicate the human hand as closely as possible. In attempting such an enormous task, she would be forced to truly understand how each part functioned. For instance, in trying to recreate all of the various bones of the hand, she came upon all kinds of seemingly irrelevant bumps and grooves. The bone at the knuckle of the index finger has a bump that makes it larger on one side. In studying this one detail, she discovered its function—giving us the ability to grasp objects in the center of the hand with more power. It seemed odd that such a bump would evolve expressly for that purpose. Probably it was some mutation that ended up becoming a part of our evolution, as the hand became increasingly important in our development.

Continuing in this line she worked on the palm of her robotic hand, which she had determined was in many ways the key to the design. For most engineers, robotic hands were designed for optimal power and maneuverability. They would build in all kinds of mechanical options, but to make it work they would have to pack all of the motors and cables in the most convenient place, the palm, rendering it completely rigid. After designing hands like this, they would then fob them off to software engineers to try to figure out to how bring back maneuverability. Because of the built-in rigidity, however, the thumb would never be able to touch the pinky, and engineers would inevitably end up with the same highly limited robotic hand.

Matsuoka started from the other end. Her goal was to discover what makes the hand dexterous, and it was clear that one critical requisite was to have a flexible, curved palm. Thinking on this higher level, it then became clear that the motors and cables had to be placed somewhere else. Instead of jamming the hand with motors everywhere so that everything could move, she determined that the most important maneuverable part of the hand was the thumb, the key to our grasping skills. That is where she would put more power.

She continued on this path, uncovering more and more of the details that went into the marvelous mechanics of the human hand. As she worked in this peculiar way, other engineers would scoff at her and her strange biological approach. What a waste of time, they would tell her. In the end, however, what she called her anatomically correct test-bed hand soon became the model for the industry, revealing whole new possibilities for prosthetic hands, vindicating her approach, and gaining her fame and recognition for her engineering skills.

This, however, was only the beginning of her quest to get at the organic nature of the hand and to literally recreate it. After graduating with a master's degree in robotics, she returned to MIT to pursue a PhD in neuroscience. Currently, armed with deep knowledge about the neuro-signals that make the hand-brain connection so unique, she is pursuing the goal of creating a prosthetic hand that can actually connect to the brain, operating and feeling as if it were real. To reach such a goal, she continues to work on high-end concepts, such as the influence of the hand-brain connection on our thinking in general.

In her lab she has done tests to see how people manipulate ambiguous objects with their eyes closed. She studies how they explore them with their hands, and records the elaborate neuro-signals that are generated in the process. She wonders if there could be a connection between such exploration and abstract thought processes (perhaps involving similar neuro-signals), such as when we are confronted with a problem that seems difficult to solve. She is interested in building such exploratory sensations into the prosthetic hand. In other experiments, in which subjects move a virtual-reality hand, she has discovered that the more people are made to feel that the hand is literally a part of their bodies, the greater the degree of control they have. Creating such sensations will be a part of the ultimate prosthetic hand she is working on. Although its realization is years away, the design of such a neurologically connected hand will have technological consequences far beyond robotics.

In many fields we can see and diagnose the same mental disease, which we shall call *technical lock*. What this means is the following: in order to learn a subject or skill, particularly one that is complex, we must immerse ourselves in many details, techniques, and procedures that are standard for solving problems. If we are not careful, however, we become locked into seeing every problem in the same way, using the same techniques and strategies that became so imprinted in us. It is always simpler to follow such a route. In the process we lose sight of the bigger picture, the purpose of what we are doing, how each problem we face is different and requires a different approach. We adopt a kind of tunnel vision.

This *technical lock* afflicts people in all fields as they lose a sense of the overall purpose of their work, of the larger question at hand, of what impels them to do their work in the first place. Yoky Matsuoka hit upon a solution to this that propelled her to the forefront of her field. It came as a reaction against the engineering approach that prevailed in robotics. Her mind naturally works better on a larger scale, continually pondering the connections between things on high levels—what makes the human hand so weirdly perfect, how the hand has influenced who we are and how we think. With these large questions governing her research, she avoids becoming narrowly focused on technical issues without understanding the bigger picture. Thinking on such a high level frees the mind up to investigate from all different angles: Why are the bones of the hand this way? What makes the palm so malleable? How does the sense of touch influence our thinking in general? It allows her to go deeply into the details without losing a sense of the why.

You must make this a model for your own work as well. Your project or the problem you are solving should always be connected to something larger—a bigger question, an overarching idea, an inspiring goal. Whenever your work begins to feel stale, you must return to the larger purpose and goal that impelled you in the first place. This bigger idea governs your smaller paths of investigation, and opens up many more such paths for you to look into. By constantly reminding yourself of your purpose, you will prevent yourself from fetishizing certain techniques or from becoming overly obsessed with trivial details. In this way you will play into the natural strengths of the human brain, which wants to look for connections on higher and higher levels.

7. The Evolutionary Hijack

In the summer of 1995, Paul Graham (see chapter 2, page 87–89) heard a story on the radio promoting the endless possibilities of online commerce, which at the time hardly existed. The promotion came from Netscape, which was trying to drum up interest in its business on the eve of its IPO. The story sounded so promising, yet so vague. At the time, Graham was at a bit of a crossroads. After graduating from Harvard with a PhD in computer engineering, he had fallen into a pattern: he would find some part-time consulting job in the software business; then, with enough money saved, he would quit the job and devote his time to his real love—art and painting—until the money ran out, and then he would scramble for another job. Now thirty-one-years old, he was getting tired of the pattern, and he hated consulting. The prospect of making a lot of money quickly by developing something for the Internet suddenly seemed very appealing.

He called up his old programming partner from Harvard, Robert Morris, and interested him in the idea of collaborating on their own startup, even though Graham had no clue where they would start or what they would develop. After a few days of discussing this, they decided they would try to write software that would enable a business to generate an online store. Once they were clear about the concept, they had to confront a very large obstacle in their way. In those days, for a program to be popular enough it would have to be written for Windows. As consummate hackers, they loathed everything about Windows and had never bothered to learn how to develop applications for it. They preferred to write in Lisp and have the program run on Unix, the open-source operating system.

They decided to postpone the inevitable and wrote the program for Unix anyway. To translate this later into Windows would be easy, but as they contemplated doing this, they realized the terrible consequences it would lead to—once the program was launched in Windows, they would have to deal with users and perfect the program based on their feedback. This would mean they would be forced to think and program in Windows for months, perhaps years. This was too awful a prospect, and they seriously considered giving up.

One morning Graham, who had been sleeping on a mattress on the floor in Morris's Manhattan apartment, woke up repeating certain words that must have come to him from a dream: "You could control the program by clicking on links." He suddenly sat bolt upright, as he realized what these words could mean—the possibility of creating a program to set up an online store that would run on the web server itself. People would download and use it through Netscape, clicking various links on the web page to set it up. This would mean he and Morris would bypass the usual route of writing a program that users would download to their desktop. It would cut out the need ever to have to dabble in Windows. There was nothing out there like this, and yet it seemed like such an obvious solution. In a state of excitement he explained his epiphany to Morris, and they agreed to give it a try. Within a few days they finished the first version, and it functioned beautifully. Clearly, the concept of a web application would work.

Over the next few weeks they refined the software, and found their own angel investor who put up an initial $10,000 for a 10 percent share in the business. In the beginning, it was quite hard to interest merchants in the concept.

Their application server provider was the very first Internet-run program for starting a business, at the very frontier of online commerce. Slowly, however, it began to take off.

As it panned out, the novelty of their idea, which Graham and Morris had come upon largely because of their distaste for Windows, proved to have all kinds of unforeseen advantages. Working directly on the Internet, they could generate a continuous stream of new releases of the software and test them right away. They could interact directly with consumers, getting instant feedback on their program and improving it in days rather than the months it could take with desktop software. With no experience running a business, they did not think to hire salespeople to do the pitching; instead, they made the phone calls to potential clients themselves. But as they were the de facto salespeople, they were also the first to hear complaints or suggestions from consumers, and this gave them a real feel for the program's weaknesses and how to improve it. Because it was so unique and came out of left field, they had no competitors to worry about; nobody could steal the idea because they were the only ones who were insane enough to attempt it.

Naturally, they made several mistakes along the way, but the idea was too strong to fail; and in 1998 they sold their company, named Viaweb, to Yahoo! for $50 million.

As the years went by and Graham looked back at the experience, he was struck by the process he and Morris had gone through. It reminded him of so many other inventions in history, such as microcomputers. The microprocessors that made the microcomputer possible had originally been developed to run traffic lights and vending machines. They had never been intended to power computers. The first entrepreneurs to attempt this were laughed at; the computers they had created looked hardly worthy of the name—they were so small and could do so little. But they caught on with just enough people for whom they saved time, and slowly, the idea took off. The same story had occurred with transistors, which in the 1930s and '40s were developed and used in electronics for the military. It was not until the early 1950s that several individuals had the idea of applying this technology to transistor radios for the public, soon hitting upon what would become the most popular electronic device in history.

What was interesting in all of these cases was the peculiar process that led to these inventions: generally, the inventors had a chance encounter with the available technology; then the idea would come to them that this technology could be used for other purposes; and finally they would try out different prototypes until the right one fell into place. What allows for this process is the willingness of the inventor to look at everyday things in a different light and to imagine new uses for them. For people who are stuck in rigid ways of seeing, the familiarity of an old application hypnotizes them into not seeing its other possibilities. What it all really comes down to is the possession of a flexible, adaptable mind—something that is often enough to separate a successful inventor or entrepreneur from the rest of the crowd.

After cashing in on Viaweb, Graham hit upon the idea of writing essays for the Internet—his rather peculiar form of blogging. These essays made him a celebrity among young hackers and programmers everywhere. In 2005 he was invited by undergraduates in the computer science department at Harvard to give a talk. Instead of boring them and himself by analyzing various programming languages, he decided to discuss the idea of technology startups themselves—why some work, why some fail. The talk was so successful, and Graham's ideas so illuminating, that the students began to besiege him with questions about their own startup ideas. As he listened, he could sense that some of their concepts were not far off the mark, but that they badly needed shaping and guidance.

Graham had always intended to try his hand at investing in other people's ideas. He had been the beneficiary of an angel investor in his project, and it was only right to return the favor by helping others. The problem was where to begin. Most angel investors had some related experience before they began investing, and they tended to start out on a small scale to get their feet wet. Graham had no such business experience. Based on this weakness, he hit upon an idea that at first glance seemed ridiculous—he would synchronously invest $15,000 in ten startups all at once. He would find these ten prospects by advertising his offer and choosing the best among the applicants. Over the course of a few months he would shepherd these novices and help guide them to the point of launching their idea. For this he would take 10 percent from any successful startup. It would be like an apprenticeship system for tech founders, but it really had another purpose—it would serve as a crash course for him in the investing business. He would be a lousy first investor and his pupils would be lousy entrepreneurs, making them a perfect match.

Yet again he recruited Robert Morris to join him in the business. A couple of weeks into the training, however, he and Morris realized that they were actually on to something powerful. Because of their experience with Viaweb they were able to give clear and effective advice. The startup ideas they were shepherding looked quite promising. Perhaps this system they had adopted as a way to learn quickly was an interesting model in itself. Most investors only handle a few startups a year; they are too overwhelmed with their own businesses to handle much more. But what if Graham and Morris were to devote their time exclusively to this apprenticeship system? They could mass-produce the service. They could fund hundreds instead of dozens of such startups. In the process they would learn in leaps and bounds, and this exponentially increasing knowledge would lead to increasing numbers of successful startups.

If it really took off, not only would they make a fortune, but they would also have a decided impact on the economy, unleashing into the system thousands of savvy entrepreneurs. They called their new company Y Combinator and considered it their ultimate hack to change the shape of the world's economy.

They coached their apprentices in all of the principles they had learned along the way—the benefit in looking for new applications of existing technology and needs that are not being met; the importance of maintaining the closest possible relationship with customers; the need to keep ideas as simple and realistic as possible; the value of creating a superior product and of winning through craftsmanship, as opposed to fixating on making money.

As their apprentices learned, they learned as well. Oddly enough, they discovered that what really makes successful entrepreneurs is not the nature of their idea, or the university they went to, but their actual character—their willingness to adapt their idea and take advantage of possibilities they had not first imagined. This is precisely the trait—fluidity of mind—that Graham had identified in himself and in other inventors. The other essential character trait was supreme tenacity.

Over the years, evolving in its own way, Y Combinator has continued to grow at an astounding rate. It is valued now at $500 million, with the clear potential for further growth.

We generally have a misconception about the inventive and creative powers of the human mind. We imagine that creative people have an interesting idea, which they then proceed to elaborate and refine in a somewhat linear process. The truth, however, is much messier and more complex. Creativity actually resembles a process known in nature as evolutionary hijacking. In evolution, accidents and contingencies play an enormous role. For instance, feathers evolved from reptilian scales, their purpose being to keep birds warm. (Birds evolved from reptiles.) But eventually, those existing feathers became adapted for the purpose of flying, transforming into wing feathers. For our own primate ancestors living in trees, the form of the hand largely evolved out of the need to grasp branches with speed and agility. Our early hominid ancestors, walking on the ground, found this intricately developed hand quite useful for manipulating rocks, making tools, and gesturing in communication. Perhaps language itself developed as a strictly social tool and became hijacked as a means of reasoning, making human consciousness itself the product of an accident.

Human creativity generally follows a similar path, perhaps indicating a kind of organic fatality to the creation of anything. Ideas do not come to us out of nowhere. Instead, we come upon something by accident—in the case of Graham, a radio announcement that he hears, or questions from the audience after a lecture. If we are experienced enough and the moment is ripe, this accidental encounter will spark some interesting associations and ideas in us. In looking at the particular materials we can work with, we suddenly see another way to use them. All along the way, contingencies pop up that reveal different paths we can take, and if they are promising, we follow them, not sure of where they will lead. Instead of a straight-line development from idea to fruition, the creative process is more like the crooked branching of a tree.

The lesson is simple—what constitutes true creativity is the openness and adaptability of our spirit. When we see or experience something we must be able to look at it from several angles, to see other possibilities beyond the obvious ones. We imagine that the objects around us can be used and co-opted for different purposes. We do not hold on to our original idea out of sheer stubbornness, or because our ego is tied up with its rightness. Instead, we move with what presents itself to us in the moment, exploring and exploiting different branches and contingencies. We thus manage to turn feathers into flying material. The difference then is not in some initial creative power of the brain, but in how we look at the world and the fluidity with which we can reframe what we see. Creativity and adaptability are inseparable.

8. Dimensional Thinking

In 1798 Napoleon Bonaparte invaded Egypt in an attempt to transform it into a colony, but the invasion bogged down as the British, seeking to block the French, became involved. A year later, as the war dragged on, a soldier working on the reinforcement of a French fort near the town of Rosetta dug into the ground and hit a rock. In extracting the rock, he discovered that it was some kind of relic from ancient Egypt—a slab of basalt covered in writing. Napoleon had been motivated to invade Egypt partially by his intense curiosity for all things Egyptian, and had taken along with his troops French scientists and historians to help analyze the relics he hoped to find.

In looking at the slab of basalt, which came to be known as the Rosetta stone, the French savants grew excited. It contained text written out in three different scripts—on the top, Egyptian hieroglyphs; in the middle, what is known as demotic (the language and script of the common people of ancient Egypt), and on the bottom, ancient Greek. In translating the ancient Greek, they discovered that the text was a mundane proclamation celebrating the reign of Ptolemy V (203–181 B.C.). At the end of the text, however, it stated that the proclamation was to be written out in three versions, meaning that the content was the same in the demotic and the hieroglyphic. With the ancient Greek text as the key, it suddenly seemed possible to decipher the other two versions. Since the last known hieroglyphs had been written in A.D. 394, anyone who could read them had long died off, making it a completely dead and untranslatable language and leaving a seemingly unsolvable mystery as to the content of so many of the writings in temples and on papyri. Now, perhaps, these secrets could finally be revealed.

The stone was carted off to an institution in Cairo, but in 1801 the English defeated the French in Egypt and threw them out. Knowing of the extremely high value of the Rosetta stone, they hunted it down in Cairo and shipped it off to London, where it remains to this day in the British Museum. As drawings of the stone began to be passed around, intellectuals from all parts of Europe became involved in a competition to be the first to decipher the hieroglyphs and unlock the mysteries. As they began to tackle the puzzle, some progress was made. Certain hieroglyphs were outlined in a rectangle, known as cartouches. It was determined that these cartouches contained the names of various royal figures. One Swedish professor had been able to make out the name of Ptolemy in the demotic, and speculated on the sound values the characters might have. But the initial enthusiasm for deciphering the hieroglyphs eventually died out, and many worried that they would remain undecipherable. The further anyone got with the puzzle, the more questions that were raised about the kind of writing system represented by the symbols themselves.

In 1814 a new figure entered the fray—an Englishman named Dr. Thomas Young—who quickly became the leading candidate to be the first to decipher the Rosetta stone. Although a medical doctor, he was a man who had dabbled in all the sciences and was considered something of a genius. He had the blessing of the English establishment and full access to all of the various papyri and relics the English had confiscated, including the stone itself. Furthermore, he was independently wealthy and could devote all of his time to the study. And so, throwing himself into the work with great enthusiasm, Young began to make some progress.

He had a computational approach to the problem. He counted the number of times a particular word, such as "god," appeared in the Greek text, then found a word that appeared the same number of times in the demotic, assuming they were the same word. He did everything he could to make the letters in demotic fit his scheme—if the apparent equivalent word of "god" seemed too long, he would simply deduce that certain letters were meaningless. He assumed that the three texts went in the same order, and that he could match words by their location. Sometimes he guessed right;

most often he got nowhere. He made some key discoveries—that demotic and hieroglyphs were related, the one being a kind of loose handwritten form of the other; and that demotic used a phonetic alphabet to spell out foreign names, but that it was mostly a system of pictograms. But he kept hitting dead ends, and he never got close to trying his hand at the hieroglyphs. After a few years, he essentially gave up.

In the meantime, there appeared on the scene a young man who seemed to be an unlikely candidate to succeed in this race—Jean-Francois Champollion (1790–1832). He came from a small town near Grenoble. His family was relatively poor, and until the age of seven Champollion had no formal education. But he had one advantage over all the others: from his earliest years he had been drawn to the history of ancient civilizations. He wanted to discover new things about the origins of mankind, and for this purpose he took up the study of ancient languages—Greek, Latin, and Hebrew, as well as several other Semitic languages—all of which he mastered with remarkable speed by the age of twelve.

Quickly his attention was drawn to ancient Egypt. In 1802 he heard about the Rosetta stone, and he told his older brother that he would be the one to decipher it. The moment he began to study the ancient Egyptians, he experienced a vivid identification with everything that had to do with the civilization. As a child, he had a powerful visual memory. He could draw with exceptional skill. He tended to see the writings in books (even books in French) as if they were drawings instead of an alphabet. When he first laid eyes on hieroglyphs they seemed almost familiar to him. Soon his relationship to hieroglyphs bordered on a fanatical obsession.

To really make progress, he decided he would have to learn the language known as Coptic. After Egypt became a Roman colony in 30 B.C., the old language, demotic, slowly died out, and was replaced by Coptic— a mix of Greek and Egyptian. After the Arabs conquered Egypt and converted it to Islam, making Arabic the official idiom, the remaining Christians in the land retained Coptic as their language. By Champollion's time only a few Christians remained who still spoke the ancient language, mostly monks and priests. In 1805 just such a monk passed through Champollion's small town, and he quickly befriended him. The monk taught him the rudiments of Coptic, and when he returned a few months later, he brought Champollion a grammar book. The boy worked at the language day and night, with a fervor that others saw as madness. He wrote his brother: "I do nothing else. I dream in Coptic. . . . I am so Coptic, that for fun, I translate into Coptic everything that comes into my head." When he later went to Paris for schooling he found more monks, and he practiced to the point where he was told that he spoke the dying language as well as any native.

With only a poor reproduction of the Rosetta stone at his disposal, he began to attack it with various hypotheses, all of which were later proven quite wrong. Unlike the others, however, Champollion's enthusiasm never dampened. The problem for him was the political turmoil of his time. An avowed son of the French Revolution, he finally came to support the cause of Napoleon just as the emperor lost power. When King Louis XVIII came to the throne as the new French king, Champollion's Napoleonic sympathies cost him his job as a professor. Years of grinding poverty and ill health forced him to abandon his interest in the Rosetta stone. But in 1821, finally rehabilitated by the government and living in Paris, Champollion returned to the quest with a renewed energy and determination.

Having been away from the study of hieroglyphics for some time, he came back with a fresh perspective. The problem, he decided, was that others were approaching decipherment as if it involved some kind of mathematical code. But Champollion, who spoke dozens of languages and could read many dead languages, understood that languages evolve in a haphazard manner, influenced by the influx of new groups into a society and shaped by the passage of time. They are not mathematical formulas, but living, evolving organisms. They are complex. He now approached the hieroglyphs in a more holistic fashion. His goal was to figure out exactly what kind of script it was—pictograms (literally the picture representing the thing), ideograms (the picture representing ideas), some kind of phonetic alphabet, or perhaps a mix of all three.

With this in mind, he tried something that strangely enough no one had thought of—he made a comparison of the number of words in the Greek and hieroglyphic sections. He counted 486 words in the Greek text, and 1,419 hieroglyphic signs. Champollion had been operating under the assumption that hieroglyphs were ideograms, each symbol representing an idea or word. With such a discrepancy in number, this assumption was no longer possible. He then tried to identify groups of hieroglyphic symbols that would constitute words, but this numbered only 180. He could find no clear numerical relationship between the two, and so the only possible conclusion from all of this was that hieroglyphic writing is a mixed system of ideograms, pictograms, and a phonetic alphabet, making it more complex than anyone had imagined.

He next decided to attempt something that anyone else would have thought insane and useless—to apply his visual powers to the demotic and hieroglyphic texts, looking exclusively at the shapes of the letters or signs. In doing so he began to see patterns and correspondences—for instance, a particular sign in the hieroglyph, such as the depiction of a bird, had a rough equivalent in demotic, the image of the bird becoming less realistic and more like an abstract shape. Because of his incredible photographic memory, he could identify hundreds of these equivalences between symbols, although he could not say what any one of them meant. They remained merely images.

Armed with this knowledge, he went on the attack. On the Rosetta stone, he examined the royal cartouche in the demotic that had been previously identified as containing the name of Ptolemy. Knowing now many equivalent signs between hieroglyphs and demotic, he transposed the demotic symbols into what they should look like in the hieroglyphic version, to create what should be the word for Ptolemy. To his surprise and delight, he found such a word—making this the first successful decipherment of a hieroglyph. Knowing that this name was probably written out in phonetics (as would be all foreign names), he deduced the sound equivalences in both demotic and hieroglyph for Ptolemy. With the letters P T L now identified, he found another cartouche in a papyrus document that he was certain would have to be that of Cleopatra, now adding new letters to his knowledge. Ptolemy and Cleopatra had two different letters for T. For others this might prove baffling, but to Champollion he understood that it merely represented homophones—much as the *f* sound in "*ph*one" and "*f*old." With growing knowledge of letters he proceeded to decipher the names of all of the royal cartouches he could find, giving him a treasure trove of alphabetic information.

Then in September 1822 it all became unlocked in the most surprising way, in the course of one day. A temple had been discovered in a desolate part of Egypt whose walls and statues were covered in hieroglyphs. Accurate drawings of the hieroglyphs fell into Champollion's hands, and in looking at them he was struck by something curious—none of the cartouches corresponded to the names he had already identified. He decided to apply the phonetic alphabet he had developed to one of them, but could only see the letter S at the end. The first symbol reminded him of the image of the sun. In Coptic, which was a distant relative of ancient Egyptian, the word for sun is *Re*. In the middle of the cartouche was a trident symbol with three prongs that looked eerily like an M. With great excitement he realized this could be the name Ramses. Ramses was a pharaoh of the thirteenth century B.C., and this would mean that the Egyptians had a phonetic alphabet dating back who knows how far in time—an earth-shattering discovery. He needed more proof to assert this.

Another cartouche in the temple drawing had the same M-shaped symbol. The first symbol in the cartouche was that of an ibis. With his knowledge of ancient Egyptian history, he knew that the bird was the symbol of the god Thoth. This cartouche could now spell out Thot-mu-sis, or Thuthmose, yet another name of an ancient pharaoh. In another part of the temple he saw a hieroglyphic word that consisted entirely of the equivalent letters of M and S. Thinking in Coptic, he translated the word as *mis*, which means to "give birth." Sure enough, in the Greek text of the Rosetta stone he found a phrase referring to a birthday, and identified the equivalent of it in the hieroglyph section.

Overwhelmed by what he had found, he ran through the streets of Paris to find his brother. He shouted upon entering the room, "I've got it!" and then fainted, falling to the floor. After nearly twenty years of a continuous obsession, through endless problems and poverty and setbacks, Champollion had uncovered the key to the hieroglyphs in a few short months of intense labor.

In the aftermath of his discovery, he would continue to translate one word after another and figure out the exact nature of the hieroglyphs. In the process he would completely transform our knowledge and concept of ancient Egypt. His earliest translations revealed that hieroglyphs, as he suspected, were a sophisticated combination of all three forms of symbols, and had the equivalent of an alphabet far before anyone had imagined the invention of an alphabet. This was not a backward civilization of priests dominating a slave culture and keeping secrets through mysterious symbols, but a vibrant society with a complicated and beautiful written language, one that could be considered the equal of ancient Greek.

When his discovery was broadcast, Champollion became an instant hero in France. But Dr. Young, his main rival in the field, could not accept defeat. He spent the ensuing years accusing Champollion of fraud and plagiarism, unable to conceive of the idea that someone from such a modest background could pull off such an amazing intellectual feat.

The story of Champollion versus Dr. Young contains an elemental lesson about the learning process, and illustrates two classic approaches to a problem. In the case of Young, he came to the hieroglyphic puzzle from the outside, fueled by the ambition to be the first to decipher the hieroglyphs and gain fame in the process. To expedite matters, he reduced the writing system of the ancient Egyptians into tidy mathematical formulas, assuming that they represented ideograms. In such a way, he could approach decipherment as if it were a computational feat. To do so, he had to simplify what ended up being revealed as an extremely complex and layered system of writing.

For Champollion, it was the opposite. He was fueled by a genuine hunger to understand the origins of mankind, and by a deep love of ancient Egyptian culture. He wanted to get at the truth, not gain fame. Because he saw the translation of the Rosetta stone as his Life's Task, he was willing to devote twenty or more years to the job, or whatever it took to solve the riddle. He did not attack the problem from the outside and with formulas, but rather went through a rigorous apprenticeship in ancient languages and

Coptic. It ended up that his knowledge of Coptic proved the decisive key to unraveling the secret. His knowledge of languages made him understand how complex they can be, reflecting the complexity of any great society. When he finally returned to the Rosetta stone with undistracted attention in 1821, his mind shifted to the Creative-Active. He reframed the problem in holistic terms. His decision to first look at the two scripts—demotic and hieroglyph—as purely visual was a stroke of creative genius. In the end, he thought in greater dimensions and uncovered enough aspects of the language to unlock it.

Many people in various fields tend to follow the Young method. If they are studying economics, or the human body and health, or the workings of the brain, they tend to work with abstractions and simplifications, reducing highly complex and interactive problems into modules, formulas, tidy statistics, and isolated organs that can be dissected. This approach can yield a partial picture of reality, much in the way that dissecting a corpse can tell you some things about the human body. But with these simplifications the living, breathing element is missing. You want to follow instead the Champollion model. You are not in a hurry. You prefer the holistic approach. You look at the object of study from as many angles as possible, giving your thoughts added dimensions. You assume that the parts of any whole interact with one another and cannot be completely separated. In your mind, you get as close to the complicated truth and reality of your object of study as possible. In the process, great mysteries will unravel themselves before your eyes.

9. Alchemical Creativity and the Unconscious

The artist Teresita Fernández (b. 1968) has long been fascinated by alchemy—an early form of science whose goal was to transform base materials into gold. (For more on Fernández, see pages 152–55.) Alchemists believed that nature itself operates through the constant interaction of opposites—earth and fire, sun and moon, male and female, dark and light. By somehow reconciling these opposites, the alchemist believed he could discover the deepest secrets of nature, gain the power to create something out of nothing, and turn dust into gold.

To Fernández, the art of alchemy resembles in many ways the artistic and creative process itself. First, a thought or idea stirs in the mind of the artist. Slowly he or she transforms this idea into a material work of art, which creates a third element, a response in the viewer—an emotion of some sort that the artist wishes to provoke. This is a magical process, the equivalent of creating something out of nothing, a kind of transmutation of dirt into gold—in this case, the artist's idea becoming realized, and leading to the stirring of powerful emotions in the spectator.

Alchemy depends on the reconciliation of various opposite qualities, and in thinking about herself, Fernández can identify many contrary impulses that are reconciled in her work. She is personally drawn to minimalism—a form of expression that communicates through the most minimal amount of material. She likes the discipline and rigor this paring down of materials imposes on her thinking process. At the same time she has a streak of romanticism, and an interest in work that produces strong emotional reactions in viewers. In her work, she likes to mix the sensual with the austere. She has noticed that expressing this and other tensions within herself gives her work a particularly disorienting and dreamlike effect upon viewers.

Since childhood, Fernández has always had a peculiar sense of scale. She would find it odd and disturbing that a relatively small space or room could evoke a much larger and even a vast space by its layout or the arrangement of windows. Children are generally obsessed with scale, playing with miniaturized versions of the adult world, yet feeling as if these miniatures represent real objects that are much larger. We generally lose this interest as we get older, but in Fernández's piece *Eruption* (2005), she brings us back to an awareness of the potentially disturbing emotions that can be evoked by playing with our sense of scale. The piece is a relatively small floor sculpture in the shape of a blob that resembles an artist's palette. It consists of thousands of clear glass beads layered on the surface. Below the beads lies an enlarged image of an abstract painting, which makes the beads reflect various colors, giving the piece the distinct look of the mouth of a bubbling volcano. We cannot see the underlying image, and we are not aware that the beads themselves are clear. Our eye is simply drawn into the effect, as we imagine much more than is actually there. In the smallest of spaces she has thus created a feeling of a deep and vast landscape. We know it is an illusion, but are moved by the sensations and tensions that the piece creates.

In making work for an outdoor public space, artists generally go in one of two directions—creating something that blends into the landscape in an interesting way, or instead making something that stands out from the surroundings and calls attention to itself. In creating her piece *Seattle Cloud Cover* (2006)—at the Olympic Sculpture Park in Seattle, Washington—Fernández navigated a space between these two opposite approaches. Along the length of an outdoor pedestrian bridge spanning railroad tracks, she placed large colored glass panes, laminated with photographic images of clouds. The panes, which also extend overhead, are semitransparent and are marked with hundreds of clear polka dots at equal lengths that reveal bits of the sky above. As people walk along the bridge, they see above them realistic photographic images of clouds, often standing out against the usual grey skies of Seattle, or sometimes brightened by the sun, or turning kaleidoscopic at sunset. Moving over the bridge, the alternation between real and unreal makes it hard for us to distinguish between the two—a surreal effect that causes powerful feelings of disorientation in the viewer.

Perhaps the ultimate expression of Fernández's alchemy can be experienced in her piece *Stacked Waters* (2009) at the Blanton Museum of Art in Austin, Texas. For this commission, she was confronted with the challenge of creating a striking piece for the vast open space of the museum's multi-layered atrium, an entryway to the rest of the museum. The atrium is generally bathed in bright light from the large skylights on the ceiling. Instead of struggling to create a sculpture for such a space, Fernández attempted to invert our whole experience of art. When people enter a museum or gallery space, it is most often with a sense of distance and coldness; they stand back and view something for a few moments, then move on. Aiming for a more visceral contact with the viewer than a traditional sculpture could provide, she decided to use the cold white walls of the atrium and its constant flow of patrons as the basis for her alchemical experiment.

She covered the walls with bands of thousands of highly reflective acrylic strips, saturated in swirls of color from shades of blue to white. The overall effect from standing in the atrium is that of being immersed in an enormous pool of blue water that shimmers from the sunlight above. As people ascend the stairs, they can see in the acrylic strips their own reflections, which are oddly distorted, similar to the effect of seeing things through water. Viewing the strips from up close, it is clear that it is all an illusion created by the most minimal amount of material, and yet the feel of water, the sense of being immersed, remains palpable and strange. The spectators thus become actual parts of the artwork itself, with their own reflections helping to create the illusion. The experience of moving through this dreamlike space makes us conscious once more of the tensions between art and nature, illusion and reality, coldness and warmth, wet and dry, and provokes a powerful intellectual and emotional response.

Our culture depends in many ways on the creation of standards and conventions that we all must adhere to. These conventions are often expressed in terms of opposites—good and evil, beautiful and ugly, painful and pleasurable, rational and irrational, intellectual and sensual. Believing in these opposites gives our world a sense of cohesion and comfort. To imagine that something can be intellectual *and* sensual, pleasurable *and* painful, real *and* unreal, good *and* bad, masculine *and* feminine is too chaotic and disturbing for us. Life, however, is more fluid and complex; our desires and experiences do not fit neatly into these tidy categories.

As the work of Teresita Fernández demonstrates, the real and the unreal are concepts that exist for us as ideas and constructions, and thus can be played with, altered, commanded, and transformed at will. Those who think in dualities—believing that there is such a thing as "real" and such a thing as "unreal," and that they are distinct entities that can never become blended into a third, alchemical element—are creatively limited, and their work can quickly become dead and predictable. To maintain a dualistic approach to life requires that we repress many observable truths, but in our unconscious and in our dreams we often let go of the need to create categories for everything, and are able to mix seemingly disparate and contradictory ideas and feelings together with ease.

Your task as a creative thinker is to actively explore the unconscious and contradictory parts of your personality, and to examine similar contradictions and tensions in the world at large. Expressing these tensions within your work in any medium will create a powerful effect on others, making them sense unconscious truths or feelings that have been obscured or repressed. You look at society at large and the various contradictions that are rampant—for instance, the way in which a culture that espouses the ideal of free expression is charged with an oppressive code of political correctness that tamps free expression down. In science, you look for ideas that go against the existing paradigm, or that seem inexplicable because they are so contradictory. All of these contradictions contain a rich mine of information about a reality that is deeper and more complex than the one immediately perceived. By delving into the chaotic and fluid zone below the level of consciousness where opposites meet, you will be surprised at the exciting and fertile ideas that will come bubbling up to the surface.

REVERSAL

In Western culture, a particular myth has evolved that drugs or madness can somehow lead to creative bursts of the highest order. How else to explain the work that John Coltrane did while hooked on heroin, or the great works of the playwright August Strindberg, who seemed clinically insane? Their work is so spontaneous and free, so far beyond the powers of the rational, conscious mind.

This is a cliché, however, that is easily debunked. Coltrane himself admitted that he did his worst work during the few years he was addicted to heroin. It was destroying him and his creative powers. He kicked the habit in 1957 and never looked back. Biographers who later examined the letters and journals of Strindberg discovered a man who was quite histrionic in public, but who in private life was extremely disciplined. The effect of madness created in his plays is very consciously crafted.

Understand: to create a meaningful work of art or to make a discovery or invention requires great discipline, self-control, and emotional stability. It requires mastering the forms of your field. Drugs and madness only destroy such powers. Do not fall for the romantic myths and clichés that abound in culture about creativity—offering us the excuse or panacea that such powers can come cheaply. When you look at the exceptionally creative work of Masters, you must not ignore the years of practice, the endless routines, the hours of doubt, and the tenacious overcoming of obstacles these people endured. Creative energy is the fruit of such efforts and nothing else.

Our vanity, our passions, our spirit of imitation, our abstract intelligence, our habits have long been at work, and it is the task of art to undo this work of theirs, making us travel back in the direction from which we have come to the depths where what has really existed lies unknown within us.

—MARCEL PROUST

VI

FUSE THE INTUITIVE WITH THE RATIONAL: MASTERY

All of us have access to a higher form of intelligence, one that can allow us to see more of the world, to anticipate trends, to respond with speed and accuracy to any circumstance. This intelligence is cultivated by deeply immersing ourselves in a field of study and staying true to our inclinations, no matter how unconventional our approach might seem to others. Through such intense immersion over many years we come to internalize and gain an intuitive feel for the complicated components of our field. When we fuse this intuitive feel with rational processes, we expand our minds to the outer limits of our potential and are able to see into the secret core of life itself. We then come to have powers that approximate the instinctive force and speed of animals, but with the added reach that our human consciousness brings us. This power is what our brains were designed to attain, and we will be naturally led to this type of intelligence if we follow our inclinations to their ultimate ends.

THE THIRD TRANSFORMATION

For the writer Marcel Proust (1871–1922), his fate seemed set at birth. He was born incredibly small and frail; for two weeks he hovered near death, but finally pulled through. As a child, he had frequent bouts of illness that kept him at home for months at a time. When he was nine years old, he suffered his first asthma attack and nearly died. His mother, Jeanne, continuously worried about his health, doted on Marcel and accompanied him on his regular trips to the countryside to convalesce.

And it was on such trips that the pattern of his life became set. Often alone, he developed a passion for reading books. He loved to read about history, and he devoured all forms of literature. His main physical outlet was taking long walks in the country, and here certain sights seemed to captivate him. He would stop and stare for hours at apple blossoms or hawthorn flowers, or at any kind of slightly exotic plant; he found the spectacle of marching ants or spiders working on their webs particularly compelling. He would soon add books on botany and entomology to his reading list. His closest companion in these early years was his mother, and his attachment to her soon went beyond all bounds. They looked alike and shared similar interests in the arts. He could not stand to be away from her for more than a day, and in the few hours in which they were separated he would write her endless letters.

In 1886 he read a book that would forever change the course of his life. It was an historical account of the Norman conquest of England written by Augustin Thierry. The narration of events was so vivid that Marcel felt himself transported back in time. The writer alluded to certain timeless laws of human nature that were revealed in this story, and the possibility of uncovering such laws made Marcel's head spin with excitement. Entomologists could discover the hidden principles that governed the behavior of insects. Could a writer do the same with humans and their complicated nature? Captivated by Thierry's ability to make history come to life, it came to Marcel in a flash that this would be his Life's Task—to become a writer and illuminate the laws of human nature. Haunted by the sense that he would not live long, he would have to hurry this process and do all that he could to develop his writing powers.

At school in Paris, where he lived, Marcel impressed his classmates with his strangeness. He had read so much that his head was teeming with ideas; he would talk about history, ancient Roman literature, and the social life of bees all in the same conversation. He would mix the past and the present, talking about a Roman writer as if he were alive, or describing a friend of theirs as if he were a character from history. His large eyes, which a friend later compared to that of a fly, would seem to bore right into the person he was talking to. In his letters to friends, he could dissect their emotions and problems with such exactitude that it was unnerving, but then he would direct his attention to himself as well, mercilessly exposing his own weaknesses. Despite his propensity for being alone, he was incredibly sociable and a real charmer. He knew how to flatter and ingratiate himself. No one could quite figure him out or gain any sense of what the future might hold for such an oddball.

In 1888 Marcel met a thirty-seven-year-old courtesan named Laure Hayman, who was the mistress of his uncle, among many others, and for him it was instant infatuation. She was like a character out of a novel. Her clothes, her coquettish manner, her power over men fascinated him. Charming her with his witty conversation and polite manners, they quickly became close friends. In France there had long been the tradition of salons—gatherings where people of like mind discussed literary and philosophical ideas. In most cases women ran these various salons, and depending on the social status of the hostess, they could attract important artists, thinkers, and political figures. Laure had her own infamous salon, frequented by artists, bohemians, actors, and actresses. Soon Marcel became a regular.

He found the social life in these upper echelons of French society endlessly fascinating. It was a world full of subtle signs—an invitation to a ball, or the particular seating position at a dinner table would indicate the status of an individual, whether they were on the rise or the decline. Clothes and gestures and certain phrases of conversation would lead to endless critiques and judgments about people. He wanted to explore this realm and learn all of its intricacies. The attention he used to direct toward history and literature he now directed toward the world of high society. He inveigled his way into other salons, and was soon mingling with upper aristocracy.

Although he was determined to become a writer, Marcel had never been able to figure out what he wanted to write about, and this had troubled him to no end. Now, however, he had his answer: this social world would be the ant colony that he would analyze as ruthlessly as an entomologist. For this purpose he began to collect characters for novels. One such character was the Count Robert de Montesquiou, a poet, aesthete, and notorious decadent who had a pronounced weakness for handsome young men. Another was Charles Haas, the epitome of high-society chicness and an expert art collector who couldn't help falling in love with lower-class women. He studied these characters, listened intently to their way of talking, followed their mannerisms, and in his notebooks he would try to bring them to life in small literary sketches. In his writing, Marcel was a master mimic.

Everything he wrote about had to be something real, something he had witnessed or experienced firsthand; otherwise, his writing came out lifeless. His own fear of intimate personal relationships, however, presented him with a problem. Attracted to both men and women, he tended to keep his distance when it came to any type of close physical and emotional relationship. This made it hard for him to write about romance and love from the inside. So he initiated a practice that served him well. If he were attracted to a particular woman, he would befriend her fiancé or boyfriend and, gaining his trust, would probe him for the most intimate details about their relationship. Since he was such an acute psychologist he could give excellent advice. Later, in his own mind, he would completely reconstruct the affair, feeling as deeply as possible the ups and downs, the bouts of jealousy, as if it were all happening to him. He would do this with either gender.

Marcel's father, a prominent doctor, began to despair for his son. Marcel would attend parties all night, return late in the morning, and sleep through the day. To fit in with high society, he was spending vast amounts of money. He seemed to have no discipline and no real career aspirations. With his health problems and his mother always spoiling him, his father feared Marcel would be a failure and a continuous burden. He tried to push him into a career. Marcel placated him as best he could—one day he told his father he would study law; the next day he talked of getting a job as a librarian. But in truth, he was banking everything on the publication of his first book, *Pleasures and Days*. It would be a collection of stories and sketches of the society he had infiltrated. Like Thierry with the Norman Conquest, he would make this world come to life. With the success of this book, he would win over his father and all the other doubters. To ensure its success and make it into more than a book, *Pleasures and Days* would feature the beautiful drawings of a high-society lady he had befriended, and it would be printed on the finest paper.

After numerous delays, the book was finally published in 1896. Although many of the reviews were positive, they kept referring to the writing as exquisite and delicate, implying a sort of superficiality to the work. More disturbing, the book hardly sold. Considering the printing costs it was an enormous financial fiasco, and the public image of Marcel Proust became permanently cemented—he was an elegant dandy, a snob who wrote of the only world he knew, a young man who had no practical sense, a social butterfly who dabbled in literature. It was an embarrassment and it demoralized him.

The family pressures to finally choose a career now grew intense. Still confident in his skills, he decided the only answer was to write another novel, but one that would be the opposite of *Pleasures and Days*. It would be much longer and weightier than the first book. In it he would mix childhood memories and recent social experiences. It would depict the lives of all classes of people and an entire period in French history. It could not be seen as superficial. But as the novel became longer and longer, he could not figure out how to make it cohere into something logical, or even into something resembling a story. He found himself getting lost in the immensity of his ambition, and despite having written hundreds of pages, by the end of 1899 he gave up the project.

He began to grow increasingly depressed and despondent. He was tired of the salons and mingling with the rich. He had no career, no position to rely upon; nearing thirty years of age, he was still living at home, dependent on his parents for money. He felt constantly anxious about his health, certain he was doomed to die within a few years. He heard endless stories of his friends from school becoming prominent members of society, with growing families of their own. In comparison he felt like a total failure. All that he had accomplished was a few articles in newspapers about high society and a book that had made him the laughingstock of Paris. The only thing he could rely on was the continued devotion of his mother.

In the midst of his despair he had an idea. For several years he had been devouring the works of the English art critic and thinker John Ruskin. He would teach himself English and translate Ruskin's work into French. This would require years of scholarly research into the various topics Ruskin specialized in, such as gothic architecture. It would consume much of his time, and he would have to put off any ideas of writing a novel. But it would show his parents that he was serious about making a living and that he had chosen a career. Clinging to this as his last hope, he poured himself into the task with all of his energy.

After several years of intense labor, a few of his translations of Ruskin were published to great acclaim. His introductions and the essays that accompanied the translations finally erased the reputation of the idle dilettante that had haunted him since *Pleasures and Days*. He was seen as a serious scholar. Through his work, he had managed to hone his own style of writing; internalizing the work of Ruskin, he could now write essays that were thoughtful and precise. He had finally gained some discipline, something to build on. But in the midst of this modest success, his network of emotional support suddenly teetered and then vanished. In 1903 his father died. Two years later his mother, unable to get over the loss, passed away as well. They had hardly ever been apart from each other, and he had dreaded the moment of her death since childhood. He felt completely alone, and he feared that he had nothing left to live for.

In the months to come he slowly withdrew from society, and as he took stock of his life up to that point he discerned a pattern that actually gave him the faintest amount of hope. To compensate for his physical weakness he had taken to reading, and in the process had discovered his Life's Task. Over the course of the last twenty years he had accumulated a vast amount of knowledge about French society—an incredibly wide variety of real-life characters of all types and classes lived inside of his head. He had written thousands of pages—including the failed novel, short sketches for newspapers, and various essays. Using Ruskin as a mentor, in translating his works he had developed discipline and some organizing skills. He had long thought of life as an apprenticeship in which we are all slowly instructed in the ways of the world. Some people learn to read the signs and heed the lessons from this apprenticeship, developing themselves in the process; others do not. He had served an elaborate twenty-year apprenticeship in writing and in human nature, and it had altered him deeply. Despite his ill health and his failures, he had never given up. This must mean something—perhaps a destiny of sorts. All of his failures had a purpose, he decided, if he knew how to exploit them. His time had not been wasted.

What he needed to do was to put all of this knowledge to work. This meant returning to the novel that had continually eluded him. What it would be about—the plot, the narrator's voice—he still had no idea. The material was all there in his head. If in his loneliness he could not bring back his mother or his childhood or his youth, he would somehow re-create these things in their entirety, here in the study of his apartment where he now holed himself up. What mattered was to get to work. Something would come of it.

In the fall of 1908 he purchased dozens of notebooks, the kind he used to use in school, and began to fill them with notes. He wrote essays on aesthetics, sketches of characters, childhood memories that he strained to recall. And as he went deep into this process, he felt a change within himself. Something clicked. He did not know where it came from, but a voice emerged, his own voice, which would be that of the narrator himself. The story would revolve around a young man who becomes too neurotically attached to his mother and cannot forge his own identity. He discovers that he wants to be a writer, but he cannot figure out what he should write about. As he grows up, he starts to explore the two social realms of bohemia and landed aristocracy. He dissects the various people he meets, uncovering the essence of their characters that lies underneath their superficial social personalities. He has several failed love affairs in which he suffers the extremes of jealousy. After numerous adventures and a creeping sense of failure as he advances in life, at the very end of the novel he discovers what he wants to write—it will be the book that we have just been reading.

The novel would be called *In Search of Lost Time*, and in the end it would recount much of Proust's own life, all of the various characters he knew disguised under different names. In the course of the narration he would cover the entire history of France from the moment he was born to the present, whatever the present was. It would be a portrait of society as a whole; he would be the entomologist uncovering the laws that governed the behavior of all the inhabitants of the anthill. His only concern now was his health. The task ahead of him was immense. Would he live long enough to complete it?

Over the course of several years, he finished the first part of the book, known as *Swann's Way*. It was published in 1913, and the reviews were extremely positive. No one had ever read a novel quite like it. It seemed that Proust had created his own genre—part novel, part essay. But as he was making plans for the final half of the book, war broke out across Europe and the publishing business essentially ground to a halt. Proust continued working on the novel unremittingly, but as he did so, something strange happened—the book kept expanding in size and scope, one volume after the next. His method of working was partially responsible for this increase. He had collected over the years thousands of bits of stories, characters, lessons on life, laws of psychology that he slowly pieced together in the novel, like tiles of a mosaic. He could not foresee the end.

And as the book grew in size, it suddenly assumed a different form— real life and the novel became inextricably interwoven. When he needed a new character, a wealthy debutante for instance, he would hunt down her equivalent in society and get himself invited to balls and soirées where he could study her. Phrases she used would find their way into the book. One evening, he reserved several boxes at the theater for his friends. In these boxes he gathered the real-life people upon whom he had based his characters. Later they attended a dinner, and around the table he could observe, like a chemist, the various elements of his book, there before his eyes. None of them of course knew what was going on. Everything became material for him—not only the past, but present events and encounters would suddenly suggest a new idea or direction.

When he wished to write about the particular plants and flowers that had obsessed him as a boy, he would drive to the country and spend hours lost in observation, trying to get at the essence of their uniqueness and at what had fascinated him, so he could recreate the original sensation for the reader. Fictionalizing the Count de Montesquiou as a character named Charlus, a notorious homosexual, he visited the most secretive male brothels in Paris that the count was known to frequent. His book had to be as real as possible, including graphic sex scenes. For things he could not personally witness, he would pay others to supply him gossip, information, even do some spying. As the book grew in length and intensity, he had the sensation that this social realm he was depicting had come alive within him, and feeling it from the inside, it would flow out of him with increasing ease. He had a metaphor to explain this sensation, which he included in the novel—he was like a spider sitting on its web, feeling the slightest vibration, knowing it so deeply as the world he had created and mastered.

After the war Proust's book continued to be published, one volume after another. Critics were completely astounded at the depth and breadth of his work. He had created, or rather recreated, an entire world. But this was not simply a realistic novel, for much of the work included discourses on art, psychology, the secrets of memory, and the workings of the brain itself. Proust had delved so deeply into his own psychology that he had made discoveries about memory and the unconscious that seemed uncannily accurate. Going through volume after volume, readers would have the sensation that they were actually living and experiencing this world from within, the narrator's thoughts becoming one's own thoughts—the boundaries between narrator and reader disappearing. It was a magical effect; it felt like life itself.

Straining to finish the final volume, the point at which the narrator would be finally able to write the novel we have been reading, Proust was in a hurry. He could feel his energy waning and death approaching. All through the publishing process, he would make the publishers stop the printing, as some new incident he had personally witnessed had to be included in the book. Now, sensing himself near death, he made his female attendant take some final notes. He finally understood how it felt to be dying, and he had to rewrite a previous deathbed scene—it was not psychologically real enough. He died two days later, never to see the full seven volumes in print.

KEYS TO MASTERY

Cook Ting was cutting up an ox for Lord Wen-hui. . . . "Ah, this is marvelous!" said Lord Wen-hui. "Imagine skill reaching such heights!" Cook Ting laid down his knife and replied, "What I care about is the Way, which goes beyond skill. When I first began cutting up oxen, all I could see was the ox itself. After three years I no longer saw the whole ox. And now—now I go at it by spirit and don't look with my eyes. Perception and understanding have come to a stop and spirit moves where it wants."

—CHUANG TZU, ANCIENT CHINESE
WRITER, FOURTH CENTURY B.C.

Throughout history we read of Masters in every conceivable form of human endeavor describing a sensation of suddenly possessing heightened intellectual powers after years of immersion in their field. The great chess Master Bobby Fischer spoke of being able to think beyond the various moves of his pieces on the chessboard; after a while he could see "fields of forces" that allowed him to anticipate the entire direction of the match. For the pianist Glenn Gould, he no longer had to focus on notes or parts of the music he was playing, but instead saw the entire architecture of the piece and could express it. Albert Einstein suddenly was able to realize not just the answer to a problem, but a whole new way of looking at the universe, contained in a visual image he intuited. The inventor Thomas Edison spoke of a vision he had for illuminating an entire city with electric light, this complex system communicated to him through a single image.

In all of these instances, these practitioners of various skills described a sensation of *seeing more.* They were suddenly able to grasp an entire situation through an image or an idea, or a combination of images and ideas. They experienced this power as *intuition,* or a *fingertip feel.*

Considering the power such intelligence can bring us, and the tremendous contributions to culture made by Masters who possess it, it would seem logical that such high-level intuition would be the subject of countless books and discussions, and that the form of thinking that goes with it would be elevated into an ideal for all of us to aim at. But oddly enough, this is not at all the case. This form of intelligence is either ignored, relegated to the inexplicable realms of the mystical and occult, or ascribed to genius and genetics. Some even try to debunk this type of power in general, claiming that these Masters are exaggerating their experiences, and that their so-called intuitive powers are nothing more than extended forms of normal thinking, based on superior knowledge.

The reason for this overall disregard is simple: we humans have come to recognize only one form of thinking and intelligence—rationality. Rational thinking is sequential by nature. We see a phenomenon A, and we deduce a cause B, and maybe anticipate a reaction C. In all cases of rational thinking, we can reconstruct the various steps that were taken to arrive at some kind of conclusion or answer. This form of thinking is extremely effective and has brought us great powers. We developed it to help make sense of our world and to gain some control over it. The process that people go through when they arrive at an answer through rational analysis can generally be examined and verified, which is why we esteem it so highly. We prefer things that can be reduced to a formula and described in precise words. But the types of intuitions discussed by various Masters cannot be reduced to a formula, and the steps they took to arrive at them cannot be reconstructed. We cannot go inside the mind of Albert Einstein and experience his sudden grasp of the nature of the relativity of time. And because we recognize rationality as the only legitimate form of intelligence, these experiences of "seeing more" must either be forms of rational thinking that just happen faster, or are simply miraculous by nature.

The problem we are facing here is that high-level intuition, the ultimate sign of mastery, involves a process that is qualitatively different from rationality, but is even more accurate and perceptive. It accesses deeper parts of reality. It is a highly legitimate type of intelligence, but one that has to be understood in its own right. And in understanding it, we can begin to see that such power is not miraculous, but intrinsically human and accessible to us all.

Let us try to make sense of this form of thinking by examining how it might operate in two very different forms of knowledge—the life sciences and warfare.

If we were to study a particular animal in order to understand it, we would break up our analysis into several parts. We would study its various organs, brain, and anatomical structure in order to see how it has adapted differently from other animals to its environment. We would study its behavior patterns, how it gathers food, and its mating rituals. We would look at how it functions within an ecosystem. In this way, we would be able to piece together an accurate picture of this animal, covering it from all angles. With warfare, we would go through a similar process, breaking it up into parts— field maneuvers, weaponry, logistics, strategy. Having deep knowledge of these subjects, we could analyze the results of a battle and come to some interesting conclusions; or, with some field experience, we could lead an army into battle and do an effective job.

In taking these analyses as far as possible, however, something is inevitably missing. An animal is not merely the sum of its parts that we can understand by adding them up. It has its own experience and emotions, which play an enormous role in its behavior, but which are elements we cannot see or measure. It has its own highly complex interactions with the environment that become distorted when we break them up into parts. The animal's continuously fluid, dimensional interaction with its environment is also something that is not visible to our eyes. With warfare, once battle is engaged, we become susceptible to what is known as the fog of war—the highly unpredictable element that comes into play when two opposing forces square up and nothing can be precisely anticipated. The situation is continuously fluid, as one side reacts to the other and the unexpected intervenes. This battle in real time has an interactive, changing element that cannot be reduced to its parts or to simple analysis, and is not something we can see and measure.

This unseen element that constitutes the animal's entire experience, and that makes battle a fluid, organic entity, can be called various things. To the ancient Chinese, who understood this very well, it was known as the Tao or Way, and this Way inhabits everything in the world and is embedded in the relationships between things. The Way is visible to the expert—in cooking, carpentry, warfare, or philosophy. We shall call it the *dynamic*, the living force that inevitably operates in anything we study or do. It is how the whole thing functions, and how the relationships evolve from within. It is not the moves of the pieces on the chessboard but the entire game, involving the psychologies of the players, their strategies in real time, their past experiences influencing the present, the comfort of the chairs they are sitting in, how their energies affect each other—in a word, everything that comes into play, all at once.

Through intense absorption in a particular field over a long period of time, Masters come to understand all of the parts involved in what they are studying. They reach a point where all of this has become internalized and they are no longer seeing the parts, but gain an *intuitive feel for the whole*. They literally see or sense the dynamic. In the living sciences, we have the example of Jane Goodall, who studied chimpanzees in the wilds of East Africa for years as she lived among them. Interacting with them constantly, she reached a point where she began to think like a chimpanzee, and could see elements of their social life that no other scientist had come close to fathoming. She gained an intuitive feel for not only how they functioned as individuals but as a group, which is an inseparable part of their lives. She made discoveries about the social life of chimpanzees that forever altered our conception of the animal, and that are no less scientific for depending on this deep level of intuition.

In warfare, we can point to the great German general Erwin Rommel, who was said to possess the highest form of the fingertip feel ever chronicled in the history of battle. He could sense exactly where the enemy was thinking of striking and foil their plans; he could launch an offensive at precisely the weak point in their lines of defense. He seemed to have eyes in the back of his head, and oracular powers for reading the future. He did all of this in the deserts of North Africa where it was nearly impossible to get any clear sense of the terrain. Rommel's power, however, was not occult in nature. He simply had a much deeper knowledge than other generals of all of the aspects of battle. He constantly flew over the desert in his own plane, gaining a bird's-eye feel for the terrain. He was a trained mechanic, and so had a complete knowledge of his tanks and what he could expect of them. He studied in depth the psychology of the opposing army and its generals. He interacted with almost all of his soldiers, and had a clear sense of how far he could push them. Whatever he studied, he did so with incredible intensity and depth. A point was reached where all of these details became internalized. They fused together in his brain, giving him a feel for the whole picture and a sense of this interactive *dynamic*.

The ability to have this intuitive grasp of the whole and feel this *dynamic* is simply a function of time. Since it has been shown that the brain is literally altered after approximately 10,000 hours of practice, these powers would be the result of a transformation that happens in the brain after some 20,000 hours and beyond. With this much practice and experience, all kinds of connections have been formed in the brain between different forms of knowledge. Masters thus have a sense of how everything interacts organically, and they can intuit patterns or solutions in an instant. This fluid form of thinking does not occur through a step-by-step process, but rather comes in flashes and insights as the brain makes sudden connections between disparate forms of knowledge, causing us to sense the *dynamic* in real time.

Some people like to imagine that such intuitions do operate sequentially, but simply happen too fast for the thinker to see the steps. This reasoning comes from the desire to reduce every form of intelligence to the same rational level. But with a discovery like the theory of simple relativity, if Albert Einstein himself could not begin to reconstruct the steps in retrospect that led to his insight on the relativity of time, then why should it be imagined that such steps exist? We must trust the experience and descriptions of these Masters, all people with high levels of self-awareness and analytical skills.

It would be a misconception, however, to imagine that Masters are simply following their intuitions and moving beyond rational thinking. First, it is through all of their hard work, the depth of their knowledge, and the development of their analytical skills that they reach this higher form of intelligence. Second, when they experience this intuition or insight, they invariably subject it to a high degree of reflection and reasoning. In science, they must spend months or years verifying their intuitions. In the arts, they must work out the ideas that come to them intuitively and rationally shape them into a form. This is hard for us to imagine, because we find intuition and rationality mutually exclusive, but in fact at this high level they operate together in a seamless fashion. The reasoning of Masters is guided by intuition; their intuition springs from intense rational focus. The two are fused.

Although time is the critical factor in attaining Mastery and this intuitive feel, the time we are talking about is not neutral or simply quantitative. An hour of Einstein's thinking at the age of sixteen does not equal an hour spent by an average high school student working on a problem in physics. It is not a matter of studying a subject for twenty years, and then emerging as a Master. The time that leads to mastery is dependent on the intensity of our focus.

The key, then, to attaining this higher level of intelligence is to make our years of study *qualitatively* rich. We don't simply absorb information—we internalize it and make it our own by finding some way to put this knowledge to practical use. We look for connections between the various elements we are learning, hidden laws that we can perceive in the apprenticeship phase. If we experience any failures or setbacks, we do not quickly forget them because they offend our self-esteem. Instead we reflect on them deeply, trying to figure out what went wrong and discern whether there are any patterns to our mistakes. As we progress, we start to question some of the assumptions and conventions we have learned along the way. Soon, we begin to experiment and become increasingly active. At all points in the various moments leading to mastery, we attack with intensity. Every moment, every experience contains deep lessons for us. We are continuously awake, never merely going through the motions.

The person who best exemplifies this usage of time for mastery is Marcel Proust, whose great novel, *In Search of Lost Time,* concerns this very subject. In French the word for "lost" is *perdu,* which equally means "wasted." And to Proust, and to many of those who knew him as a young man, he seemed the least likely person ever to attain mastery, because on the surface he appeared to waste so much valuable time. All he ever seemed to do was read books, take walks, write interminable letters, attend parties, sleep during the day, and publish frothy society articles. When he finally applied himself to translating Ruskin, he took an incredibly long time and involved himself in seemingly irrelevant tasks, like traveling to locations Ruskin described, something no other translator would think of doing.

Proust himself complained endlessly about the time that he had wasted as a young man and how little he had accomplished, but these complaints cannot be taken at face value, because he never gave up. Despite his physical weakness and bouts of depression, he continued to try new endeavors and kept widening the scope of his knowledge. He was tireless and tenacious. These moments of self-doubt were his way of propelling himself forward and reminding himself of the short amount of time remaining to him. He had a deep awareness of a sense of destiny, of an overall purpose for his strangeness, that he was called to fulfill through his writing.

What made those twenty years qualitatively different from those of an ordinary person was the intensity of his attention. He did not simply read books—he took them apart, rigorously analyzed them, and learned valuable lessons to apply to his own life. All of this reading implanted in his brain various styles that would enrich his own writing style. He did not merely socialize—he strained to understand people at their core and to uncover their secret motivations. He did not just analyze his own psychology, but went so deeply into the various levels of consciousness he found within himself that he developed insights about the functioning of memory that foreshadowed many discoveries in neuroscience. He did not merely translate, but strove to inhabit the mind of Ruskin himself. In the end, he even used the death of his mother to intensify his development. With her gone, he would have to write himself out of his depression, and find a way to re-create the feelings between them in the book he was to write. As he later described it, all of these experiences were like seeds, and once he had started his novel he was like a gardener tending and cultivating the plants that had taken root so many years before.

Through his own efforts, he transformed himself from an apprentice to a mature writer and translator, and from there to a novelist who figured out what to write about, which voice to assume, and how to attack his subject. At some point after he began writing his novel, he underwent a third transformation. Memories and ideas came flooding into his mind. Even as the book kept expanding, he could intuit its overall shape and the relationships between the many tiles of the mosaic. This immense novel had a living, breathing dynamic that was now completely alive within him. He was inside his characters and the whole slice of French society he was writing about. More important, he was completely inside the narrator (who is Proust himself), and in his novel it's as if we are literally, from the inside, experiencing the thoughts and sensations of another person. He was able to achieve this effect through the intuitive powers he had gained from close to thirty years of perpetual work and analysis.

Like Proust, you must also maintain a sense of destiny, and feel continuously connected to it. You are unique, and there is a purpose to your uniqueness. You must see every setback, failure, or hardship as a trial along the way, as seeds that are being planted for further cultivation, if you know how to grow them. No moment is wasted if you pay attention and learn the lessons contained in every experience. By constantly applying yourself to the subject that suits your inclinations and attacking it from many different angles, you are simply enriching the ground for these seeds to take root. You may not see this process in the present, but it is happening. Never losing your connection to your Life's Task, you will unconsciously hit upon the right choices in your life. Over time, mastery will come to you.

The high-level intuitive powers we are talking about have roots in our development as the thinking animal; they have an evolutionary purpose that is extremely helpful to understand, and one that is highly relevant to the times in which we live.

The Roots of Masterly Intuition

For nearly all animals, speed is the critical factor in survival. A few seconds can spell the difference between avoiding a predator or meeting death. And for the purposes of such speed, organisms have evolved elaborate instincts. An instinctual response is immediate and is generally triggered by certain stimuli. Sometimes organisms possess instincts that are so finely calibrated to circumstances that they seem to have uncanny abilities.

Take, for instance, the Ammophila wasp. With incredible speed the female Ammophila is able to sting her various victims—spiders, beetles, caterpillars—in precisely the right place to paralyze but not kill them. Into the paralyzed flesh she lays her eggs, providing her larvae with fresh meat to feast upon for several days. In each of these victims the stinging points are different—for instance, with the caterpillar, she must hit at three separate points to paralyze the entire creature. Because it is such a delicate operation, sometimes the Ammophila misses and kills the victim, but generally, her success rate is high enough to ensure the survival of her offspring. In this process there is no time for calculating the kind of victim and the exact spot to hit. It is instant, as if the wasp has a feel for the nerve centers of her various victims, and can sense them from the inside.

Our primitive ancestors had their own sets of instincts, many of which remain buried within us to this day. But as these ancestors slowly developed reasoning powers, they had to detach themselves from their immediate circumstances and depend less on instinct. To notice behavior patterns in the animals they were tracking, they had to connect them to other actions that were not immediately apparent. They had to make similar calculations when it came to locating food sources, or to navigating the long distances they traveled on foot. With this ability to detach themselves from the environment and see patterns, they gained tremendous mental powers, but this development also presented a great danger—increasing amounts of information for the brain to process and a consequent loss of speed in reacting to events.

Such slowness could have spelled doom for us as a species if not for a compensatory power that the human brain developed. Years of tracking particular animals and observing their surroundings gave our ancestors a feel for their environment in all of its complexity. Knowing the behavior patterns of various animals, they could anticipate where predators might strike, and sense where prey might lie. They came to know so well the long distances they traveled that they could negotiate these spaces quickly and effectively, without having to calculate. In other words, they developed a primitive form of intuition. Through continual experience and practice, our ancestors recovered some of the immediacy and speed they had lost. They could respond intuitively instead of instinctually. On this level, intuition was more powerful than instinct in that it was not tied to very specific circumstances or stimuli, but could be applied to a much wider arena of action.

These ancestors' brains were not yet burdened by all of the information that comes through language or the complexities of living in large groups. Interacting so directly with their environment, they could develop an intuitive feel over the course of a handful years. But for us, living in a much more complex environment, this process can take fifteen to twenty years. Our *high-level intuition*, however, has its roots firmly in the primitive version.

Intuition, primitive or high level, is essentially driven by memory. When we take in information of any kind, we store it in mnemonic networks in the brain. The stability and durability of these networks depends on repetition, intensity of experience, and how deeply we pay attention. If we are half listening to a vocabulary lesson in a foreign language, we are not likely to retain it on any level. But if we are in the country where the language is spoken, we will hear the same words repeated in context; we will tend to pay deeper attention because we need to, and the memory trace will be that much more stable.

According to the model developed by the psychologist Kenneth Bowers, whenever we encounter a problem—a face we need to recognize, a word or phrase we need to recall—mnemonic networks within the brain become activated as the search for the answer is guided along certain pathways. All of this occurs below the level of consciousness. When a particular network is sufficiently activated, we suddenly become conscious of a possible name for the face, or a phrase that might be appropriate. These are low-level forms of intuition that come to us in our everyday life; we cannot reconstruct the steps that went into recognizing a person's face and remembering their name.

People who spend years studying a particular subject or field develop so many of these memory networks and pathways that their brains are constantly searching for and discovering connections between various pieces of information. When confronted with a high-level problem, the search goes in a hundred directions below conscious awareness, guided by an intuitive sense of where the answer might lie. All kinds of networks become activated, ideas and solutions suddenly rising to the surface. Those that seem particularly fruitful and appropriate stick in the memory and are acted upon. Instead of having to reason an answer through a step-by-step process, the answer comes to consciousness with a feeling of immediacy.

The extremely high number of experiences and memory networks that become hardwired allow the brains of Masters to explore an area that is so wide that it has the dimensions and feel of reality itself, of the *dynamic*.

For someone like the chess Master Bobby Fischer, the number of times he experienced similar sets of circumstances and witnessed the various movements and reactions of different opponents created powerful memory traces. He internalized incredible numbers of patterns. At some point in his development, all of these memories fused into a feel for the overall dynamic of the game. He was no longer seeing simple moves on the chessboard and recalling various countermoves he had made in the past, but rather was able to see and recollect long sequences of potential moves that presented themselves as fields of force, sweeping the board as a whole. With such a sense for the game, he could entrap his opponents well before they were aware of what was happening, and could finish them off as quickly and precisely as the Ammophila delivered her sting.

In fields such as sports or warfare, or any competitive endeavor where time is of the essence, Masters' decisions based on intuition will be much more effective than if they had tried to analyze all of the components and figure out the best answer. There is too much information to consider in too short a time. Although the power of intuition was originally developed for the rapidity it brought, it has become something that can be applied to the sciences or the arts, or to any field in which there are complex elements and time is not necessarily the critical factor.

This high-level intuition, like any skill, requires practice and experience. At first, our intuitions might be so faint that we do not pay attention to them or trust them. All Masters talk of this phenomenon. But over time they learn to notice these rapid ideas that come to them. They learn to act on them and verify their validity. Some lead nowhere, but others lead to tremendous insights. Over time, Masters find that they can call up more and more of these high-level intuitions, which are now sparking all over the brain. Accessing this level of thinking on a more regular basis, they can fuse it even more deeply with their rational forms of thinking.

Understand: this intuitive form of intelligence was developed to help us process complex layers of information and gain a sense of the whole. And in the world today, the need to attain such a level of thinking is more critical than ever before. To follow any career path is difficult, and requires the cultivation of much patience and discipline. We have so many elements to master that it can be intimidating. We must learn to handle the technical aspects, the social and political gamesmanship, the public reactions to our work, and the constantly changing picture in our field. When we add to this already-daunting quantity of study the vast amounts of information now available to us, and that we must keep on top of, it all seems beyond our capability.

What happens to many of us when faced with such complexity is that we feel subtly discouraged before we even try anything. More and more people in this overheated environment will be tempted to opt out. They will develop a greater taste for ease and comfort; they will increasingly settle on simplified ideas of reality and conventional ways of thinking; they will fall prey to seductive formulas that offer quick and easy knowledge. They will lose a taste for developing skills that require time and a resilient ego—it can hurt our self-esteem in the initial phases of learning a skill, as we are made so aware of our awkwardness. Such people will rail against the world and blame others for their problems; they will find political justifications for opting out, when in truth they simply cannot handle the challenges of engaging with complexity. In trying to simplify their mental lives, they disconnect themselves from reality and neutralize all of the powers developed by the human brain over so many millions of years.

This desire for what is simple and easy infects all of us, often in ways we are mostly unaware of. The only solution is the following: We must learn how to quiet the anxiety we feel whenever we are confronted with anything that seems complex or chaotic. In our journey from apprenticeship to mastery we must patiently learn the various parts and skills that are required, never looking too far ahead. In moments of perceived crisis, we must develop the habit of maintaining our cool and never overreacting. If the situation is complex and others are reaching for simple black-and-white answers, or for the usual conventional responses, we must make a point of resisting such a temptation. We maintain our Negative Capability and a degree of detachment. What we are doing is gaining a tolerance and even a taste for chaotic moments, training ourselves to entertain several possibilities or solutions. We are learning to manage our anxiety, a key skill in these chaotic times.

To go along with this self-control, we must do whatever we can to cultivate a greater memory capacity—one of the most important skills in our technologically oriented environment. The problem that technology presents us is that it increases the amount of information at our disposal, but slowly degrades the power of our memory to retain it. Tasks that used to exercise the brain—remembering phone numbers, doing simple calculations, navigating and remembering streets in a city—are now performed for us, and like any muscle the brain can grow flabby from disuse. To counteract this, in our spare time we should not simply look for entertainment and distractions. We should take up hobbies—a game, a musical instrument, a foreign language—that bring pleasure but also offer us the chance to strengthen our memory capacities and the flexibility of our brain. In doing so, we can train ourselves to process large amounts of information without feeling anxious or overtaxed.

Faithfully pursuing this course over enough time, we will eventually be rewarded with intuitive powers. That whole living, breathing, changing beast that is our field will become internalized and live within us. Possessing even a part of such power will instantly separate us from all of the others who find themselves overwhelmed and straining to simplify what is inherently complex. We will be able to respond faster and more effectively than others. What seemed chaotic to us before will now seem to be simply a fluid situation with a particular dynamic that we have a feel for and can handle with relative ease.

What is interesting to note is that many Masters who come to possess this high-level intuitive power seem to become younger in mind and spirit with the passing years—something that should be encouraging to us all. They do not need to expend a great deal of energy in order to understand phenomena, and can think creatively with increasing speed. Unless debilitated by disease, they can maintain their spontaneity and mental fluidity well into their seventies and beyond. Among such types are the Zen Master and artist Hakuin, who made paintings in his sixties that are now considered among the greatest works of his time, remarkable for the spontaneity of expression they reveal. Another example is the Spanish filmmaker Luis Buñuel, whose surrealist films seemed to get richer and more startling as he reached his sixties and seventies. But the quintessence of this phenomenon would have to be Benjamin Franklin.

Franklin had always been an acute observer of natural phenomena, but these powers only increased with the years. In his seventies and on into his eighties he continued with a series of speculations that are now considered uncannily ahead of his time—including advanced ideas on health and medicine, weather, physics, geophysics, evolution, the use of aircraft for military and commercial purposes, and more. As he aged, he applied his renowned inventiveness to his growing physical weaknesses. Trying to improve his eyesight and quality of life, he invented bifocals. Unable to reach books on the tops of his shelves, he invented an extendible mechanical arm. Needing copies of his own work and not wanting to leave his house, he invented a rolling press that could make an accurate copy of a document in less than two minutes. In his last years, he had insights into politics and the future of America that made people think of him as a seer, as someone with magical abilities. William Pierce, a delegate to the Constitutional Convention, met Franklin near the end of his life and wrote: "Dr. Franklin is well known to be the greatest philosopher of the present age; all the operations of nature he seems to understand. . . . He is eighty-two years old, and possesses an activity of mind equal to a youth of twenty-five years of age."

It is interesting to speculate what depths of understanding such Masters could have reached if they had lived even longer. Perhaps in the future, with life expectancy increasing, we will witness examples of the Benjamin Franklin variety stretching to even more advanced ages.

The Return to Reality

People can argue endlessly about what constitutes reality, but let us start our definition with a simple, undeniable fact: some 4 billion years ago, life began on this planet in the shape of simple cells. These cells, perhaps even one cell in particular, were the common ancestors to all life forms that followed. From that single source, various branches of life emerged. Some 1.2 billion years ago there appeared the first multicellular creatures; 600 million years ago there emerged perhaps the greatest development of all—organisms with a central nervous system, the starting point that eventually led to the brains we now possess. From the Cambrian explosion of life some 500 million years ago came the first simple animals, followed by the first vertebrates. Some 360 million years ago we see the first traces on land of amphibious creatures, and 120 million years ago the first mammals. Branching off in a new mammalian direction about 60 million years ago, we see signs of the earliest primates from whom we are directly descended. The earliest human ancestors arrived some 6 million years ago, and 4 million years later our most recent ancestor, *Homo erectus*. And just 200,000 years ago the anatomically modern human emerged, with more or less the same brain size that we now possess.

In this remarkably complex chain of circumstances, we can identify, at certain turning points, a single ancestor from whom we humans have evolved (the first cells, simple animals, mammals, then primates). Some archeologists have speculated about a single female ancestor from whom all modern humans have descended. Moving up the chain, backwards in time, it is clear that who we are today—our particular physiological makeup—is intimately connected to each one of these original ancestors, as far back as the first cells of life. Since all life forms are descended from this common beginning, they are all interconnected in some way, and we humans are intimately implicated in this network. This is undeniable.

Let us call this interrelatedness of life the *ultimate reality*. And in relation to this reality, the human mind tends to go in one of two directions. On the one hand, the mind tends to move away from this interconnectedness and focus instead on the distinctions between things, taking objects out of their contexts and analyzing them as separate entities. At the extreme this tendency leads to highly specialized forms of knowledge. In the world today, we can see many signs of this tendency—the microscopic divisions between fields in our universities, the narrowest of specializations in the sciences. In the culture at large, people will make the finest distinctions between closely related or overlapping subjects, and argue endlessly about the differences. They will distinguish between military and civilian society, even though in a democracy such a distinction is not so easy to make. (Perhaps keeping people and fields of study so rigorously separated can be considered the ultimate ploy of those in power, a version of divide and conquer.) At this level of thinking, a sense of the interrelatedness of life and phenomena is lost, and in becoming so specialized ideas can become quite weird and disconnected from reality.

On the other hand, there is the opposing tendency of the brain to want to make connections between everything. This generally occurs among individuals who pursue knowledge far enough that these associations come to life. Although this tendency is easier to spot in Masters, we can see in history certain movements and philosophies in which this return to reality becomes widespread in a culture, part of the zeitgeist. For instance, in the ancient world there was Taoism in the East, and Stoicism in the West, both movements that endured for centuries. In Taoism, there is the concept of the Way, and in Stoicism, that of the Logos—the ordering principle of the universe that connects all living things. As Marcus Aurelius expresses it, "Keep reminding yourself of the way things are connected, of their relatedness. All things are implicated in one another and in sympathy with each other. This event is the consequence of some other one. Things push and pull on each other, and breathe together, and are one."

Perhaps the greatest example of this was the Renaissance, a cultural movement for which the ideal was the Universal Man—a person who has managed to connect all branches of knowledge and approximate the intellectual reach of the Creator.

Perhaps today we are witnessing the early signs of a return to reality, a Renaissance in modern form. In the sciences, the first seeds of this began with Faraday, Maxwell, and Einstein, who focused on the relationships between phenomena, fields of force instead of individual particles. In the larger sense, many scientists are now actively seeking to connect their various specializations to others—for instance, how neuroscience intersects so many other disciplines. We see signs of this also in the growing interest in theories of complexity applied to such disparate fields as economics, biology, and computers. We can see it in the broadening of our thinking to ecosystems, as a way to truly conceptualize the dynamic interactions in nature. We can see it in health and medicine, in the sane approach many are taking to consider the body as a whole. This trend is the future, because the purpose of consciousness itself has always been to connect us to reality.

As individuals, we can participate in this trend simply by pursuing mastery. In our apprenticeships, we naturally begin by learning the parts and making various distinctions—the right and wrong way to proceed, the individual skills to master and their particular techniques, the various rules and conventions that govern the group. In the Creative-Active we begin to melt these distinctions as we experiment with, shape, and alter these conventions to suit our purposes. And in mastery we come full circle, returning to a sense of the whole. We intuit and see the connections. We embrace the natural complexity of life, making the brain expand to the dimensions of reality instead of shrinking it to the narrowest of specializations. This is the inevitable outcome of deep immersion in a field. We can define intelligence as moving toward thinking that is more contextual, more sensitive to the relationships between things.

Think of it this way: the ultimate distinction you make is between yourself and the world. There is the inside (your subjective experience) and there is the outside. But every time you learn something, your brain is altered as new connections are formed. Your experience of something that occurs in the world physically alters your brain. The boundaries between you and the world are much more fluid than you might imagine. When you move toward mastery, your brain becomes radically altered by the years of practice and active experimentation. It is no longer the simple ecosystem of years gone by. The brain of a Master is so richly interconnected that it comes to resemble the physical world, and becomes a vibrant ecosystem in which all forms of thinking associate and connect. This growing similarity between the brain and complex life itself represents the ultimate return to reality.

STRATEGIES FOR ATTAINING MASTERY

The intuitive mind is a sacred gift and the rational mind is a faithful servant.
We have created a society that honors the servant and has forgotten the gift.

—ALBERT EINSTEIN

Mastery is not a function of genius or talent. It is a function of time and intense focus applied to a particular field of knowledge. But there is another element, an X factor that Masters inevitably possess, that seems mystical but that is accessible to us all. Whatever field of activity we are involved in, there is generally an accepted path to the top. It is a path that others have followed, and because we are conformist creatures, most of us opt for this conventional route. But Masters have a strong inner guiding system and a high level of self-awareness. What has suited others in the past does not suit them, and they know that trying to fit into a conventional mold would only lead to a dampening of spirit, the reality they seek eluding them.

And so inevitably, these Masters, as they progress on their career paths, make a choice at a key moment in their lives: they decide to forge their own route, one that others will see as unconventional, but that suits their own spirit and rhythms and leads them closer to discovering the hidden truths of their objects of study. This key choice takes self-confidence and self-awareness—the X factor that is necessary for attaining mastery. The following are examples of this X factor in action and the strategic choices it leads to. The examples given are meant to show the importance of this quality and how we might adapt it to our own circumstances.

1. Connect to your environment—Primal Powers

Among the many feats of human navigation of the sea, perhaps none are more remarkable and mysterious than the voyages of the indigenous peoples in the area known as Oceania—comprising the islands of Micronesia, Melanesia, and Polynesia. In an area that is 99.8 percent water, the inhabitants of this region were able for many centuries to deftly navigate the vast spaces between the islands. Some 1,500 years ago they managed to travel the several thousand miles to Hawaii, and perhaps at one point even voyaged as far as parts of North and South America, all in canoes with the same design and technology as those of the Stone Age. During the nineteenth century, mostly because of Western interference and the introduction of charts and compasses, these ancient navigating skills died out, and the source of their uncanny skill remained mostly a mystery. But in the area of Micronesia known as the Caroline Islands, certain islanders maintained the ancient traditions well into the twentieth century. And the first Westerners who traveled with them were astonished at what they witnessed.

The Islanders would travel in outrigger canoes fitted with a sail with three or four men aboard, one serving as the chief navigator. They had no charts or instruments of any kind, and for the Westerners who accompanied them this could be a disconcerting experience. Taking off at night or day (it didn't matter to them), there would be apparently nothing to guide them along the way. The islands were so far apart that one could travel for days without spotting land. To go off course only slightly (and storms or weather changes could certainly cause that) would mean never spotting their destination, and probably death—it would take too long to find the next island in the chain, and supplies would run out. And yet they would embark on their sea voyages with a remarkably relaxed spirit.

The chief navigator would occasionally glance at the night sky or the position of the sun, but mostly he talked with the others or stared straight ahead. Sometimes one of the men would lie belly down in the middle of the outrigger canoe and report some information he had gleaned. In general they gave the impression of being passengers on a train, serenely taking in the passing scenery. They seemed even calmer at night. When they were supposedly getting closer to their destination, they would become slightly more alert. They would follow the paths of birds in the sky; they would look deeply into the water, which they would sometimes cup in their hands and smell. When they arrived at their destination, it was all with the air of pulling into the train station on time. They seemed to know exactly how long it would take and how many supplies were required for the voyage. Along the way, they would make perfect adjustments to any changes in weather or currents.

Curious as to how this was possible, some Westerners asked to be initiated into their secrets, and over the decades such travelers managed to piece together the system the Islanders used. As these Westerners discovered, one of their principal means of navigation was following the paths of stars in the night sky. Over the course of centuries, they had devised a chart comprising the path of fourteen different constellations. These constellations, along with the sun and the moon, described arcs in the sky that could translate into thirty-two different directions around the circle of the horizon. These arcs remained the same, no matter the season. From their own island, they could map out the location of all of the islands in their area by locating what stars they should be under at particular moments at night, and they knew how this position would change to another star as they traveled toward their destination. The Islanders had no writing system. Apprentice navigators simply had to memorize this elaborate map, which was in continual motion.

During the day, they would chart a course by the sun. Toward the middle of the day they could read the exact direction they were headed in by the shadows that were cast on the mast. At dawn or at sunset they could use the moon, or the stars sinking below the horizon or starting to rise. To help them measure the distance they had covered, they would choose an island somewhere off to the side as a reference point. By following the stars in the sky they could calculate when they would be passing by this reference island, and how much time remained to reach their destination.

As part of this system, they envisioned that their canoe was completely still—the stars moved above them, and the islands in the ocean were moving toward and then away from them as they passed them. Acting as if the canoe were stationary made it easier to calculate their position within their reference system. Although they knew that islands did not move, after many years of traveling this way, they would literally experience the trip as if they were sitting still. This would account for the impression they gave of looking like passengers in a train viewing the passing landscape.

Their sky chart was complemented by dozens of other signs they had learned to read. In their apprenticeship system, young navigators would be taken to sea and made to float in the ocean for several hours. In this way, they could learn to distinguish the various currents by how they felt on their skin. After much practice, they could read these currents by lying down on the floor of the canoe. They had developed a similar sensitivity to winds, and could identify various wind currents by how they moved the hairs on their head, or the sail on the outrigger.

Once they approached an island, they knew how to interpret the paths of land birds, which left in the morning to fish or returned at dusk to their homes. They could read the changes in the phosphorescence of the water that indicated closeness to land, and they could gauge whether the clouds in the distance were reflecting land beneath them, or simply ocean. They could touch the water to their lips, sensing any changes in temperature that indicated they were approaching an island. There were many more such indicators; the Islanders had learned to see everything in this environment as a potential sign.

What was most remarkable was that the chief navigator hardly seemed to be paying attention to this complex network of signs. Only an occasional glance upward or downward would indicate any kind of reading that was going on. Apparently, Master navigators knew the sky chart so well that with the sight of one star in the sky they could immediately sense where all of the others were located. They had learned how to read the other navigational signs so well that it all had become second nature. They had a complete feel for this environment, including all of the variables that seemed to make it so chaotic and dangerous. As one Westerner put it, such Masters could travel hundreds of miles from island to island as easily as an experienced cab driver could negotiate the labyrinthine streets of London.

At some point in history, the original navigators in this region must have felt a great degree of fear as they confronted the need to travel to find other food sources, realizing the tremendous dangers this involved. The ocean must have seemed much more chaotic than the tiny patch of land on their islands. They slowly overcame this fear and evolved a system that was magnificently suited to the environment they lived in. In this part of the world, the night sky is particularly clear through much of the year, giving them the ability to use the changing position of stars to great effect. Using smaller craft allowed them to maintain closer contact with the water, which they had learned to read as accurately as the undulating earth on their island. Imagining themselves as stationary and the islands as moving helped them keep track of their reference points and had a calming effect. They did not depend on a single tool or instrument; this elaborate system existed entirely in their minds. By building a deep connection to the environment and reading all of the available signs, the Islanders could approximate the remarkable instinctual powers of animals, such as various bird species that can navigate around the globe through their extreme sensitivity to the earth's geomagnetic field.

Understand: the ability to connect deeply to your environment is the most primal and in many ways the most powerful form of mastery the brain can bring us. It applies equally well to the waters of Micronesia as it does to any modern field or office. We gain such power by first transforming ourselves into consummate observers. We see everything in our surroundings as a potential sign to interpret. Nothing is taken at face value. Like the Islanders, we can break these observations down into various systems. There are the people with whom we work and interact—everything they do and say reveals something hidden below the surface. We can look at our interactions with the public, how they respond to our work, how people's tastes are constantly in flux. We can immerse ourselves in every aspect of our field, paying deep attention, for example, to the economic factors that play such a large role. We become like the Proustian spider, sensing the slightest vibration on our web. Over the years, as we progress on this path, we begin to merge our knowledge of these various components into an overall feel for the environment itself. Instead of exerting and overtaxing ourselves to keep up with a complex, changing environment, we know it from the inside and can sense the changes before they happen.

For the Caroline Islanders, there was nothing unconventional in their approach to mastery; their method fit perfectly their circumstances. But for us, in our advanced technological age, such mastery involves making an unconventional choice. To become such sensitive observers, we must not succumb to all of the distractions afforded by technology; we must be a little primitive. The primary instruments that we depend on must be our eyes for observing and our brains for analyzing. The information afforded to us through various media is only one small component in our connection to the environment. It is easy to become enamored with the powers that technology affords us, and to see them as the end and not the means. When that happens, we connect to a virtual environment, and the power of our eyes and brain slowly atrophy. You must see your environment as a physical entity and your connection to it as visceral. If there is any instrument you must fall in love with and fetishize, it is the human brain—the most miraculous, awe-inspiring, information-processing tool devised in the known universe, with a complexity we can't even begin to fathom, and with dimensional powers that far outstrip any piece of technology in sophistication and usefulness.

2. Play to your strengths—Supreme Focus

A. In the first years of the life of their child, the parents of Albert Einstein (1879–1955) had cause for concern. It took longer than usual for little Albert to talk, and his first attempts at language were always so halting. (See pages 30 and 66 for more on Einstein.) He had a strange habit of first muttering to himself the words he was going to speak out loud. His parents were concerned that their son might have a mental deficiency, and they consulted a doctor. Soon, however, he lost his hesitancy with words and revealed some hidden mental strengths—he was good with puzzles, had a knack for certain sciences, and he loved playing the violin, particularly anything by Mozart, whose music he would play over and over.

The problems began again, however, as he advanced his way through school. He was not a particularly good student. He hated having to memorize so many facts and numbers. He hated the stern authority of the teachers. His grades were mediocre and, concerned for his future, the parents decided to send their sixteen-year-old son to a more liberal-minded school in the town of Aarau, near their home in Zurich. This school used a method developed by the Swiss educational reformer Johann Pestalozzi, which emphasized the importance of learning through one's own observations, leading to the development of ideas and intuitions. Even mathematics and physics were taught in this manner. There were no drills or facts to memorize; instead, the method placed supreme importance on visual forms of intelligence, which Pestalozzi saw as the key to creative thinking.

In this atmosphere, young Einstein suddenly thrived. He found the place intensely stimulating. The school encouraged students to learn on their own, wherever their inclinations would take them, and for Einstein this meant delving even more deeply into Newtonian physics (a passion of his) and recent advances in the study of electromagnetism. In his studies of Newton while at Aarau, he came upon some problems in the Newtonian concept of the universe that deeply troubled him and caused him many sleepless nights.

According to Newton, all phenomena in nature can be explained through simple mechanical laws. Knowing them, we can deduce the causes for almost everything that happens. Objects move through space according to these mechanical laws, such as laws of gravity, and all of these movements can be measured mathematically. It is a universe that is highly ordered and rational. But Newton's concept relied upon two assumptions that could never be proven or verified empirically: the existence of absolute time and space, both of which were thought to exist independently of living beings and objects. Without these assumptions there would be no supreme standard of measurement. The brilliance of his system, however, was hard to call into question, considering that based on his laws scientists could accurately measure the movements of sound waves, the diffusion of gases, or the motion of stars.

In the late nineteenth century, however, certain cracks began to emerge in Newton's concept of the mechanical universe. Based on the work of Michael Faraday, the great Scottish mathematician James Maxwell made some interesting discoveries about the properties of electromagnetism. Developing what became known as field theories, Maxwell asserted that electromagnetism should not be described in terms of charged particles, but rather in terms of fields in space that have the continual potential to be converted into electromagnetism; this field consists of vectors of stress that can be charged at any point. By his calculations, electromagnetic waves move at the speed of 186,000 miles per second, which happens to be the speed of light. This could not simply be some coincidence. Light must therefore be a visible manifestation of an entire spectrum of electromagnetic waves.

This was a groundbreaking and novel concept of the physical universe, but to make it consistent with Newton, Maxwell and others assumed the existence of a "light-bearing ether," a substance that could oscillate and produce these electromagnetic waves, analogous to water for ocean waves, or air for sound waves. This concept added one more absolute to the Newtonian equation—that of absolute rest. The speed of the movement of these waves could only be measured against the backdrop of something at rest, which would be the ether itself. This ether would have to be something strange—covering the entire universe but not in any way interfering with the movement of planets or objects.

Scientists around the world had been struggling for decades to prove somehow the existence of this ether, concocting all sorts of elaborate experiments, but it seemed an impossible quest, and this raised increasingly more questions about the Newtonian universe and the absolutes on which it depended. Albert Einstein devoured everything he could about Maxwell's work and the questions it raised. Einstein himself had a basic need to believe in laws, in the existence of an ordered universe, and experiencing doubts on these laws caused him great anxiety.

One day, in the midst of all of these thoughts and while still attending the school at Aarau, an image appeared in his mind: that of a man moving at the speed of light itself. As he pondered this image, it turned into a sort of puzzle, or what he would later call a thought experiment: if the man were moving at the speed of light alongside a light beam, he should be able to "observe such a beam of light as an electromagnetic field at rest though spatially oscillating."

Intuitively, however, this made no sense to him for two reasons. The moment the man would look at the light source to see the beam, the light pulse would be moving ahead of him at the speed of light; he could not perceive it otherwise, since visible light travels at that constant speed. The speed of the light pulse with respect to the observer would still be 186,000 miles per second. The law governing the speed of light or any electromagnetic wave would have to be the same to someone standing still on Earth, or someone theoretically moving at the speed of light. There could not be two separate laws. And yet in theory it still could be supposed that one could catch up with and see the wave itself before it appeared as light. It was a paradox, and it made him unbearably anxious as he contemplated it.

The next year Einstein entered the Zurich Polytechnic Institute, and once again his dislike for traditional schooling returned. He did not do particularly well at math. He disliked the way physics was taught, and he started taking many classes in totally unrelated fields. He was not a promising student, and had not attracted the attention of any important professor or mentor. He quickly developed a disdain for academia and the constrictions it placed on his thinking. Still deeply troubled by his thought experiment, he continued to work on it on his own. He spent months devising an experiment that could perhaps allow him to detect the ether and its effects on light, but a professor at the Polytechnic revealed to him that his experiment was unworkable. He gave Einstein a paper describing all of the failed attempts to detect ether that had been attempted by eminent scientists, perhaps trying to deflate the pretensions of a twenty-year-old student who thought he could uncover what the greatest scientists in the world had failed to accomplish.

A year later, in 1900, Einstein came to a life-changing decision about himself: He was not an experimental scientist. He was not good at devising experiments and he did not enjoy the process. He had several strengths—he was a marvel at solving abstract puzzles of any kind; he could turn them over in his mind, converting them into images he could manipulate and shape at will. And because of his natural disdain of authority and conventions, he could think in ways that were novel and flexible. This meant of course that he would never succeed in the slippery world of academia. He would have to blaze his own path, but this could be an advantage. He would not be burdened by the need to fit in or adhere to the standard paradigm.

Continuing to work on his thought experiment day and night, he finally came to a conclusion—something had to be wrong with the entire notion of the physical universe as described by Newton. Scientists were going at the problem from the wrong end: they were straining to prove the existence of the ether in order to maintain the Newtonian edifice. Although Einstein admired Newton, he had no ties to any school of thought. Considering his decision to work on his own, he could be as daring as he liked. He would throw out the idea of the ether itself and all of the absolutes that could not be verified. His way forward would be to deduce the laws, the principles that governed motion, through his reasoning powers and through mathematics. He did not need a university position or any laboratory to do this. Wherever he found himself, he could work on these problems.

As the years went by, it would seem to others that Einstein was a bit of a failure. He had graduated from the Polytechnic close to the bottom of his class. He could not find any kind of teaching job and had settled for a mediocre, low-paid position as an evaluator of inventions for the Swiss patent office in Bern. But free to continue on his own, he worked with unbelievable tenacity at this one problem. Even while apparently on the job at the patent office, he would focus for hours on the theory that was forming in his mind; even when out for a walk with friends, he would continue to ponder his ideas—he had the unusual ability to listen on one track and think on another. He carried with him a little notebook and filled it up with all kinds of ideas. He reflected on his original paradox and all of the embellishments it had undergone and played around with them endlessly in his mind, imagining a thousand different possibilities. During almost every waking hour he contemplated the problem from some angle or other.

In the course of his deep thinking, he came up with two important principles that would guide him further. First, he determined that his original intuition had to be correct—the laws of physics had to apply equally to someone at rest as to someone traveling at a uniform speed in a spaceship. Nothing else would make sense. And second, that the speed of light was a constant. Even if a star moving at several thousand miles per hour emitted light, the speed of such light would remain at 186,000 miles per second and not any faster. In this way he would adhere to Maxwell's law on the invariable speed of electromagnetic waves.

As he contemplated these principles further, however, another paradox emerged in his mind in the shape of yet another image. He imagined a train speeding along a track with its lights beaming. A man standing on the embankment would see the light of the beam moving at the expected speed. But what if a woman were running toward or away from the train on the tracks? The woman's speed relative to the train would depend on how quickly she was moving and in which direction, but wouldn't it be the same with the light beam? Certainly, the light beam from the train relative to the woman would travel at a different speed if she were running away or running toward it, and the speed of this beam would be different from the speed relative to the man on the tracks. This one image seemingly called into question all of his guiding principles up until then.

For months he pondered this paradox, and by May 1905 he had decided to give up the entire matter. It seemed beyond solution. On a beautiful, sunny day in Bern, he walked with a friend and colleague from the patent office, explaining to him the dead end he had reached, his frustration, and his decision to give up. Just as he said all of this, as Einstein later recalled, "I suddenly understood the key to the problem." It came to him in a grand, intuitive flash, first with an image and then with words—a split-second insight that would forever alter our own concept of the universe.

Later Einstein would illustrate his insight through the following image: Suppose a train is moving past an embankment at a constant velocity. A man stands in the center of the embankment. Just as the train moves by, lightning strikes simultaneously at two equidistant points, A and B, to the right and left of the man. Suppose there is a woman seated in the middle of the train, who is passing just in front of the man on the embankment as the lightning strikes. She will be moving closer to point B as the light signal travels. She will see it strike ever so slightly ahead of the lightning at point A. What is simultaneous for the man on the embankment is not so for the woman on the train. No two events can ever be said to be simultaneous, because every moving reference frame has its own relative time, and everything in the universe is moving in relation to something else. As Einstein put it, "There is no audible tick-tock everywhere in the world that can be considered as time." If time is not absolute, then neither is space or distance. Everything is relative to everything else—speed, time, distance, and so on— except for the speed of light, which never changes.

This was called his theory of Simple Relativity, and in the years to come it would shake the foundations of physics and science. Several years later, Einstein would repeat the exact same process for his discovery of General Relativity and what he called the "curvature of spacetime," applying relativity to gravitational force. He again began with an image, a thought experiment that he pondered for close to ten years, leading to his breakthrough theory in 1915. From this theory alone he deduced that the course of light rays must be bent by the curvature of spacetime, and had gone even further to speculate the exact bend of the arc for rays of starlight grazing the sun. To the astonishment of scientists and the public alike, during the solar eclipse of 1919, astronomers were able to precisely verify Einstein's speculation. It seemed that only someone with superhuman brain capabilities could deduce such a measurement simply through abstract reasoning. The fame and reputation of Albert Einstein as a freakish genius was born at that moment and has remained ever since.

Although we like to assume that a genius like Albert Einstein had powers far beyond our capabilities, his great discoveries depended on two very simple decisions he made as a young man. First, at the age of twenty he determined that he would be a mediocre experimental scientist. Even though a heavy immersion in mathematics and experimentation was the conventional route in physics, he would go his own way—a daring decision. Second, he would consider his primal distaste for authority and conventions as a great strength. He would attack from the outside and unburden himself of all the assumptions that were torturing scientists in relation to Newton. These two decisions allowed him to play to his strengths. A third factor can be identified as well: his love of the violin and the music of Mozart. To others who would marvel at his feel for Mozart, he would reply, "It's in my blood." He meant that he had played this music so often that it had become part of him, his essence. He had an inside understanding of the music. This would become the unconscious model for his approach to science: he would think himself inside complex phenomena.

Although we tend to imagine Einstein as the ultimate abstract thinker, his way of thinking was remarkably concrete—almost always in terms of images that related to the everyday objects around him, such as trains, clocks, and elevators. Thinking in this concrete way, he could turn a problem over and over in his mind, consider it from all angles while walking, talking to others, or sitting at his desk at the patent office. He would later explain that imagination and intuition played a far larger role in his discoveries than his knowledge of science and mathematics. If he had any qualities that were extraordinary, they were his patience mixed with his extreme tenacity. After what can only be considered as well beyond 10,000 hours of contemplation of one problem, he reached a transformation point. The various aspects of a supremely complicated phenomenon had become internalized, leading to an intuitive grasp of the whole—in this case, the sudden image that came to him revealing the relativity of time. His two theories of relativity have to be considered as perhaps the greatest intellectual feats in history, the fruits of intense labor and not of some extraordinary, inexplicable genius.

There are many paths to mastery, and if you are persistent you will certainly find one that suits you. But a key component in the process is determining your mental and psychological strengths and working with them. To rise to the level of mastery requires many hours of dedicated focus and practice. You cannot get there if your work brings you no joy and you are constantly struggling to overcome your own weaknesses. You must look deep within and come to an understanding of these particular strengths and weaknesses you possess, being as realistic as possible. Knowing your strengths, you can lean on them with utmost intensity. Once you start in this direction, you will gain momentum. You will not be burdened by conventions, and you will not be slowed down by having to deal with skills that go against your inclinations and strengths. In this way, your creative and intuitive powers will be naturally awakened.

B. In thinking back to her earliest years in the 1950s, Temple Grandin could only recall a dark and chaotic world. Born with autism, she could remember spending hours on the beach watching grains of sand pour through her hands. (For more on Grandin see pages 43–45 and 156–58.) She lived in a world of constant terrors—any sudden noise would overwhelm her. It took her much longer than other children to learn language, and as she slowly did, she became painfully aware of how different she was from other children. Often alone, she naturally gravitated toward animals, particularly horses. It was more than just a need for companionship—she somehow felt an unusual identification and empathy with the world of animals. Her great passion was to go horseback riding in the country around Boston where she was raised. In riding horses, she could deepen her connection to them.

Then one summer, as a young girl, she was sent to visit her Aunt Ann, who had a ranch in Arizona. Temple felt an instant connection with the cattle on the ranch, and she would watch them for hours. What particularly intrigued her was the squeeze chute they would enter to be vaccinated. The pressure from the side panels of the chute was designed to help relax them while they were injected.

As far back as she could remember, she had always been trying to wrap herself in blankets or bury herself under cushions and pillows to somehow feel squeezed. As with the cows, any sort of gradual compression would relax her. (As is common for autistic children, being hugged by humans was overstimulating for her and induced anxiety; she had no control over the experience.) She had long dreamed about some kind of device that could squeeze her, and seeing the cattle in the chute she realized the answer. One day she begged her aunt to let her into the chute to be squeezed like a cow, and the aunt agreed. For thirty minutes she experienced what she had always wanted, and afterwards felt a complete calmness. It was at such a moment that she realized that she had some kind of strange connection to cattle, that her destiny was somehow tied up with these animals.

Curious about this connection, a few years later in high school she decided to research the subject of cattle. She also wanted to find out whether other autistic children and adults felt the same way. She could find very little information on cattle and their emotions or how they might experience the world; there was much more on autism, and she devoured books on the subject. In this way, she discovered an interest in the sciences; doing research allowed her to channel her nervous energy and learn about the world. She had tremendous powers to focus completely on one subject.

Slowly, she transformed herself into a promising student, which allowed her to gain admittance into a liberal arts school in New Hampshire where she majored in psychology. She had chosen the field because of her interest in autism—she had a personal, inside knowledge of the subject, and following this major would help her to understand more of the science behind the phenomenon. After graduating, she decided to pursue a PhD in psychology at Arizona State University, but when she went back to the Southwest and visited her aunt, she reconnected with her childhood fascination with cattle. Not really knowing why or what it would lead to, she decided to switch her major to animal sciences. For her thesis, she would focus largely on cattle.

Grandin had always done much of her thinking in visual terms, often having to translate words into images before she could understand them. Perhaps this was the result of the unique wiring of her brain. As part of the fieldwork for her major, she visited a couple of cattle feedlots in the state, and she was appalled by what she saw. It suddenly became clear to her that her propensity to think in visual terms was not shared by most others. How else to explain the highly irrational design of many of these feedlots and the remarkable lack of attention paid to details that were so visible to her eyes?

She would watch with dismay as the animals were herded through cattle chutes that were far too slippery. She would imagine what it must feel like to be a 1,200 pound animal suddenly sensing a loss of control on surfaces that were clearly too slick. The animals would bellow and stop in their tracks as they slid into one another, causing a sudden pileup. At one feedlot, almost all of the cows would stop at the same point; something in their visual field was obviously terrifying them. Didn't anyone stop to consider what was causing this? At another feedlot, she witnessed the horrifying spectacle of cattle being herded onto ramps leading to a dip vat—a pool of water full of disinfectant to help rid them of ticks and parasites. The ramp was too steep and the drop into the water too great; some of the cattle would tumble upside down into the pool and drown.

Based on what she had seen, she decided to do a detailed analysis of the efficiency of these feedlots, and how they could be improved, for her master's thesis. She now visited dozens of these sites, and each time she would stand close to the chutes, recording the reactions of the cattle as they were branded and vaccinated. On her own, she would approach the cattle and touch them. When she used to ride horses as a girl, she often could sense the mood of the horse just by the contact with her legs and hands. She began to experience the same with the cattle, as she would press her hands on their sides and feel their relaxing response. She noticed that when she was calm, they would react to her in a calmer manner. Slowly, she was getting a sense of their perspective, and how so much of their behavior was guided by perceived threats that we could not necessarily notice.

It soon became obvious to Grandin that in the animal sciences department she was essentially alone in her interest in the emotions and experience of animals. Such subjects were considered beneath scientific interest. She persisted, however, in these lines of investigation—for her own sake and because she felt they had relevance to her thesis. She began to carry a camera with her on her tours of the feedlots. Knowing that cattle are very sensitive to any contrasts in their visual field, she would follow the course of the animals through the various chutes, kneeling and taking black-and-white photographs from their point of view. Her camera would pick up all kinds of sharp contrasts in their field of vision—bright reflections from the sun, sudden shadows, the glare from a window. It was clear to her that seeing these sharp contrasts is what caused the cattle to stop repeatedly in their tracks. Sometimes the sight of a suspended plastic bottle or a dangling chain would cause the same reaction—somehow these things represented dangers to them.

The instincts of these animals were obviously not designed for living in an industrial feedlot, and this created a great strain. Whenever the animals would become instinctively frightened by something and react, the fieldworkers would grow irritated and hurry them along, which only exacerbated the cattle's fear. The number of injuries and deaths was rather appalling, and the time lost when they all piled up into gridlock was incredibly high; and yet, as she knew now, this was all quite easy to fix.

After graduating, she got her first series of jobs working on various design elements for feedlots throughout the Southwest. For meatpacking plants, she devised cattle ramps and restrainer systems that were infinitely more humane than what was there before. Some of this was accomplished through attention to simple details, such as making a ramp curved so the cattle could not see anything to the sides or too far ahead, which kept them calmer. At another site, she redesigned the dip vat so that the incline leading to it sloped gently and had deep grooves in the concrete to help them with their footing. The drop into the water was ever so slight. She also redesigned the area where they dried off, making it a much more placid environment for them.

In the case of the dip vat, the cowboys and fieldworkers would stare at her as if she were from Mars. They secretly mocked her "touchy-feely" approach to farm animals. But when her design was finished, they would watch in amazement as the cattle would blithely approach the dip vat and plop into it with hardly a sound or a complaint. There were no injuries or deaths, and no time lost with pileups or group panic. Such an increase in efficiency would occur in all of her other designs, and this would win her begrudging respect from the skeptical men on the job. Slowly, she was making a name for herself in the field, and considering how far she had come from her earliest days as a severely impaired autistic child, such achievements gave her an incredible feeling of pride.

As the years went by, her knowledge of cattle continued to grow, both through research and through frequent contact with them. Soon her work expanded to other farm animals, such as hogs, and later to antelope and elk. She became a sought-after consultant to farms and zoos. She seemed to possess a sixth sense for the inner lives of the animals she dealt with and a remarkable power to calm them down. She herself felt that she had reached a point where she could imagine the thought processes of these various animals. This was based both on her intense scientific investigations and a great deal of thinking inside their minds. She determined, for instance, that animals' memory and thinking is largely driven by images and other sense traces. Animals are more than capable of learning, but their reasoning process cycles through images. Although we might find it hard to imagine such thinking, before the invention of language we reasoned in a similar way. The distance between humans and animals is not nearly as great as we like to believe, and this connection fascinated her.

With cattle, she could read their moods by the movement of their ears, the look in their eyes, the tension she could feel through their skin. In studying the brain dynamics of cattle, she had the strange feeling that they resembled people with autism in many ways. A scan of her own brain revealed that she possessed fear centers that were three times larger than normal. She always had to manage higher levels of anxiety than most other people, and she would see continual threats in the environment. Cattle, as prey species, were continually on guard and anxious. Perhaps her own enlarged fear center, she reasoned, was a throwback to the deep past, when humans were prey as well. These reactions are now largely blocked or hidden to us, but because of her autism, her brain had retained this ancient trait. She noticed other similarities between cattle and people with autism, such as the dependence on habit and routine.

Thinking in this way led her back to her early interest in the psychology behind autism, and to deepening studies of the neuroscience involved. Her condition as someone who had emerged from autism to a career in science gave her a unique perspective on the subject. As she had done with animals, she could explore it both from the outside (science) and the inside (empathy). She could read about the latest discoveries on autism and relate them to her own experiences. She could illuminate aspects of the condition that no other scientist was able to describe or understand. As she delved deeply into the subject and wrote books on her experiences, she quickly became an extremely popular consultant and lecturer on the subject, as well as a role model for young people with autism.

As she looks back on her life from the present, Temple Grandin has a strange sensation. She emerged from the darkness and chaos of her earliest years of autism, her mind partially guided out of it by her love of animals and her curiosity about their inner lives. Through her experience on her aunt's ranch with cattle, she became interested in science, which then opened her mind to studying autism itself. Returning to animals for her career, through science and deep observation, she made innovative designs and unique discoveries. These discoveries led her back to autism yet again, a field to which she could now apply her scientific training and thinking. It would appear that some form of destiny kept directing her to the particular fields that she could explore and understand with single-minded purpose, and master in her own ingenious way.

For someone like Temple Grandin, the possibility of achieving mastery in any field would normally seem like an impossible dream. The obstacles in the path of someone with autism are enormous. And yet she managed to find her way to the two subjects that opened up possibilities for advancement. Although it might seem as if luck or blind fate led her there, even as a child she intuited her natural strengths—her love and feel for animals, her visual powers of thinking, her ability to focus on one thing—and leaned on them with all of her energy. Moving with these strengths gave her both the desire and resiliency to put up with all of the doubters, all those who saw her as strange and different and who found the subject matters she chose to study too unconventional. Working in a field where she could use her natural empathy and her particular way of thinking to great effect, she was able to delve deeper and deeper into her chosen subject, arriving at a powerful inside sense of the world of animals. Once she had mastery in this realm, she was able to apply her skills to her other great interest—autism.

Understand: achieving mastery in life often depends on those first steps that we take. It is not simply a question of knowing deeply our Life's Task, but also of having a feel for our own ways of thinking and for perspectives that are unique to us. A deep level of empathy for animals or for certain types of people may not seem like a skill or an intellectual strength, but in truth it is. Empathy plays an enormous role in learning and knowledge. Even scientists, renowned for their objectivity, regularly engage in thinking in which they momentarily identify with their subject. Other qualities we might possess, such as a penchant for visual forms of thinking, represent other possible strengths, not weaknesses. The problem is that we humans are deep conformists. Those qualities that separate us are often ridiculed by others, or criticized by teachers. People with a high visual sense are often labeled as dyslexic, for example. Because of these judgments, we might see our strengths as disabilities and try to work around them in order to fit in. But anything that is peculiar to our makeup is precisely what we must pay the deepest attention to and lean on in our rise to mastery. Mastery is like swimming—it is too difficult to move forward when we are creating our own resistance or swimming against the current. Know your strengths and move with them.

3. Transform yourself through practice—The Fingertip Feel

As narrated in chapter 2 (page 75), after graduating from the Citadel in 1981, Cesar Rodriguez decided to enter the pilot training program for the United States Air Force. But soon he had to confront a harsh reality—he was not naturally gifted for flying a jet plane. Among those in the program were some who were known as "golden boys." They seemed to have a knack for flying at high speeds. They were in their element. From the very beginning Rodriguez loved to fly, and he had ambitions to become a fighter pilot, the most elite and coveted position within the air force. But he would never reach such a goal unless he somehow managed to raise himself up to the skill level of the golden boys. His problem was that he was quickly overwhelmed by the glut of information that a pilot had to process. The key was to learn how to take a scan pattern of all the instruments—a quick reading here and there—while maintaining a feel for one's overall position in the sky. Losing situational awareness could prove fatal. For him, this scanning ability could only come through endless hours of practice on the simulator and in flying, until it became relatively automatic.

Rodriguez had played sports in high school and he knew the value of practice and repetition, but this was a lot more complex than any sport or any skill he had ever tried to master. As soon as he became comfortable with the instruments, he would be faced with the daunting task of learning to execute various flying maneuvers (like rolls), and to develop a feel for the exact speeds needed to enter them. All of this required extremely rapid mental calculations. The golden boys would ace these maneuvers in no time. For Rodriguez, it would require a lot of repetition and intense focus every time he entered the cockpit. He noticed sometimes that his body would get there ahead of his mind; his nerves and his fingers would intuit a sense of what command of the maneuver should feel like; he would then consciously aim to recreate that feeling.

Once this mark was passed, he would have to learn how to fly in formation, working with other pilots in an intricately coordinated team. Flying in formation meant juggling several skills at the same time, and the complexity of it all could be mind-boggling. Part of him was motivated by the great excitement he felt commanding such a jet and working with the team, and part of him was also motivated by the challenge. He had noticed that in gaining control of the jet and the various maneuvers, he had developed acute powers of concentration. He could tune everything out and immerse himself completely in the moment. This made every new skill set a little easier to master.

Slowly, through sheer tenacity and practice, he rose to the top of his class, and was considered among the few who could serve as fighter pilots. But there remained one last hurdle in his ascent to the top: flying in the high-scale exercises run by all branches of the military. In this case it was a matter of understanding the overall mission and operating in an intricately orchestrated land-air-sea campaign. It required an even higher level of awareness, and at moments during these exercises Rodriguez had an odd sensation—he was no longer focusing on the various physical elements of flying or on the individual skill components, but was thinking and feeling the overall campaign and how he fit into it in a seamless fashion. It was a sensation of mastery, and it was fleeting. He also noticed a slight gap between himself and the golden boys. They had relied for so long on their natural skills that they had not cultivated the same level of concentration that he now possessed. In many ways, he had surpassed them. After participating in a few of these exercises, Rodriguez had risen to elite status.

On January 19, 1991, in the space of a few minutes, all of his elaborate training and practice would be put to the ultimate test. A few days before, the United States and allied forces had launched Operation Desert Storm in response to Sadaam Hussein's invasion of Kuwait. The morning of the 19th Rodriguez and his wingman, Craig "Mole" Underhill, flew into Iraq as part of a thirty-six-aircraft strike force, heading toward a target near Baghdad. It was his first real taste of combat. Flying F-15s, he and Mole quickly spotted a pair of Iraqi MiG fighters in the distance and decided to give chase. Within seconds they realized that they had been lured into a trap, the pursuer turning into the pursued, as two MiGs now bore down on them from an unexpected direction.

Realizing how quickly one of the enemy planes was approaching, Rodriguez suddenly jettisoned his fuel tanks for greater speed and maneuverability. He then dove toward the ground, below the level of the approaching MiG, doing everything he could to make it difficult for the enemy to get a read on him with his radar, including flying at a right angle to the ground to make his plane as skinny as possible. Without a radar reading, the MiG could not launch a missile. Everything was happening so fast. At any moment his own radar could light up, indicating the enemy had locked into him and he was as good as dead. He had one chance to make it: evading the MiG until it got too close to fire, and drawing it into a dogfight—a circular battle in the air that was a rare occurrence in modern warfare. At the back of his mind he was also trying to buy enough time for his wingman to help him out, and he could somehow sense Mole's presence following him from a distance. But time would bring another danger—the presence of the second MiG on the scene.

He tried every evasive maneuver in the book. He saw the MiG getting closer and closer when suddenly he heard from Mole, who had been following him and had now maneuvered into position. As Rodriguez looked over his shoulder, he could see the enemy MiG exploding—Mole's missile had struck it. As the chase had unfolded, everything had gone as Rodriguez wanted, but there was not a second to relax. The second MiG was now rapidly approaching.

Mole ascended to 20,000 feet. As the MiG bore down on Rodriguez's plane, its pilot realized Mole's presence above him, and began to maneuver up and down to somehow escape being trapped between the two of them. Using this instant of confusion, Rodriguez was able to get inside the MiG's turning circle. It had now turned into a classic two-circle dogfight in which each plane tried to circle onto the tail of the other and into firing range, moving closer to the ground with each succeeding loop. They circled and circled around each other. Finally, at 3,600 feet, Rodriguez got a reading and locked his missiles on the MiG. The Iraqi pilot went into a hard evasive maneuver, turning directly toward the ground, flipping upside down and trying to circle into a reverse direction to escape, but in the few seconds of the dogfight the pilot had lost awareness of how close they had drifted to the ground, and he crashed into the desert below.

Mole and Rodriguez returned to the base to debrief their superiors on the mission, but as Rodriguez went over it all and watched video of the encounters, he had a strange sensation. He could not really recall any moment of it. It had happened so fast. The entire encounter with the MiGs had only lasted three to four minutes, and the final dogfight a matter of seconds. He must have been thinking in some way—he had executed some nearly perfect maneuvers. For instance, he had no recollection of deciding to jettison the fuel tanks nor where such an idea came from. It must have been something he had learned, and somehow in the moment it had simply occurred to him, and very easily might have saved his life. The evasive maneuvers he executed with the first MiG astounded his superiors—they were so fast and effective. His awareness during the dogfight must have been exceptionally keen; he had circled to his opponent's tail in ever-faster cycles, never losing sight of the desert floor they were approaching. How could he explain all of these maneuvers? He could hardly remember them. All he knew was that in the moment he hadn't been experiencing fear, but rather an intense adrenalin rush that made his body and mind operate in total harmony, with a kind of thinking that moved in milliseconds and was too fast for him to analyze.

For three days after the encounter he could not sleep, the adrenalin still coursing through his veins. It made him realize that the body possesses latent physiological powers—unleashed in such dramatic moments—that elevate the mind to an even higher level of focus. Rodriguez would go on to have one more kill in Desert Storm, and another in the 1999 Kosovo campaign, more than any pilot in recent combat, earning him the nickname the Last American Ace.

In our daily, conscious activity we generally experience a separation between the mind and the body. We *think* about our bodies and our physical actions. Animals do not experience this division. When we start to learn any skill that has a physical component, this separation becomes even more apparent. We have to think about the various actions involved, the steps we have to follow. We are aware of our slowness and of how our bodies respond in an awkward way. At certain points, as we improve, we have glimpses of how this process could function differently, of how it might feel to practice the skill fluidly, with the mind not getting in the way of the body. With such glimpses, we know what to aim for. If we take our practice far enough the skill becomes automatic, and we have the sensation that the mind and the body are operating as one.

If we are learning a complex skill, such as flying a jet in combat, we must master a series of simple skills, one on top of the other. Each time one skill becomes automatic, the mind is freed up to focus on the higher one. At the very end of this process, when there are no more simple skills to learn, the brain has assimilated an incredible amount of information, all of which has become internalized, part of our nervous system. The whole complex skill is now inside us and at our fingertips. We are thinking, but in a different way—with the body and mind completely fused. We are transformed. We possess a form of intelligence that allows us to approximate the instinctual power of animals, but only through a conscious, deliberate, and extended practice.

In our culture we tend to denigrate practice. We want to imagine that great feats occur naturally—that they are a sign of someone's genius or superior talent. Getting to a high level of achievement through practice seems so banal, so uninspiring. Besides, we don't want to have to think of the 10,000 to 20,000 hours that go into such mastery. These values of ours are oddly counterproductive—they cloak from us the fact that almost anyone can reach such heights through tenacious effort, something that should encourage us all. It is time to reverse this prejudice against conscious effort and to see the powers we gain through practice and discipline as eminently inspiring and even miraculous. The ability to master complicated skills by building connections in the brain is the product of millions of years of evolution, and the source of all of our material and cultural powers. When we sense the possible unity of mind and body in the early stages of practice, we are being guided toward this power. It is the natural bent of our brain to want to move in this direction, to elevate its powers through repetition. To lose our connection to this natural inclination is the height of madness, and will lead to a world in which no one has the patience to master complex skills. As individuals we must resist such a trend, and venerate the transformative powers we gain through practice.

4. Internalize the details—The Life Force

As the illegitimate son of the notary Ser Piero da Vinci, Leonardo da Vinci (see pages 21–25, for more on the artist) was essentially barred from studying and practicing the traditional professional careers—medicine, law, and so on—and from higher education. And so as a boy growing up in the town of Vinci, near Florence, he received little formal education. He spent much of his time roaming around the countryside and venturing into the forests outside his town. He was enchanted by the incredible variety of life he found there, and the dramatic rock formations and waterfalls that were part of the landscape. As his father was a notary, there was a fair amount of paper (a rare commodity at the time) in the family house, and feeling a great desire to draw all that he saw on his walks, he began stealing sheets of paper and carrying them with him.

He would sit on a rock and draw the insects, birds and flowers that fascinated him. He never received any instruction. He simply drew what he saw, and he began to notice that in trying to capture these things on paper, he had to think deeply. He had to focus on the details that the eye would often pass over. In drawing plants, for instance, he began to notice the subtle distinctions in the stamens of various flowers and how they were different from one another. He would notice the transformations these plants went through on their way to blossoming, and he would capture these changes in sequential drawings. In going so deeply into their details, he had fleeting intimations of what animated these plants from within, what made them distinct and alive. Soon, thinking and drawing became fused in his mind. Through drawing things in the world around him, he came to understand them.

His progress at drawing was so astounding that his father thought of finding him a position as an apprentice in one of the various studios in Florence. Working in the arts was one of the few professions open to illegitimate sons. In 1466, using his influence as a respected notary in Florence, he managed to secure a position for his fourteen-year-old son in the workshop of the great artist Verrocchio. For Leonardo, this was a perfect fit. Verrocchio was deeply influenced by the enlightened spirit of the times, and his apprentices were taught to approach their work with the seriousness of scientists. For instance, plaster casts of human figures would be placed about the studio with various pieces of fabric draped over them. The apprentices had to learn to concentrate deeply, and recognize the different creases and shadows that would form. They had to learn how to reproduce them realistically. Leonardo loved learning in this way, and soon it became apparent to Verrocchio that his young apprentice had developed an exceptional eye for detail.

By 1472 Leonardo was one of Verrocchio's top assistants, helping him on his large-scale paintings and taking on a fair amount of responsibility. In Verrocchio's *The Baptism of Christ,* Leonardo was given the task of painting one of the two angels off to the side, and this work is now the oldest example we have of his painting. When Verrocchio saw the results of Leonardo's work he was astounded. The face of the angel had a quality he had never seen before—it seemed to literally glow from within. The look on the angel's face seemed uncannily real and expressive.

Although it might have seemed like magic to Verrocchio, recent X-rays have revealed some of the secrets to Leonardo's early technique. The layers of paint he applied were exceptionally thin, his brush strokes invisible. He had gradually added more layers, each ever so slightly darker than the last. Operating in this way, and experimenting with different pigments, he had taught himself how to capture the delicate contours of human flesh. Because of the thin layers, any light hitting the painting seemed to pass through the angel's face and illuminate it from within.

What this revealed was that in the six years that he had been working in the studio, he must have applied himself to an elaborate study of the various paints and perfected a style of layering that made everything seem delicate and lifelike, with a feeling of texture and depth. He must have also spent a great deal of time studying the composition of human flesh itself. What this also revealed was the incredible patience of Leonardo, who must have felt a great deal of love for such detailed work.

Over the years, after he left Verrocchio's studio and established a name for himself as an artist, Leonardo da Vinci developed a philosophy that would guide his artwork and, later, his scientific work as well. He noticed that other artists generally started with an overall image they planned to depict, one that would create a startling or spiritual effect. His mind operated differently. He would find himself beginning with a keen focus on details—the various shapes of noses, the possible turnings of the mouth to indicate a mood, the veins in a hand, the intricate knots of trees. These details fascinated him. He had come to believe that by focusing on and understanding such details he was actually getting closer to the secret of life itself, to the work of the Creator who infused his presence into every living thing and every form of matter. The bones of the hand or the contours of human lips were as inspiring to him as any religious image. For him, painting was a quest to get at the life force that animates all things. In the process of doing so, he believed he could create work that was much more emotional and visceral. And to realize this quest, he invented a series of exercises that he followed with incredible rigor.

During the day he would take endless walks through the city and countryside, his eyes taking in all of the details of the visible world. He would make himself notice something new in every familiar object that he saw. At night, before falling asleep, he would review all of these various objects and details, fixing them in his memory. He was obsessed with capturing the essence of the human face in all of its glorious diversity. For this purpose, he would visit every conceivable place where he could find different types of people—brothels, public houses, prisons, hospitals, prayer corners in churches, country festivals. With his notebook always at hand, he would sketch grimacing, laughing, pained, beatific, leering expressions on an incredible variety of faces. He would follow people in the streets who had a type of face he had never seen before, or some kind of physical deformity, and would sketch them as he walked. He would fill single sheets of paper with dozens of different noses in profile. He seemed particularly interested in lips, finding them just as expressive as eyes. He would repeat all of these exercises at different times of the day, to make sure he could capture the different effects that changing light would have on the human face.

For his great painting *The Last Supper*, his patron, the duke of Milan, grew increasingly angry with Leonardo for the time he was taking to finish it. It seemed that all that remained was to fill in the face of Judas, but Leonardo could not find an adequate model. He had taken to visiting the worst parts of Milan to find the most perfectly villainous expression to translate onto Judas, but was having no luck. The duke accepted his explanation, and soon enough Leonardo had found the model he wanted.

He applied this same rigor to capturing bodies in motion. Part of his philosophy was that life is defined by continual movement and constant change. The artist must be able to render the sensation of dynamic movement in a still image. Ever since he was a young man he had been obsessed with currents of water, and had become quite proficient at capturing the look of waterfalls, cascades, and rushing water. With people, he would spend hours seated on the side of a street, watching pedestrians as they moved by. He would hurriedly sketch the outlines of their figures, capturing their various movements in a stop-action sequence. (He had reached the point where he could sketch with incredible rapidity.) At home, he would fill in the outlines. To develop his eye for following movement in general, he invented a whole series of different exercises. For instance, one day in his notebook he wrote, "Tomorrow make some silhouettes out of cardboard in various forms and throw them from the top of the terrace through the air; then draw the movements each makes at different stages of descent."

His hunger to get at the core of life by exploring its details drove him into elaborate research on human and animal anatomy. He wanted to be able to draw a human or a cat from the inside out. He personally dissected cadavers, sawing through bones and skulls, and he religiously attended autopsies so that he could see as closely as possible the structure of muscles and nerves. His anatomical drawings were far in advance of anything of his time for their realism and accuracy.

To other artists, Leonardo seemed insane for all of this attention to detail, but in the few paintings that he actually completed, the results of such rigorous practice can be seen and felt. More than the work of any other artist of his time, the landscapes in the backgrounds of his paintings seemed infused with life. Every flower, branch, leaf or stone was rendered in intense detail. But these backgrounds were not simply there to decorate. In an effect known as *sfumato,* and one that was peculiar to his work, he would soften parts of these backgrounds to the point at which they would melt into the figure in the foreground, giving a dreamlike effect. It was part of his idea that all of life is deeply interconnected and fused on some level.

The faces of the women he painted had a pronounced effect on people, and particularly on men, who often fell in love with the female figures he depicted in religious scenes. It wasn't any obvious sensual quality in their expression, but in their ambiguous smiles and their beautifully rendered flesh the men would recognize a powerfully seductive quality. Leonard heard many stories of them finding their way to his paintings in various houses and secretly fondling the women in the images and kissing their lips.

Much of Leonardo's *Mona Lisa* has been damaged by attempts to clean and restore it in the past, making it hard to imagine it as it originally appeared, and how its startling qualities shocked the public. Fortunately, we have the critic Vasari's description of it, before it became hopelessly altered: "The eyebrows, growing thickly in one place and thinly in another, following the pores of the skin, could not have been more lifelike. The nose, with its ravishingly delicate pink nostrils, was life itself. The shaping of the mouth, where the red of the lips merged with the skin tones of the face, seemed not to be made from colors but from living flesh. In the hollow of the throat, the observant onlooker could see the pulsing of the veins."

Long after Leonardo's death, his paintings continue to have haunting and disturbing effects on viewers. Numerous security guards in museums around the world have been fired for their weird, obsessive relationships to his work, and Leonardo's paintings remain the most vandalized in the history of art, all of this attesting to the power of his work to stir up the most visceral emotions.

<hr/>

The primary problem for artists in Leonardo da Vinci's day was the constant pressure to produce more and more work. They had to produce at a relatively high rate in order to keep the commissions coming and remain in the public eye. This influenced the quality of their work. A style had developed in which artists could quickly create effects in their painting that would superficially excite viewers. To create such effects they would depend on bright colors, unusual juxtapositions and compositions, and dramatic scenes. In the process, they would inevitably gloss over the details in the background and even in the people they portrayed. They did not pay much attention to the flowers or trees or the hands of figures in the foreground. They had to dazzle on the surface. Leonardo recognized this fact early in his career and it distressed him. It went against his grain in two ways—he hated the feeling of having to hurry with anything, and he loved immersing himself in details for their own sake. He was not interested in creating surface effects. He was animated by a hunger to understand life forms from the inside out and to grasp the force that makes them dynamic, and to somehow express all of this on a flat surface. And so, not fitting in, he went on his own peculiar path, mixing science and art.

To complete his quest, Leonardo had to become what he termed "universal"—for each object he had to be able to render all of its details, and he had to extend this knowledge as far as possible, to as many objects in the world as he could study. Through sheer accumulation of such details, the essence of life itself became visible to him, and his understanding of this life force became visible in his artwork.

In your own work you must follow the Leonardo path. Most people don't have the patience to absorb their minds in the fine points and minutiae that are intrinsically part of their work. They are in a hurry to create effects and make a splash; they think in large brush strokes. Their work inevitably reveals their lack of attention to detail—it doesn't connect deeply with the public, and it feels flimsy. If it gets attention, the attention is momentary. You must see whatever you produce as something that has a life and presence of its own. This presence can be vibrant and visceral, or it can be weak and lifeless. A character in a novel, for instance, will come to life for the reader if the writer has put great effort into imagining the details of that character. The writer does not need to literally lay out these details; readers will *feel* it in the work and will intuit the level of research that went into the creation of it. All living things are an amalgam of intricate levels of details, animated by the dynamic that connects them. Seeing your work as something alive, your path to mastery is to study and absorb these details in a universal fashion, to the point at which you feel the life force and can express it effortlessly in your work.

5. Widen your vision—the Global Perspective

Early in his career as a boxing trainer, Freddie Roach felt like he knew the business well enough to become highly successful at it. (For more information on Roach see chapter 1, pages 38–40, and chapter 3, pages 119–21.) He had fought for years as a professional; he had a boxer's feel for the game. His own trainer had been the legendary Eddie Futch, who had trained Joe Frazier, among others. When Roach's career as a boxer had ended in the mid-1980s, he had served as an apprentice trainer for several years under Futch himself. On his own, Roach had created a novel training technique based on the use of sparring mitts. Wearing these large mitts, he could spar with and teach his fighters in the ring, in real time. This added another dimension to his instruction. He worked hard at building a personal rapport with his fighters. And finally, he developed the practice of poring over videos of opposing fighters, studying their styles in depth, and devising an effective counter-strategy based on this study.

And yet despite all of this work, he sensed that something was missing. Everything would go well in practice, but in actual fights he would often watch from the corner with a helpless feeling as his boxers would go their own way, or would enact only a part of the strategy he had devised. Sometimes he and his fighters would be on the same page, sometimes not. All of this was reflected in the winning percentage of his boxers—good but not great. He could remember back to his own days as a fighter under Futch. He too had done well in practice, but in actual fights and in the heat of the moment, all strategy and preparation would go out the window and he would try to punch his way to a victory. He had always missed something from Futch's training. Futch had trained him well in all of the separate components of a fight (like offense, defense, and footwork), but Roach never had had a sense of the whole picture or the overall strategy. The connection between himself and Futch had never been that great, and so under pressure in the ring, he would suddenly just revert to his own natural way of fighting. And he now seemed to be having a similar problem with his own fighters.

Trying to feel his way through to a process that would bring better results, Roach decided he needed to do for his fighters what had never been done for himself in his own career—namely, to give them a feel for the complete picture of the fight. He wanted them to enact this script over all the rounds, and to deepen the connection between fighter and trainer. He began by expanding the mitt work, making it not just a component in the training process, but the focal point. Now he would spend hours sparring with his fighters over several rounds. Day after day, feeling their punches and getting a sense of the rhythm of their footwork, he could almost get inside their skin. He could feel their moods, the level of their focus, and the degree to which they were open to instruction. Without ever having to say a word, he could alter their moods and focus by the intensity of the mitt work he did with them.

Having trained as a fighter since he was six years old, Roach had a feel for every square inch of the ring. With his eyes closed he could gauge exactly where he stood in the ring at any moment. Training his fighters for hours with the mitt work, he could imprint into them his own sixth sense for the space itself, deliberately maneuvering them into bad positions so they could feel in advance how they were approaching such a dangerous space. In the same way, he would impart to them several ways to avoid such dead positions.

One day, as he was studying a video of an opposing fighter, he had an epiphany—his way of watching videos was all wrong. In general, he would focus on a fighter's style, which is something boxers can control and alter for strategic purposes. This suddenly seemed like a superficial way of studying the opponent. A far better strategy would be to look for their habits or tics, the things they couldn't control no matter how hard they tried. Every fighter has such tics—they are signs of something deeply wired into their rhythms—and they translate into potential weaknesses. Discovering these tics and habits would give Roach a much deeper read on the opponent, cutting to his psyche and to his heart.

He began to look for signs of this in the tapes he watched, and in the beginning it would take him several days to see anything. But in the course of watching so many hours on the opposing fighter, he would get a feel for his ways of moving and thinking. Eventually, he would find the habit he was looking for—for instance, a slight motion of the head that always foreshadowed a particular punch. Now that he had found it, he would see it everywhere on the tapes. After doing this for many different fights over several years, he developed a feel for identifying such tics much more quickly.

Based on these discoveries, he would craft a complete strategy that had built-in flexibility. Depending on what the opponent showed in the first round, Roach would have ready several options for his own fighter that would surprise and upset the opponent, keeping him on his heels and in react mode. His strategy would encompass the entire fight. If necessary, his own fighter could sacrifice a round or two without ever losing control of the overall dynamic. Now, in the mitt work, he would go over the strategy endlessly. Carefully mimicking the tics and rhythms of the opponent he had come to know so well, he could show his fighters how to mercilessly take advantage of their habits and weaknesses; he would go over the various options to adopt, depending on what the opponent revealed in the first round. By the time the fight itself approached, his fighters would feel as if they had already fought and destroyed this opponent, having faced Roach so many times in preparation.

During the progress of the fights themselves, Roach now had a completely different feeling than in the years before. The connection with his fighters was absolute. His vision of the whole picture—the spirit of the opponent, the way to dominate the ring space within each round, the overall strategy to win the fight—was now deeply imprinted into the footwork, punching, and thinking of his own fighter. He could almost feel himself in the ring exchanging punches, but now he had the ultimate satisfaction of controlling both the mind of his own fighter and that of the opponent's. He would watch with mounting excitement as his fighters would slowly wear down their opponents, exploiting their habits and getting inside their heads just as he had taught them to.

His winning percentage started to climb to a level that was unprecedented in the sport. His success extended beyond the main fighter in his stable, Manny Pacquiao, to include nearly all of his boxers. Since 2003 he has been named Boxing Trainer of the Year five times, no other previous trainer having received the award more than twice. It seems that in modern boxing he is now in a class all by himself.

If we look closely at the career path of Freddie Roach, we can see a transparent example of the development of mastery. His father, a former New England featherweight champion himself, had pushed all of his sons into the sport at a very early age. Freddie Roach himself had begun serious training as a boxer at the age of six, and this continued all the way to the age of eighteen, when he turned professional. Those twelve years added up to an extremely deep level of practice and immersion in the sport. For the next eight years of his life, until he retired from the sport, he fought fifty-three bouts, an intense fighting schedule. As someone who enjoyed practicing and training, the number of hours he spent in the gym as a professional boxer was much higher than that of other fighters. After retirement he stayed around the sport, working as an apprentice trainer for Eddie Futch. By the time he began his own career as a trainer, he had accumulated so many overall hours of work in the sport that he already saw boxing from a perspective that was much wider and deeper than that of other trainers. And so when he felt that there was an even higher level to aim for, this intuition was based on the depth of all those years of practical experience. Inspired by this feeling, he was able to analyze his own work up to that point and see its limitations.

Roach knew from his own career that so much of boxing is mental. A fighter who enters the ring with a clear sense of purpose and strategy, and with the confidence that comes from complete preparation, has a much better chance of prevailing. It was one thing to imagine giving his fighters such an advantage, but it was quite another to bring it to pass. Before a fight there are so many distractions, and during a match it is so easy to simply react emotionally to the punches and lose any sense of strategy. To overcome these problems, he developed a two-pronged approach—he crafted a comprehensive and fluid strategy based on his perception of the opponent's habits, and he imprinted this strategy into the nervous system of his fighters through hours of mitt work. On this level, his training did not consist of individual elements that he worked on with his boxers, but of an integrated, seamless form of preparation that closely simulated the experience of a fight, repeated over and over again. It took many years of a hit-and-miss process to create this high-level training, but when it all came together his success rate skyrocketed.

In any competitive environment in which there are winners or losers, the person who has the wider, more global perspective will inevitably prevail. The reason is simple: such a person will be able to think beyond the moment and control the overall dynamic through careful strategizing. Most people are perpetually locked in the present. Their decisions are overly influenced by the most immediate event; they easily become emotional and ascribe greater significance to a problem than it should have in reality. Moving toward mastery will naturally bring you a more global outlook, but it is always wise to expedite the process by training yourself early on to continually enlarge your perspective. You can do so by always reminding yourself of the overall purpose of the work you are presently engaged in and how this meshes with your long-term goals. In dealing with any problem, you must train yourself to look at how it inevitably connects to a larger picture. If your work is not having the desired effect, you must look at it from all angles until you find the source of the problem. You must not merely observe the rivals in your field, but dissect and uncover their weaknesses. "Look wider and think further ahead" must be your motto. Through such mental training, you will smooth the path to mastery while separating yourself ever further from the competition.

6. Submit to the other—The Inside-out Perspective

As narrated in chapter 2 (page 72), in December 1977, Daniel Everett, along with his wife, Keren, and their two children, arrived in a remote village in the Amazonian jungles of Brazil, where they would end up spending a good part of the next twenty years of their lives. The village belonged to a tribe scattered in the area known as the Pirahã. Everett had been sent there by the Summer Institute of Languages (SIL)—a Christian organization that trains future missionaries in the linguistic skills that will enable them to translate the Bible into indigenous languages and help spread the Gospel. Everett himself was an ordained minister.

The directors at SIL considered Pirahã one of the last frontiers in their quest to translate the Bible into all languages; it represented perhaps the most challenging language for any outsider to learn. The Pirahã had lived for centuries in the same Amazonian basin, resisting all attempts to assimilate or learn Portuguese. Living in such isolation, a point was reached in which no one outside of the Pirahã could speak or understand their language. Several missionaries had been sent there after World War II, and all had failed to make much progress; despite their training and linguistic talents, they found the language maddeningly elusive.

Daniel Everett was one of the most promising linguists the SIL had seen in a long time, and when the institute presented him with the challenge of the Pirahã he was more than excited. His wife's parents had been missionaries stationed in Brazil, and Keren had grown up in an environment not too dissimilar to a Pirahã village. It seemed the family was up to the task, and in his first months there Everett made good progress. He attacked the Pirahã language with great energy. Using the methods he had learned at SIL, he slowly built up a vocabulary and the ability to speak some rudimentary sentences. He copied everything down on index cards and carried them in his belt loop. He was a tireless researcher. Although life in the village presented some challenges for him and his family, he was comfortable with the Pirahã and hoped they had accepted his presence. But soon he began to feel that all was not right.

Part of the SIL method was to encourage immersion in the indigenous culture as the best means for learning the language. Missionaries are essentially abandoned to their fate, to sink or swim in the local culture without any crutches to lean on. Perhaps unconsciously, however, Everett could not help but keep some distance and feel ever so slightly superior to the backward culture of the Pirahã. He became aware of this inner distance after several incidents that occurred in the village.

First, several months into their stay, his wife and daughter nearly died from malaria. He was rather perturbed by the lack of empathy from the Pirahã about this. A little later, Everett and his wife tried desperately to nurse back to health a Pirahã infant that was gravely ill. The Pirahã were certain the baby would die, and seemed bothered by the missionaries' efforts. Then one day, Everett and his wife discovered the baby was dead; the Pirahã had forced alcohol down its throat to kill it. Although he tried to rationalize this event to himself, he could not help but feel some disgust. On another occasion, for apparently no reason, a group of Pirahã men had gotten very drunk and were looking for him in order to kill him. He managed to escape the threat, and nothing else ever happened, but it made him wonder about the safety of his family.

More than anything, however, he began to feel disappointed by the Pirahã themselves. He had read much about Amazonian tribes, and by any standards the Pirahã did not measure up. They had virtually no material culture—no important tools, artwork, costumes, or jewelry. If women needed a basket, they would find some moist palm leaves, quickly weave them together, use the basket once or twice, and then abandon it. They placed no value on material things, and nothing in their villages was designed to last very long. They had few rituals, and as far as he could tell no real folklore or creation myths. One time he had been woken up by excitement in the village—apparently a spirit who lived above the clouds had been sighted and was warning them not to go into the jungle. He looked at what they were looking at and saw nothing. There were no colorful stories being told about this, no relation to any myth, just some villagers excitedly staring off into empty space. They seemed to him like Boy Scouts on a camping trip, or a group of hippies—a tribe that had somehow lost its own culture.

This disappointment and unease coincided with frustration in his own work. He had made some progress with the language, but it seemed that the more words and phrases he learned, the more questions and puzzles he uncovered. He would think that he had mastered a particular expression, only to find it meant something different or something larger than he had imagined. He could see the children learning the language so easily, but to him who now lived among them, it seemed beyond his reach. Then one day he experienced what he would later realize was a turning point.

The thatch roof of his family's hut needed replacing, and he decided to enlist some villagers in the effort. Although he felt he had integrated himself into their lives, he had never ventured very far into the surrounding jungles with the Pirahã men. Finally, on this occasion he would go much farther than before to gather the necessary materials. Suddenly, during this trip, he saw an entirely different side to them. While he was stomping and whacking his way through the brush, they seemed to glide through the thick jungle without being touched by a single branch. He was not able to keep up with them, and so he stopped and rested. In the distance he could hear strange sounds—the Pirahã men were clearly speaking to one another, but their words were somehow transposed into whistles. He realized that in the jungle they used this different form of communication, one that would not stand out from the jungle hum. It was a marvelous way to talk without attracting attention, and must have been a great help in hunting.

Now he joined them on subsequent forays into the jungle, and his respect for them increased. They could hear and see things he could not perceive at all—dangerous animals, signs of something different or suspicious. Occasionally, it would rain when it was not the rainy season, and in the jungle they had a sixth sense for the weather and knew when a heavy rain was coming hours before it arrived. (They could even predict the arrival of a plane several hours in advance, although he never figured out how.) They could identify every plant and its possible medicinal purposes, and knew every square inch of the jungle. If they saw bubbles or ripples in the river, they could instantly tell whether the movement was from a falling rock or from some dangerous animal lurking below the surface. They had a mastery of their environment that he could not sense by seeing them in the village. And as he became aware of this, he began to understand that their life and culture, which at first glance had seemed rather poor according to our standards, was actually something remarkably rich. Over the course of hundreds of years they had adapted a way of life that was perfectly wedded to the harsh circumstances of their environment.

Now, as he looked back on the same incidents that had troubled him before, he could see them in a new light. Living so closely to death on a daily basis (the jungle was teeming with dangers and diseases), they had developed a rather stoic attitude. They could not afford to waste time or energy on mourning rituals or on too much empathy. They could sense when someone was going to die, and being certain that the infant the Everetts had tried to nurse was doomed, they thought it easier and better to hasten its death and not look back. The village men who had thought of killing him had heard that he did not like their drinking; they feared that he was yet another outsider who was going to impose his values and authority on them. They had their reasons for behaving as they did, but only with time could he see them clearly.

He extended his participation in their lives to other aspects—hunting and fishing excursions, gathering roots and vegetables in the fields, and so on. He and his family would share meals with them and interacted with them as much as possible, and in this way he slowly immersed himself in the Pirahã culture. Although it was not immediately apparent, this also initiated a change in his learning of the language itself. It started to come more naturally—less from the tireless work of a field researcher and more from within, from simply living inside their culture. He began to think like a Pirahã, to foresee their reactions to what some visiting Westerner would ask of them; he got inside their sense of humor, and the kinds of stories they liked to relate around the campfire.

And as he began to understand more aspects of their culture and to communicate with a higher degree of proficiency, he noticed more and more peculiarities to the Pirahã language. Everett had been indoctrinated in the prevailing beliefs in linguistics championed by Noam Chomsky. According to Chomsky all languages share certain features, which he designates as Universal Grammar. This grammar implies a common neurological trait to the brain that allows for the learning of languages among children. According to this theory, we are hardwired for language. But the more time Everett spent among the Pirahã, the more signs he saw that their language did not share some of these common features. They had no numbers and no system for counting. They had no specific words for colors, but rather described colors through phrases that related to real objects.

According to Universal Grammar, the most important trait shared by all languages is what is known as *recursion,* the embedding of phrases within phrases that gives language an almost infinite potential to relate experiences. An example would be, "the food you are eating smells good." Everett could find absolutely no evidence for recursion in Pirahã. They would express such ideas in simple, assertive phrases, such as "You are eating food. That food smells good." These exceptions to Universal Grammar began to pile up as he looked for them.

At the same time, the Pirahã culture began to make increasing sense to him, which altered his conception of their language. For instance, one time he learned a new word that a Pirahã explained to him meant "what is in your head when you sleep." The word then means to dream. But the word was used with a special intonation that Pirahã use when they are referring to a new experience. Questioning further, he saw that to them dreaming is simply a different form of experience, not at all a fiction. A dream is as real and immediate to them as anything they encounter in waking life. With more and more of these examples, a theory began to stir in his head, one that he would call the Immediate Experience Principle (IEP). What this means is that for the Pirahã all that concerns them are things that can be experienced in the here and now, or that relate to something that someone personally has experienced in the very recent past.

This would account for the peculiarities of their language—colors and numbers are abstractions that do not fit IEP. Instead of recursion, they have simple declarative statements on what they have seen. His theory would account for their lack of material culture, or of creation myths and stories that refer to something in the past. They had developed this form of culture as the perfect adaptation to their environment and needs; it made them profoundly immersed in the present and remarkably happy. It helped them to psychologically transcend the difficulties of their environment. Because they had no need for anything beyond their immediate experience, they had no words for such things. Everett's theory was the fruit of years and years of deep immersion in their culture. As it came together in his mind, it explained so many things. It could not have been seen or understood in the course of a few months or years observing them from the outside.

The conclusion that he drew from this, one that would provoke much controversy within the field of linguistics, is that culture plays an enormous role in the development of language, and that languages are more different than we have imagined. Although there are certainly common aspects to all human languages, there can be no universal grammar that overrides the relevance of culture. Such a conclusion, he determined, can only come through years of intense fieldwork. Those who make assumptions from far away, based on universal theories, do not see the whole picture. It takes great time and effort to see the differences, to participate in a culture. And because it is so much harder to perceive these differences, culture has not been given its due as one of the primary shaping forces for language and for how we experience the world.

The deeper he immersed himself into Pirahã culture, the more it changed him. He not only grew disenchanted with the top-down form of research in linguistics and the ideas it led to, but also with his work as a missionary. These were both attempts to impose on the Pirahã alien ideas and values. He could only imagine that spreading the Gospel and converting them to Christianity would completely ruin their culture, which had shaped itself so perfectly to their circumstances and made them so content. With these ideas, he lost his faith in Christianity itself, and finally left the church. Learning an alien culture from so deeply inside it, he could no longer accept the superiority of one particular belief or value system. To hold such an opinion, he determined, is merely an illusion that comes from remaining on the outside.

For many researchers in circumstances similar to Daniel Everett's, the natural response is to rely on the skills and concepts they have learned for research purposes. This would mean studying the Pirahã as closely as Everett had done in the beginning, taking extensive notes, and trying to make this alien culture fit into the framework already designated by the prevailing theories in linguistics and anthropology. Doing so, such researchers would be rewarded with articles in prestigious journals and solid positions within academia. But in the end they would remain on the outside looking in, and a good portion of their conclusions would simply be confirmations of what they had already assumed. The wealth of information that Everett had uncovered about their language and culture would remain unnoticed. Imagine how often this has occurred in the past and still occurs in the present, and how many secrets of indigenous cultures have been lost to us because of this outsider approach.

Part of this predilection for the outside perspective originates from a prejudice among scientists. Studying from the outside, many would say, preserves our objectivity. But what kind of objectivity is it when the researcher's perspective is tainted by so many assumptions and predigested theories? The reality of the Pirahã could only be seen from within and from participating in their culture. This does not taint the observer with subjectivity. A scientist can participate from within and yet retain his or her reasoning powers. Everett could stand back from their culture and devise his IEP theory. The intuitive and the rational, the inside perspective and science, can easily coexist. For Everett, choosing this inside path required a great deal of courage. It meant physically subjecting himself to the dangers of their life in the jungle. It led to a difficult confrontation with other linguists and all of the problems such conflict presented for his future career as a professor. It led to a profound disenchantment with Christianity, which had meant so much to him as a young man. But he felt compelled to do so by his desire to uncover the reality. And by moving in this unconventional direction, he was able to master an unbelievably complex language system and gain invaluable insights into their culture and the role of culture in general.

Understand: we can never really experience what other people are experiencing. We always remain on the outside looking in, and this is the cause of so many misunderstandings and conflicts. But the primal source of human intelligence comes from the development of mirror neurons (see page 7), which gives us the ability to place ourselves in the skin of another and *imagine* their experience. Through continual exposure to people and by attempting to think inside them we can gain an increasing sense of their perspective, but this requires effort on our part. Our natural tendency is to project onto other people our own beliefs and value systems, in ways in which we are not even aware. When it comes to studying another culture, it is only through the use of our empathic powers and by participating in their lives that we can begin to overcome these natural projections and arrive at the reality of their experience. To do so we must overcome our great fear of the Other and the unfamiliarity of their ways. We must enter their belief and value systems, their guiding myths, their way of seeing the world. Slowly, the distorted lens through which we first viewed them starts to clear up. Going deeper into their Otherness, feeling what they feel, we can discover what makes them different and learn about human nature. This applies to cultures, individuals, and even writers of books. As Nietzsche once wrote, "As soon as you feel yourself *against me* you have ceased to understand my position and consequently my arguments! You have to be the victim of the *same passion*."

7. Synthesize all forms of knowledge— The Universal Man/Woman

Johann Wolfgang von Goethe (1749–1832) grew up in an unhappy home in Frankfurt, Germany. His father had a failed career in local politics that had left him embittered, and he had become estranged from his young wife. To make up for his own lack of success, Johann's father made certain that his son received the finest education possible. He learned the arts, the sciences, numerous languages, various crafts, fencing, and dancing. But Johann found life in the house under the watchful eye of his father unbearable and stultifying. When he finally left home to study at the university in Leipzig, it was as if he had been set free from prison. All of his pent-up energies, his restlessness, his hunger for women and adventures, were suddenly released and he went wild.

He lived the life of a dandy, dressing in the most fashionable clothes and seducing as many young women as he could find. He threw himself into the intellectual life of Leipzig; he could be seen in all of the taverns arguing about this or that philosophy with professors and fellow students. His ideas went against the grain—he ranted against Christianity and yearned for the pagan religion of the ancient Greeks. As one professor noted, "It was the well-nigh universal opinion that he had a slate loose in the upper story."

And then young Johann fell in love, and any remnant of self-control was finally gone. His letters to friends about this love affair caused them great concern. He swung from elation to deep depression, from adoration to distrust. He stopped eating. He proposed marriage, then broke it off. To many it looked like he was on the edge of madness. "I'm going downhill faster every day," he wrote to a friend. "Three months will see the end of me." Then suddenly in 1768, in the middle of all this, he collapsed. He awoke to find himself bathed in blood. He had suffered a lung hemorrhage, and for days he was near death. To the doctors, his recovery seemed miraculous; fearful of a relapse, they made him return to his home in Frankfurt, where he was to be confined to his bed for many months.

As he emerged from his illness, young Goethe felt like a different person. He was struck now by two ideas that would remain with him for the rest of his life. First, he had the sensation that he possessed a type of inner spirit that he named his *daemon*. This spirit was an incarnation of all of his intense, restless, demonic energy. It could turn destructive, as it had done in Leipzig. Or he could master it and channel it into something productive. This energy was so powerful that it made him swing from one mood or idea to the opposite—from spirituality to sensuality, from naïveté to craftiness. This daemon, he decided, was a spirit implanted in him at birth and it encompassed his whole being. How he managed this daemon would determine the length of his life and the success of his endeavors.

Second, coming so close to death at such an early age made him feel the presence of death in his bones, and this feeling stayed with him for weeks after recovering. As he returned to life, he was suddenly struck by the strangeness of being alive—of possessing a heart and lungs and brain that functioned beyond his conscious control. He felt that there was a life force that transcended the individual incarnations of life, a force not from God (Goethe would remain a pagan his entire life), but from nature itself. In his convalescence he would take long walks in the country, and his personal sense of the strangeness of life was transferred to the sight of plants and trees and animals. What force brought them to their present, perfectly adapted states of life? What was the source of the energy that made them grow?

Feeling as if he had been reprieved from a death sentence, he experienced an insatiable curiosity for this life force. An idea came to him for a story based on the famous German legend of a scholar named Faust, who desperately wants to discover the secret of life, and who meets an incarnation of the devil named Mephistopheles who helps him in this quest in exchange for possession of his soul. If ever the restless Faust experiences a moment of contentment and wants nothing more from life, then he is to die and the devil will own his soul. Goethe began to take notes on this drama, and in the dialogues he wrote between the devil and Faust he could hear his own inner voices, his own demonic dualities talking to each other.

Several years later, Goethe began life as a lawyer in Frankfurt. And as before in Leipzig, his daemon seemed to take control of him. He hated the conventional life of a lawyer, and he hated all of the conventions that seemed to dominate social life and to disconnect people from nature. He entertained deeply rebellious thoughts, which he channeled into an epistolary novel—*The Sorrows of Young Werther*. Although the story was loosely based on people he knew and on a young friend who had committed suicide over a failed romance, most of the ideas in it came from his experiences. The novel promoted the superiority of the emotions, and advocated a return to a life of sensation and to living closer to nature. It was the precursor of the movement that would come to be known throughout Europe as Romanticism, and it created a powerful reaction in Germany and beyond. Overnight, young

Goethe became a celebrity. Almost everyone read the book. Hundreds of young people committed suicide in imitation of the despairing Werther.

For Goethe, this success surprised and baffled him. Suddenly, he was hobnobbing with the most famous writers of his time. Slowly, the daemon reared its ugly head. He gave himself up to a life of wine, women, and parties. His moods began to swing wildly back and forth. He felt a rising disgust—at himself and the world he was frequenting. The circle of writers and intellectuals who dominated his social life annoyed him to no end. They were so smug, and their world was as disconnected from reality and nature as that of lawyers. He felt increasingly constricted by his reputation as a sensational writer.

In 1775, a year after the publication of *Werther,* he received an invitation from the duke of Weimar to stay in his duchy and serve as a personal adviser and minister. The duke was a great admirer of his writing, and was trying to recruit more artists to his rather dull court. For Goethe, however, this was the opportunity he was waiting for. He could say good-bye to the literary world and bury himself in Weimar. He could pour his energies into political work and into science, taming that damnable inner daemon. He accepted the invitation, and except for one later trip to Italy, he would spend the rest of his life in Weimar.

In Weimar Goethe had the idea of trying to modernize the local government, but he quickly realized that the duke was weak and undisciplined and that any attempt at reforming the duchy was doomed. There was too much corruption. And so slowly he poured his energies into his new passion in life, the sciences. He focused on geology, botany, and anatomy. His years of writing poetry and novels were over. He began to collect a large amount of stones, plants, and bones that he could study in his house at all hours. And as he looked deeply into these sciences, he began to see strange connections between them. In geology, changes in the earth occur with great slowness, over immensely long periods of time, too slowly to be observed in the span of a single lifetime. Plants are in a continual state of metamorphosis, from the most primitive beginnings of the seed to the flower or tree. All life on the planet is in an ever-present state of development, one life form growing out of another. He began to entertain the radical idea that humans themselves evolved from primitive life forms—that was the way, after all, of nature.

One of the main arguments of the time against such evolutionary theory was the nonexistence of the intermaxillary bone in humans. It exists in all lower animals in the jaw, including primates, but at the time could not be found in the human skull. This was paraded as evidence that man is separate and created by a divine force. Based on his idea that all of nature is interconnected, Goethe could not accept such a hypothesis, and through much research he discovered remnants of the intermaxillary bone in the upper cheekbones of human infants, the ultimate indication of our connection to all other life forms.

His style of science was unconventional for the time. He had the idea that there existed a form of archetypal plant that could be deduced from the shape and development of all plants. In his study of bones, he liked to compare all life forms to see whether there were similarities in the construction of parts such as the vertebral column. He was obsessed with the connections between life forms, the result of his Faustian desire to get at the essence of all life. He felt that phenomena in nature contained the theory of their essence in their own structure, if we could only grasp it with our senses and our minds. Almost all scientists at the time ridiculed his work, but in the decades to follow it was recognized that he had developed perhaps the first real concept of evolution, and his other work was the precursor to such later sciences as morphology and comparative anatomy.

In Weimar, Goethe was a changed man—a sober scientist and thinker. But in 1801 another bout of illness came close to killing him yet again. It took years to recover, but by 1805 he felt his strength returning, and with it a return to sensations he had not experienced since his youth. That year initiated one of the strangest and most amazing periods of productivity in the history of the human mind, stretching from his midfifties to his late sixties. The daemon he had repressed for several decades broke loose once more, but now he had the discipline to channel it into all kinds of work. Poems, novels, and plays came pouring out of him. He took up *Faust* again, writing most of it in this period. His day was an almost insane medley of different studies—writing in the morning, experiments and scientific observations (which were now expanded to chemistry and meteorology) in the afternoon, discussions with friends about aesthetics, science, and politics in the evening. He seemed to be tireless, and to be going through a second youth.

Goethe had now come to the conclusion that all forms of human knowledge are manifestations of the same life force he had intuited in his near-death experience as a young man. The problem with most people, he felt, is that they build artificial walls around subjects and ideas. The real thinker sees the connections, grasps the essence of the life force operating in every individual instance. Why should any individual stop at poetry, or find art unrelated to science, or narrow his or her intellectual interests? The mind was designed to connect things, like a loom that knits together all of the threads of a fabric. If life exists as an organic whole and cannot be separated into parts without losing a sense of the whole, then thinking should make itself equal to the whole.

Friends and acquaintances noticed a strange phenomenon in this twilight period of Goethe's life—he loved to talk about the future, decades and centuries ahead. In his Weimar years he had added to his studies, reading many books on economics, history, and political science. Gaining new insights from these readings and adding to them his own reasoning, he loved to predict the tide of historical events, and those who witnessed these predictions were later shocked at his prescience. Years before the French Revolution he had predicted the fall of the Bourbon monarchy, intuiting that it had lost its legitimacy in the eyes of the people. Participating on the German side in battles to overturn the French Revolution, and witnessing the victory of the French civilian army at the battle of Valmy, he exclaimed, "Here and now begins a new historical era; and you can all say you have seen it." He meant the coming era of democracies and civilian armies.

Now in his seventies, he would tell people that petty nationalism was a dying force and that one day Europe would form a union like the United States, a development he welcomed. He talked excitedly of the United States itself, predicting that it would some day be the great power in the world, its borders slowly expanding to fill the continent. He discussed his belief that a new science of telegraphy would connect the globe, and that people would have access to the latest news by the hour. He called this future "the velocipedic age," one determined by speed. He was concerned that it could lead to a deadening of the human spirit.

Finally, at the age of eighty-two, he could sense that the end was near, even though his mind was sparking with more ideas than ever before. He said to a friend that it was a shame that he could not live another eighty years—what new discoveries he could make, with all of his accumulated experience! He had been postponing it for years, but now it was time to finally write the ending to *Faust* itself: the scholar would find a moment of happiness, the devil would take his soul, but divine forces would forgive Faust for his great intellectual ambition, for his relentless quest for knowledge, and would save him from hell—perhaps Goethe's own judgment on himself.

A few months later, he wrote his friend, the great linguist and educator Wilhelm von Humboldt, the following: "The human organs, by means of practice, training, reflection, success or failure, furtherance or resistance . . . learn to make the necessary connections unconsciously, the acquired and the intuitive working hand-in-hand, so that a unison results which is the world's wonder . . . The world is ruled by bewildered theories of bewildering operations; and nothing is to me more important than, so far as is possible, to turn to the best account what is in me and persists in me, and keep a firm hand upon my idiosyncrasies." These would be the last words he would write. Within a few days he was dead, at the age of eighty-three.

For Goethe, a turning point came in his life with the great success of *The Sorrows of Young Werther*. He could not help but be dazzled by his sudden fame. The people around him were clamoring for an encore. He was only twenty-five at the time. For the rest of his life he would deny the public such an encore, and none of his subsequent writings would approach the success of *Werther*, although in his last years he was recognized as Germany's great genius. To deny the public what it wanted was an act of tremendous courage. To decline to exploit such fame would mean that it would probably never return. He would have to give up all of that attention. But Goethe felt something within him that was much stronger than the lure of fame. He did not want to be imprisoned by this one book, devoting his life to literature and creating a sensation. And so he chose his own unique and strange path in life, guided by an inner force that he called his daemon—a spirit of restlessness that impelled him to explore beyond literature, to the core of life itself. All that was necessary was to master and channel this spirit, implanted in him at birth.

In the sciences, he followed his unique path, looking for deep patterns in nature. He extended his studies to politics, economics and history. Returning to literature in the last phase of his life, his head now teemed with links between all forms of knowledge. His poetry, novels, and plays were suffused with science, and his scientific investigations were suffused with poetic intuitions. His insights into history were uncanny. His mastery was not over this subject or that one, but in the connections between them, based on decades of deep observation and thinking. Goethe epitomizes what was known in the Renaissance as the Ideal of the Universal Man— a person so steeped in all forms of knowledge that his mind grows closer to the reality of nature itself and sees secrets that are invisible to most people.

Today some might see a person such as Goethe as a quaint relic of the eighteenth century, and his ideal of unifying knowledge as a Romantic dream, but in fact the opposite is the case, and for one simple reason: the design of the human brain—its inherent need to make connections and associations—gives it a will of its own. Although this evolution might take various twists and turns in history, the desire to connect will win out in the end because it is so powerfully a part of our nature and inclination. Aspects of technology now offer unprecedented means to build connections between fields and ideas. The artificial barriers between the arts and the sciences will melt away under the pressure to know and to express our common reality. Our ideas will become closer to nature, more alive and organic. In any way possible, you should strive to be a part of this universalizing process, extending your own knowledge to other branches, further and further out. The rich ideas that will come from such a quest will be their own reward.

REVERSAL

The reversal to mastery is to deny its existence or its importance, and therefore the need to strive for it in any way. But such a reversal can only lead to feelings of powerlessness and disappointment. This reversal leads to enslavement to what we shall call *the false self.*

Your false self is the accumulation of all the voices you have internalized from other people—parents and friends who want you to conform to their ideas of what you should be like and what you should do, as well as societal pressures to adhere to certain values that can easily seduce you. It also includes the voice of your own ego, which constantly tries to protect you from unflattering truths. This self talks to you in clear words, and when it comes to mastery, it says things like, "Mastery is for the geniuses, the exceptionally talented, the freaks of nature. I was simply not born that way." Or it says, "Mastery is ugly and immoral. It is for those who are ambitious and egotistical. Better to accept my lot in life and to work to help other people instead of enriching myself." Or it might say, "Success is all luck. Those we call Masters are only people who were at the right place at the right time. I could easily be in their place if I had a lucky break." Or it might also say, "To work for so long at something that requires so much pain and effort, why bother? Better to enjoy my short life and do what I can to get by."

As you must know by now, these voices do not speak the truth. Mastery is not a question of genetics or luck, but of following your natural inclinations and the deep desire that stirs you from within. Everyone has such inclinations. This desire within you is not motivated by egotism or sheer ambition for power, both of which are emotions that get in the way of mastery. It is instead a deep expression of something natural, something that marked you at birth as unique. In following your inclinations and moving toward mastery, you make a great contribution to society, enriching it with discoveries and insights, and making the most of the diversity in nature and among human society. It is in fact the height of selfishness to merely consume what others create and to retreat into a shell of limited goals and immediate pleasures. Alienating yourself from your inclinations can only lead to pain and disappointment in the long run, and a sense that you have wasted something unique. This pain will be expressed in bitterness and envy, and you will not recognize the true source of your depression.

Your *true self* does not speak in words or banal phrases. Its voice comes from *deep* within you, from the substrata of your psyche, from something embedded physically within you. It emanates from your uniqueness, and it communicates through sensations and powerful desires that seem to transcend you. You cannot ultimately understand why you are drawn to certain activities or forms of knowledge. This cannot really be verbalized or explained. It is simply a fact of nature. In following this voice you realize your own potential, and satisfy your deepest longings to create and express your uniqueness. It exists for a purpose, and it is your Life's Task to bring it to fruition.

Because we think well of ourselves, but nonetheless never suppose ourselves capable of producing a painting like one of Raphael's or a dramatic scene like one of Shakespeare's, we convince ourselves that the capacity to do so is quite extraordinarily marvelous, a wholly uncommon accident, or, if we are still religiously inclined, a mercy from on high. Thus our vanity, our self-love, promotes the cult of the genius: for only if we think of him as being very remote from us, as a miraculum, does he not aggrieve us. . . . But, aside from these suggestions of our vanity, the activity of the genius seems in no way fundamentally different from the activity of the inventor of machines, the scholar of astronomy or history, the master of tactics. All these activities are explicable if one pictures to oneself people whose thinking is active in one direction, who employ everything as material, who always zealously observe their own inner life and that of others, who perceive everywhere models and incentives, who never tire of combining together the means available to them. Genius too does nothing but learn first how to lay bricks then how to build, and continually seek for material and continually form itself around it. Every activity of man is amazingly complicated, not only that of the genius: but none is a 'miracle.'

—FRIEDRICH NIETZSCHE

CONTEMPORARY
MASTER BIOGRAPHIES

Santiago Calatrava was born in 1951, in Valencia, Spain. He earned his architecture degree from the Polytechnic University of Valencia, and then went on to obtain a PhD in civil engineering from the Swiss Federal Institute of Technology, in Zurich, Switzerland. Because of his civil engineering background, Calatrava has focused primarily on large-scale public projects such as bridges, train stations, museums, cultural centers, and sports complexes. Inspired by organic shapes in nature, Calatrava has sought to infuse these public projects with a mythic, yet futuristic quality, featuring parts of buildings that move and change shape. Among his notable designs are BCE Place Galleria in Toronto, Canada (1992), Oriente Railway Station in Lisbon, Portugal (1998), the extension to the Milwaukee Art Museum (2001), the Puente de la Mujer in Buenos Aires, Argentina (2001), Auditorio de Tenerife in Santa Cruz, the Canary Islands (2003), the Athens Olympic Sports Complex (2004), the Turning Torso Tower in Malmo, Sweden (2005), and the Light Railway Bridge in Jerusalem, Israel (2008). He is currently designing the Transportation Hub at the World Trade Center in New York City, expected to open in 2014. Calatrava is also a renowned sculptor whose work has been shown in galleries all around the world. Among his numerous awards, he has received the Gold Medal from the Institution of Structural Engineers (1992) and the Gold Medal from the American Institute of Architects (2005).

Daniel Everett was born in 1951, in Holtville, California. He received a degree in foreign missions from the Moody Bible Institute of Chicago, and became an ordained minister. After studying linguistics at the Summer Institute of Languages, a Christian organization, Everett and his family were sent as missionaries to the Amazon basin, to live with a small group of hunter and gatherers known as the Pirahã, whose language is not related to any other living dialect. After spending many years among the Pirahã, Everett was finally able to crack the code of their seemingly indecipherable language, and in the process made some discoveries about the nature of human language that continue to stir controversy in linguistics. He has also conducted research, and published articles, on more than a dozen distinct Amazonian languages. Everett has a PhD in linguistics from the State University of Campinas in Brazil. He served as professor of Linguistics and Anthropology at the University of Pittsburgh, where he was also chairman of the Department of Linguistics. He has also taught at the University of Manchester (England) and Illinois State University. Everett is currently the dean of Arts and Sciences at Bentley University. He has published two books: the best-selling *Don't Sleep, There are Snakes: Life and Language in the Amazonian Jungle* (2008), and *Language: The Cultural Tool* (2012). His work with the Pirahã is the subject of a documentary, *The Grammar of Happiness* (2012).

Teresita Fernández was born in 1968, in Miami, Florida. She received a BFA from Florida International University, and her MFA from Virginia Commonwealth University. Fernández is a conceptual artist who is best known for her public sculptures and for her large-scale pieces in unconventional materials. In her work she likes to explore how psychology impacts our perception of the world around us; for this purpose, she creates immersive environments that challenge our conventional views of art and nature. Her work has been exhibited in prominent museums around the world, including the Museum of Modern Art in New York, the San Francisco Museum of Modern Art, and the Corcoran Gallery of Art in Washington, D.C. Her large-scale commissions include a recent site-specific work titled *Blind Blue Landscape* at the renowned Bennesee Art site in Naoshima, Japan. Fernández has received numerous awards, including a Guggenheim Fellowship, an American Academy in Rome Affiliated Fellowship, and a National Endowment for the Arts Artist's Grant. In 2005 she was awarded a MacArthur Foundation Fellowship, also known as the "genius grant." In 2011 President Barack Obama appointed Fernández to serve on the U.S. Commission on Fine Arts.

Paul Graham was born in 1964, in Weymouth, England. His family moved to the United States when he was four, and he was raised in Monroeville, Pennsylvania. Graham obtained a BA in philosophy from Cornell University, and a PhD in computer science from Harvard University. He studied painting at the Rhode Island School of Design and the Accademia di Belle Arti in Florence, Italy. In 1995 he cofounded Viaweb, the first application service provider that allowed users to set up their own Internet stores. After Yahoo! acquired Viaweb for close to $50 million (and renamed it Yahoo! Store), Graham went on to write a highly popular series of online essays about programming, tech startups, the history of technology, and art. Inspired by the reaction to a talk he gave at the Harvard Computer Society in 2005, Graham created Y Combinator, an apprenticeship system that provides seed funding, advice, and mentorship to young tech entrepreneurs. It has since become one of the most successful tech incubators in the world. Its portfolio of over two hundred companies is currently worth more than $4 billion, and includes DropBox, Reddit, loopt, and AirBnB. He has published two books: *On Lisp* (1993) about the computer programming language, and *Hackers and Painters* (2004). His online essays can be viewed at PaulGraham.com.

Temple Grandin was born in 1947, in Boston, Massachusetts. At the age of three she was diagnosed with autism. Through special mentoring and work with a speech therapist, she slowly mastered the language skills that allowed her to develop intellectually and to attend various schools, including a high school for gifted children, where she excelled in science. Grandin went on to receive a bachelor's degree in psychology from Franklin Pierce College, a master's degree in animal science from Arizona State University, and a doctorate in animal science from the University of Illinois at Urbana-Champaign. After graduation, she worked as a designer of livestock-handling facilities. Half the cattle in the United States are handled by equipment she has designed. Her work in this area is devoted to making more humane, stress-free environments for animals in slaughterhouses. For this purpose, she has created a series of guidelines for handling cattle and pigs at meat plants that are now used by companies such as McDonald's. Grandin has become a popular lecturer on animal rights and on autism. She has written several best-selling books, including *Thinking in Pictures: My Life with Autism* (1996), *Animals in Translation: Using the Mysteries of Autism to Decode Animal Behavior* (2005), and *The Way I See It: A Personal Look at Autism and Aspergers* (2009). In 2010 she was the subject of an HBO biopic about her life, titled *Temple Grandin*. She is currently a professor of animal science at Colorado State University.

Yoky Matsuoka was born in 1972, in Tokyo, Japan. As a promising young tennis player, Matsuoka came to the United States to attend a high-level tennis academy. She ended up staying, completing her high school studies in the States, and then attending the University of California at Berkeley, where she received a BS in electrical engineering and computer science. She received her PhD in electrical engineering and artificial intelligence from

MIT. While at MIT she was the chief engineer at Barrett Technology, where she developed a robotic hand that became an industry standard. She has served as a professor of robotics and mechanical engineering at Carnegie Mellon University and professor of computer science and engineering at the University of Washington at Seattle. At the University of Washington, Matsuoka created a new field, which she called "neurobotics," and established the university's neurobotics laboratory, where robotic models and virtual environments are used to understand the biomechanics and neuromuscular control of human limbs. In 2007, Matsuoka was awarded a MacArthur Foundation Fellowship, or "genius grant." She was a cofounder of Google's X division, where she served as Head of Innovation. Matsuoka is currently the vice president of technology at Nest Labs, a green technology firm that develops energy-efficient consumer products such as the Nest Learning Thermostat.

Vilayanur S. Ramachandran was born in 1951, in Madras, India. He trained as a doctor, then switched fields to study visual psychology at Trinity College at the University of Cambridge in England, where he received his PhD. In 1983 he was appointed assistant professor of psychology at the University of California at San Diego (UCSD). He is currently a Distinguished Professor in the Psychology Department and Neurosciences Program at UCSD, and also serves as the director of the university's Center for Brain and Cognition. He is best known for his work on bizarre neurological syndromes such as phantom limbs, various body-identity disorders, Capgras delusion (in which the sufferer believes that family members have been replaced by impostors), and for his theories on mirror neurons and synesthesia. Among his numerous awards, he has been elected to an honorary life membership to the Royal Institution of Great Britain, fellowships from Oxford University and Stanford University, and the annual Ramon Y Cajal award from the International Neuropsychiatry Society. In 2011 *Time* magazine listed him as "one of the most influential people in the world." He is the author of the best-selling *Phantoms in the Brain* (1998), as well as *A Brief Tour of Human Consciousness: From Impostor Poodles to Purple Numbers* (2005), and *The Tell-Tale Brain: A Neuroscientist's Quest for What Makes Us Human* (2010).

Freddie Roach was born in 1960, in Dedham, Massachusetts. He began training as a boxer at the age of six. By the time he turned professional in 1978, Roach had fought 150 amateur bouts. Training under the legendary Eddie Futch, as a professional Roach compiled a record of 41 wins (17 by knockout) and 13 losses. After retiring as a fighter in 1986, Roach apprenticed as a trainer under Futch, then started his own career several years later, opening in 1995 his Wild Card Boxing Club in Hollywood, California, where he now trains his stable of fighters. As a trainer Roach has worked with 28 world champion boxers including Manny Pacquiao, Mike Tyson, Oscar De La Hoya, Amir Khan, Julio César Chávez Jr., James Toney, and Virgil Hill. He is also the coach of UFC Welterweight Champion Georges St. Pierre, and one of the top female boxers in the world, Lucia Rijker. In 1990 Roach was diagnosed with Parkinson's disease, but has been able to largely control the effects of it through medication and his rigorous training regimen. Among his numerous awards, he has been named Trainer of Year by the Boxing Writers Association of America an unprecedented five times, and was recently inducted into the International Boxing Hall of Fame. Roach is the focus of the current HBO series *On Freddie Roach*, directed by Peter Berg.

Cesar Rodriguez Jr. was born in 1959, in El Paso, Texas. After graduating from the Citadel, the Military College of South Carolina, with a degree in business administration, Rodriguez entered the Air Force Undergraduate Pilot Training Program. Trained as a command fighter pilot on the F-15, among other jets, he slowly rose through the ranks, becoming major in 1993, lieutenant colonel in 1997, and full colonel in 2002. He compiled over 3,100 fighter flight hours, 350 of which were in combat operations. He distinguished himself in aerial combat, as he is credited with downing three enemy aircraft—two Iraqi MiG fighters during Operation Desert Storm (1991) and a Yugoslavian Air Force MiG during the Yugoslav War (1999). His three kills in active duty are the most of any American pilot since the Vietnam War. Rodriguez commanded the 332nd Expeditionary Operations Group during Operation Iraqi Freedom (2003). Rodriguez retired from the air force in 2006. He is a graduate of the U.S. Air Force Air Command and Staff College, and the U.S. Naval War College. Among his numerous medals, he has been awarded three Distinguished Flying Crosses, the Legion of Merit, and the Bronze Star. He is currently employed by Raytheon as the director of International Programs and Growth for their Air Warfare Systems Product line.

ACKNOWLEDGMENTS

First and foremost I would like to thank Anna Biller for all of her invaluable contributions to this book—including her many insightful ideas, her skillful editing, her help with the research, and her loving support throughout the long writing process. Her work and assistance made this book possible, and I am eternally grateful.

I would like to thank my agent, Michael Carlisle at Inkwell Management, for deftly navigating this project past the occasional obstacles that came up, and for all of his editorial and life advice. He is truly the Master agent. Also at Inkwell, my thanks go to Lauren Smythe for all of her help, and to Alexis Hurley for bringing the book to a worldwide audience.

I would like to thank Molly Stern for setting the whole project in motion, and all of those at Viking who played such an important role in the production of the book. That would include my editor Josh Kendall, who helped and influenced the project on so many levels; Carolyn Carlson, who took over the editorial reins and worked her magic; Maggie Payette, who designed the cover; Daniel Lagin, who designed the layout; Noirin Lucas, who ably shepherded the book through production; marketing director Nancy Sheppard and publicity director Carolyn Coleburn, who both did such a wonderful job in promoting the book; and last but not least Margaret Riggs, who lent all of her logistical support. I must also thank Clare Ferraro for her patience and her overall masterful direction of the project.

I would like to thank Ryan Holiday, author of *Trust Me I'm Lying: Confessions of a Media Manipulator* (Penguin 2012), for his invaluable assistance on the research and for helping find and coordinate interviews with the various contemporary Masters.

Along the way, several people contributed with their advice and ideas. First on the list would have to be 50 Cent. Our discussions back in 2007 planted the seed for this book. 50's literary agent, Marc Gerald, played his usual midwife role in the early stages. In this vein, I would also like to thank Casper Alexander, Keith Ferrazzi, and Neil Strauss; Professor William Ripple; Francisco Gimenez; my great friends Eliot Schain, Michiel Schwarz, and Joost Elffers; and Katerina Kantola, whose memory will live on forever. I would also like to thank my sister Leslie for all of her inspiring ideas about animals and our Pleistocene ancestors.

I am, of course, eternally grateful to the contemporary Masters who agreed to be interviewed for this book. I had made it a condition that all interviews be conducted in person, with no real time limit, and that the interview subjects had to be as candid as possible about their creative process, their early struggles, and even failures along the way. All of the people I interviewed were extremely generous with their time and gracious in dealing with my often-irritating questions. They displayed the kind of open spirit that I believe plays an essential role in mastery and success in life.

In helping me to set up these interviews I must thank graduate student Elizabeth Seckel, who works with Professor V.S. Ramachandran at UCSD; Jessica Livingston, wife of Paul Graham and founding partner of Y Combinator; Andrew Franklin, my extraordinary publisher at Profile Books in the United Kingdom, who helped with the Daniel Everett interview; David Gordon, former director of the Calatrava-enhanced Milwaukee Art Museum, who helped set up the Santiago Calatrava interview; Mrs. Tina Calatrava; Cheryl Miller, executive assistant to Temple Grandin; Stephanie Smith, partner at Lehmann Maupin, who helped with the Teresita Fernández interview; and agents Nick Khan and Evan Dick at CAA, who both represent Freddie Roach.

I must also thank my mother, Laurette, for all of her patience and love, and for being my biggest fan. And, of course, I cannot fail to mention Brutus, the greatest cat who has ever lived and Master hunter.

Finally, I would like to thank all those in the past—masters, mentors, and teachers—who over the years slowly opened my eyes to so many ideas, and taught me how to think. Their presence and spirit are suffused throughout this book.

SELECTED BIBLIOGRAPHY

Abernathy, Charles M. and Robert M. Hamm. *Surgical Intuition: What It Is and How to Get It*. Philadelphia, PA: Hanley & Belfus, Inc., 1995.

Adkins, Lesley and Roy. *The Keys of Egypt: The Race to Crack the Hieroglyph Code*. New York: Perennial, 2001.

Aurelius, Marcus. *Meditations*. Trans. Gregory Hays. New York: The Modern Library, 2003.

Bate, Walter Jackson. *John Keats*. Cambridge, MA: Harvard University Press, 1963.

Bazzana, Kevin. *Wondrous Strange: The Life and Art of Glenn Gould*. Oxford, UK: Oxford University Press, 2004.

Bergman, Ingmar. *The Magic Lantern: An Autobiography*. Chicago, IL: The University of Chicago Press, 2007.

Bergson, Henri. *Creative Evolution*. Trans. Arthur Mitchell. New York: Henry Holt and Company, 1911.

Beveridge, W. I. B. *The Art of Scientific Investigation*. Caldwell, NJ: The Blackburn Press, 1957.

Boden, Margaret A. *The Creative Mind: Myths and Mechanisms*. London, UK: Routledge, 2004.

Bohm, David, and F. David Peat. *Science, Order, and Creativity*. London, UK: Routledge, 1989.

Boyd, Valerie. *Wrapped in Rainbows: The Life of Zora Neale Hurston*. New York: Scribner, 2004.

Bramly, Serge. *Leonardo: The Artist and the Man*. Trans. Sian Reynolds. New York: Penguin Books, 1994.

Brands, H. W. *The First American: The Life and Times of Benjamin Franklin*. New York: Anchor Books, 2002.

Capra, Fritjof. *The Science of Leonardo: Inside the Mind of the Great Genius of the Renaissance*. New York: Doubleday, 2007.

Carter, William C. *Marcel Proust: A Life*. New Haven, CT: Yale University Press, 2000.

Chuang Tzu, *Basic Writings*. Trans. Burton Watson. New York: Columbia University Press, 1996.

Corballis, Michael C. *The Lopsided Ape: Evolution of the Generative Mind*. Oxford, UK: Oxford University Press, 1991.

Curie, Eve. *Madame Curie: A Biography*. Cambridge, MA: Da Capo Press, 2001.

De Mille, Agnes. *Martha: The Life and Work of Martha Graham*. New York: Random House, 1991.

Donald, Merlin. *Origins of the Modern Mind: Three Stages in the Evolution of Culture and Cognition*. Cambridge, MA: Harvard University Press, 1993.

Dreyfus, Hubert L., and Stuart E. Dreyfus. *Mind Over Machine: The Power of Human Intuition and Expertise in the Era of the Computer*. New York: Free Press, 1986.

Ehrenzweig, Anton. *The Hidden Order of Art: A Study in the Psychology of Artistic Imagination*. Berkeley, CA: University of California Press, 1971.

Ericsson, K. Anders, ed. *The Road to Excellence: The Acquisition of Expert Performance in the Arts, Sciences, Sports and Games*. Mahwah, NJ: Lawrence Erlbaum Associates, Publishers, 1996.

Gardner, Howard. *Frames of Mind: The Theory of Multiple Intelligences*. New York: Basic Books, 2004.

Gregory, Andrew. *Harvey's Heart: The Discovery of Blood Circulation*. Cambridge, U.K: Icon Books, 2001.

Hadamard, Jacques. *The Mathematician's Mind: The Psychology of Invention in the Mathematical Field*. Princeton, NJ: Princeton University Press, 1996.

Hirshfeld, Alan. *The Electric Life of Michael Faraday*. New York: Walker & Company, 2006.

Hogarth, Robin M. *Educating Intuition*. Chicago, IL: The University of Chicago Press, 2001.

Howe, Michael J. A. *Genius Explained*. Cambridge, UK: Cambridge University Press, 2001.

Humphrey, Nicholas. *The Inner Eye: Social Intelligence in Evolution*. Oxford, UK: Oxford University Press, 2008.

Isaacson, Walter. *Einstein: His Life and Universe*. New York: Simon & Schuster, 2007.

Johnson-Laird, Philip. *How We Reason*. Oxford, UK: Oxford University Press, 2008.

Josephson, Matthew. *Edison: A Biography*. New York: John Wiley & Sons, Inc., 1992.

Klein, Gary. *Sources of Power: How People Make Decisions*. Cambridge, MA: The MIT Press, 1999.

Koestler, Arthur. *The Act of Creation*. London, UK: Penguin Books, 1989.

Kuhn, Thomas S. *The Structure of Scientific Revolutions*. Chicago, IL: The University of Chicago Press, 1996.

Leakey, Richard E., and Roger Lewin. *Origins: What New Discoveries Reveal About the Emergence of Our Species and Its Possible Future*. New York: Penguin Books, 1991.

Lewis, David. *We, the Navigators: The Ancient Art of Landfinding in the Pacific*. Honolulu, HI: The University Press of Hawaii, 1972.

Ludwig, Emil. *Goethe: The History of a Man.* Trans. Ethel Colburn Mayne. New York: G.P. Putnam's Sons, 1928.

Lumsden, Charles J., and Edward O. Wilson. *Promethean Fire: Reflections on the Origin of Mind.* Cambridge, MA: Harvard University Press, 1983.

McGilchrist, Iain. *The Master and His Emissary: The Divided Brain and the Making of the Western World.* New Haven, CT: Yale University Press, 2009.

McKim, Robert H. *Experiences in Visual Thinking.* Belmont, CA: Wadsworth Publishing Company, Inc., 1972.

McPhee, John. *A Sense of Where You Are: A Profile of Bill Bradley at Princeton.* New York: Farrar, Straus and Giroux, 1978.

Moorehead, Alan. *Darwin and the Beagle.* New York: Harper & Row, Publishers, 1969.

Nietzsche, Friedrich. *Human, All Too Human: A Book for Free Spirits.* Trans. R. J. Hollingdale. Cambridge, UK: Cambridge University Press, 1986.

Nuland, Sherwin B. *The Doctor's Plague: Germs, Childbed Fever, and the Strange Story of Ignác Semmelweis.* New York: W. W. Norton & Company, 2004.

Ortega y Gasset, José. *Man and People.* Trans. Willard R. Trask. New York: W. W. Norton & Company, 1963.

Polanyi, Michael. *Personal Knowledge: Toward a Post–Critical Philosophy.* Chicago, IL: The University of Chicago Press, 1974.

Popper, Karl R., and John C. Eccles. *The Self and Its Brain.* London, UK: Routledge, 1990.

Prigogine, Ilya. *The End of Certainty: Time, Chaos, and the New Laws of Nature.* New York: The Free Press, 1997.

Quammen, David. *The Reluctant Mr. Darwin: An Intimate Portrait of Charles Darwin and the Making of His Theory of Evolution.* New York: W. W. Norton & Company, 2007.

Ratey, John J. *A User's Guide to the Brain: Perception, Attention, and the Four Theaters of the Brain.* New York: Vintage Books, 2002.

Ratliff, Ben. *Coltrane: The Story of a Sound.* New York: Picador, 2007.

Rothenberg, Albert. *The Emerging Goddess: The Creative Process in Art, Science, and Other Fields.* Chicago, IL: The University of Chicago Press, 1990.

Schrödinger, Erwin. *What Is Life: The Physical Aspect of the Living Cell.* Cambridge, UK: Cambridge University Press, 1992.

Schultz, Duane. *Intimate Friends, Dangerous Rivals: The Turbulent Relationship Between Freud & Jung.* Los Angeles, CA: Jeremy P. Tarcher, Inc., 1990.

Sennett, Richard. *The Craftsman.* New Haven, CT: Yale University Press, 2008.

Shepard, Paul. *Coming Home to the Pleistocene.* Washington, D.C.: Island Press, 1998.

Sieden, Lloyd Steven. *Buckminster Fuller's Universe.* New York: Basic Books, 2000.

Simonton, Dean Keith. *Origins of Genius: Darwinian Perspectives on Creativity.* New York: Oxford University Press, 1999.

Solomon, Maynard. *Mozart: A Life.* New York: Harper Perennial, 1996.

Steiner, Rudolf. *Nature's Open Secret: Introductions to Goethe's Scientific Writings.* Trans. John Barnes and Mado Spiegler. Great Barrington, MA: Anthroposophic Press, 2000.

Storr, Anthony. *The Dynamics of Creation*. New York: Ballantine Books, 1993.

Von Goethe, Johann Wolfgang, and Johann Peter Eckermann. *Conversations of Goethe*. Trans. John Oxenford. Cambridge, MA: Da Capo Press, 1998.

Von Sternberg, Josef. *Fun in a Chinese Laundry*. San Francisco, CA: Mercury House, 1988.

Waldrop, M. Mitchell. *Complexity: The Emerging Science at the Edge of Order and Chaos*. New York: Simon & Schuster Paperbacks, 1992.

Watts, Steven. *The People's Tycoon: Henry Ford and the American Century*. New York: Vintage Books, 2006.

Wilson, Colin. *Super Consciousness: The Quest for the Peak Experience*. London, UK: 2009.

Zenji, Hakuin. *Wild Ivy: The Spiritual Autobiography of Zen Master Hakuin*. Trans. Norman Waddell. Boston, MA: Shambhala, 2001.

INDEX

childhood, 4, 11, 243
  dependency of, 54, 134–35
  genius in, 36
  limitations evidenced in, 43
  primal inclination evidenced in, 30–32
  as reflected in mentors, 107–8
  reverting to, 73–74
  sense of wonder in, 28, 31, 74,
    175–77, 202
  uniqueness expressed in, 25–26
chimpanzees, 8, 258
Chomsky, Noam, 162, 301
Christianity, 27, 71–72, 95–96, 161,
    238, 302–3, 304
Chuang Tzu, 255–56
Cleopatra, 240
Coltrane, John, 15, 31, 187, 206–9, 245
communication:
  nonverbal, 30, 138–39, 224
  social, 146
complacency, 202, 224
computer science, 87–90, 164, 193, 229
confirmation bias, 183
conflict avoidance, 161
conformism, 227, 285
  as Deadly Reality, 141, 142
  as impediment to uniqueness, 26–27,
    29, 42
confrontation, indirect, 145
consciousness, expanding of, 4–5
conservatism, emotional pitfall of,
    202–3, 212, 225
contagious disease, 148, 185, 194
contradictions, 244–45
Conventional Mind, 176–77, 191
Conversations with Goethe (Eckermann),
    102
Coptic language, 238, 240, 242
court, rituals of, 23, 159–60
craftsmanship, craftspeople, 64, 219
Creative-Active Phase, 3, 135, 167–246
  keys to mastery of, 175–205
  nine strategies for, 205–45
  six emotional pitfalls in, 202–5

Creative Breakthrough, 179, 199–201
Creative Dynamic, Primary Law of,
    180–81
creative process, 24, 199–201
  compared to alchemy, 242–45
  in developing new ideas, 227–28
  evolution of, 223–24
Creative Strategies, 179, 181–99
Creative Task, 179–81
creative thinking, 3, 62, 127, 204
  adaptability as essential to, 234–36
  analogies in, 187
  childhood spirit in, 176–78
  compared to expanded vision, 191
  going beyond language in, 196–99
  heightened consciousness in, 205
  imagining new uses in, 233–34
  impediments to, 176–77, 181,
    191–96
  misconception about, 235
  models and diagrams in, 197–98
  Negative Capability as key to, 183
  openness in, 185, 236
  outburst and frenzy of, 172–75
  in science, 98, 100, 101
  social intelligence and, 146
  subverting shorthands in, 191–96
  synesthesia in, 198–99
  transformation to, 52–56
  transforming spirit of, 173–75
Crick, Francis, 197–98
criticism:
  of authority, 102–3
  as constructive, 62, 76, 115–16, 163
  derisive, 230, 285
  exposing self to, 62–63
  public, 162–63
Curie, Marie, 30, 193
Curie, Pierre, 193
cycle of accelerated returns, 60, 61,
    77–78

dance, 30–31, 66–67, 224–28
Dance, William, 97, 98

Darwin, Charles, 10, 15, 110, 192, 197
anomalies recognized by, 194
Apprenticeship Phase for, 49–54
Beagle voyage of, 11, 50–54, 62,
187–88
and first transformation, 49–54
as model for apprenticeship, 55–56,
58, 62
see also evolution, theory of
Darwinian strategy, 32–36
Das Rheingold (Wagner), 200
Davis, Miles, 207
Davy, Humphry, 97–101, 104–6, 111
Deep Observation (The Passive Mode),
56–58
democratization, 102
in mentoring, 121–22
demotic language, 236–38, 242
Denishawn method, 225, 228
destiny, sense of, 25–26, 261
detachment, 7, 265
in social interactions, 130, 139
in view of self, 55, 61, 63, 80, 155,
157–59, 203
determination, 76–77, 79–80,
90–91, 123
Dimensional Mind, 167–246
Creative Breakthrough for, 199–201
Creative Strategies for, 181–99
Creative Task for, 179–81
dimensional thinking, 236–42
discipline, 13, 38, 75, 115–16, 128, 177,
246, 253
diversity, 28–29
Dogood, Silence, 127–28, 130
Don Giovanni (Mozart), 173–75
Don't Sleep, There Are Snakes (Everett),
162–63
doubt, in creative process, 199, 201,
204, 260
Doyle, Arthur Conan, 194
dreams, 245, 301
inspiration from, 198, 200–201,
223, 232

drugs, 4, 14, 71, 205, 245–46
Duncan, Isadora, 225

Eckermann, Johann Peter, 102
Edison, Thomas Alva, 15, 185–86, 197,
201, 256
Creative Task of, 179–80
self-apprenticeship of, 122–23
education, formal, 49–50, 54, 69–70,
84–86, 87–88, 122, 276
ego, 55, 182, 204
Einstein, Albert, 15, 25, 30, 31, 64, 66,
90, 146, 185, 192, 197, 198, 205,
256, 257, 259–60, 268, 269, 274–79
mastery achieved through focus on
strengths by, 274–79
Negative Capability of, 182–83
see also relativity, theories of
electricity, 96, 122
electromagnetism, 8, 100–101, 105, 197,
274–75, 277
emotions, 14, 55, 135, 145–46, 163, 179,
180, 195
as impediments in Creative-Active
Phase, 202–5
empathy, 134, 136, 139, 157
for animals, 283–84
as nonverbal communication, 138–39
Pirahã's lack of, 299–300
Endymion (Keats), 79–80
enlightenment, 113–15, 201
entrepreneurs, 83–84, 89, 194–95, 235
environmental connection, achieving
mastery through, 270–73
envy, 15, 38, 107, 141–42, 241
Ernst, Max, 186
Ernsting warehouse, 220–22
Eruption (Fernández), 243
ether, 275–77
Everett, Daniel, 15, 31, 162, 312–13
Apprenticeship Phase of, 71–74
mastery achieved through
submission to other, 298–304
public criticism of, 161–63

golden boys, 76–77, 288–89
Gould, Glenn, 15, 116–19, 256
Graham, Martha, 15, 30–31
  apprenticeship of, 66–67
  Creative-Active strategy of, 224–28
Graham, Paul, 15, 164
  Apprenticeship Phase of, 87–90
  Creative-Active strategy of, 213–35
Grandin, Temple, 16, 314
  evolving social intelligence of, 156–59
  limitations overcome by, 43–45,
    156–58, 284
  mastery achieved through focus on
    strengths by, 280–84
  see also autism
grandiosity, 204
Greek, 236–37
Gregory, Richard, 33, 109–10
Guerrero, Alberto, 116–18
Gutenberg, Johannes, 185

habit, 181, 296
hackers, hacking, 87–89, 232, 234, 235
Hadamard, Jacques, 197
hands:
  and brain, 35, 64, 198, 210–11,
    219, 230
  prosthetic, 230
  robotic, 34–35, 228–31
hardwiring:
  of brain connections, 211, 264, 301
  of skills, 60–61, 77, 209
Harvard University, 41, 87–88, 89, 164,
  231–32, 234
Harvey, William, agility of, 149–52
Hayman, Laure, 250
heart function, 149–50
heightened intellect, 256–57
hieroglyphs, 236–42
high end, 228–31
Hill, Virgil, 39
Hillman, James, 45–46
Hobbes, Thomas, 151
Homo erectus, 267

Homo magister, 9
Hook, Sidney, 196
Hopkins, Frederick Gowland, 194
human behavior:
  extreme, 139–40
  overall patterns of, 137–38, 141–46
human beings:
  early evolution of, 5–10
  learning in animals vs., 4
  as ultimate opportunists, 213–14
Humboldt, Wilhelm von, 308
humility, 102–3, 115, 183
Hurston, Zora Neale, 68–71
Hussein, Saddam, 286

identification, 8
  empathy as, 134, 136, 138–39
imagination, 188–89, 195
imitation:
  learning through, 59–60, 79
  pitfall of, 206, 209, 227
Immediate Experience Principle (IEP),
  301–2
impatience, 203–4
Improvement of the Mind (Watts), 96–97,
  104, 107, 122
inclination, 112, 206, 274
  in choice of career path, 27–28, 229
  as inner calling, 12–14, 29
  primal, 30–32
  as reflection of uniqueness, 11–12,
    25–26
independence, 74, 100–101, 107–8,
  117–19
inferiority, sense of, 71–74
inflexibility, 204
In Search of Lost Time (Proust), 180,
  254–55, 260–61
inside-out perspective, 298–304
instinct, 4, 262–63, 273, 288
intelligence:
  as heightened in Masters, 256–62
  intuition in, 257–58
  mechanical, 215–19

Massachusetts Institute of Technology
(MIT), 111, 162, 228, 230
artificial-intelligence lab of, 34
Masterly intuition, 256–67
Masters:
fusion of intuition and rational
thinking in, 247–311
heightened intuition of, *see* Masterly
intuition
productive old age of, 266–67
X factor of, 269–70
mastery:
through connection to environment,
270–73
following one's own path in, 22,
24–25, 42
fusion of intuitive and rational in,
247–311
keys to, 10–17, 25–29, 54–64, 102–8,
133, 175–205, 255–69
learning as basic value in, 67–68
profound love for subject of, 31,
169–70
sense of the whole in, 268, 294–96
seven strategies for attaining, 269–311
social class as impediment to, 96–97
time as critical factor in, 259–60, 269
as ultimate power, 1–17
mathematics, 197, 201
Matsuoka, Yoky, 16, 33–36, 111,
228–31, 314–15
Maxwell, James, 268, 275, 277
mechanical intelligence, 215–19
Medici, Lorenzo de', 23
Melville, Herman, 179
memory, 197, 263–66, 288–89
Mendeleyev, Dmitry, 197
Mentor Dynamic, 103–7, 112
mentoring, mentors, 15, 107, 93–123
back-and-forth dynamic in, 119–22
dependency on, 203
four strategies for, 108–22
independence from, 100–101, 107–8,
117–19

keys to mastery in, 102–8
lack of, 122–23
submission to, 102–3, 108
transfiguring ideas of, 116–19
two-way dynamic in, 103–7, 112
Mephistopheles, 305
Michelangelo, 24
Middle Ages, apprenticeship in, 59, 89
Milan, duke of, 291
Milton, John, 69
Milwaukee Art Museum, 86, 222
mirror experiment, 211–12
mirror neurons, 7–8, 59, 104, 134, 146
missionaries, 71–72, 161, 298
mitt work, 39, 119–20, 294–95
Moby-Dick (Melville), 179
molecular biology, 197–98
Mona Lisa (Leonardo), 292–93
money, 42, 65–68
monkeys, 210–11
Montesquiou, Count de, 255
Morris, Robert, 88, 232–34
movement:
in architecture, 84–87, 220
in art, 291–92
Mozart, Anna Maria, 169–73
Mozart, Leopold, 36–37, 38, 169–73
Mozart, Wolfgang Amadeus, 10, 15,
274, 171, 172, 175, 182, 279
Creative-Active Phase of, 169–74, 178
genius of, 90, 169–70, 178
parental control of, 169–73
rebellion of, 36–37
second transformation and, 169–75
multitasking, dangers of, 60
Murphy, William H., 82

Naïve Perspective, 135–38
naïveté, 129–31, 165, 202
Napoleon I, Emperor of the French,
25, 107, 236, 239
NASA, 85, 220
National Public Radio, 162
natural powers, 219–24

natural selection, 188

nature, 21–22, 24, 25, 51, 95–96, 210, 305, 309

navigation, Caroline Islanders' mastery of, 270–73

Negative Capability, 175, 265
  as source of creative power, 182–84

negative cues, 194

neoteny, 74

Netscape, 88, 231–32

neurobiotics, 35, 111

neurons, 60–61
  mirror, 7–8, 59

neuroscience, 33, 211–13, 229–30, 268

Newton, Isaac, 187, 274–75

Nietzsche, Friedrich, 17, 304, 311

Norman Conquest, 249, 251

Norris, Isaac, 132–33

observation, 7, 15, 58
  as basis for literature, 160, 251, 254–55
  in creative thinking, 52, 274
  deep, 56–58
  of Leonardo, 22–23
  of mentors, 106–7
  nonjudgmental, 183
  opinion vs., 183
  of rules and procedures, 57
  social, 130–31, 136, 137–40, 152
  as step toward mastery, 273
  verification of, 188–89
  and visual thinking, 198

obsession, in Creative Task, 179–80

obstetrics, 147–49

Oceania, 270

Olympic Sculpture Park, 243–44

open field, as Creative-Active strategy, 224–28

opera, 37, 171–75, 178, 179, 200

Operation Desert Storm, 286–88

optical illusions, 210–11

Original Mind, 175–77

Ortega y Gasset, José, 25

ostinato rigore, 203

Other:
  achieving mastery through submission to, 298–304
  fear of, 303

Pacquiao, Manny, mentoring of, 120–22, 296

Page, Larry, anomalies recognized by, 193–94

pain, brain in, 212

Pantheon, 85

paradigms:
  examining of, 193–94, 245
  as impediment to creativity, 227

Paradise Lost (Milton), 69

parents:
  accepting, 65
  critical, 38, 49
  defying of, 37, 38, 50–51
  exploitation by, 36–37, 169–73
  guidance from, 54
  idealization of, 134–35
  influence of, 11, 32, 33, 49–51, 251–52
  mentors as reflection of, 107–8, 112
  as obstacles, 36–38

Parker, Charlie "Bird," 31, 206, 208

passion, as element of mastery, 11

passive aggression, as Deadly Reality, 141, 145

passivity:
  in observation, 57
  pitfalls of, 13–14

Pasteur, Louis, 185

patience, 43, 62, 179, 223, 224

Penfeld, Wilder, 210

penicillin, 185

perdu, 260

periodic table, 197

persistence, 3, 114–15, 121, 123

persona:
  as art form, 155
  crafting of, 152–56

perspective, altering of, 191–96

Pestalozzi, Johann, 274

phantom limb paralysis, 211–12
phantom limb syndrome, 33, 210–12
Philip II, king of Macedonia, 106
philosopher's stone, 4
 mentors compared to, 104
phonograph, 186
piano, 116
Pierce, William, 266
Pindar, 29
Pirahã, 72–74, 161–63, 298–303
Planck, Max, 189
Pleasures and Days (Proust), 251–52
poetry, 79–80
Polanyi, Michael, 123
political behavior, politicking, 15, 54–55
 avoidance of, 164–65
 in court, 23, 159–60
 money and, 212
 in work environment, 57, 129–30,
  135, 152, 156–57
politics:
 Franklin's career in, 132–33
 French, 239
Pons, Timothy, 210–11
power:
 keys to mastery of, 10–17
 mastery as ultimate, 1–17
power relationships, 57
practice, 11, 34, 58–62, 206, 246
 achieving mastery through, 285–89,
  296–97
 as denigrated, 288–89
 in intuition, 254
 love of, 36, 38, 170–71, 296–97
 moving toward resistance and pain
  in, 78–81
 trusting in, 76–78
prehendere, 59
preverbal intelligence, 8, 59, 175,
 196, 283
primal inclination strategy, 30–32
primal intelligence, 196–99
primal powers, achieving mastery
 through, 270–73

primates:
 humans vs. other, 6–7, 134
 visual development of, 6
printing press, 185, 215
programming, 87–90
prototypes, 190
Proust, Jeanne, 249, 251,
 252, 253
Proust, Marcel, 15, 246
 apprenticeship of, 253
 bisexuality of, 251
 charm of, 250
 Creative Task of, 180
 death of, 255
 despair of, 252, 261
 evolution to mastery of, 249–55,
  260–61
 frailty of, 249, 251, 252, 253
 Life's Task of, 250, 253
 mastery achieved through time for,
  260–61
 setbacks for, 252
 strangeness of, 250
psychology, 109–10
Ptolemy V, 237, 240

Quadricycle, 81

radioactivity, 193
radium, 30
Ramachandran, V. S., 15, 315
 and fact of great yield, 210–14
 mentoring of, 110–11
 personal niche discovered by,
  32–33, 35
 strategic experimental guidelines
  for, 212
Ramses, pharaoh of Egypt, 240
rational thinking:
 fusion of intuition and, 247–310
 instinct vs., 4
 intuition vs., 256–57
reality, return to, 267–69
rebellion strategy, 36–38, 111

vitamin, C, 194
vocation, 25, 27
  see also Life's Task

Wagner, Richard, Creative
  Breakthrough of, 200–201
warfare, seeing more in, 257–59
War of Independence, 133
Watson, James D., 197–98
Watts, Isaac, 96–97, 104
Way (Tao), 91, 256, 258, 268
weaknesses, practice to overcome, 81
web applications, 232–33
Weimar, court of, 159–60, 306
Weimar, duke of, 306
whale, as architectural model, 221
Wheeler, Wheels, 76
Windows, 232–33
Wollaston, William Hyde, 100–101
women, in Leonardo's art, 292–93

World War I, 41, 254, 255
World War II, 298
Wright, Frank Lloyd, mentoring
  of, 109
Wright, Orville, mechanical
  intelligence of, 215–18
Wright, Wilber:
  mechanical intelligence of,
    215–19
  visualization skills of, 216

X factor, 269–70
X-rays, 185, 290

Yahoo!, 88, 233
Y Combinator, 89, 164, 235
Young, Thomas, 237–38, 241–42

Zen Buddhism, 113–15, 201
Zenji, Hakuin, 15, 90–91, 112–15, 266

3 1901 05411 6654